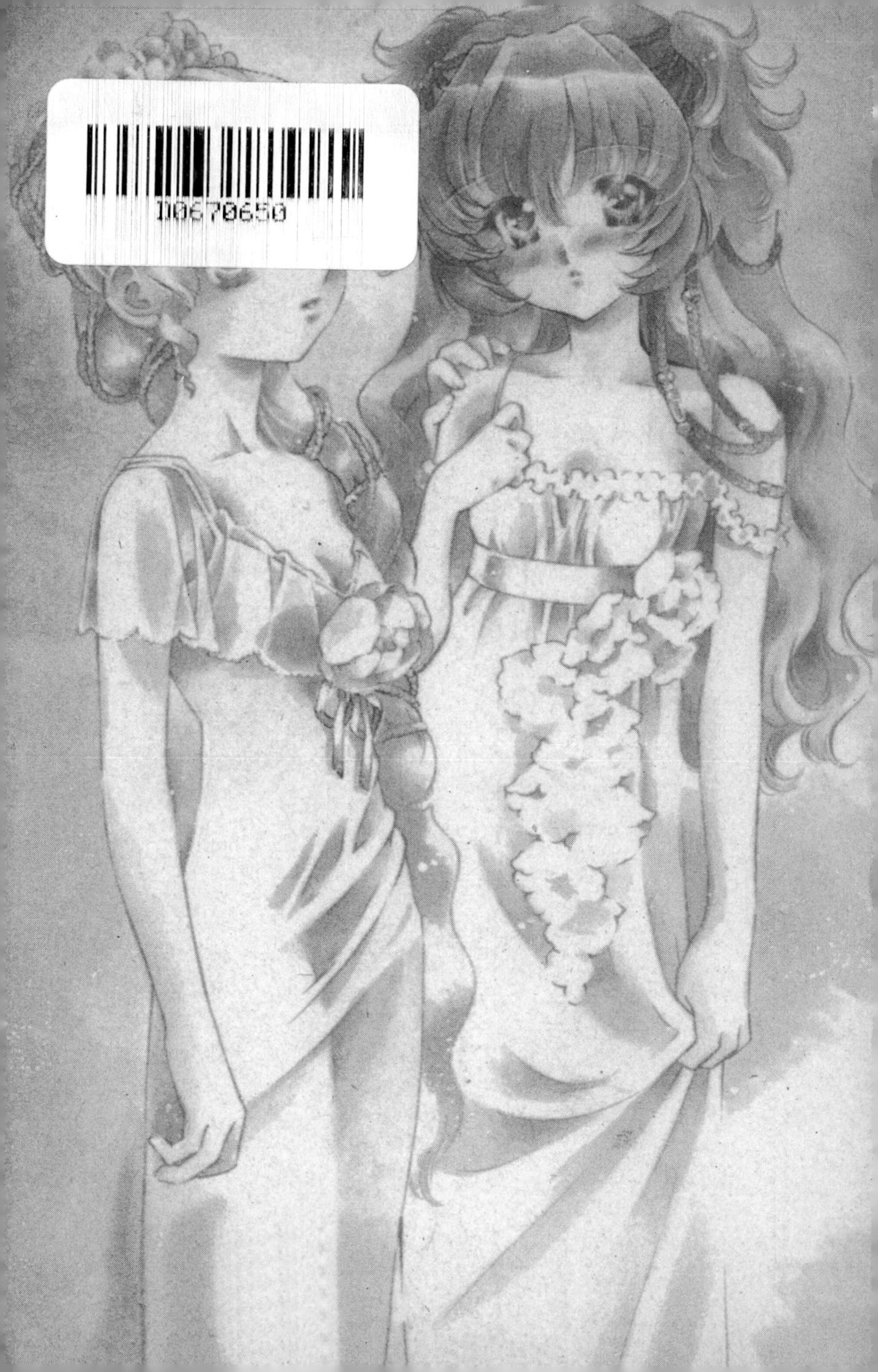

The Good Witch Of The West Vol. 1
written by Noriko Ogiwara
illustrated by Haruhiko Momokawa

Translation - Adrienne Beck
English Adaptation - Barbara Randall Kesel
Retouch and Lettering - Courtney Geter
Production Artist - Courtney Geter
Cover Design - John Lo

Editor - Hope Donovan
Digital Imaging Manager - Chris Buford
Production Manager - Elisabeth Brizzi
Managing Editor - Vy Nyugen
Editor-in-Chief - Rob Tokar
VP of Production - Ron Klamert
Publisher and E.I.C. - Mike Kiley
President and C.O.O. - John Parker
C.E.O. and Chief Creative Officer - Stuart Levy

A 🔵 **TOKYOPOP**® Manga

TOKYOPOP Inc.
5900 Wilshire Blvd. Suite 2000
Los Angeles, CA 90036

E-mail: info@TOKYOPOP.com
Come visit us online at www.TOKYOPOP.com

ISBN: 1-59816-620-4

First TOKYOPOP printing: October 2006
10 9 8 7 6 5 4 3 2 1
Printed in the USA

THE GOOD WITCH OF THE WEST™

Story by Noriko Ogiwara
Art by Haruhiko Momokawa

Volume 1

HAMBURG // LONDON // LOS ANGELES // TOKYO

Contents

Chapter 1
The Girl from Sera Field 5

Chapter 2
Edilene's Necklace 59

Chapter 3
Gideon's Escape 107

Chapter 4
Where Have All the Little Goats Gone? (Part 1) 145

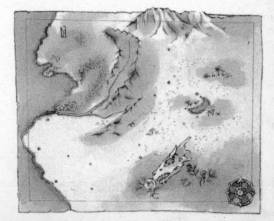

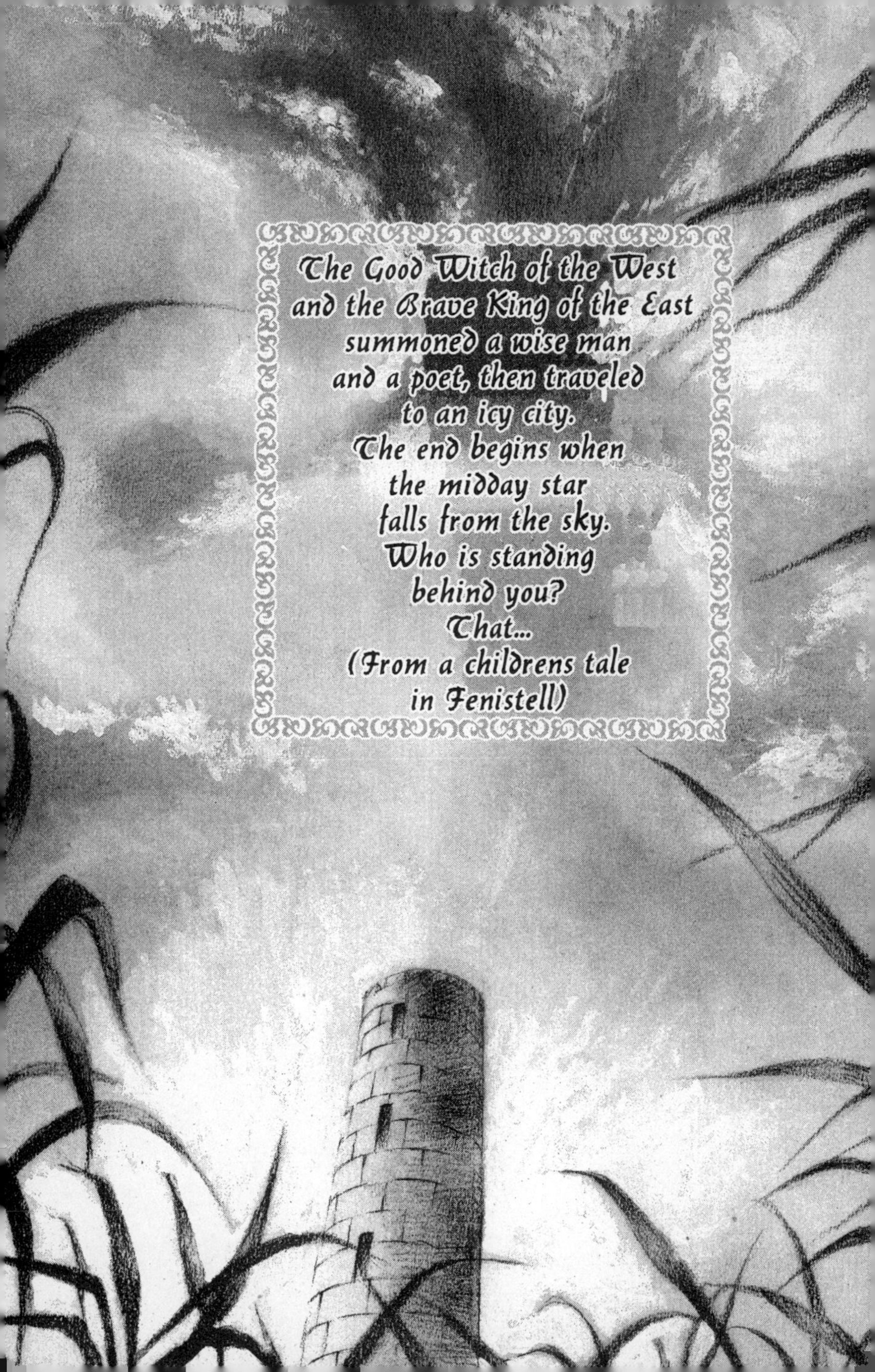
The Good Witch of the West
and the Brave King of the East
summoned a wise man
and a poet, then traveled
to an icy city.
The end begins when
the midday star
falls from the sky.
Who is standing
behind you?
That...
(From a childrens tale
in Fenistell)

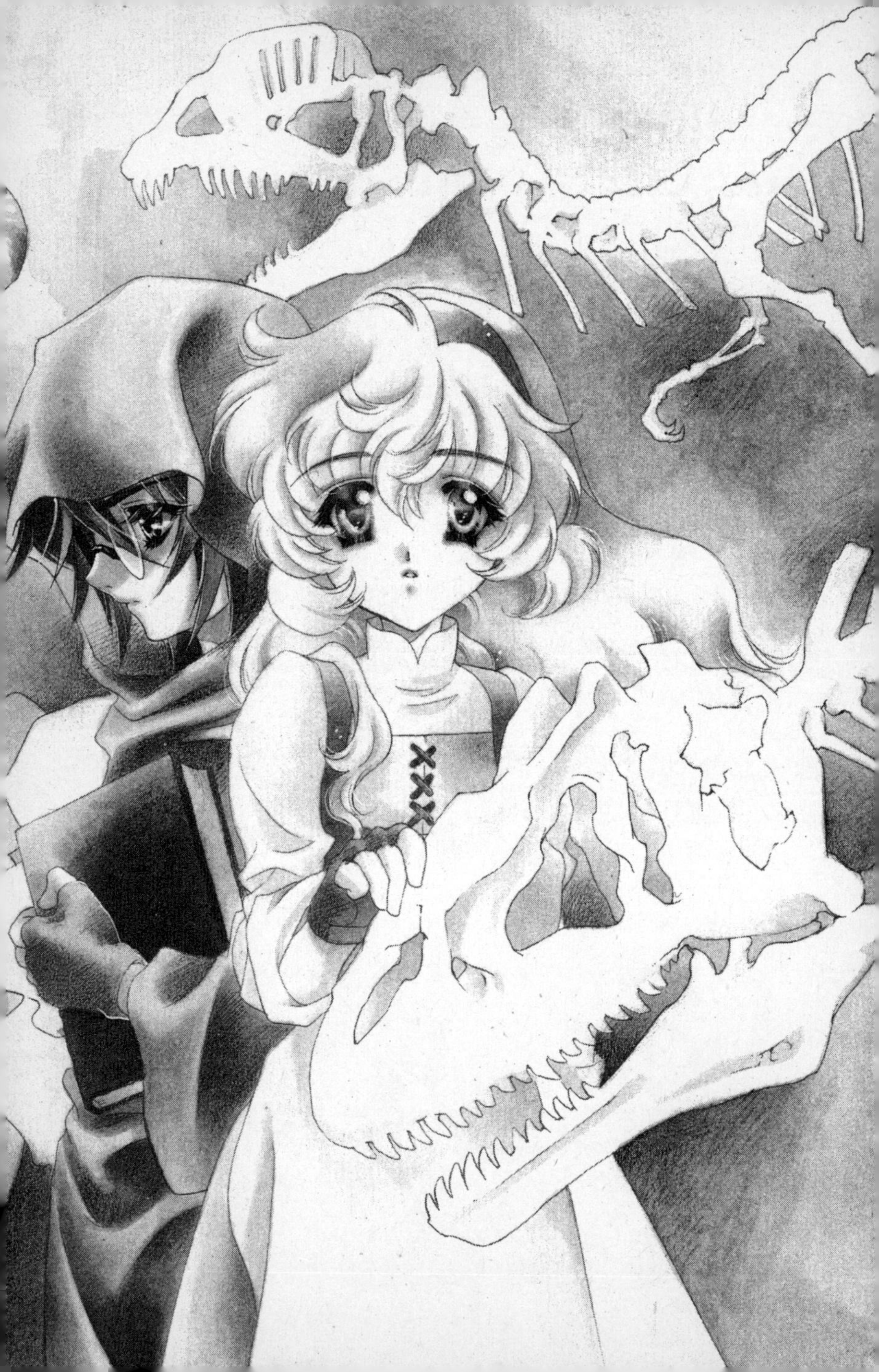

Chapter 1: The Girl From Sera Field

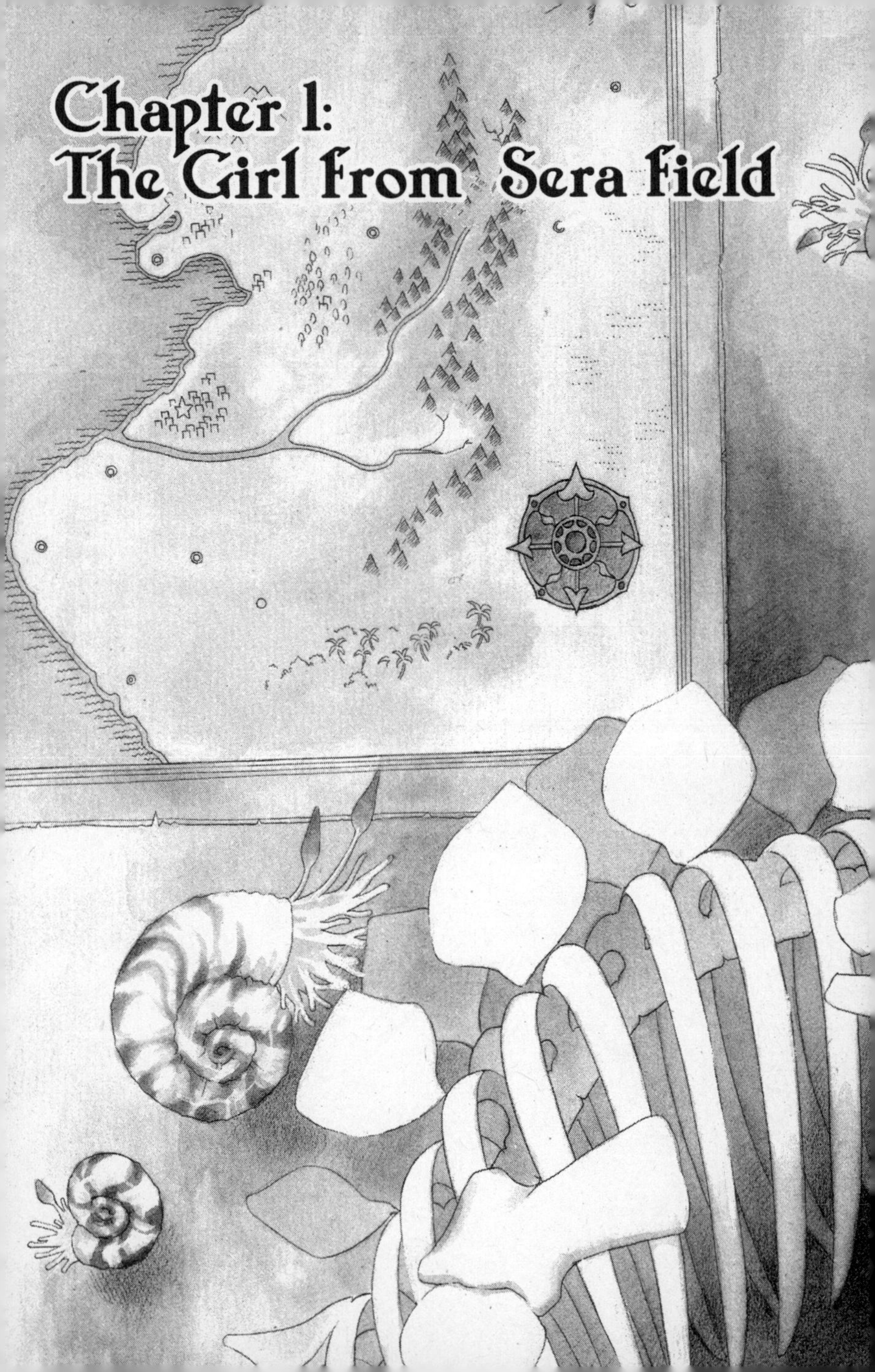

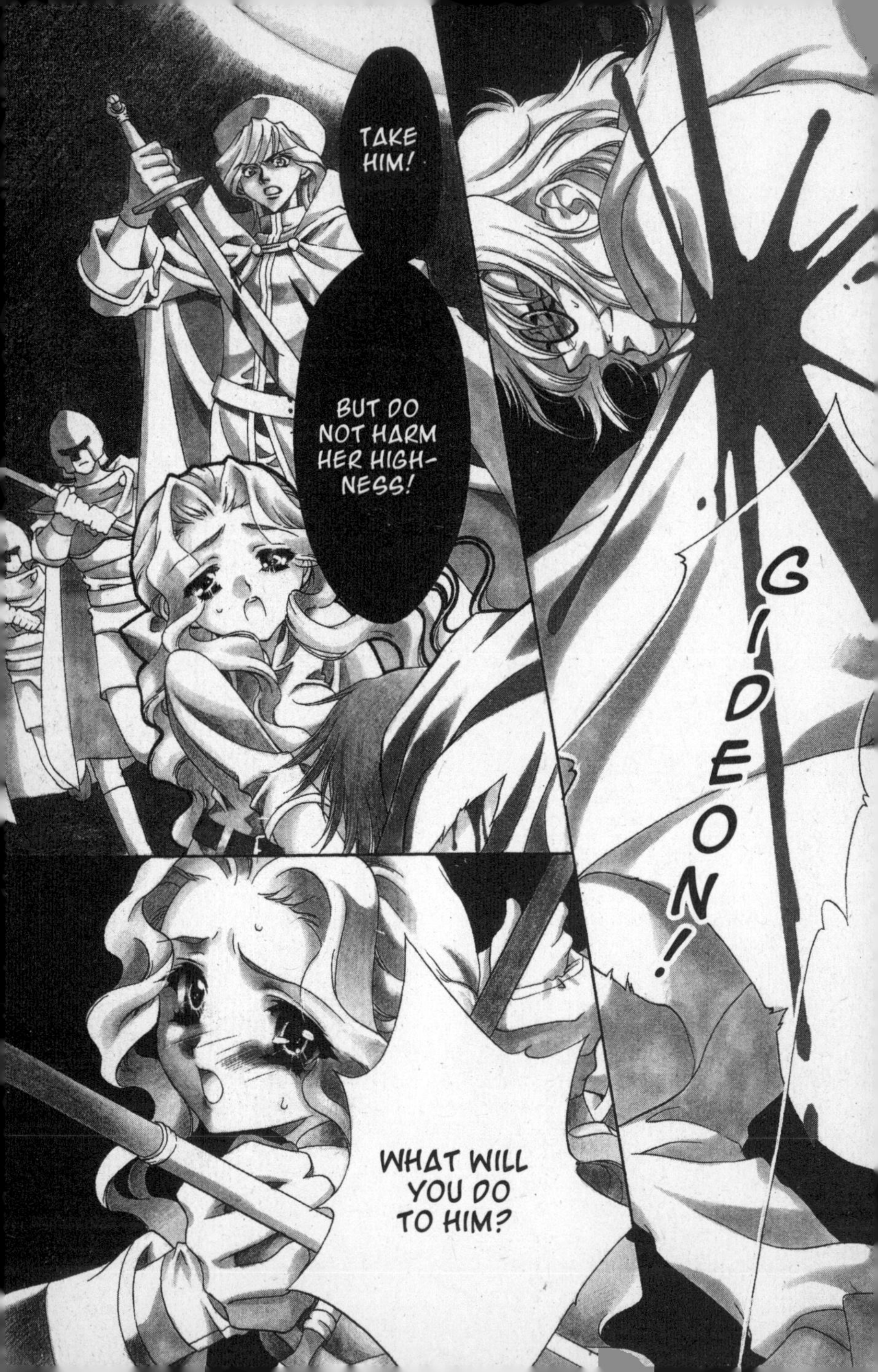
GIDEON!
TAKE HIM!
BUT DO NOT HARM HER HIGHNESS!
WHAT WILL YOU DO TO HIM?

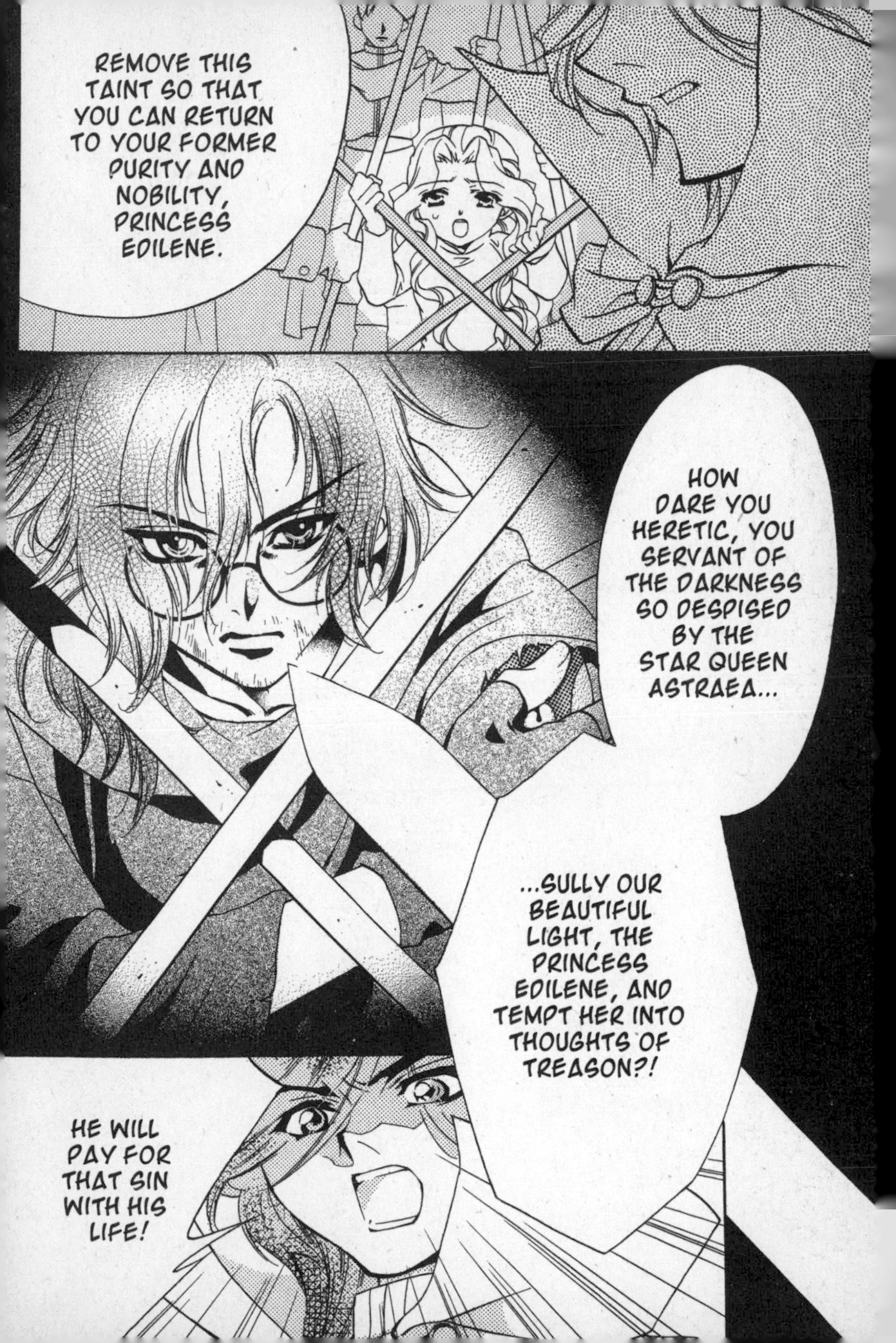
REMOVE THIS TAINT SO THAT YOU CAN RETURN TO YOUR FORMER PURITY AND NOBILITY, PRINCESS EDILENE.
HOW DARE YOU HERETIC, YOU SERVANT OF THE DARKNESS SO DESPISED BY THE STAR QUEEN ASTRAEA...
...SULLY OUR BEAUTIFUL LIGHT, THE PRINCESS EDILENE, AND TEMPT HER INTO THOUGHTS OF TREASON?!
HE WILL PAY FOR THAT SIN WITH HIS LIFE!

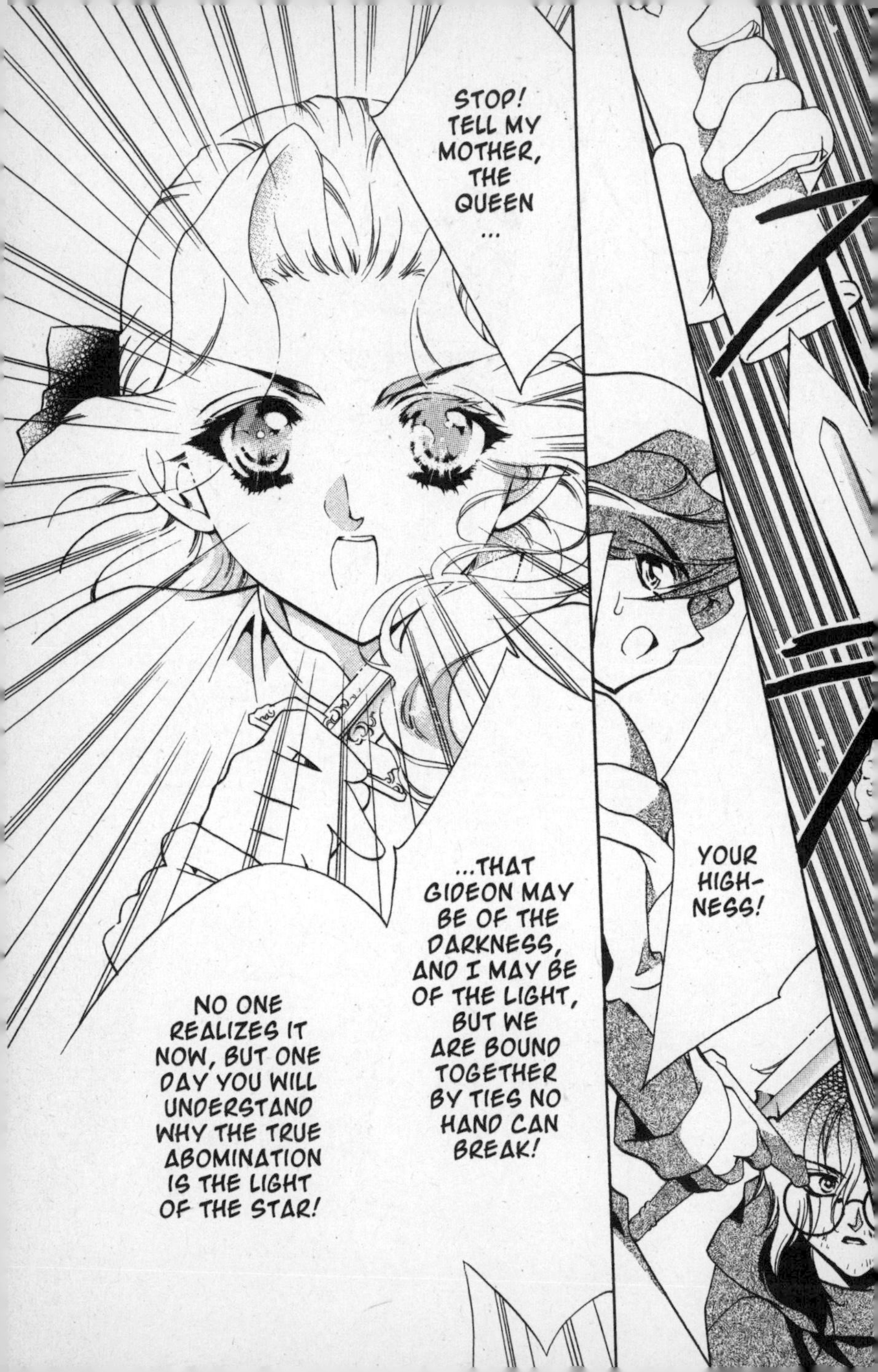
YOUR HIGHNESS!
STOP! TELL MY MOTHER, THE QUEEN ...
...THAT GIDEON MAY BE OF THE DARKNESS, AND I MAY BE OF THE LIGHT, BUT WE ARE BOUND TOGETHER BY TIES NO HAND CAN BREAK!
NO ONE REALIZES IT NOW, BUT ONE DAY YOU WILL UNDERSTAND WHY THE TRUE ABOMINATION IS THE LIGHT OF THE STAR!

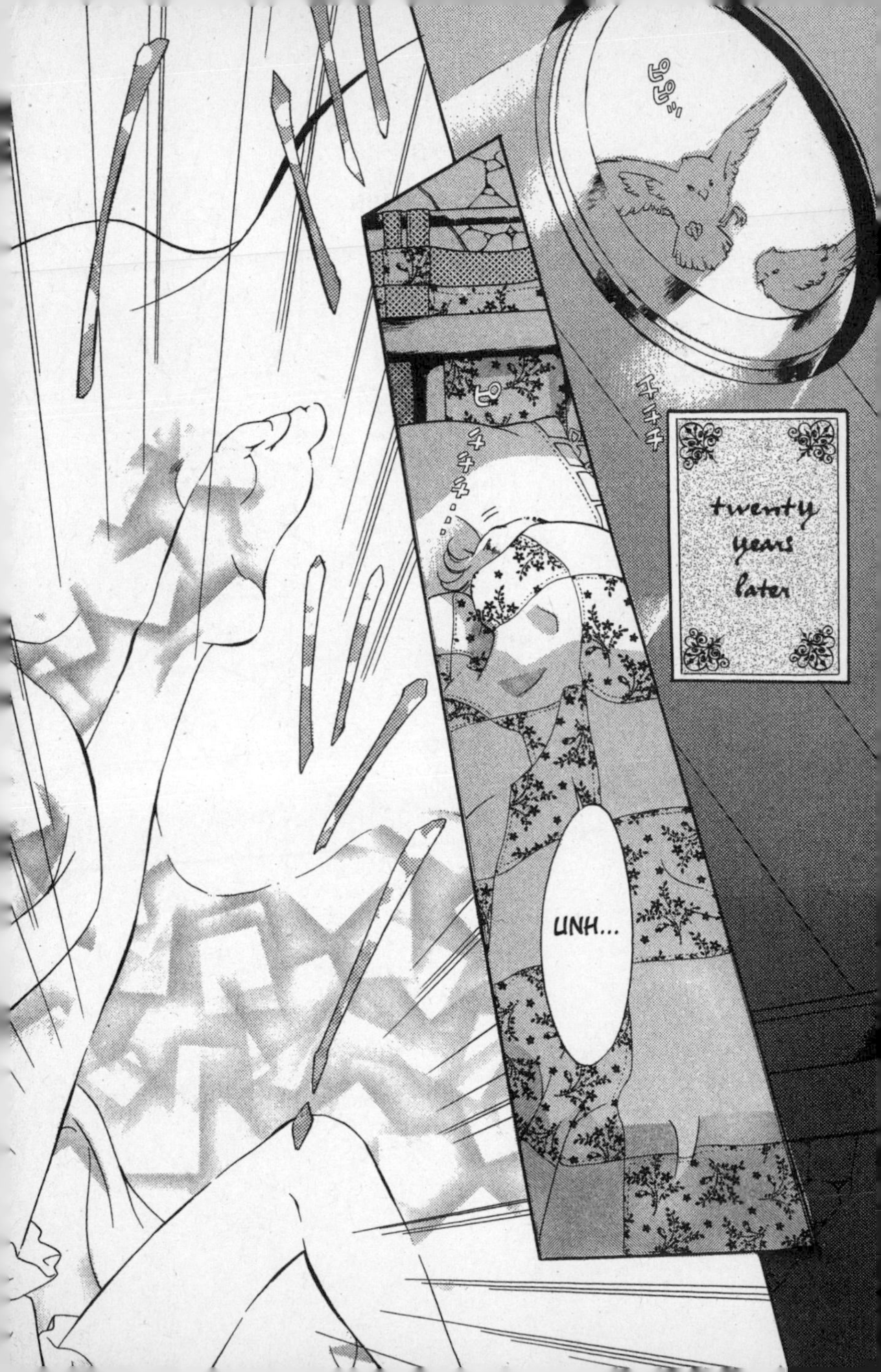
twenty years later
UNH...

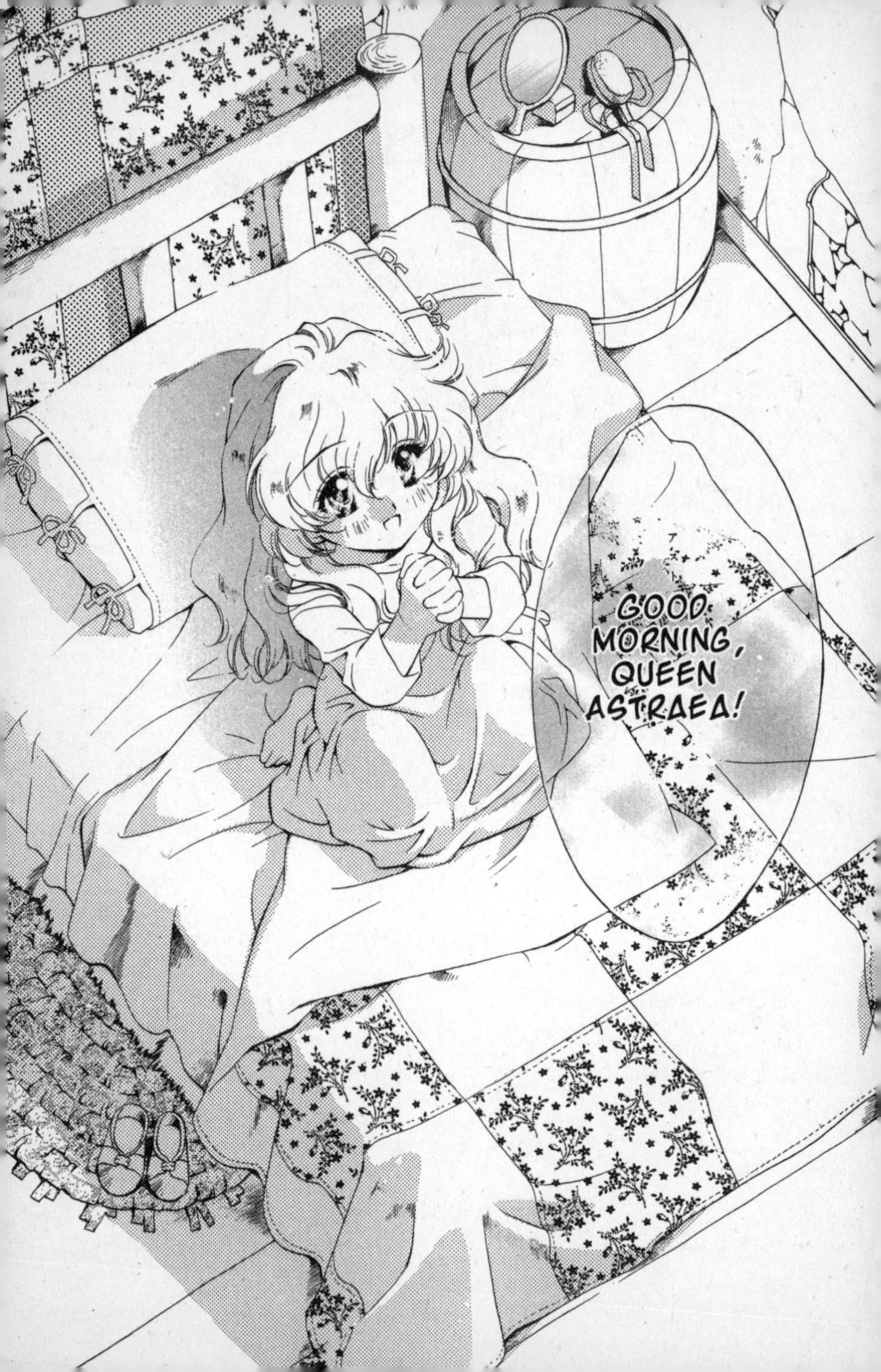
GOOD MORNING, QUEEN ASTRAEA!

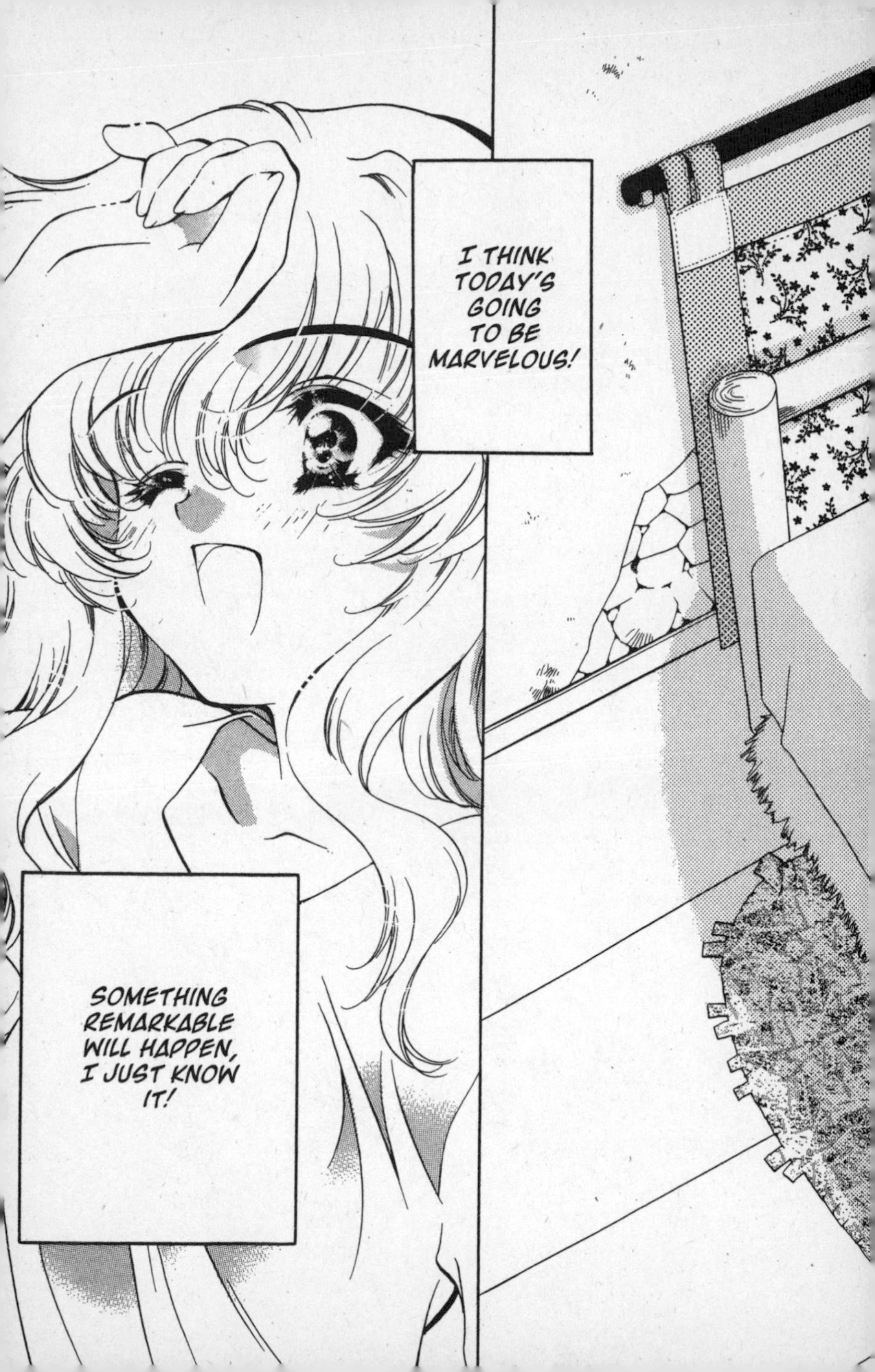
I THINK TODAY'S GOING TO BE MARVELOUS!
SOMETHING REMARKABLE WILL HAPPEN, I JUST KNOW IT!

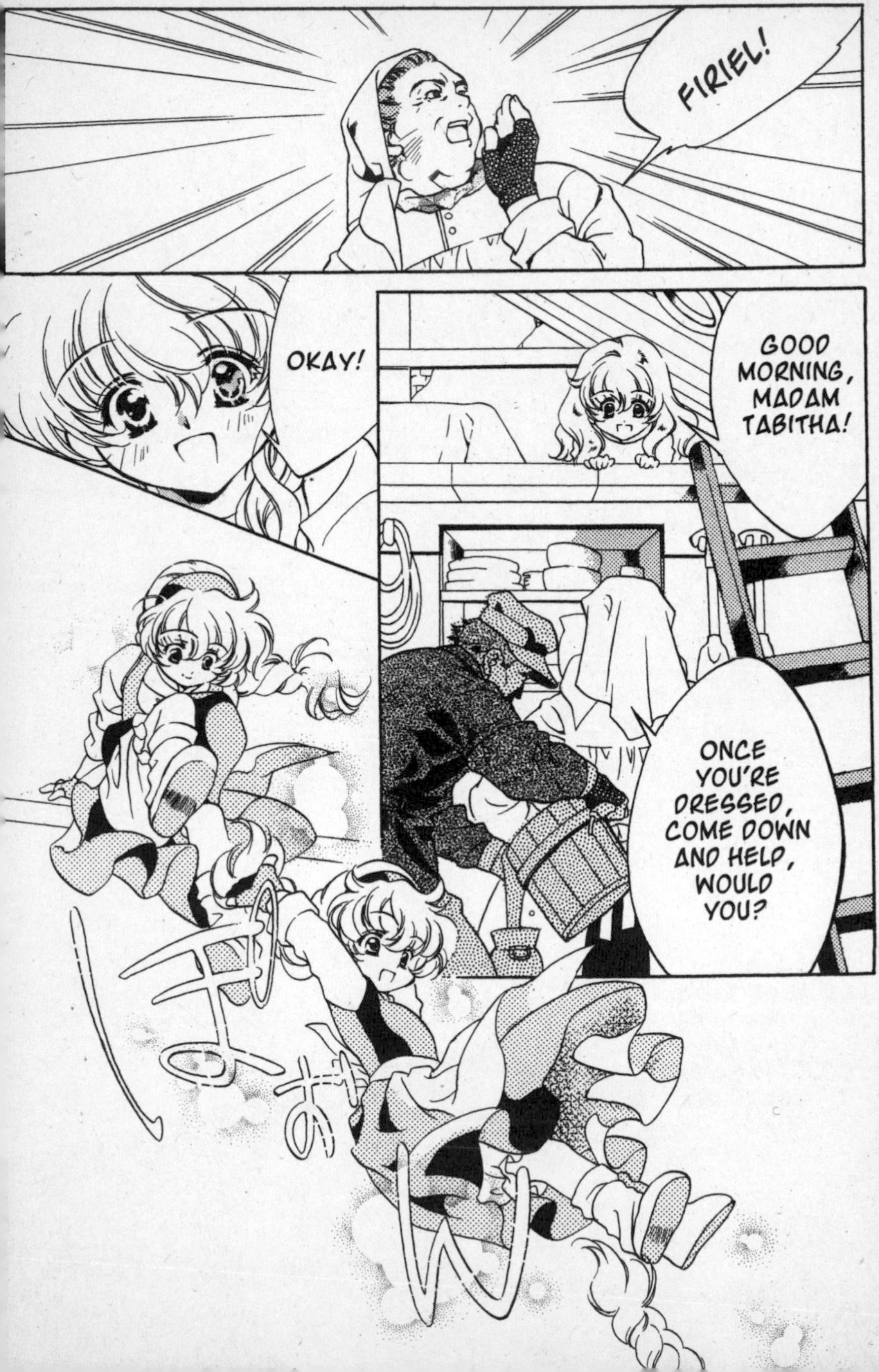
FIRIEL!
GOOD MORNING, MADAM TABITHA!
ONCE YOU'RE DRESSED, COME DOWN AND HELP, WOULD YOU?
OKAY!

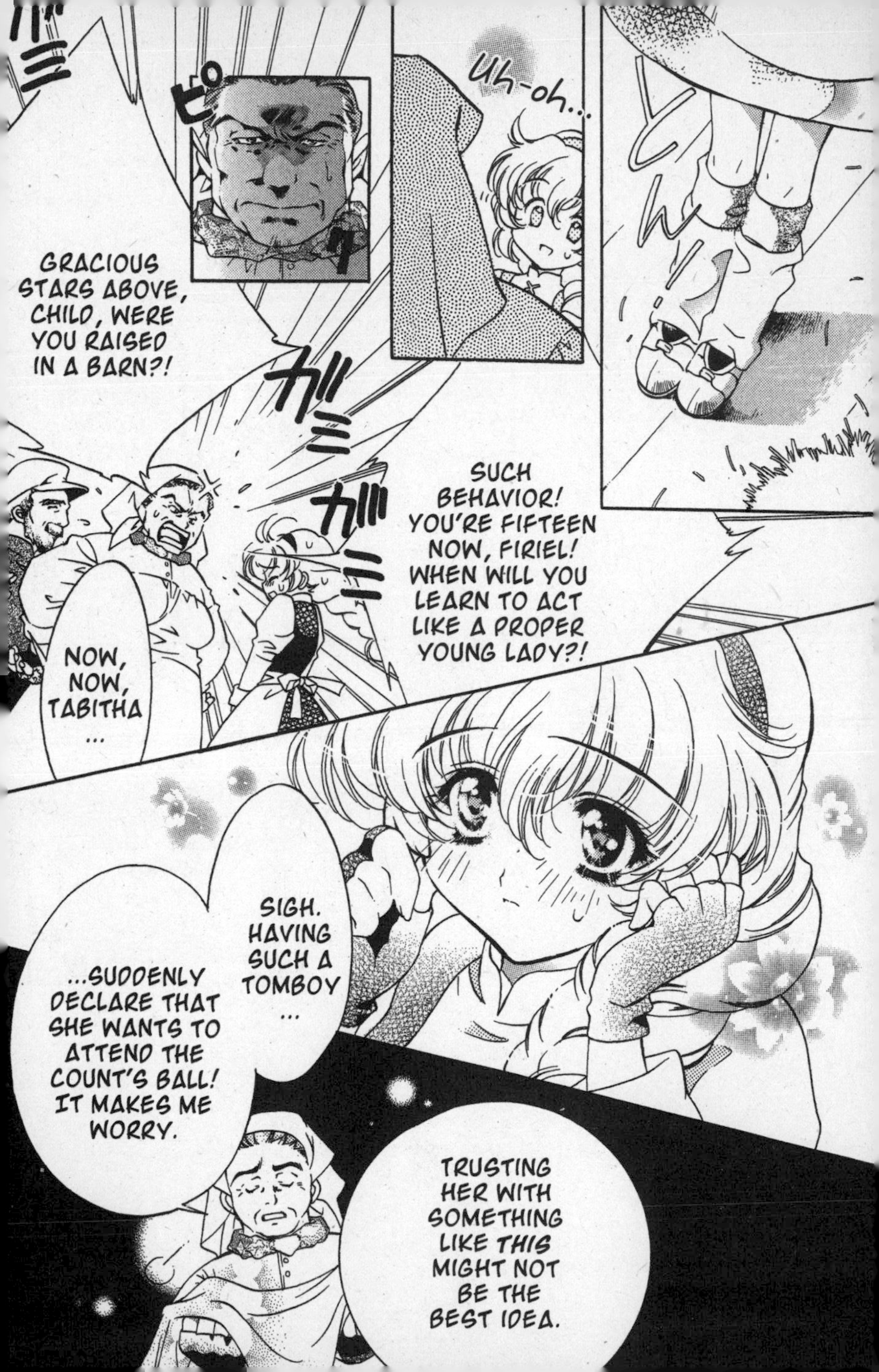
Uh-oh...
GRACIOUS STARS ABOVE, CHILD, WERE YOU RAISED IN A BARN?!
SUCH BEHAVIOR! YOU'RE FIFTEEN NOW, FIRIEL! WHEN WILL YOU LEARN TO ACT LIKE A PROPER YOUNG LADY?!
NOW, NOW, TABITHA ...
SIGH. HAVING SUCH A TOMBOY ...
...SUDDENLY DECLARE THAT SHE WANTS TO ATTEND THE COUNT'S BALL! IT MAKES ME WORRY.
TRUSTING HER WITH SOMETHING LIKE THIS MIGHT NOT BE THE BEST IDEA.

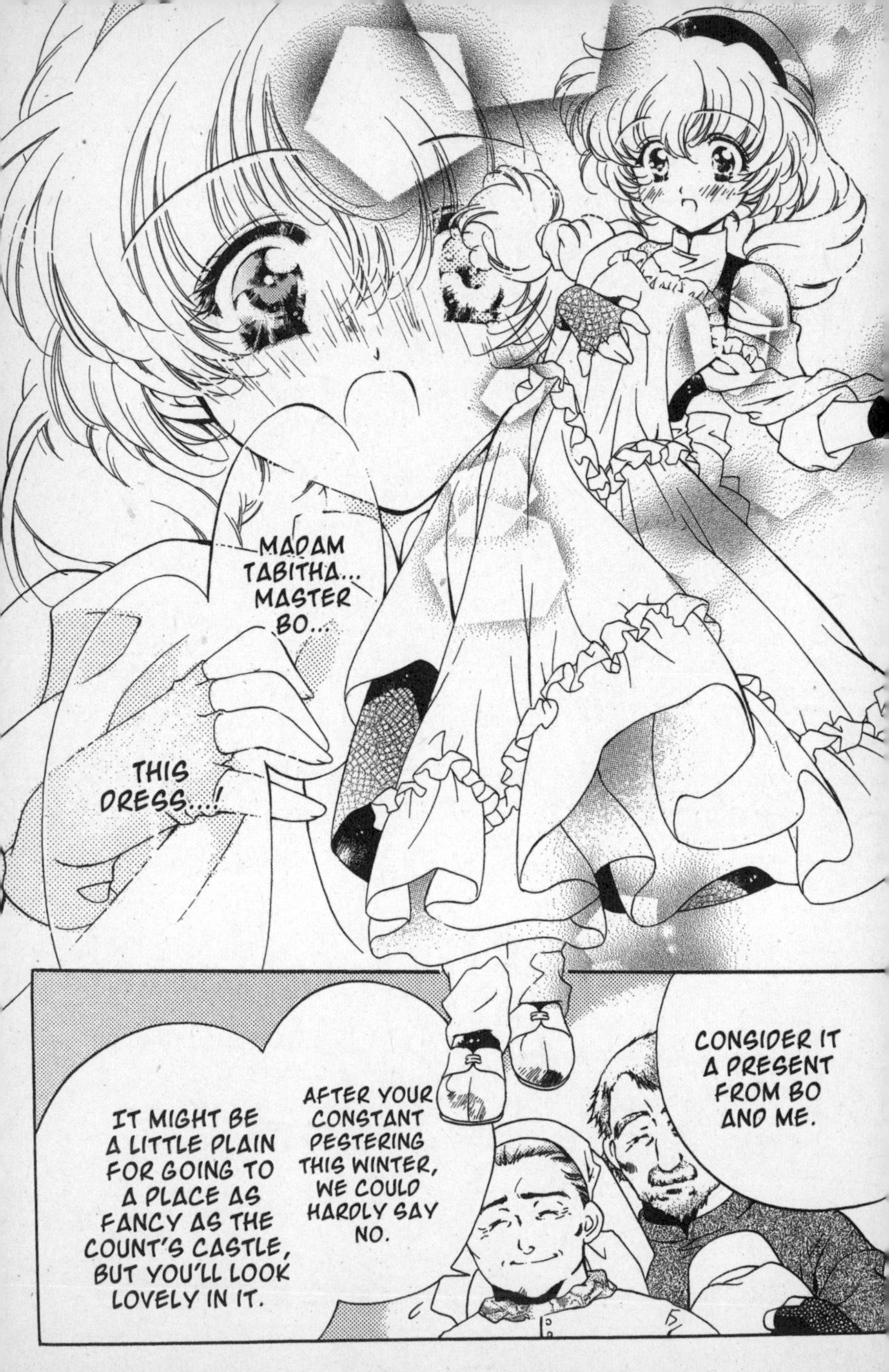
MADAM TABITHA... MASTER BO...
THIS DRESS...!
CONSIDER IT A PRESENT FROM BO AND ME.
AFTER YOUR CONSTANT PESTERING THIS WINTER, WE COULD HARDLY SAY NO.
IT MIGHT BE A LITTLE PLAIN FOR GOING TO A PLACE AS FANCY AS THE COUNT'S CASTLE, BUT YOU'LL LOOK LOVELY IN IT.

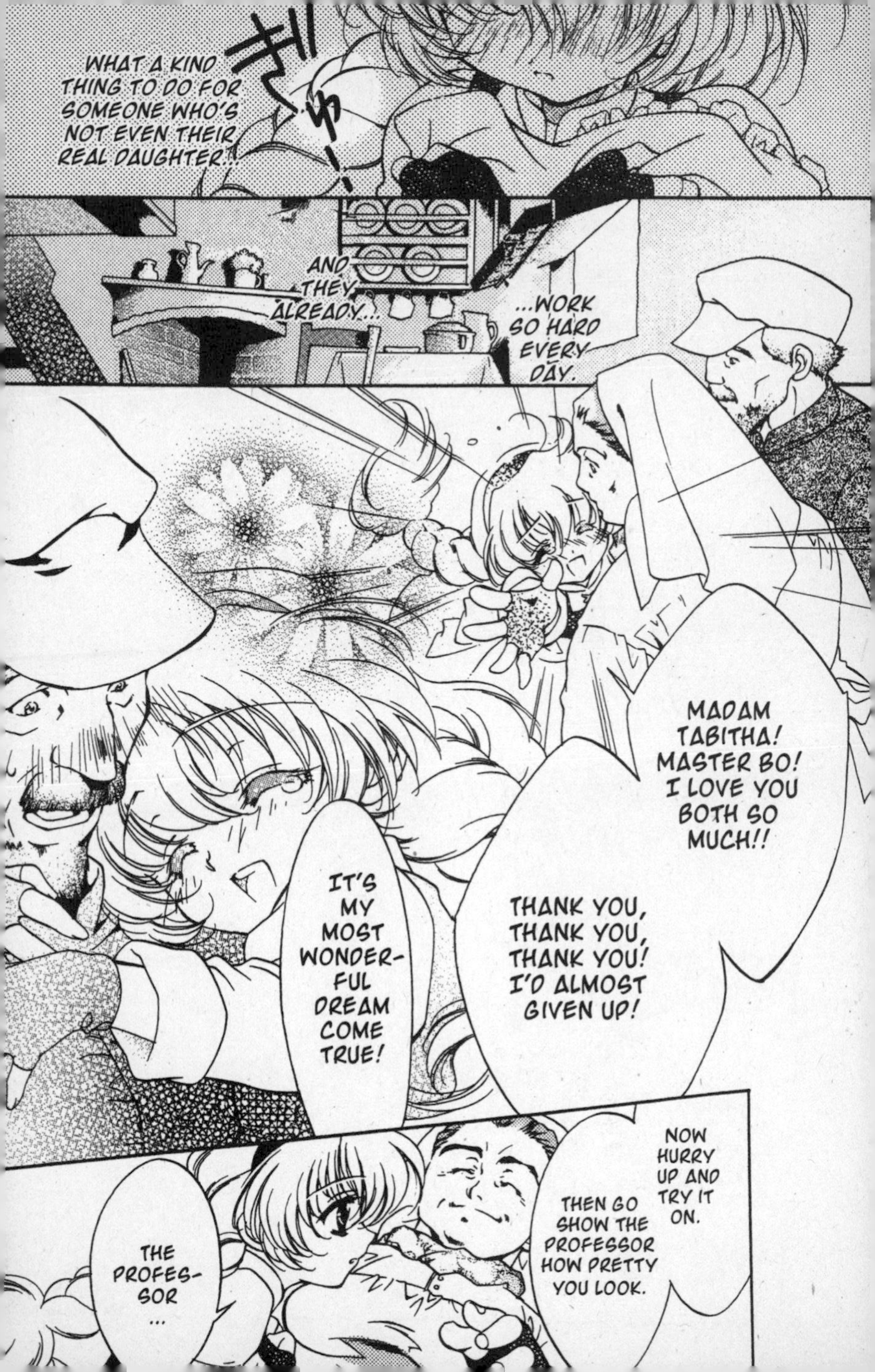
WHAT A KIND THING TO DO FOR SOMEONE WHO'S NOT EVEN THEIR REAL DAUGHTER...
ぎゅー!
AND THEY ALREADY...
...WORK SO HARD EVERY DAY.
MADAM TABITHA! MASTER BO! I LOVE YOU BOTH SO MUCH!!
THANK YOU, THANK YOU, THANK YOU! I'D ALMOST GIVEN UP!
IT'S MY MOST WONDER-FUL DREAM COME TRUE!
NOW HURRY UP AND TRY IT ON.
THEN GO SHOW THE PROFESSOR HOW PRETTY YOU LOOK.
THE PROFES-SOR ...

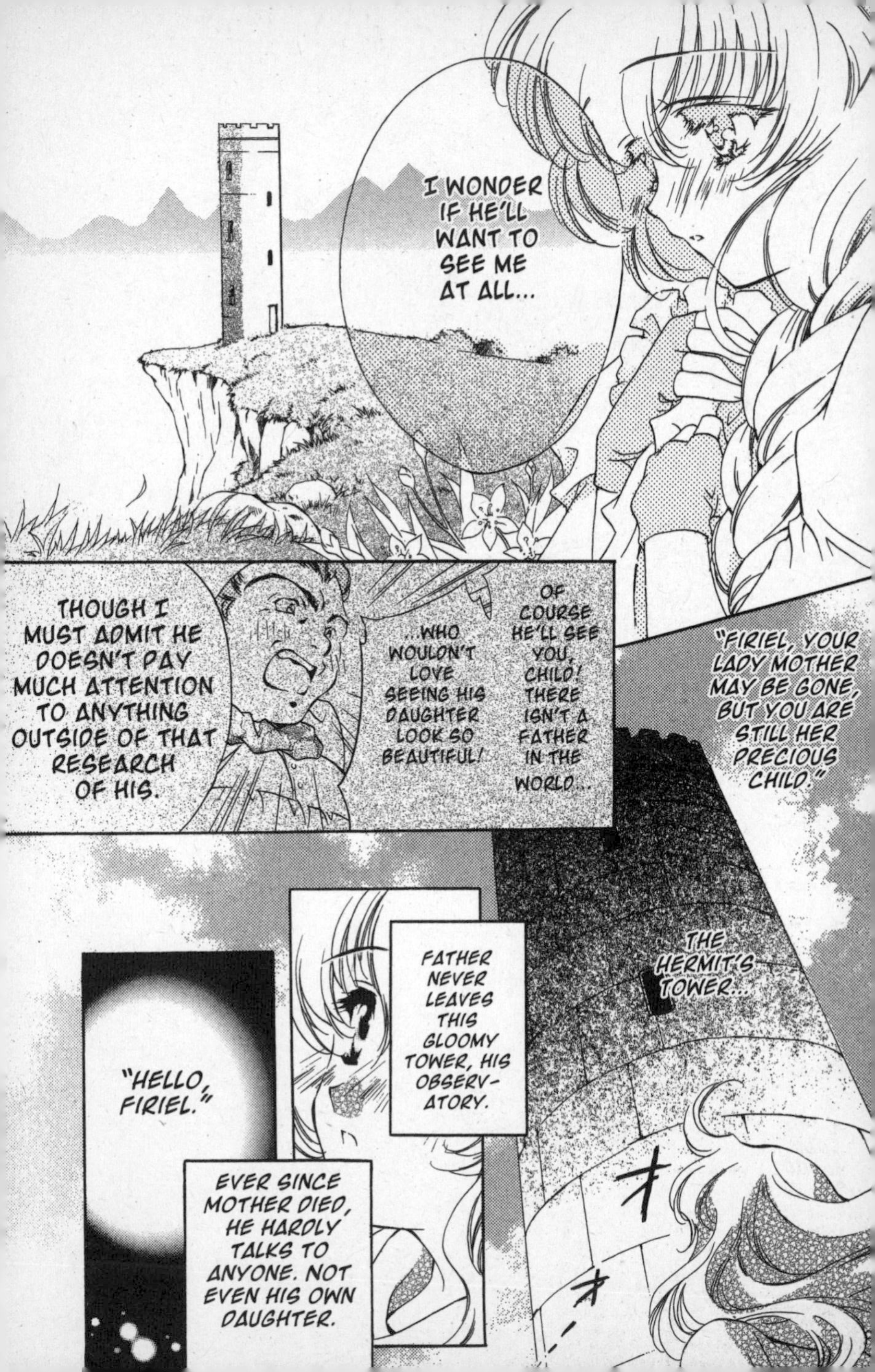
I WONDER IF HE'LL WANT TO SEE ME AT ALL...
OF COURSE HE'LL SEE YOU, CHILD! THERE ISN'T A FATHER IN THE WORLD...
...WHO WOULDN'T LOVE SEEING HIS DAUGHTER LOOK SO BEAUTIFUL!
THOUGH I MUST ADMIT HE DOESN'T PAY MUCH ATTENTION TO ANYTHING OUTSIDE OF THAT RESEARCH OF HIS.
"FIRIEL, YOUR LADY MOTHER MAY BE GONE, BUT YOU ARE STILL HER PRECIOUS CHILD."
THE HERMIT'S TOWER...
FATHER NEVER LEAVES THIS GLOOMY TOWER, HIS OBSERVATORY.
EVER SINCE MOTHER DIED, HE HARDLY TALKS TO ANYONE. NOT EVEN HIS OWN DAUGHTER.
"HELLO, FIRIEL."

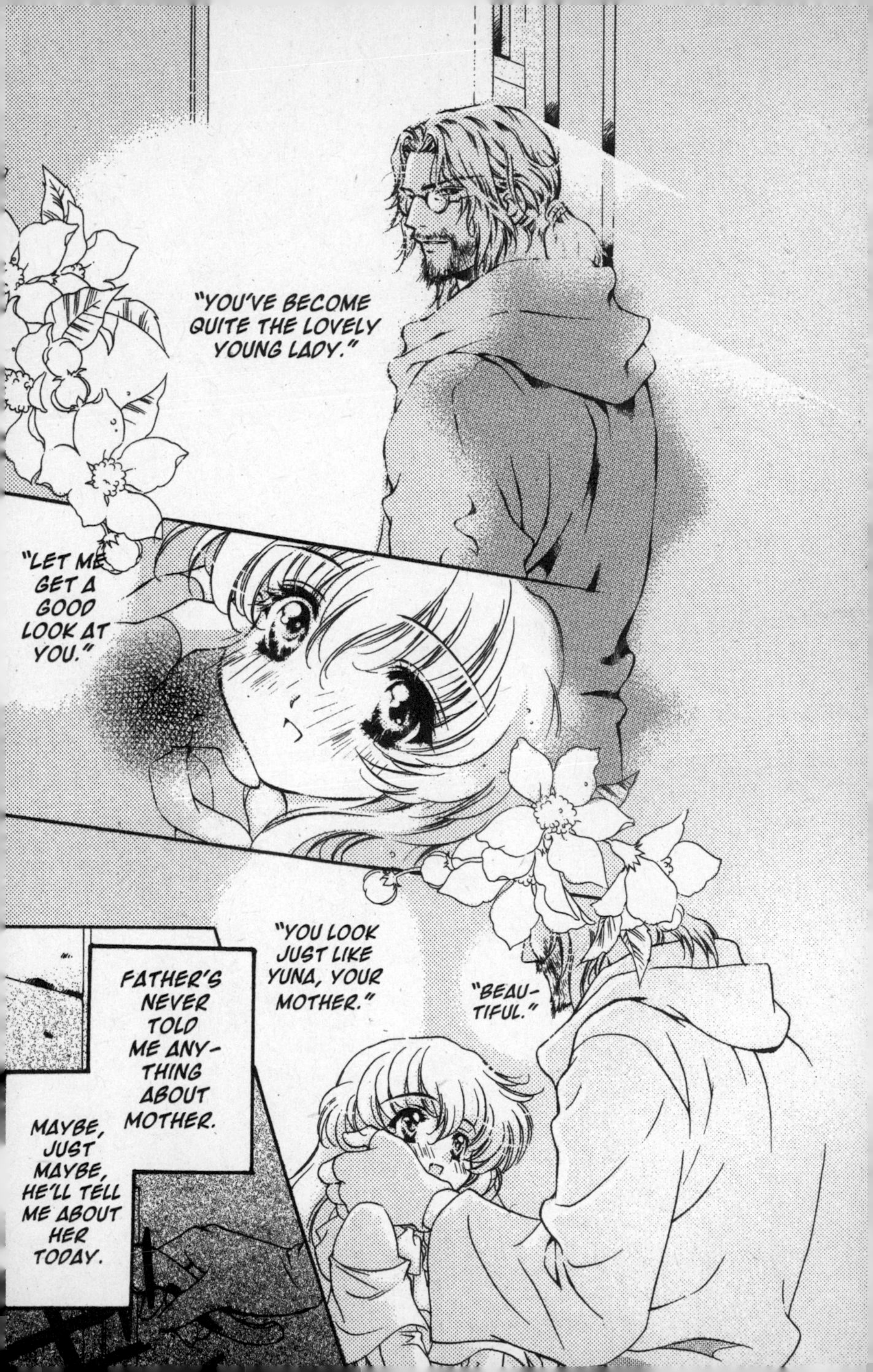
"YOU'VE BECOME QUITE THE LOVELY YOUNG LADY."
"LET ME GET A GOOD LOOK AT YOU."
"BEAU-TIFUL."
"YOU LOOK JUST LIKE YUNA, YOUR MOTHER."
FATHER'S NEVER TOLD ME ANY-THING ABOUT MOTHER.
MAYBE, JUST MAYBE, HE'LL TELL ME ABOUT HER TODAY.

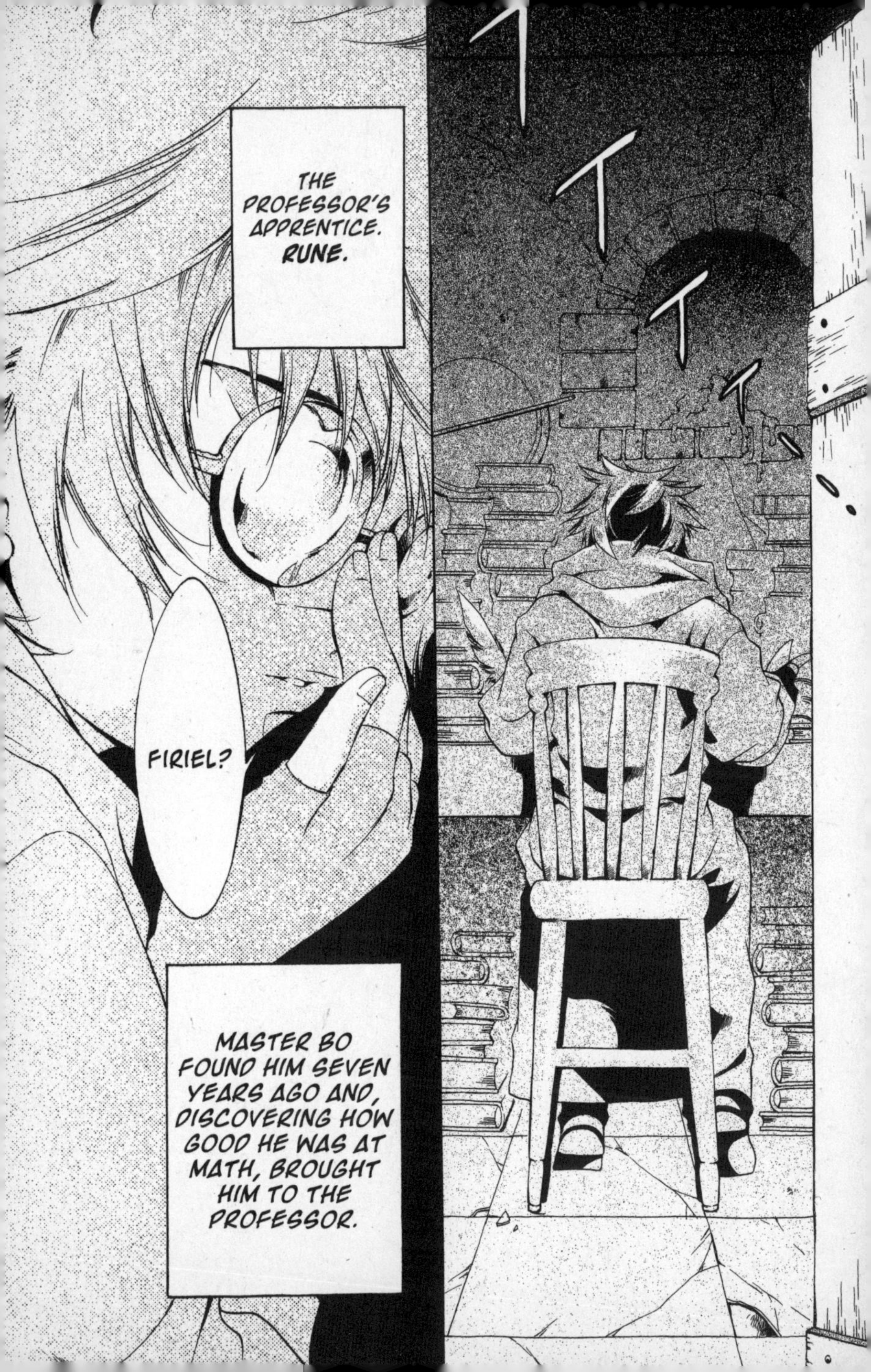
THE PROFESSOR'S APPRENTICE. RUNE.
FIRIEL?
MASTER BO FOUND HIM SEVEN YEARS AGO AND, DISCOVERING HOW GOOD HE WAS AT MATH, BROUGHT HIM TO THE PROFESSOR.

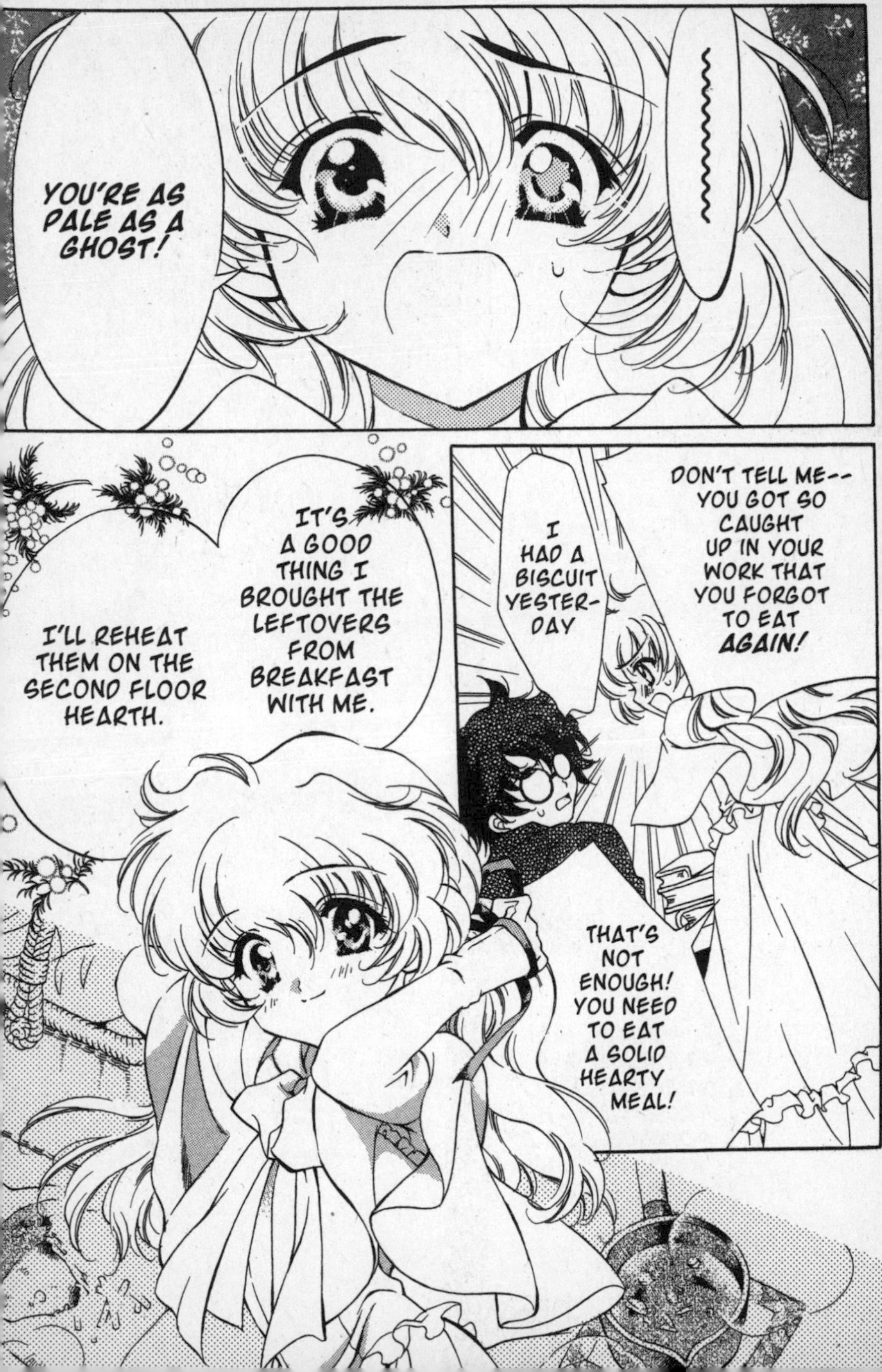
YOU'RE AS PALE AS A GHOST!
DON'T TELL ME-- YOU GOT SO CAUGHT UP IN YOUR WORK THAT YOU FORGOT TO EAT AGAIN!
I HAD A BISCUIT YESTER-DAY
THAT'S NOT ENOUGH! YOU NEED TO EAT A SOLID HEARTY MEAL!
IT'S A GOOD THING I BROUGHT THE LEFTOVERS FROM BREAKFAST WITH ME.
I'LL REHEAT THEM ON THE SECOND FLOOR HEARTH.

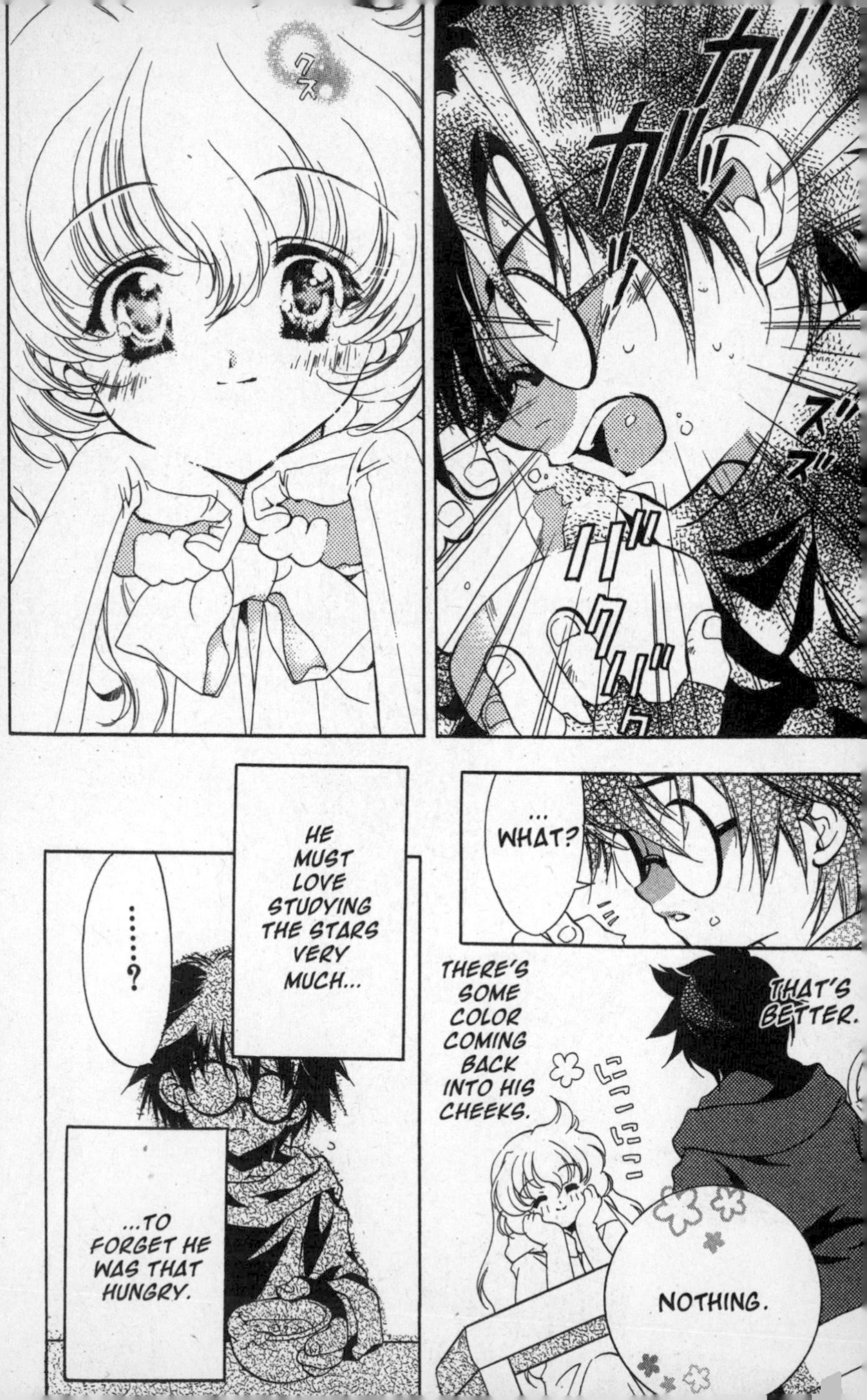
クス
...WHAT?
THAT'S BETTER.
THERE'S SOME COLOR COMING BACK INTO HIS CHEEKS.
NOTHING.
HE MUST LOVE STUDYING THE STARS VERY MUCH...
.....?
...TO FORGET HE WAS THAT HUNGRY.

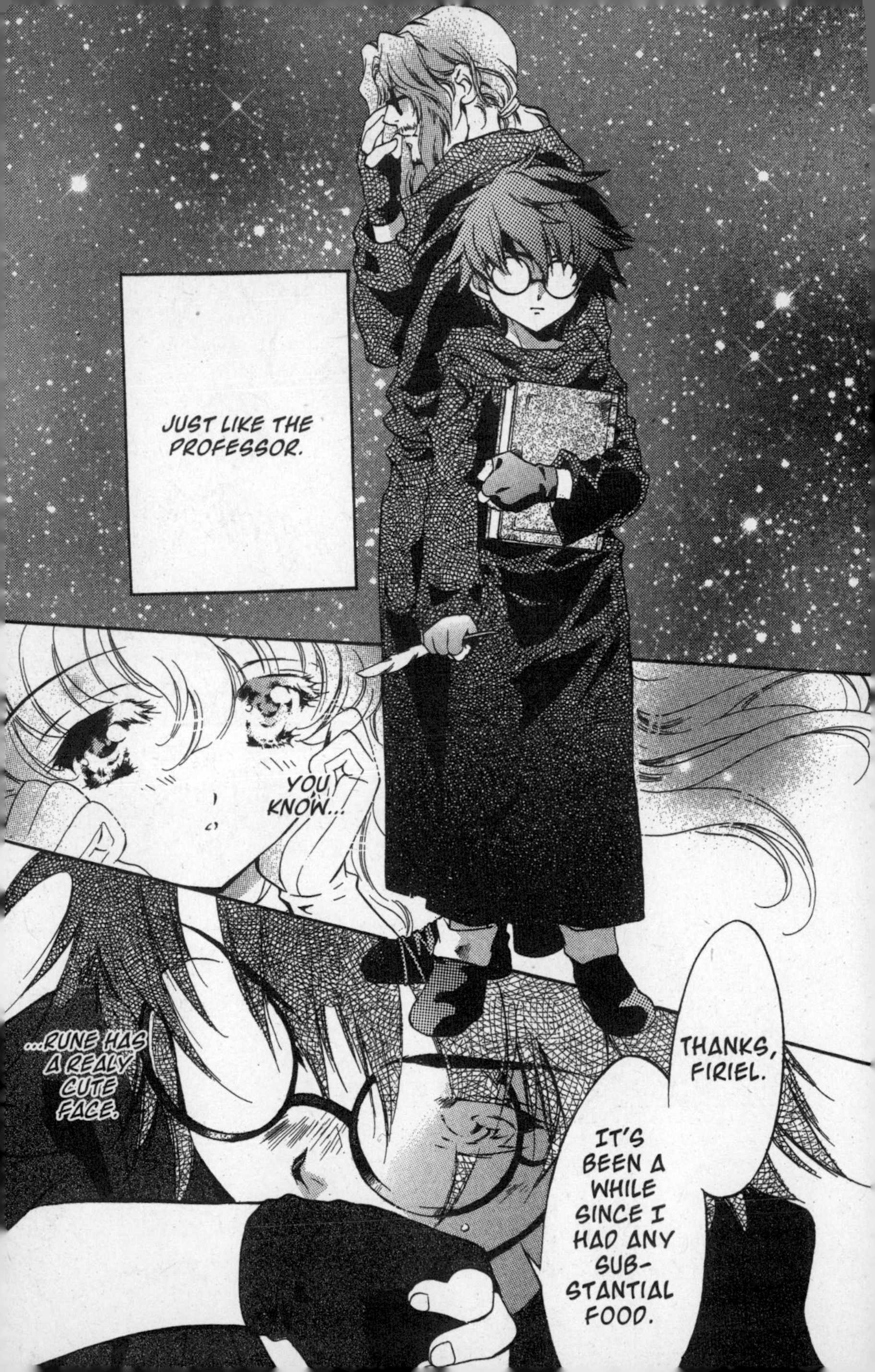
JUST LIKE THE PROFESSOR.
YOU KNOW...
THANKS, FIRIEL.
IT'S BEEN A WHILE SINCE I HAD ANY SUB-STANTIAL FOOD.
...RUNE HAS A REALY CUTE FACE.

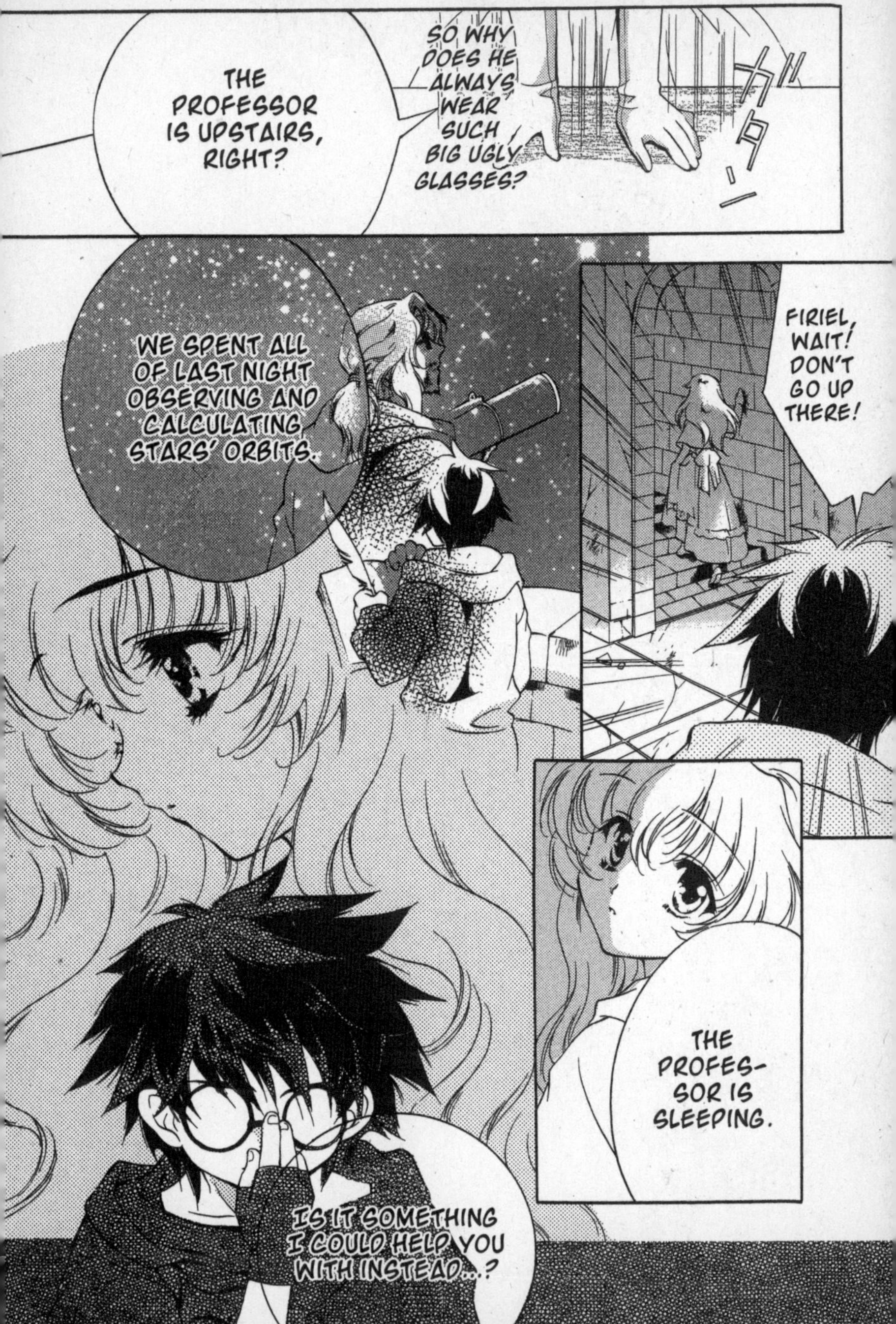
ガタン
SO WHY DOES HE ALWAYS WEAR SUCH BIG UGLY GLASSES?
THE PROFESSOR IS UPSTAIRS, RIGHT?
FIRIEL, WAIT! DON'T GO UP THERE!
THE PROFES-SOR IS SLEEPING.
WE SPENT ALL OF LAST NIGHT OBSERVING AND CALCULATING STARS' ORBITS.
IS IT SOMETHING I COULD HELP YOU WITH INSTEAD...?

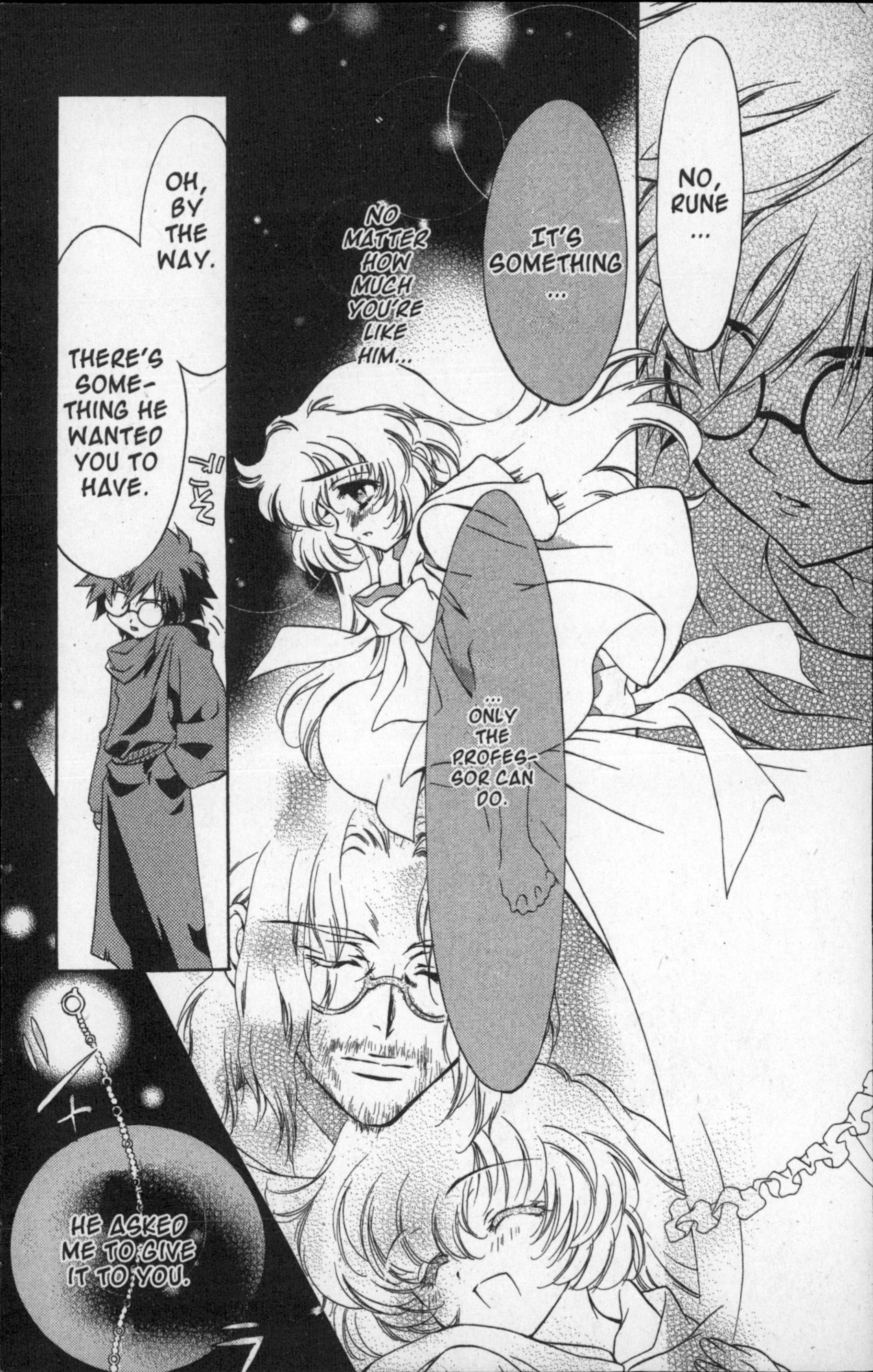
NO, RUNE ...
IT'S SOMETHING ...
... ONLY THE PROFES-SOR CAN DO.
NO MATTER HOW MUCH YOU'RE LIKE HIM...
OH, BY THE WAY.
THERE'S SOME-THING HE WANTED YOU TO HAVE.
HE ASKED ME TO GIVE IT TO YOU.

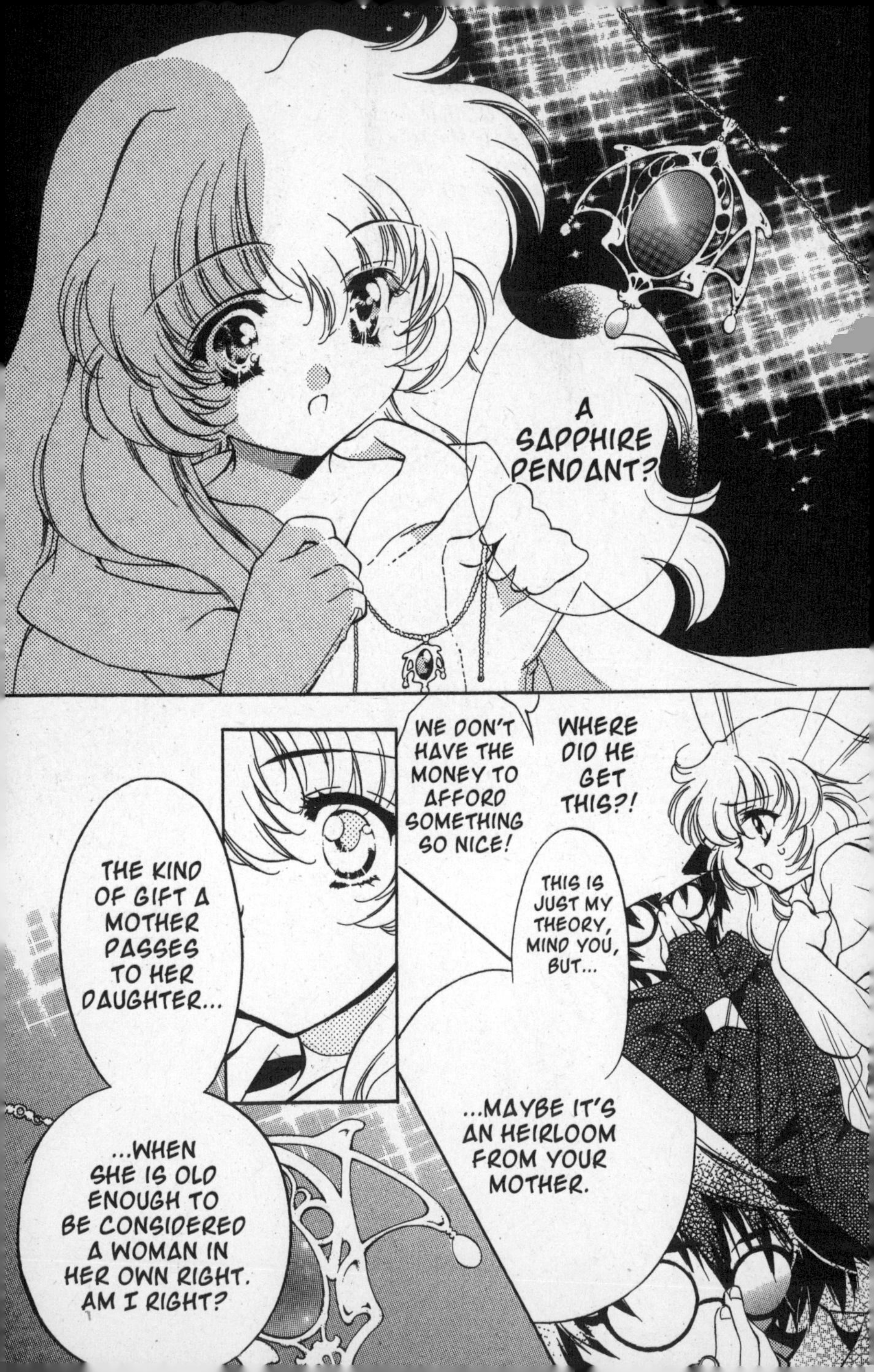
A SAPPHIRE PENDANT?
WHERE DID HE GET THIS?!
WE DON'T HAVE THE MONEY TO AFFORD SOMETHING SO NICE!
THIS IS JUST MY THEORY, MIND YOU, BUT...
...MAYBE IT'S AN HEIRLOOM FROM YOUR MOTHER.
THE KIND OF GIFT A MOTHER PASSES TO HER DAUGHTER...
...WHEN SHE IS OLD ENOUGH TO BE CONSIDERED A WOMAN IN HER OWN RIGHT. AM I RIGHT?

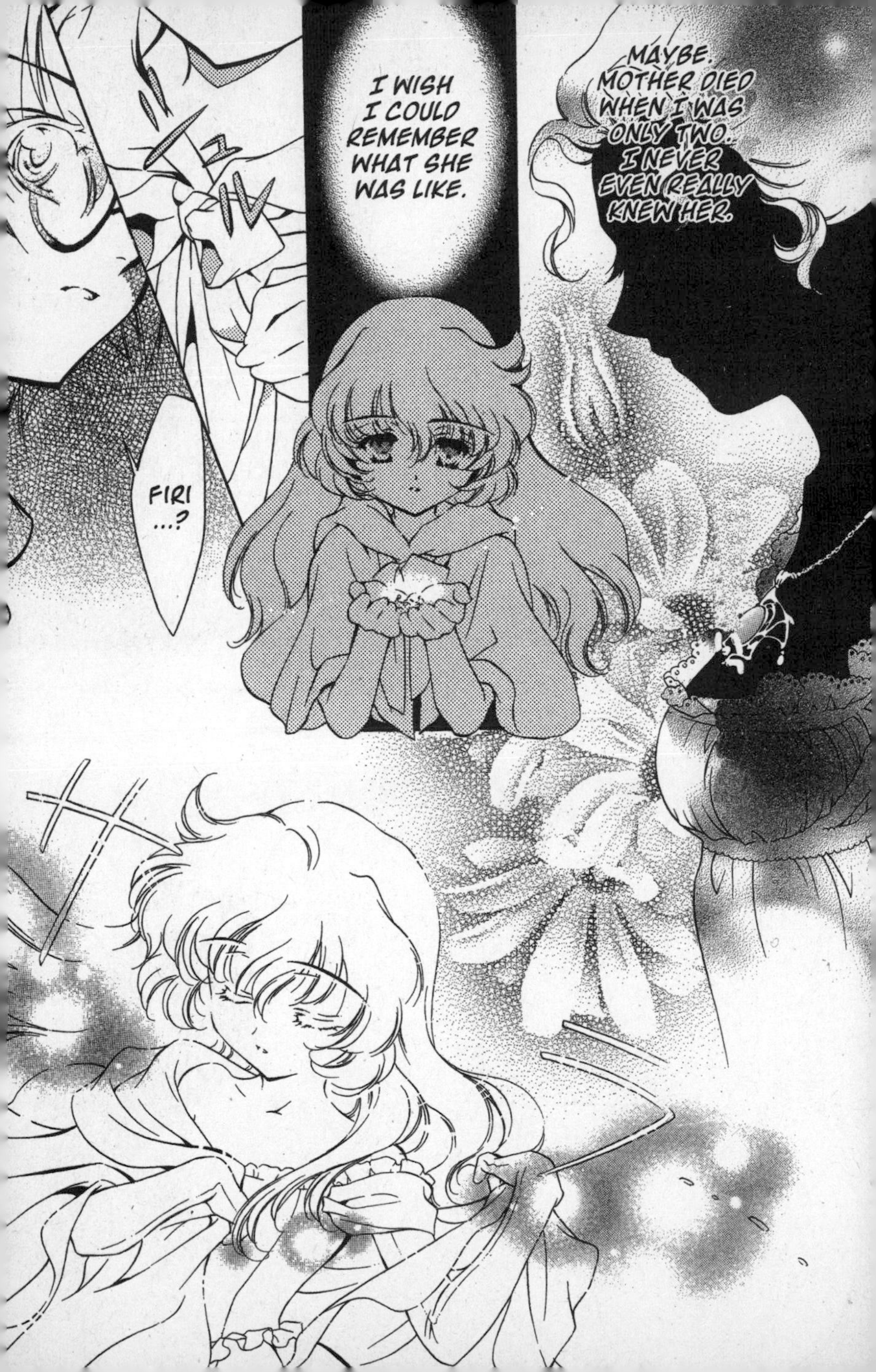
MAYBE. MOTHER DIED WHEN I WAS ONLY TWO. I NEVER EVEN REALLY KNEW HER.
I WISH I COULD REMEMBER WHAT SHE WAS LIKE.
FIRI ...?

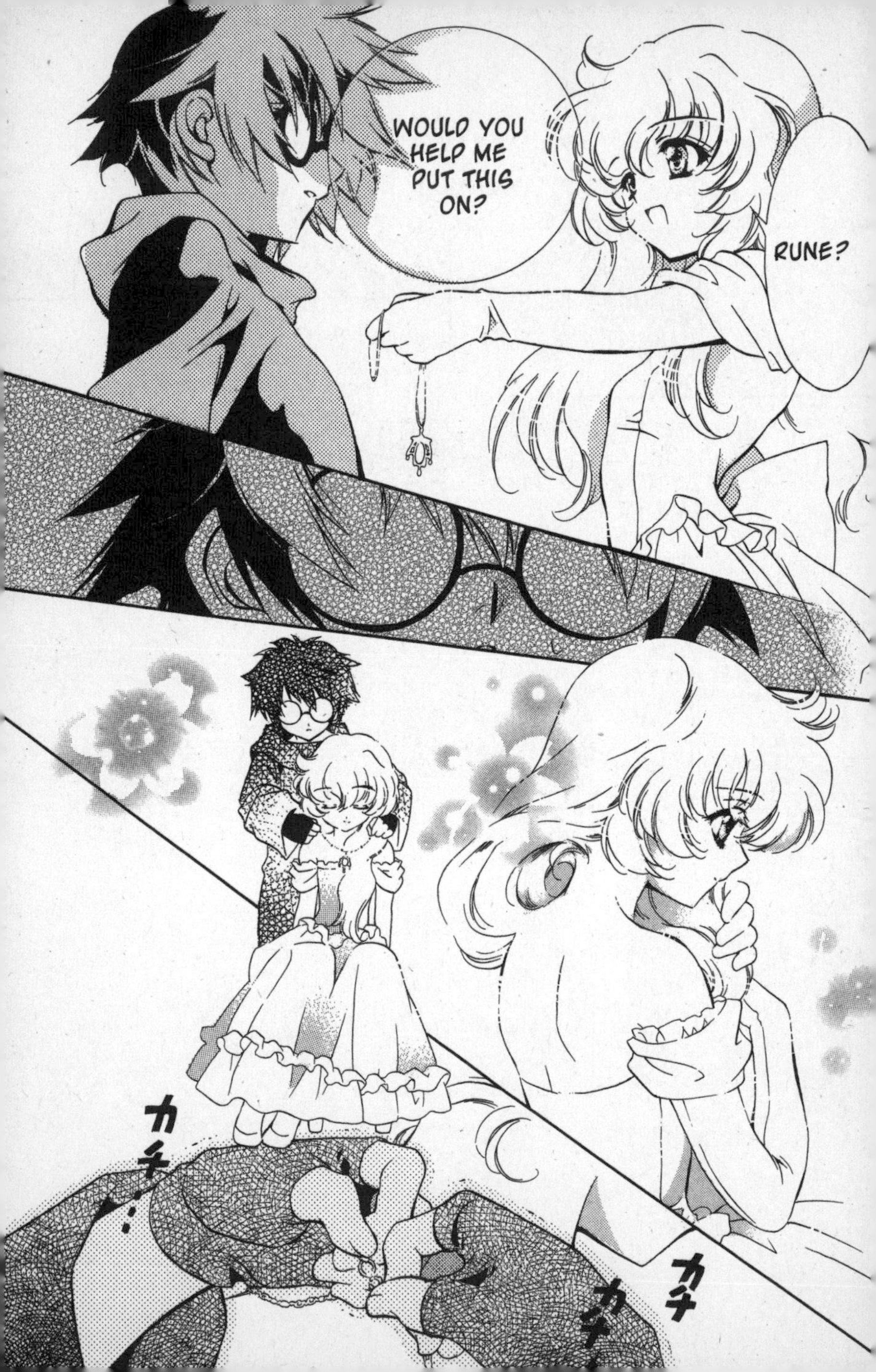
RUNE?
WOULD YOU HELP ME PUT THIS ON?
カチ
カチ
カチ…

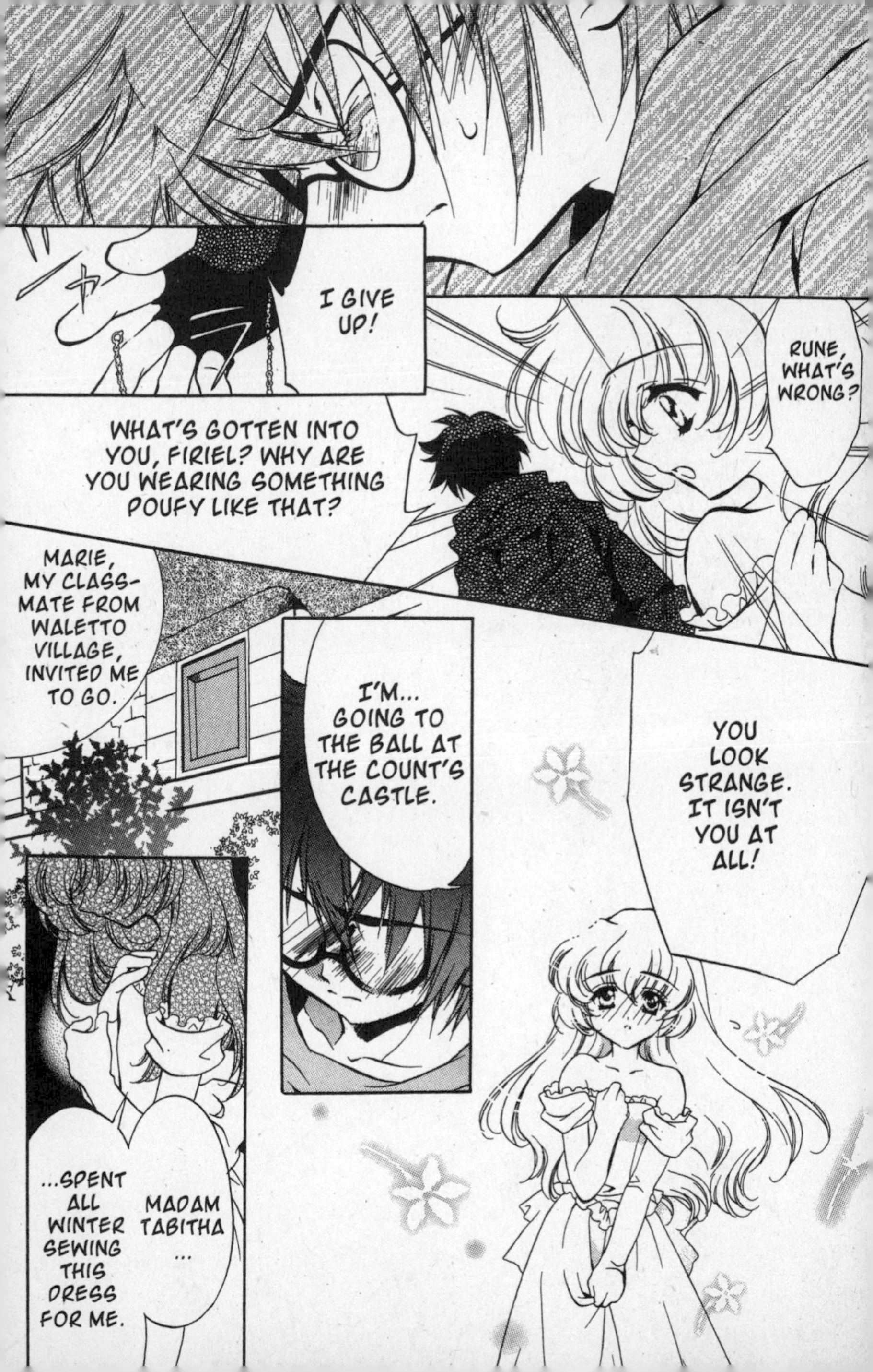
I GIVE UP!
RUNE, WHAT'S WRONG?
WHAT'S GOTTEN INTO YOU, FIRIEL? WHY ARE YOU WEARING SOMETHING POUFY LIKE THAT?
YOU LOOK STRANGE. IT ISN'T YOU AT ALL!
I'M... GOING TO THE BALL AT THE COUNT'S CASTLE.
MARIE, MY CLASSMATE FROM WALETTO VILLAGE, INVITED ME TO GO.
MADAM TABITHA ...
...SPENT ALL WINTER SEWING THIS DRESS FOR ME.

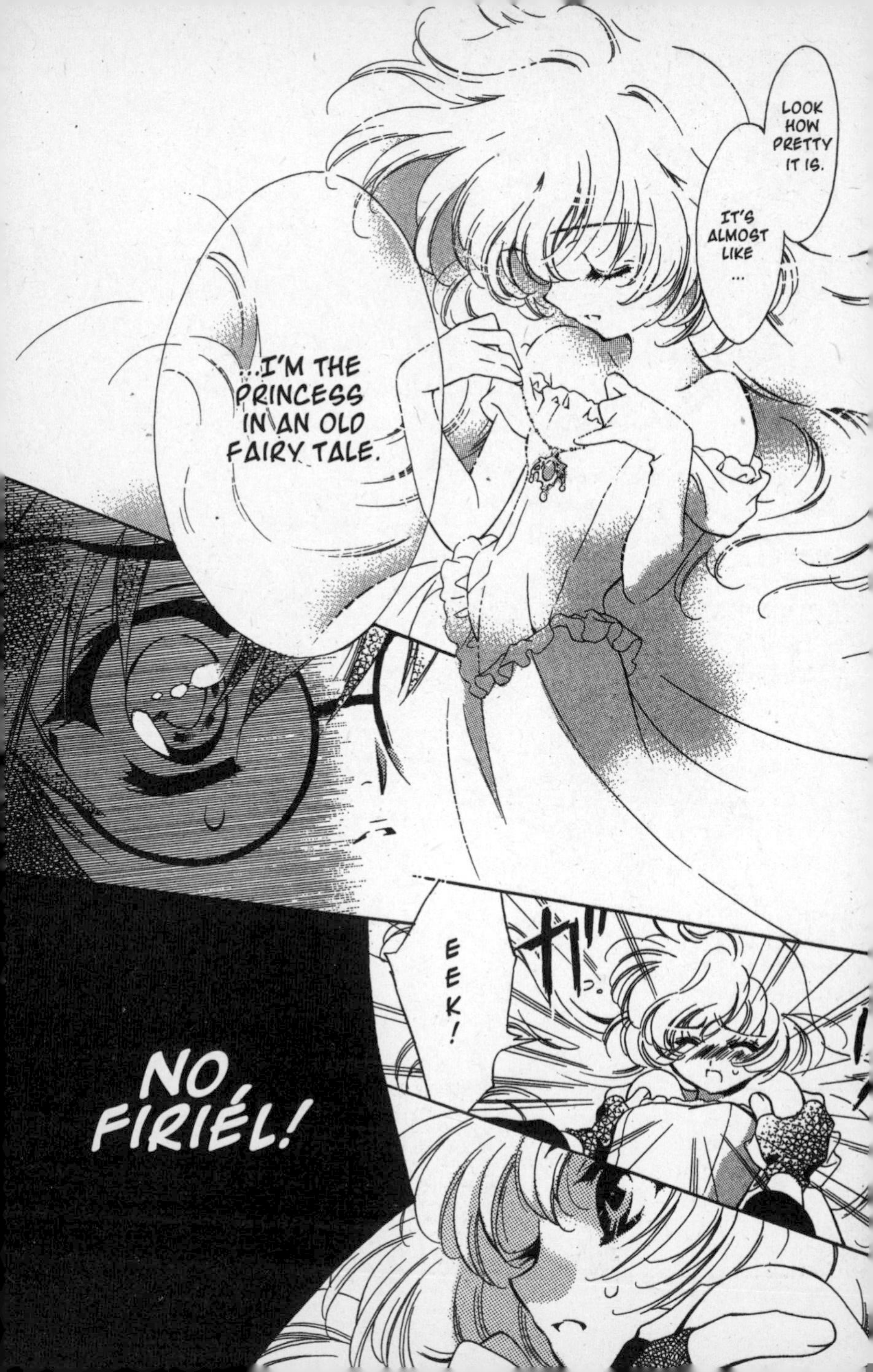
LOOK HOW PRETTY IT IS.
IT'S ALMOST LIKE ...
...I'M THE PRINCESS IN AN OLD FAIRY TALE.
EEK!
NO FIRIÉL!

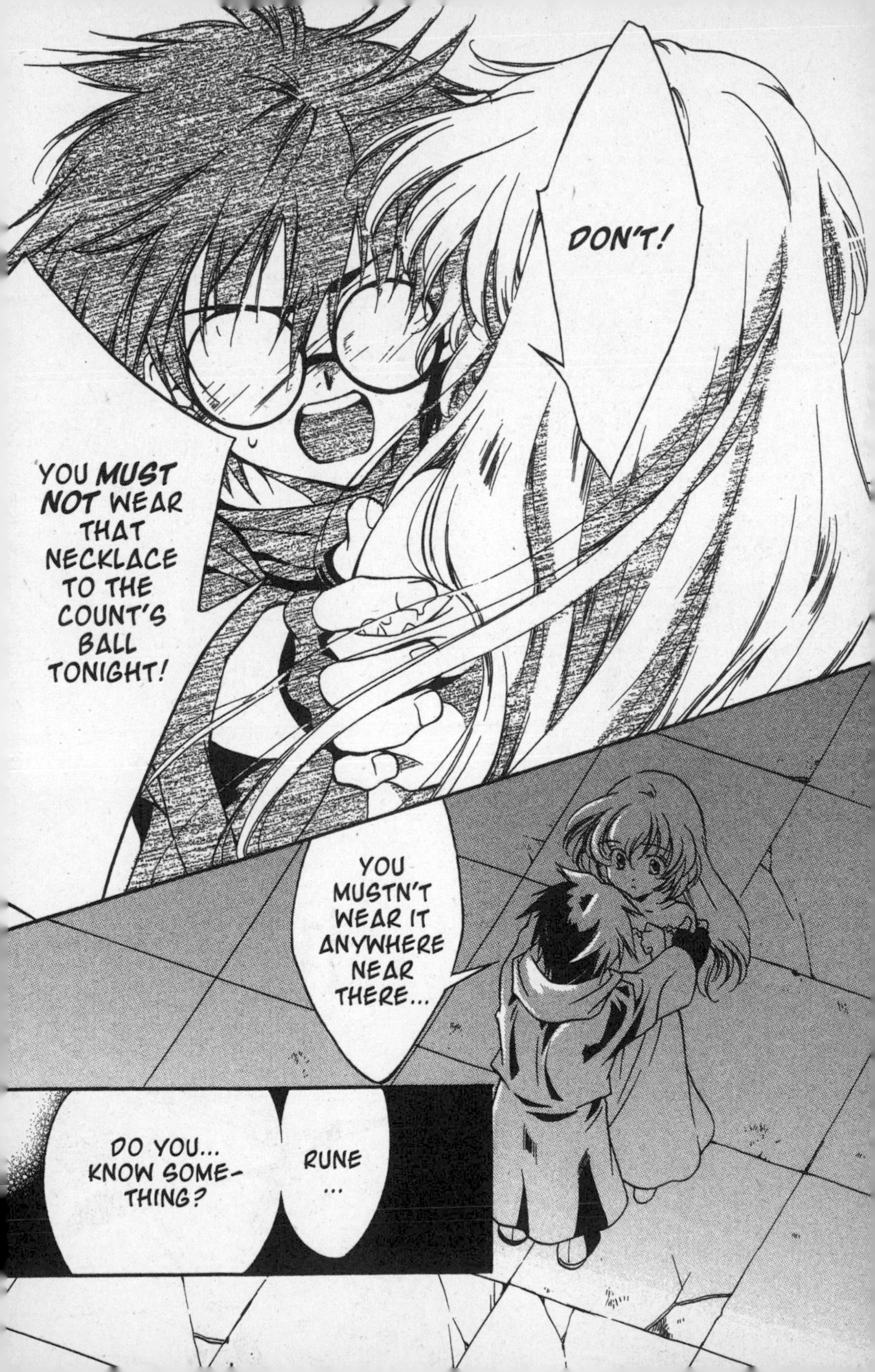
DON'T!
YOU MUST NOT WEAR THAT NECKLACE TO THE COUNT'S BALL TONIGHT!
YOU MUSTN'T WEAR IT ANYWHERE NEAR THERE...
RUNE ...
DO YOU... KNOW SOME-THING?

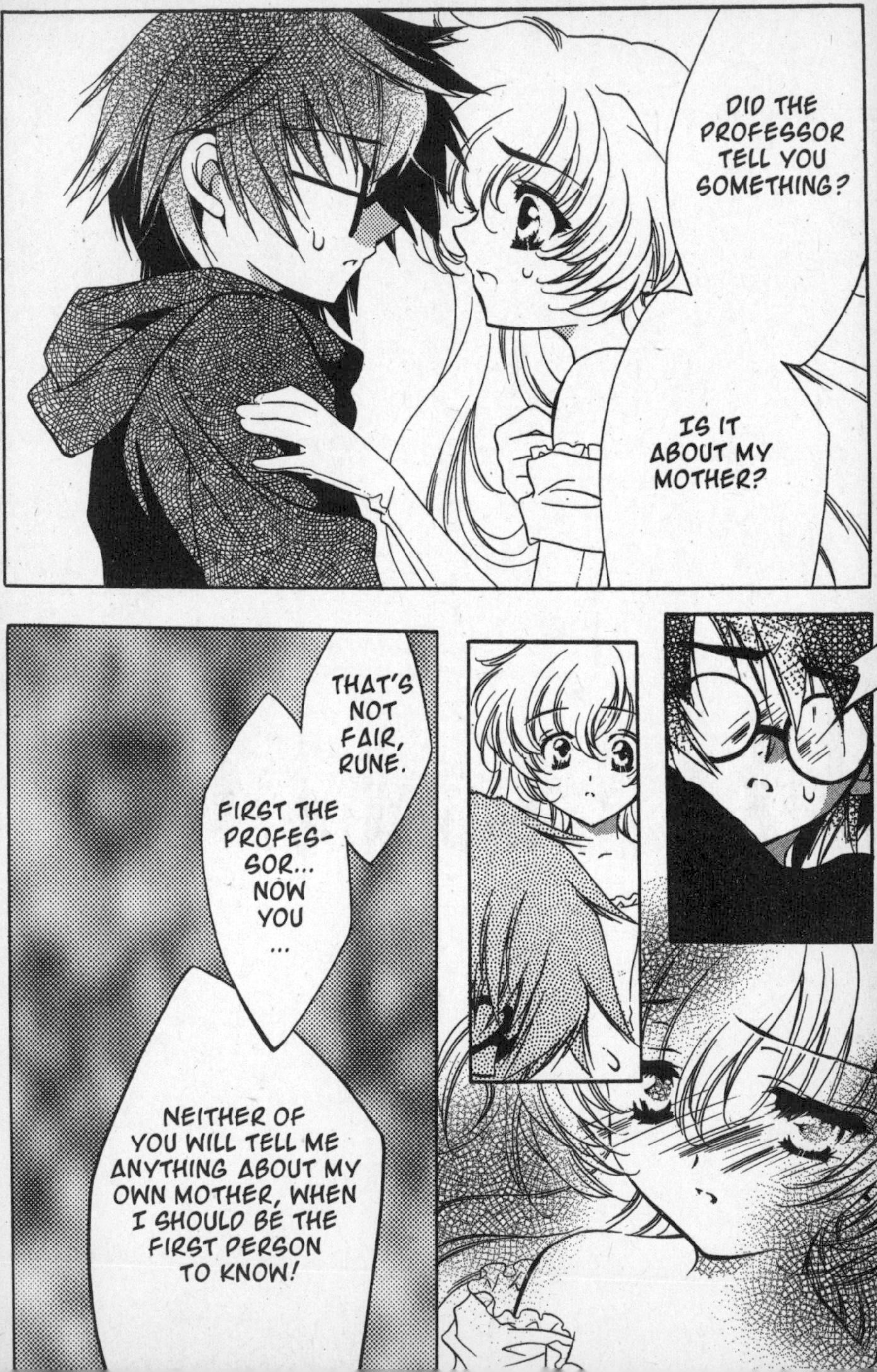
DID THE PROFESSOR TELL YOU SOMETHING?
IS IT ABOUT MY MOTHER?
THAT'S NOT FAIR, RUNE.
FIRST THE PROFES-SOR... NOW YOU ...
NEITHER OF YOU WILL TELL ME ANYTHING ABOUT MY OWN MOTHER, WHEN I SHOULD BE THE FIRST PERSON TO KNOW!

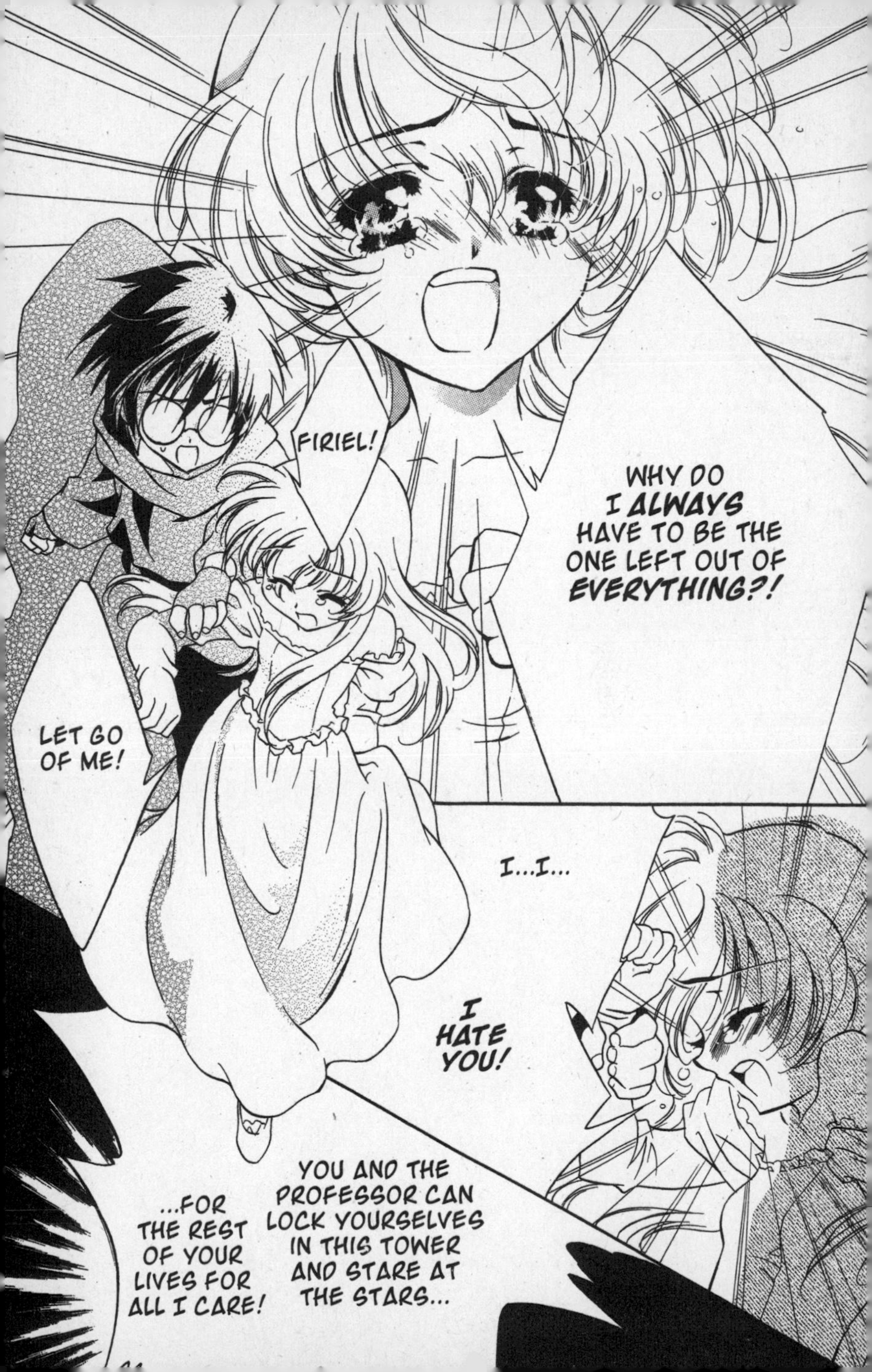
WHY DO I ALWAYS HAVE TO BE THE ONE LEFT OUT OF EVERYTHING?!
FIRIEL!
LET GO OF ME!
I...I...
I HATE YOU!
YOU AND THE PROFESSOR CAN LOCK YOURSELVES IN THIS TOWER AND STARE AT THE STARS...
...FOR THE REST OF YOUR LIVES FOR ALL I CARE!

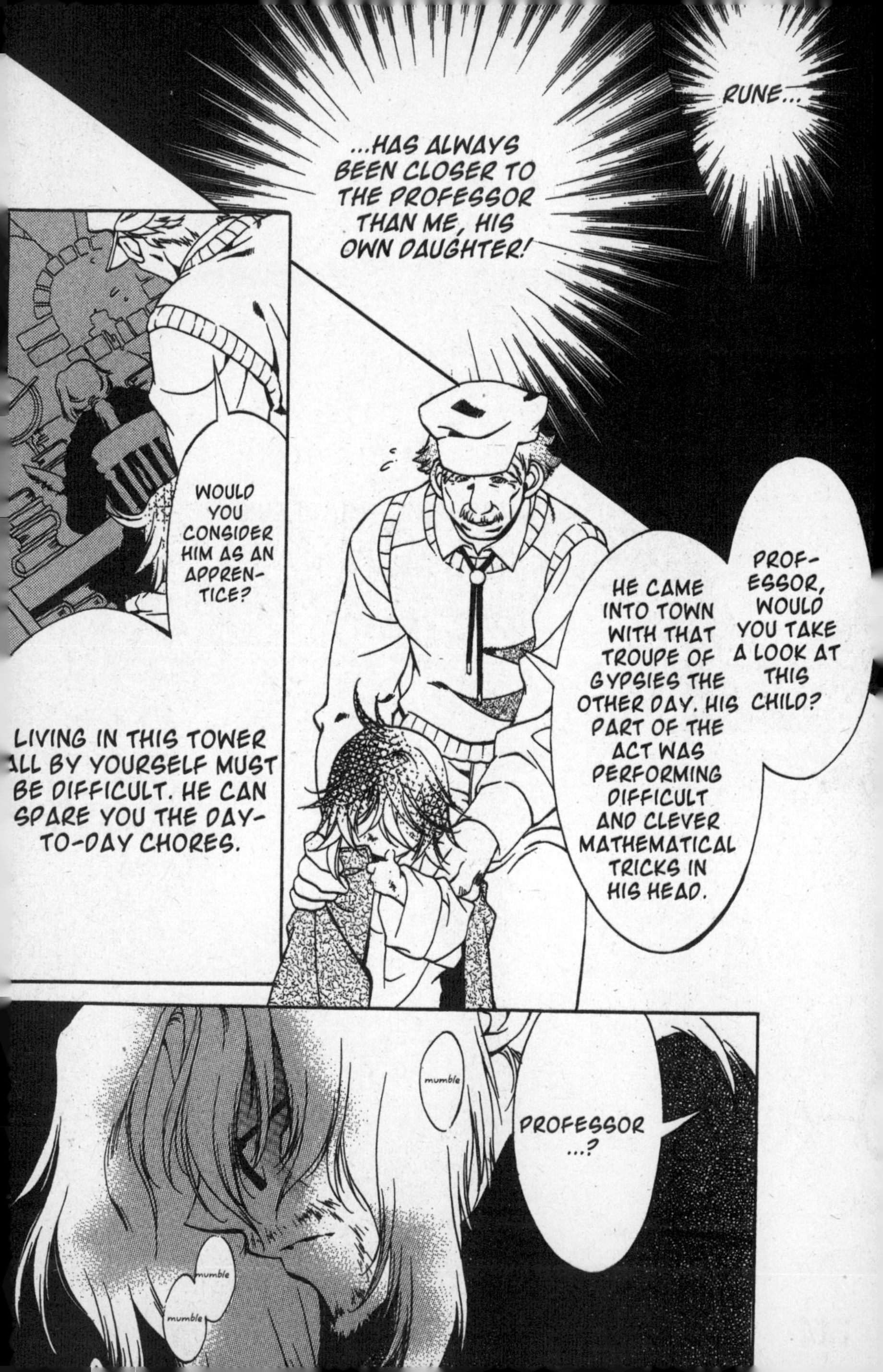
RUNE...
...HAS ALWAYS BEEN CLOSER TO THE PROFESSOR THAN ME, HIS OWN DAUGHTER!
PROFESSOR, WOULD YOU TAKE A LOOK AT THIS CHILD?
HE CAME INTO TOWN WITH THAT TROUPE OF GYPSIES THE OTHER DAY. HIS PART OF THE ACT WAS PERFORMING DIFFICULT AND CLEVER MATHEMATICAL TRICKS IN HIS HEAD.
WOULD YOU CONSIDER HIM AS AN APPRENTICE?
LIVING IN THIS TOWER ALL BY YOURSELF MUST BE DIFFICULT. HE CAN SPARE YOU THE DAY-TO-DAY CHORES.
PROFESSOR ...?
mumble
mumble
mumble

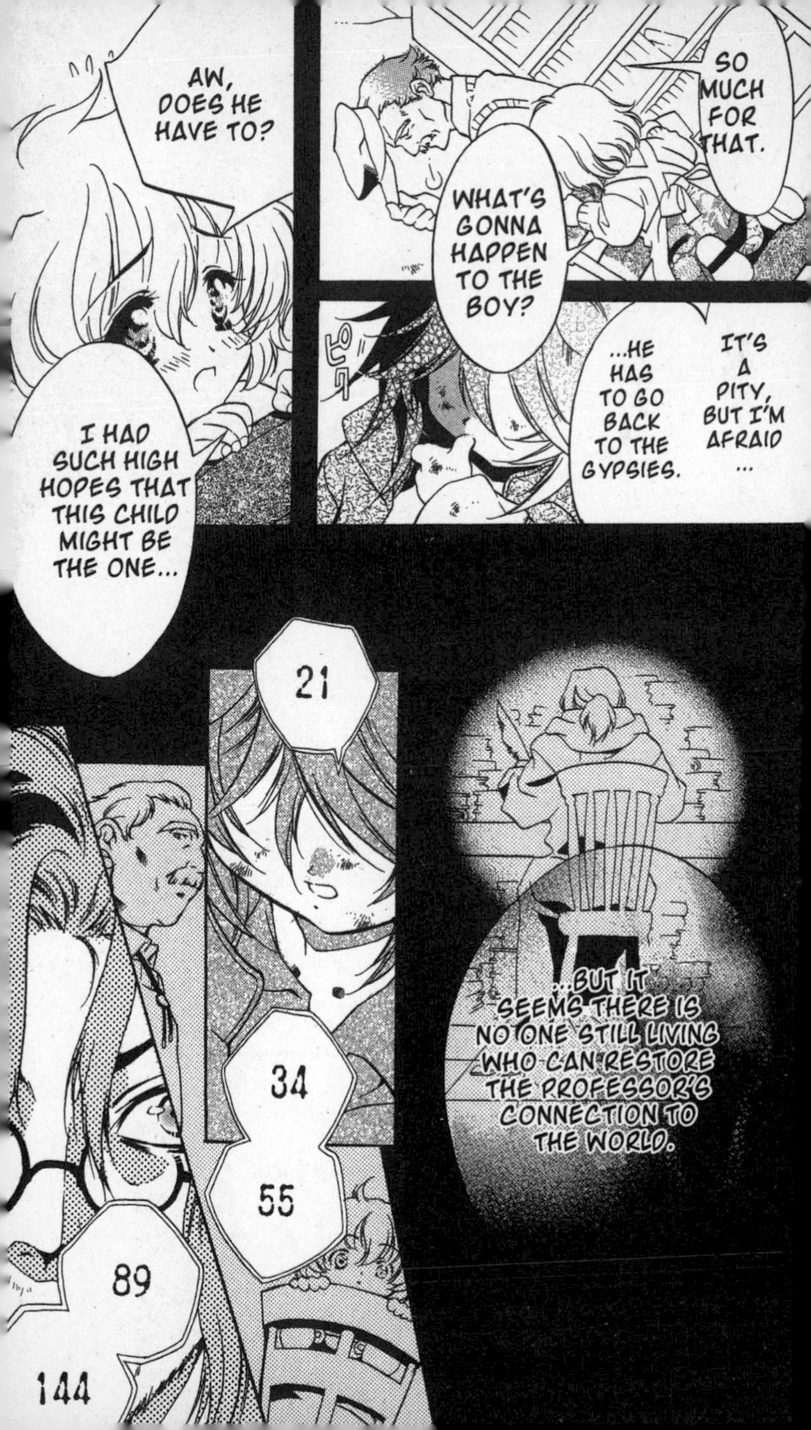
SO MUCH FOR THAT.
WHAT'S GONNA HAPPEN TO THE BOY?
IT'S A PITY, BUT I'M AFRAID ...
...HE HAS TO GO BACK TO THE GYPSIES.
AW, DOES HE HAVE TO?
I HAD SUCH HIGH HOPES THAT THIS CHILD MIGHT BE THE ONE...
...BUT IT SEEMS THERE IS NO ONE STILL LIVING WHO CAN RESTORE THE PROFESSOR'S CONNECTION TO THE WORLD.
21
34
55
89

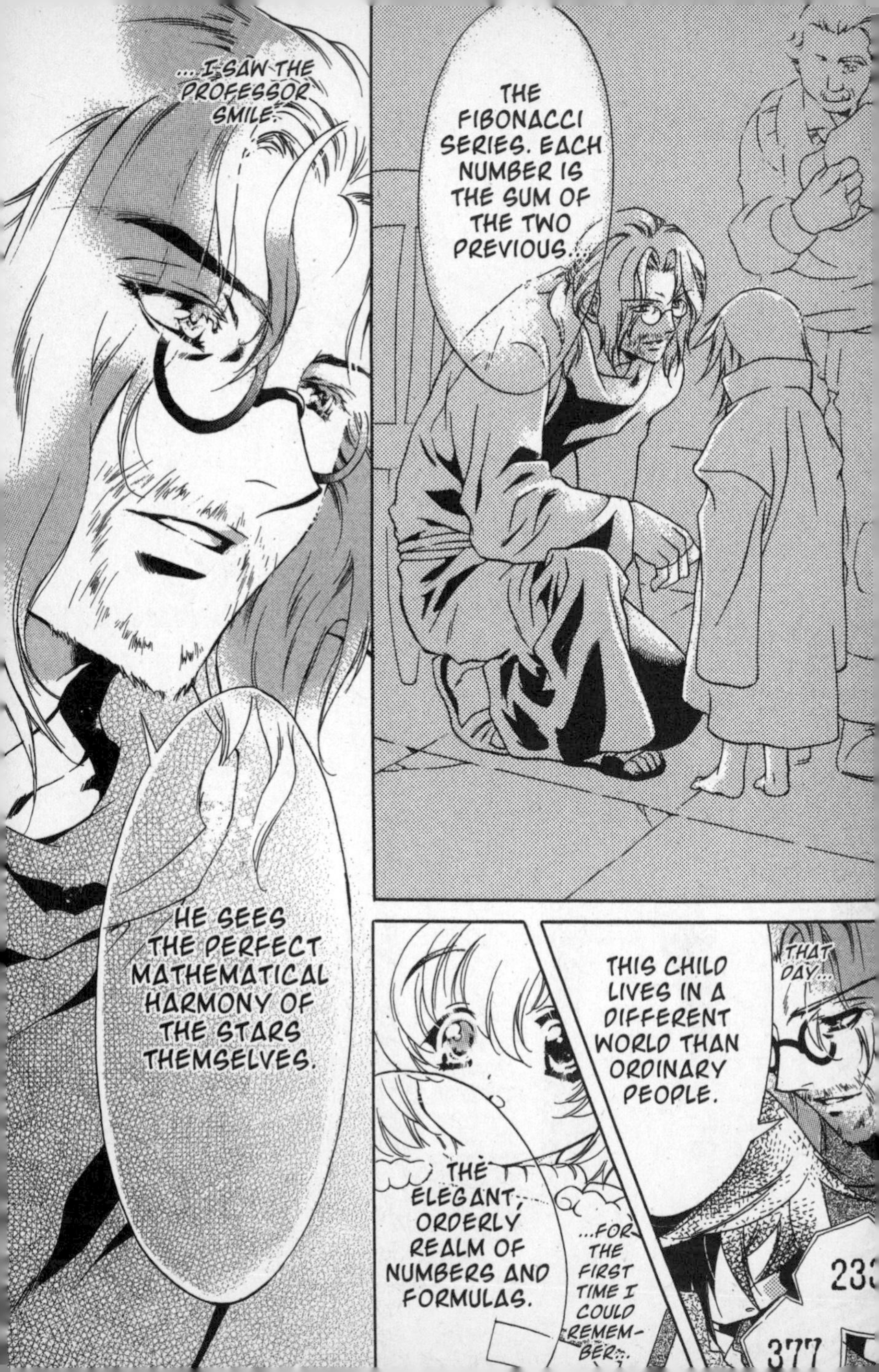
THE FIBONACCI SERIES. EACH NUMBER IS THE SUM OF THE TWO PREVIOUS...
THAT DAY...
THIS CHILD LIVES IN A DIFFERENT WORLD THAN ORDINARY PEOPLE.
THE ELEGANT, ORDERLY REALM OF NUMBERS AND FORMULAS.
...FOR THE FIRST TIME I COULD REMEMBER...
377
...I SAW THE PROFESSOR SMILE.
HE SEES THE PERFECT MATHEMATICAL HARMONY OF THE STARS THEMSELVES.

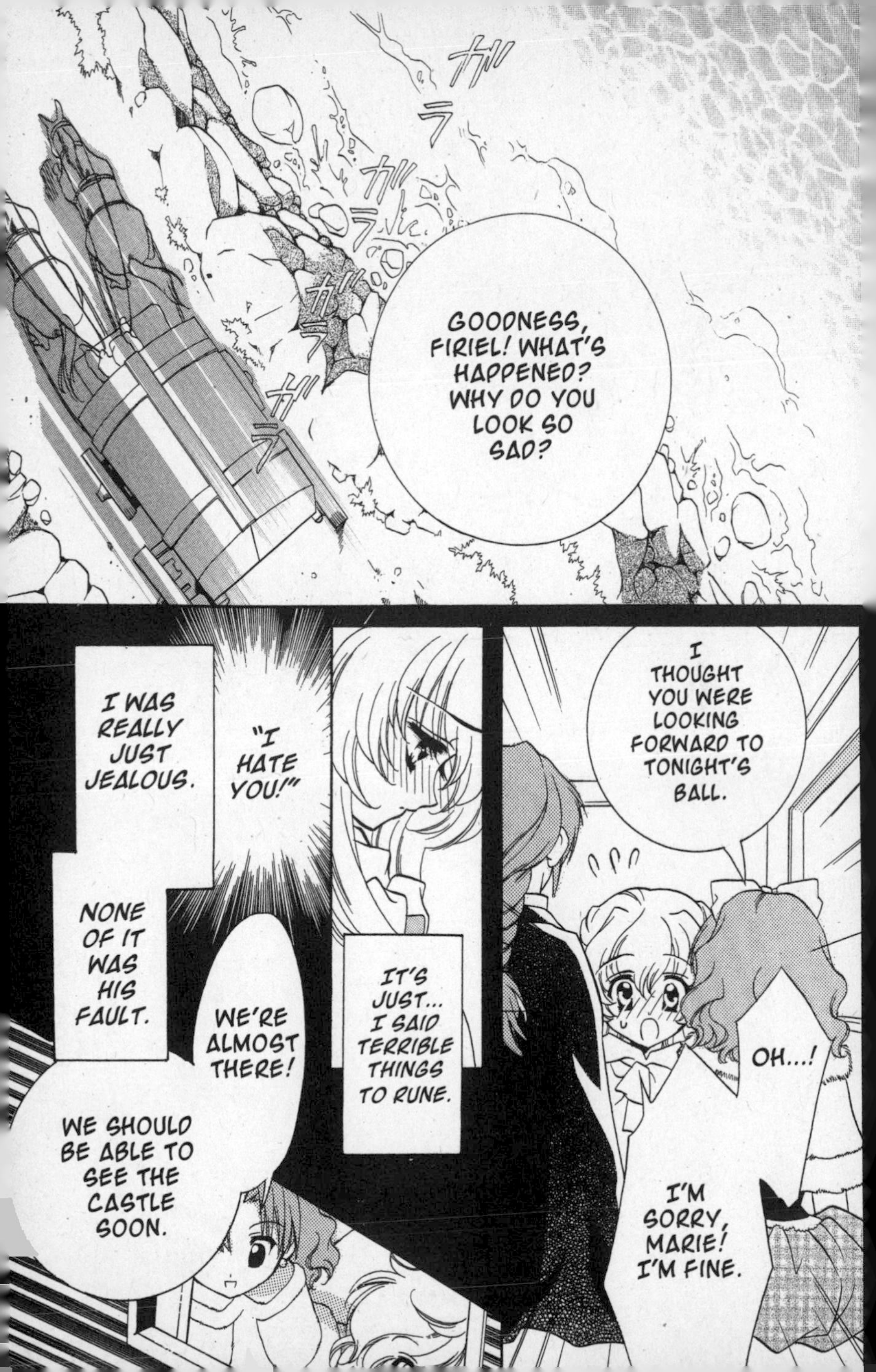
ガラ
ガラ
ガラ
ガラ
GOODNESS, FIRIEL! WHAT'S HAPPENED? WHY DO YOU LOOK SO SAD?
I THOUGHT YOU WERE LOOKING FORWARD TO TONIGHT'S BALL.
OH...!
I'M SORRY, MARIE! I'M FINE.
IT'S JUST... I SAID TERRIBLE THINGS TO RUNE.
"I HATE YOU!"
I WAS REALLY JUST JEALOUS.
NONE OF IT WAS HIS FAULT.
WE'RE ALMOST THERE!
WE SHOULD BE ABLE TO SEE THE CASTLE SOON.

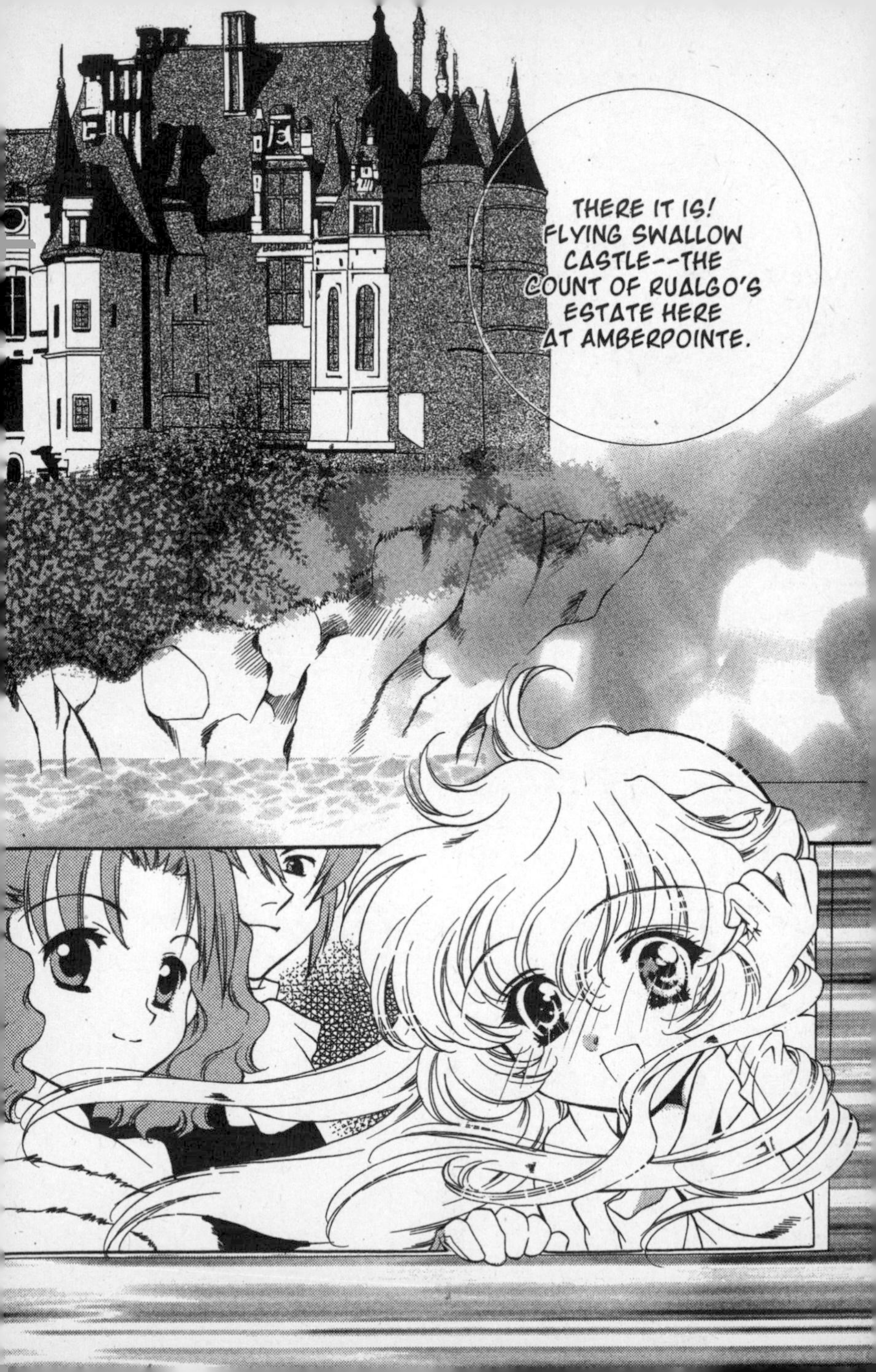
THERE IT IS! FLYING SWALLOW CASTLE--THE COUNT OF RUALGO'S ESTATE HERE AT AMBERPOINTE.

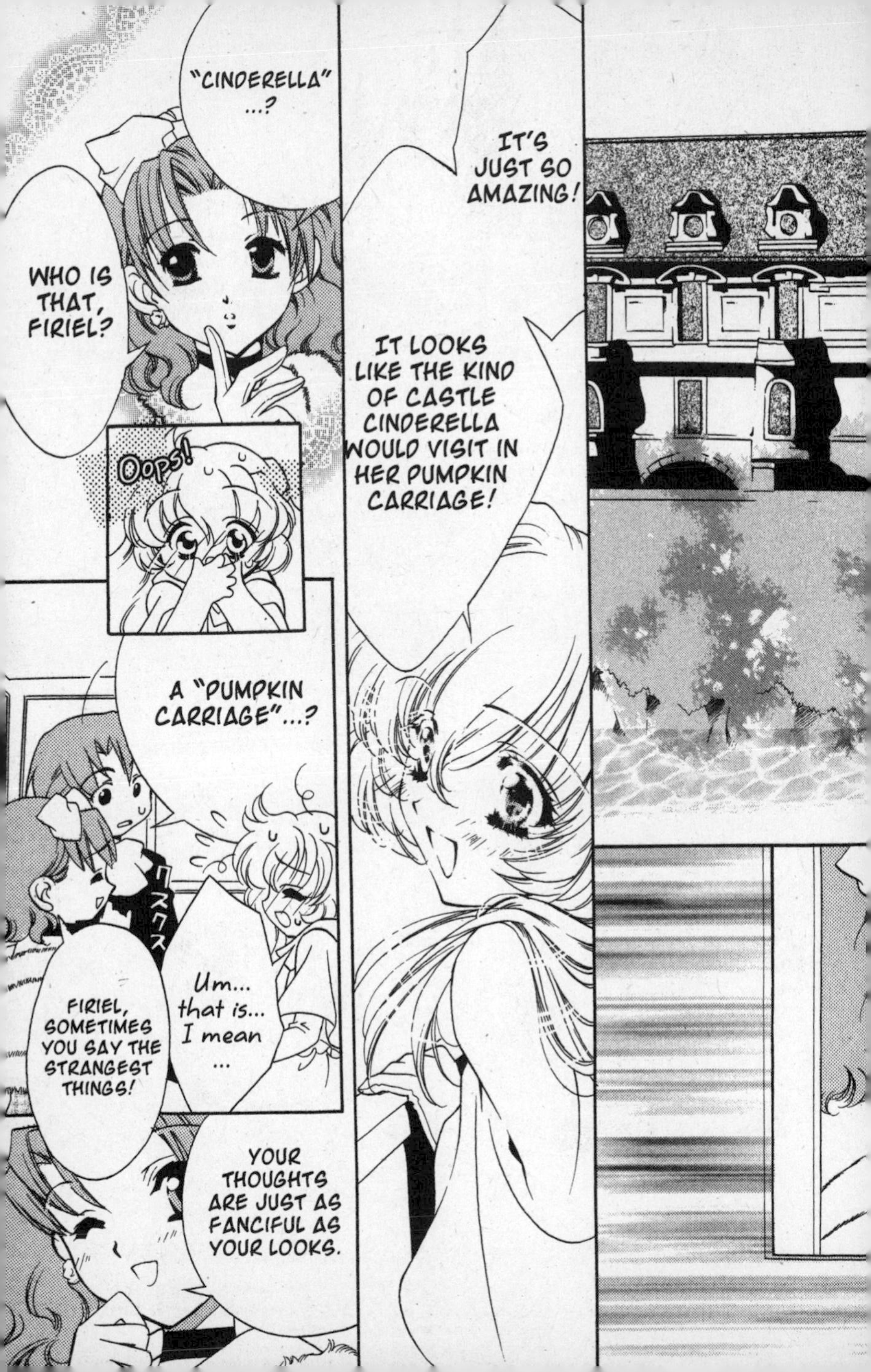
IT'S JUST SO AMAZING!
IT LOOKS LIKE THE KIND OF CASTLE CINDERELLA WOULD VISIT IN HER PUMPKIN CARRIAGE!
"CINDERELLA" ...?
WHO IS THAT, FIRIEL?
Oops!
A "PUMPKIN CARRIAGE"...?
Um... that is... I mean ...
クスクス
FIRIEL, SOMETIMES YOU SAY THE STRANGEST THINGS!
YOUR THOUGHTS ARE JUST AS FANCIFUL AS YOUR LOOKS.

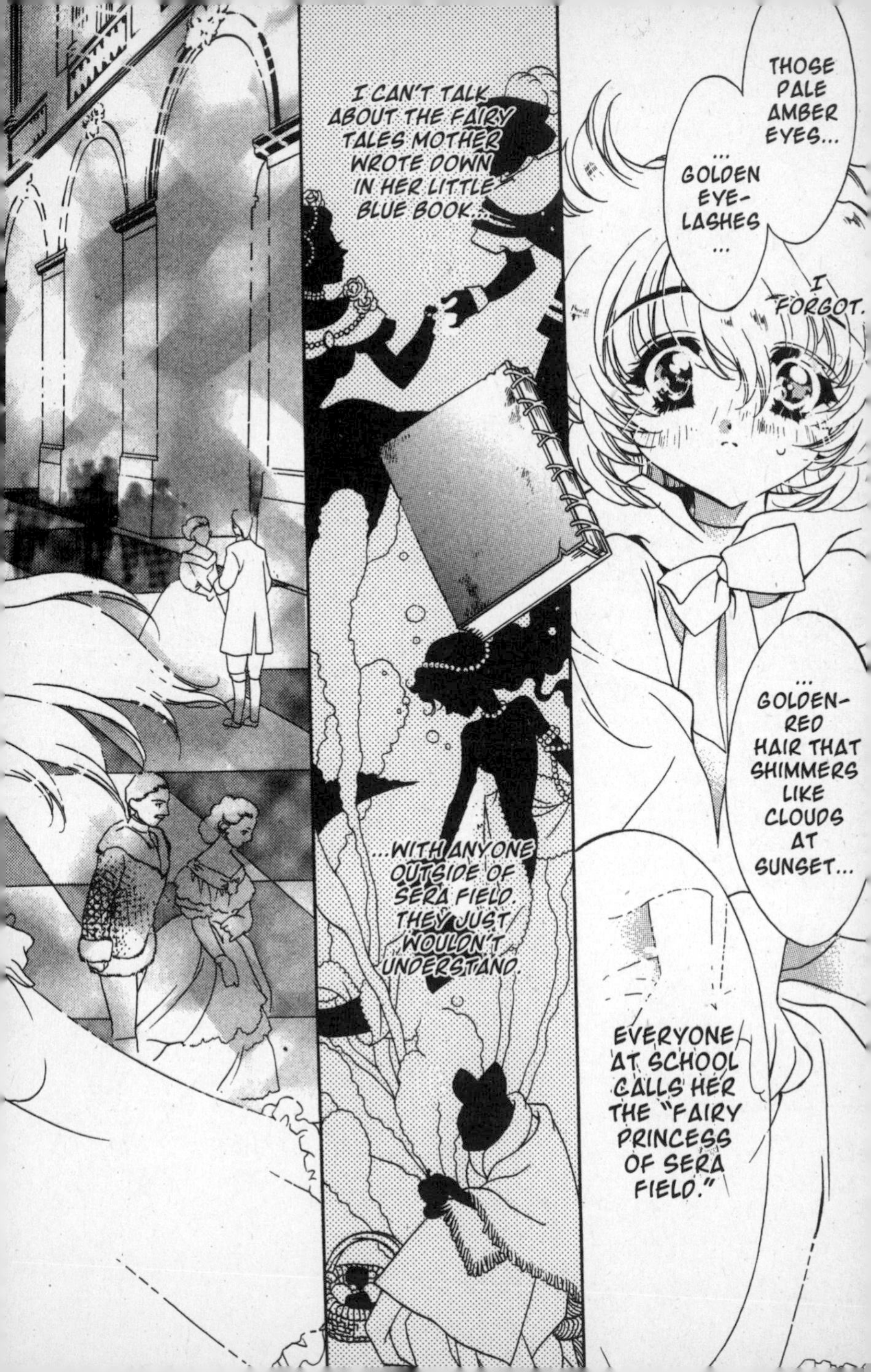
THOSE PALE AMBER EYES...
... GOLDEN EYE-LASHES ...
I FORGOT.
... GOLDEN-RED HAIR THAT SHIMMERS LIKE CLOUDS AT SUNSET...
EVERYONE AT SCHOOL CALLS HER THE "FAIRY PRINCESS OF SERA FIELD."
I CAN'T TALK ABOUT THE FAIRY TALES MOTHER WROTE DOWN IN HER LITTLE BLUE BOOK...
...WITH ANYONE OUTSIDE OF SERA FIELD. THEY JUST WOULDN'T UNDERSTAND.

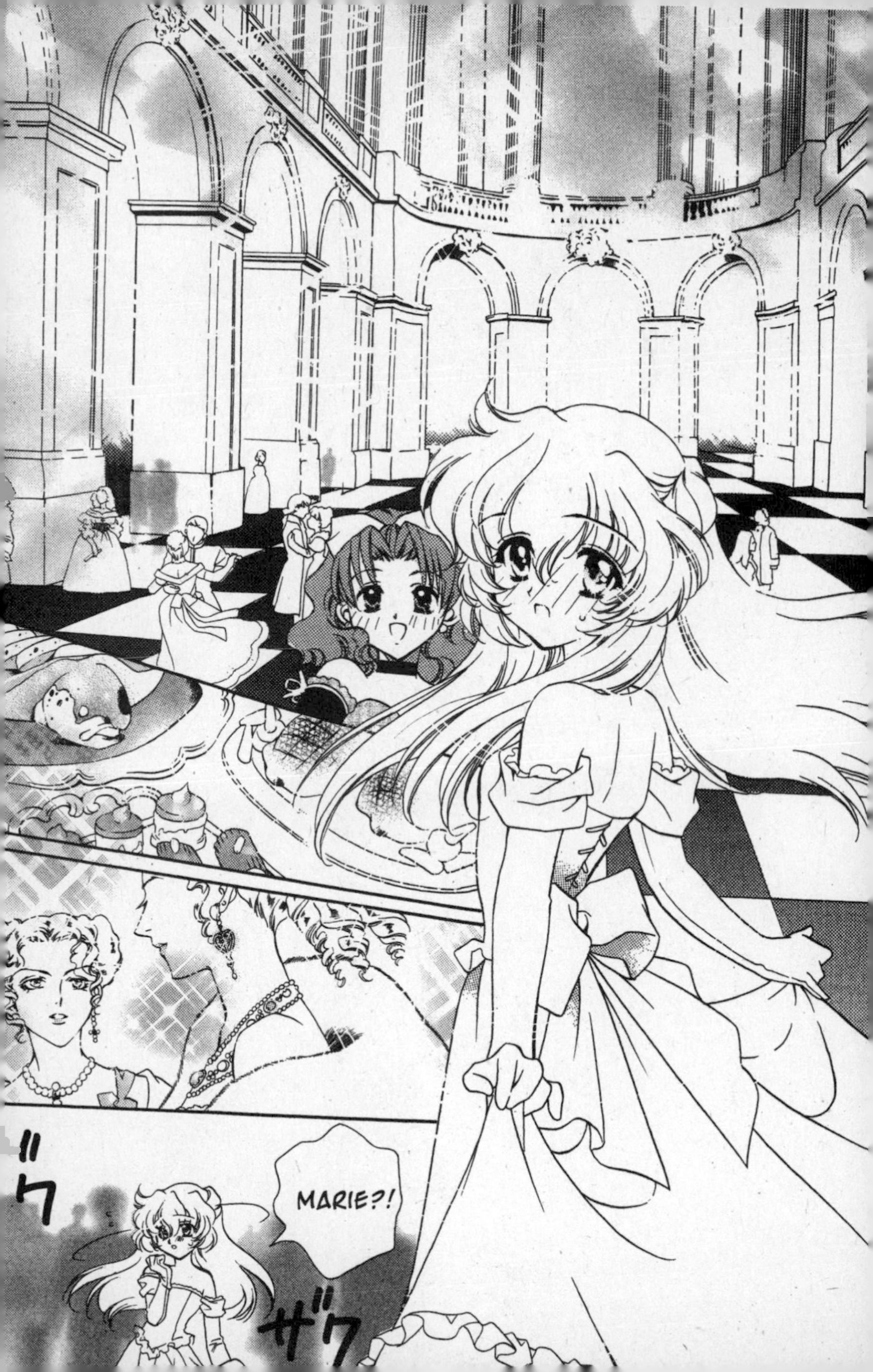
MARIE?!
ザワ
ザワ

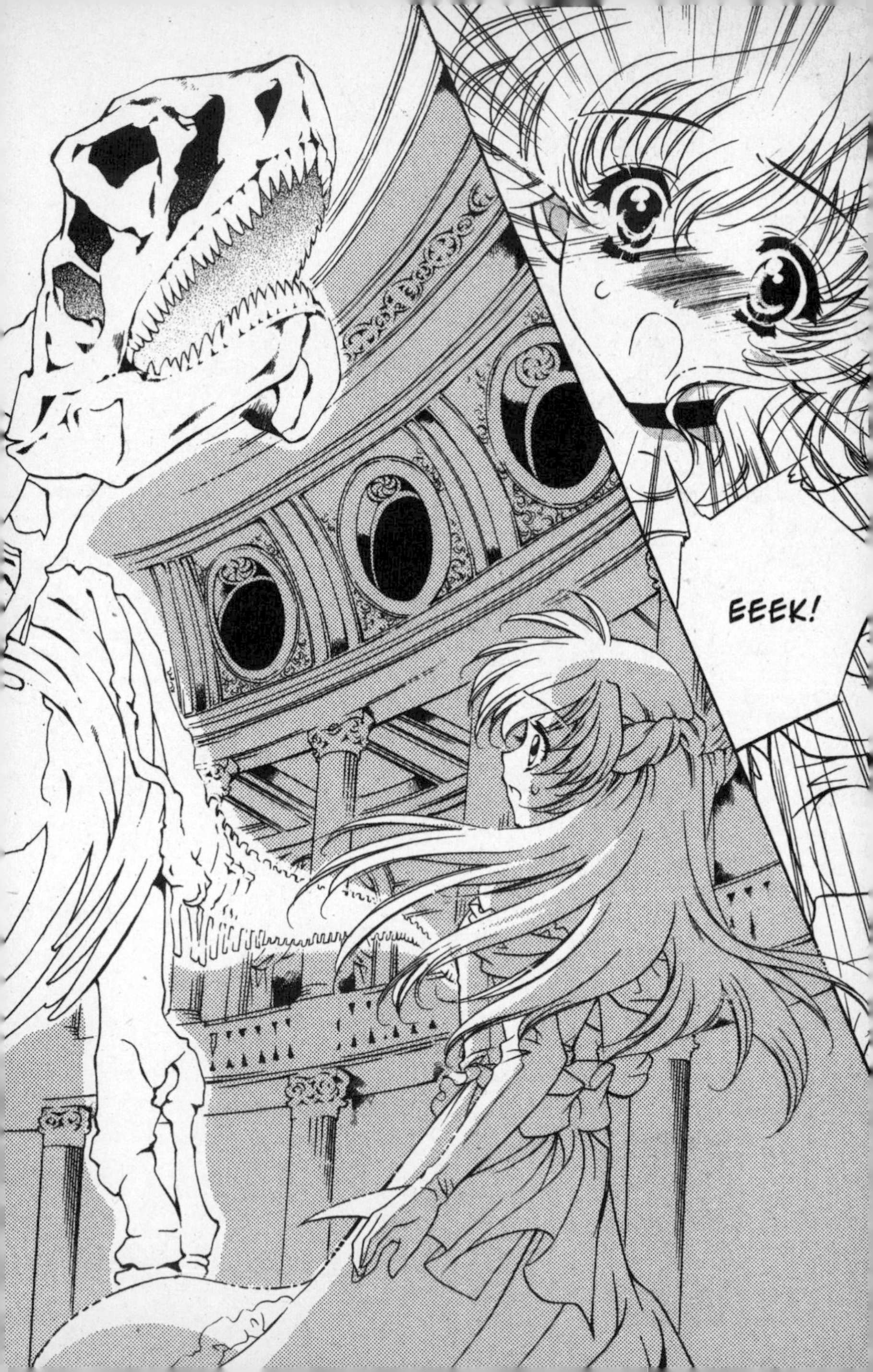
EEEK!

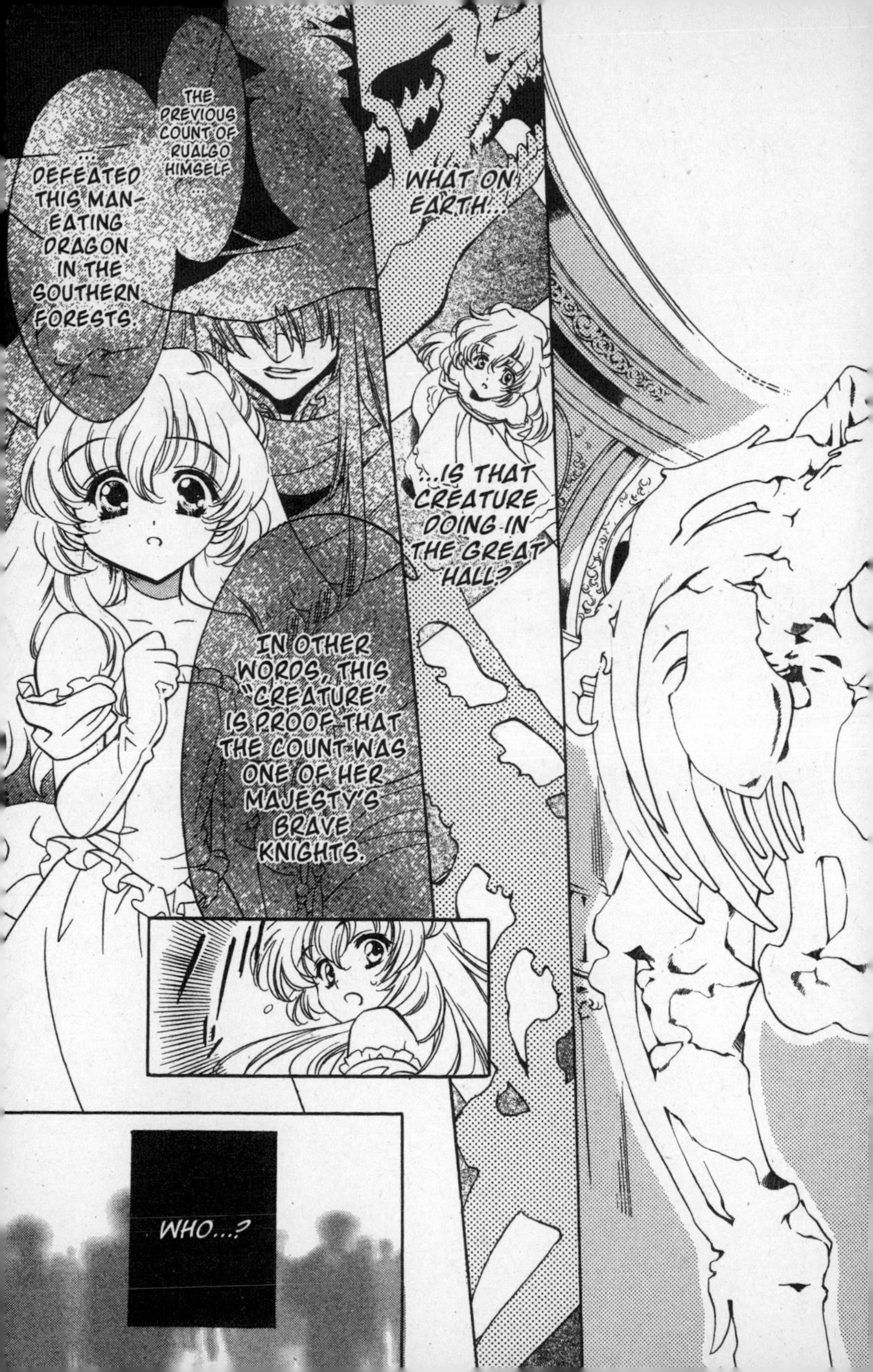
WHAT ON EARTH...
...IS THAT CREATURE DOING IN THE GREAT HALL?
THE PREVIOUS COUNT OF RUALGO HIMSELF...
...DEFEATED THIS MAN-EATING DRAGON IN THE SOUTHERN FORESTS.
IN OTHER WORDS, THIS "CREATURE" IS PROOF THAT THE COUNT WAS ONE OF HER MAJESTY'S BRAVE KNIGHTS.
WHO...?

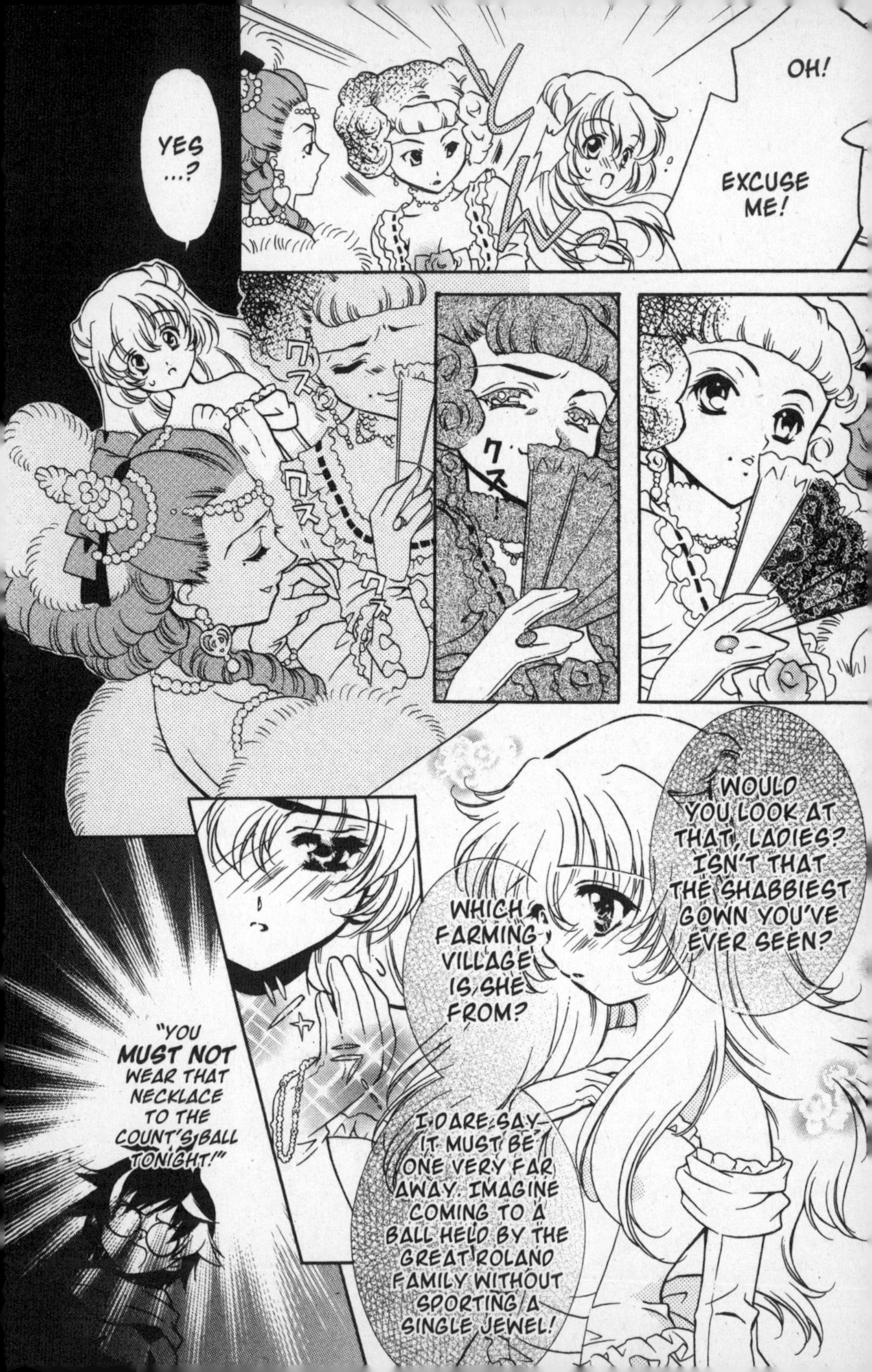
OH!
EXCUSE ME!
YES ...?
WOULD YOU LOOK AT THAT, LADIES? ISN'T THAT THE SHABBIEST GOWN YOU'VE EVER SEEN?
WHICH FARMING VILLAGE IS SHE FROM?
I DARE SAY IT MUST BE ONE VERY FAR AWAY. IMAGINE COMING TO A BALL HELD BY THE GREAT ROLAND FAMILY WITHOUT SPORTING A SINGLE JEWEL!
"YOU **MUST NOT** WEAR THAT NECKLACE TO THE COUNT'S BALL TONIGHT!"

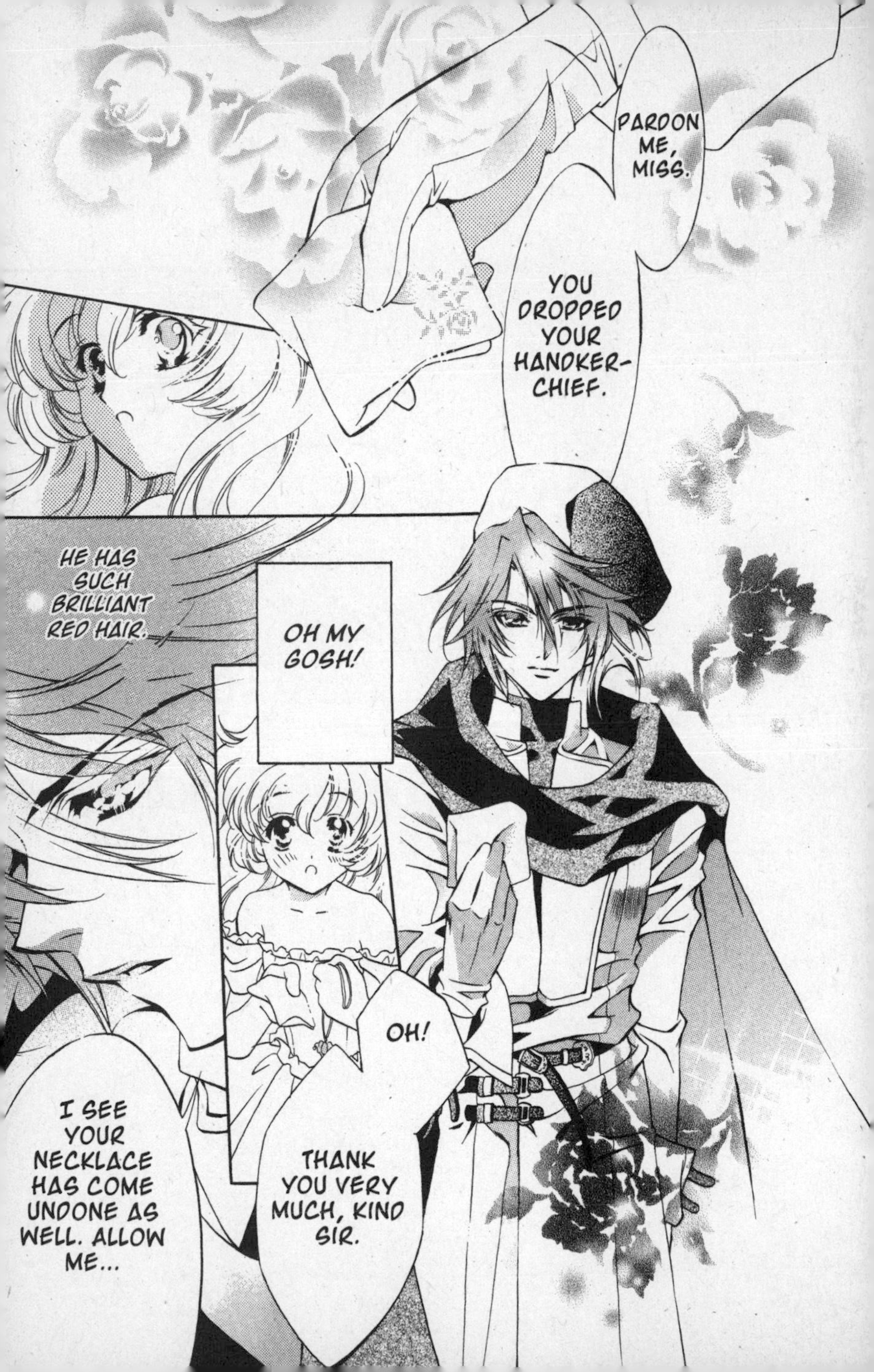
PARDON ME, MISS.
YOU DROPPED YOUR HANDKER-CHIEF.
OH MY GOSH!
HE HAS SUCH BRILLIANT RED HAIR.
OH!
THANK YOU VERY MUCH, KIND SIR.
I SEE YOUR NECKLACE HAS COME UNDONE AS WELL. ALLOW ME...

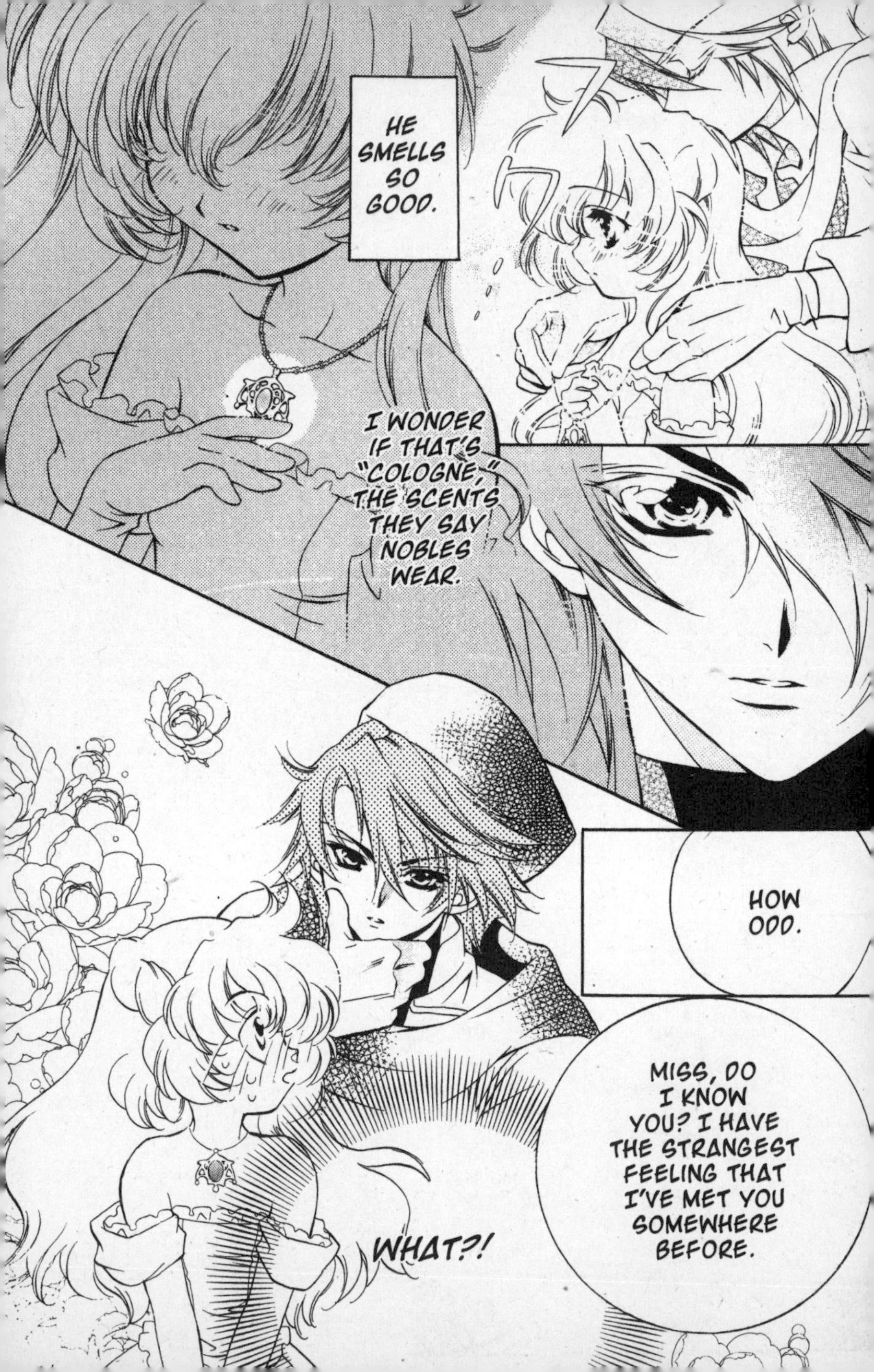
HE SMELLS SO GOOD.
I WONDER IF THAT'S "COLOGNE," THE SCENTS THEY SAY NOBLES WEAR.
HOW ODD.
MISS, DO I KNOW YOU? I HAVE THE STRANGEST FEELING THAT I'VE MET YOU SOMEWHERE BEFORE.
WHAT?!

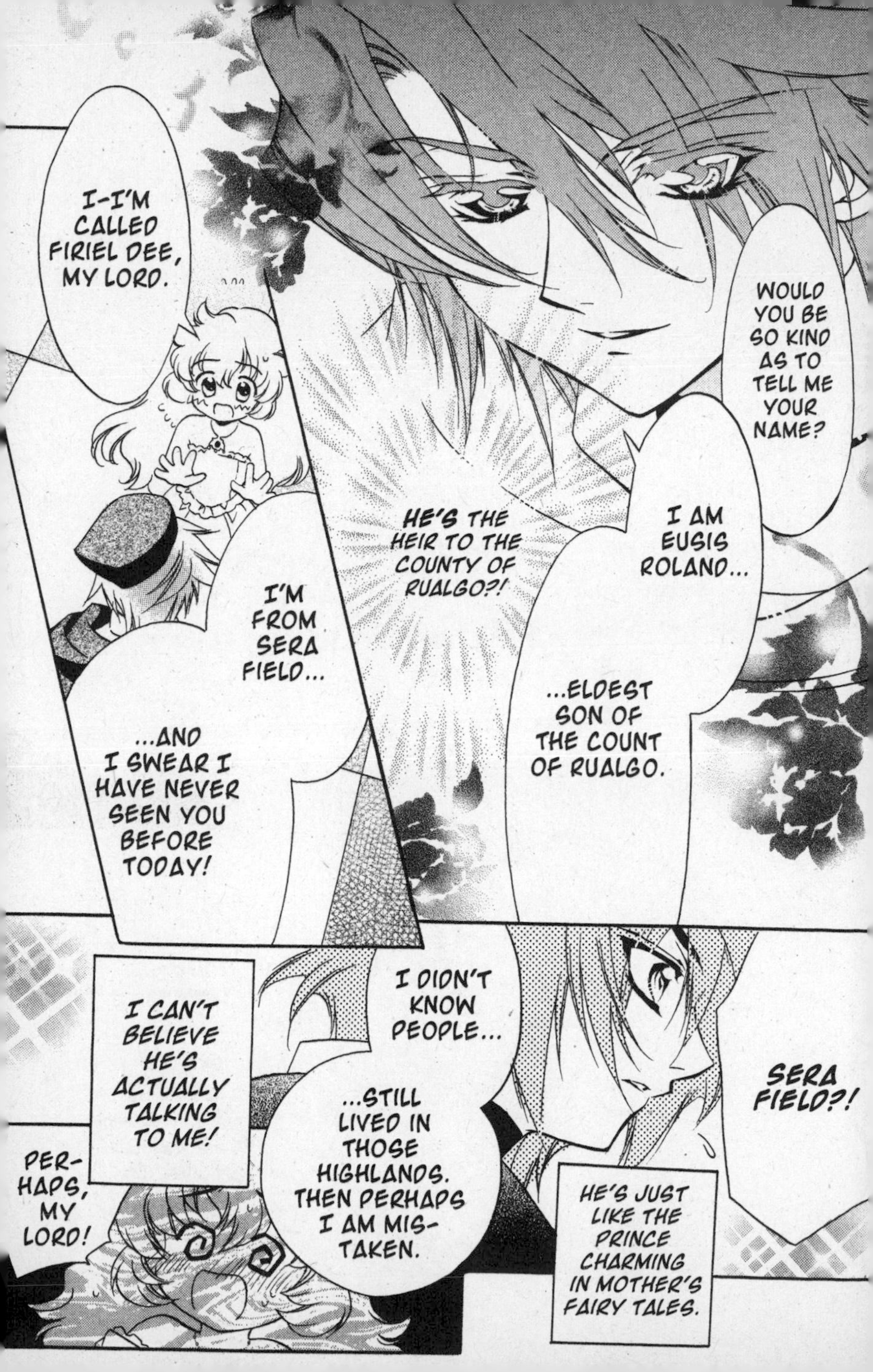
WOULD YOU BE SO KIND AS TO TELL ME YOUR NAME?
I AM EUSIS ROLAND...
...ELDEST SON OF THE COUNT OF RUALGO.
HE'S THE HEIR TO THE COUNTY OF RUALGO?!
I-I'M CALLED FIRIEL DEE, MY LORD.
I'M FROM SERA FIELD...
...AND I SWEAR I HAVE NEVER SEEN YOU BEFORE TODAY!
SERA FIELD?!
HE'S JUST LIKE THE PRINCE CHARMING IN MOTHER'S FAIRY TALES.
I DIDN'T KNOW PEOPLE...
...STILL LIVED IN THOSE HIGHLANDS. THEN PERHAPS I AM MIS-TAKEN.
I CAN'T BELIEVE HE'S ACTUALLY TALKING TO ME!
PER-HAPS, MY LORD!

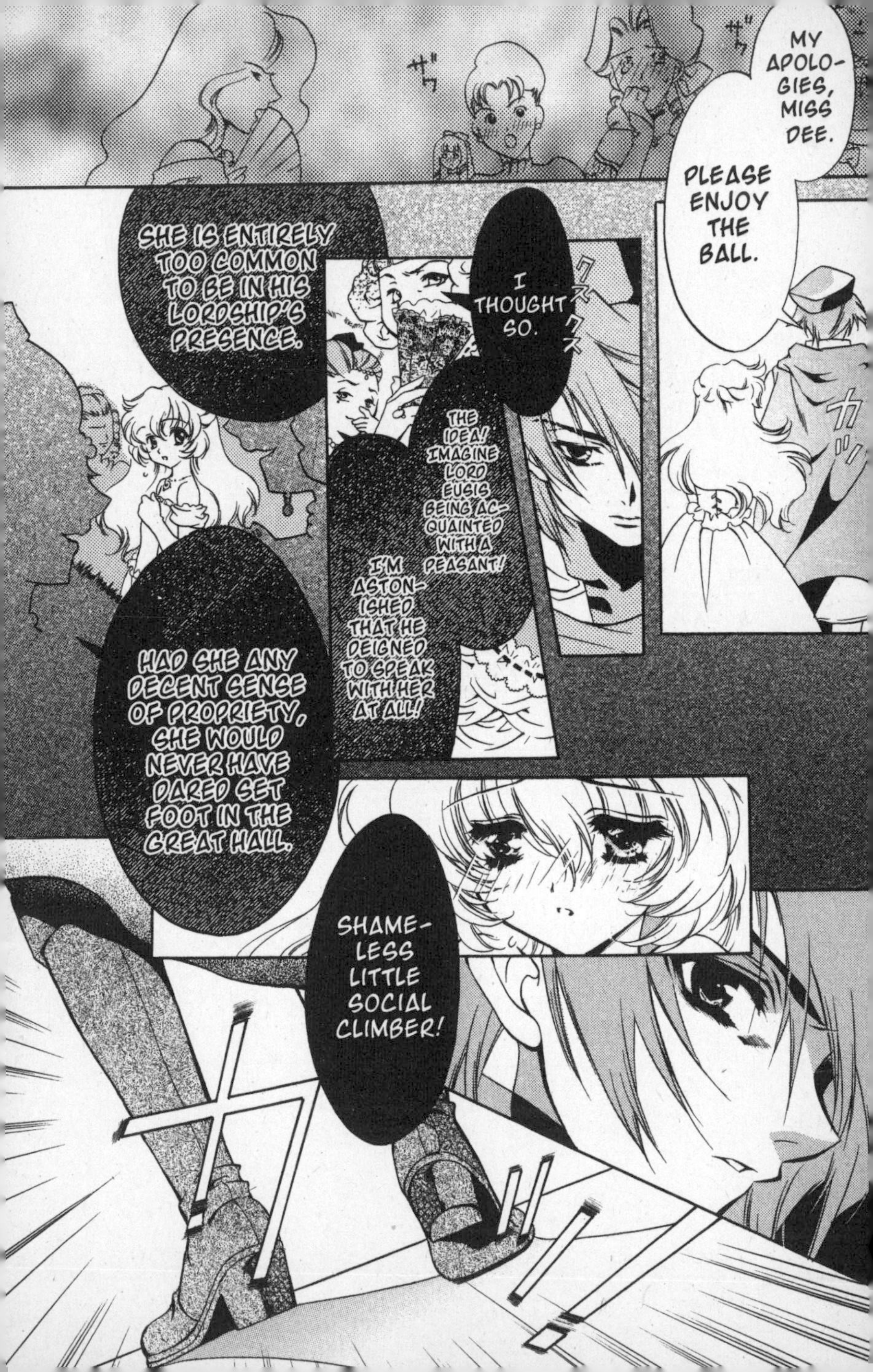
MY APOLOGIES, MISS DEE.
PLEASE ENJOY THE BALL.
I THOUGHT SO.
THE IDEA! IMAGINE LORD EUSIS BEING ACQUAINTED WITH A PEASANT!
I'M ASTONISHED THAT HE DEIGNED TO SPEAK WITH HER AT ALL!
SHE IS ENTIRELY TOO COMMON TO BE IN HIS LORDSHIP'S PRESENCE.
HAD SHE ANY DECENT SENSE OF PROPRIETY, SHE WOULD NEVER HAVE DARED SET FOOT IN THE GREAT HALL.
SHAMELESS LITTLE SOCIAL CLIMBER!

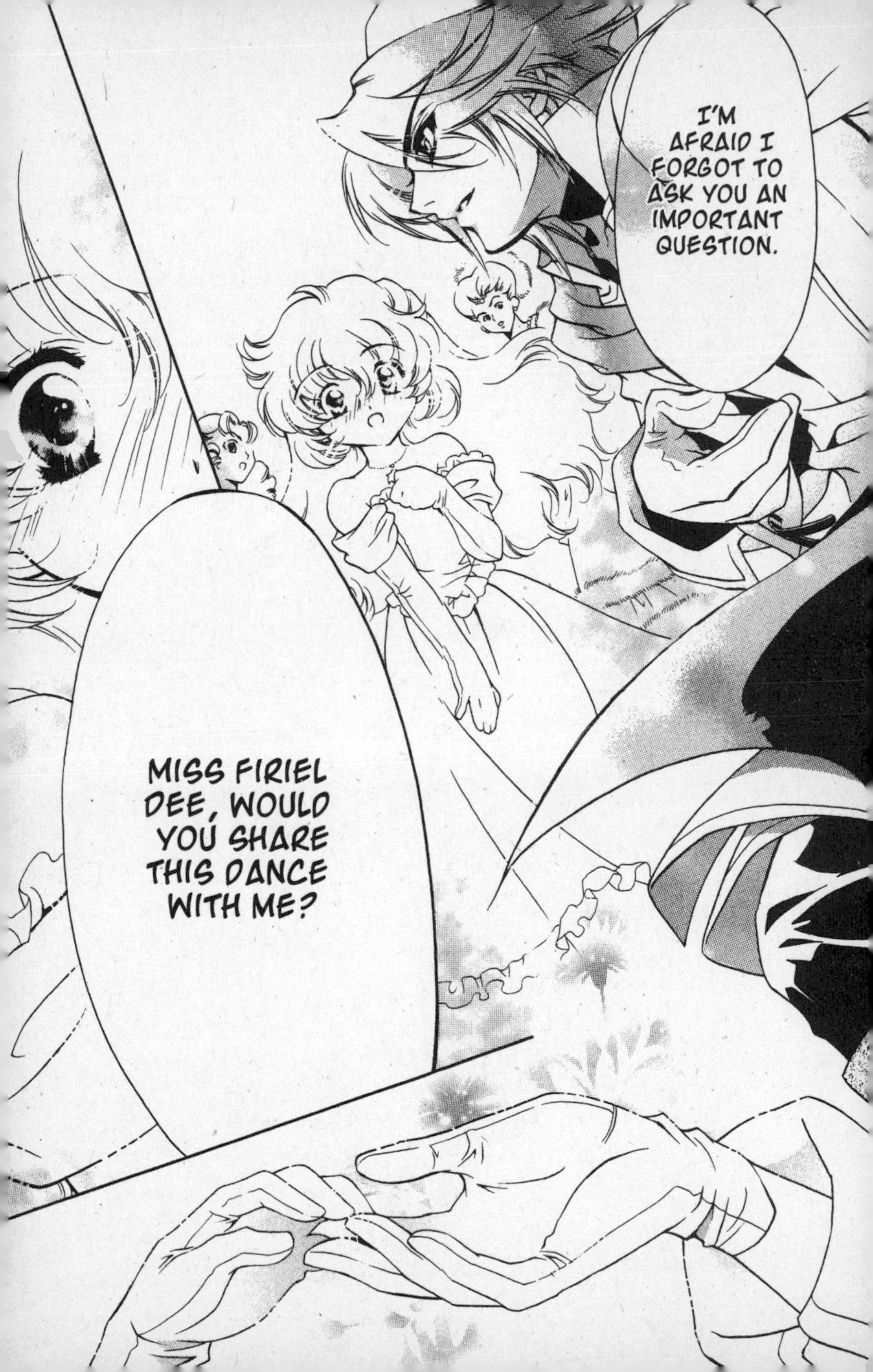
I'M AFRAID I FORGOT TO ASK YOU AN IMPORTANT QUESTION.
MISS FIRIEL DEE, WOULD YOU SHARE THIS DANCE WITH ME?

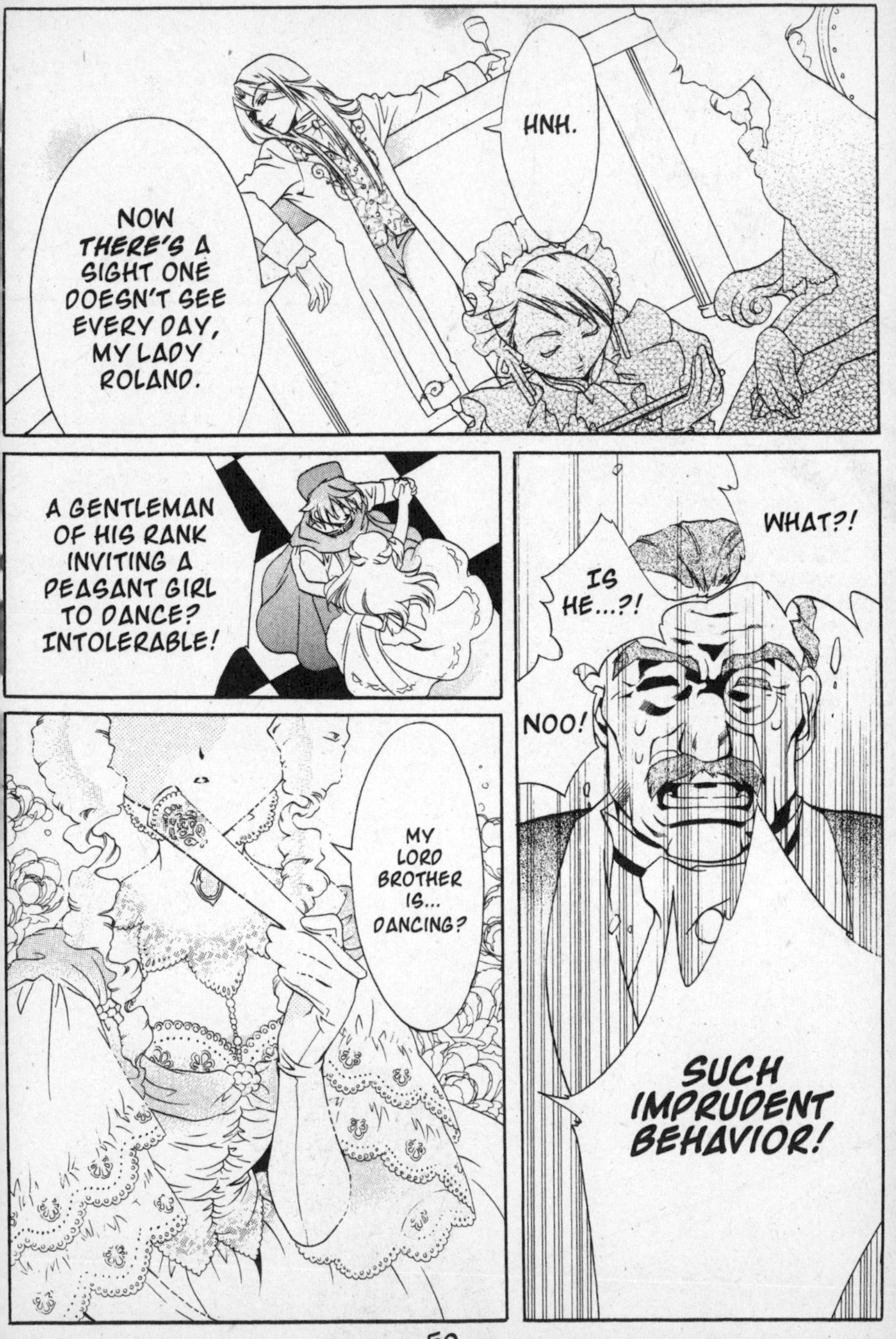
NOW THERE'S A SIGHT ONE DOESN'T SEE EVERY DAY, MY LADY ROLAND.
HNH.
A GENTLEMAN OF HIS RANK INVITING A PEASANT GIRL TO DANCE? INTOLERABLE!
MY LORD BROTHER IS... DANCING?
WHAT?!
IS HE...?!
NOO!
SUCH IMPRUDENT BEHAVIOR!

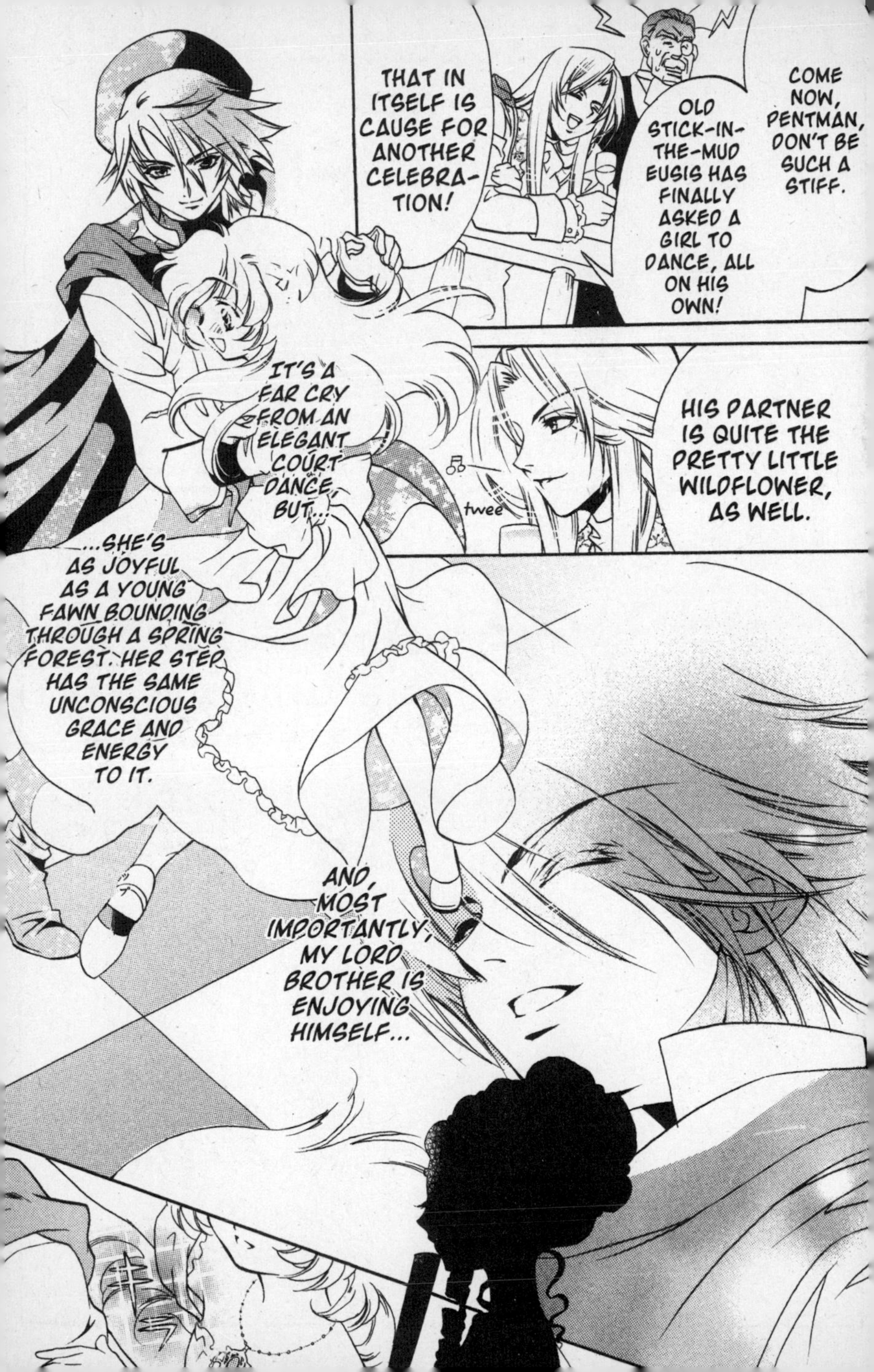
COME NOW, PENTMAN, DON'T BE SUCH A STIFF.
OLD STICK-IN-THE-MUD EUSIS HAS FINALLY ASKED A GIRL TO DANCE, ALL ON HIS OWN!
THAT IN ITSELF IS CAUSE FOR ANOTHER CELEBRATION!
HIS PARTNER IS QUITE THE PRETTY LITTLE WILDFLOWER, AS WELL.
twee
IT'S A FAR CRY FROM AN ELEGANT COURT DANCE, BUT...
...SHE'S AS JOYFUL AS A YOUNG FAWN BOUNDING THROUGH A SPRING FOREST. HER STEP HAS THE SAME UNCONSCIOUS GRACE AND ENERGY TO IT.
AND, MOST IMPORTANTLY, MY LORD BROTHER IS ENJOYING HIMSELF...

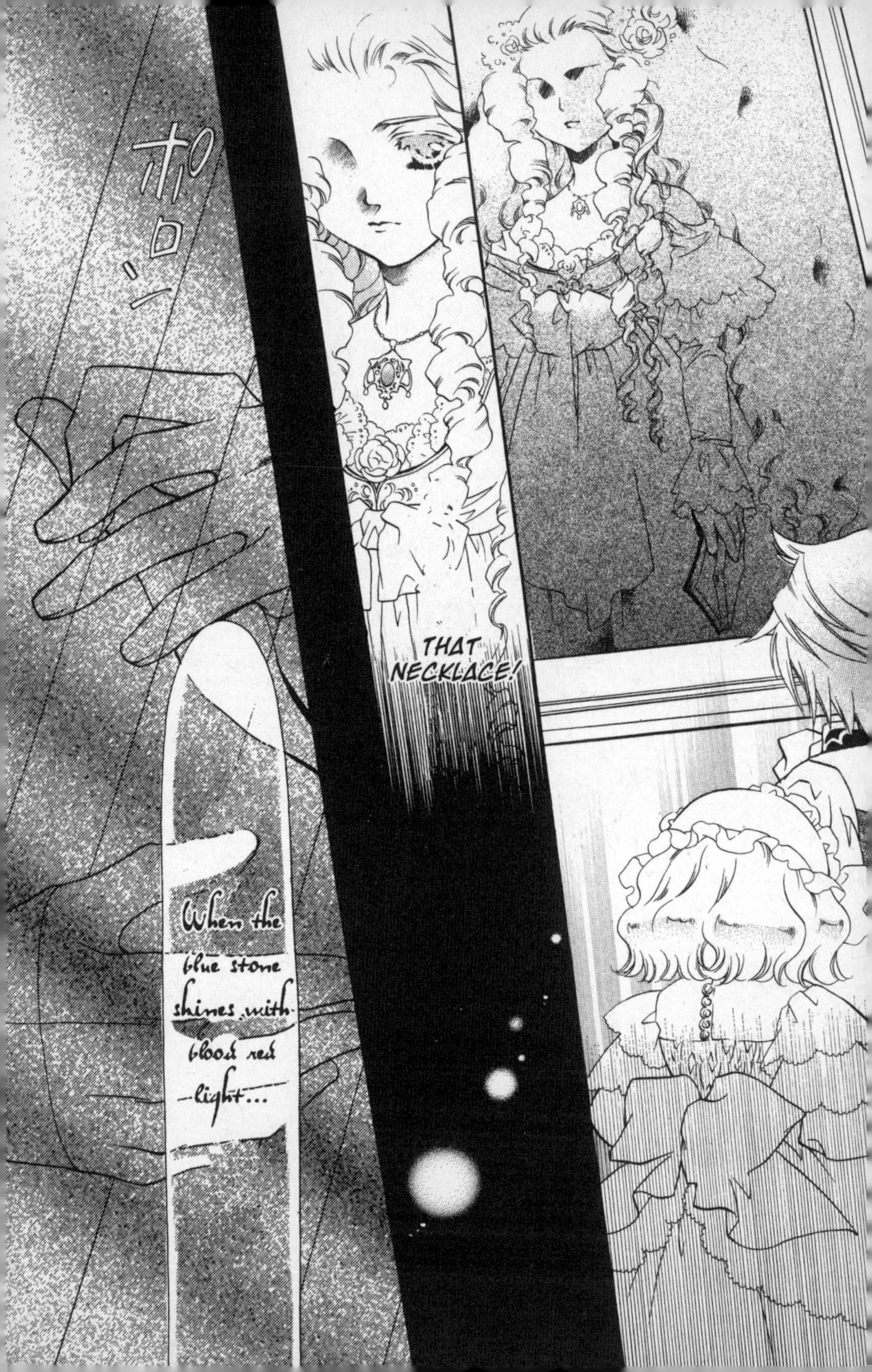
THAT NECKLACE!
ポロン
When the blue stone shines with blood red light...

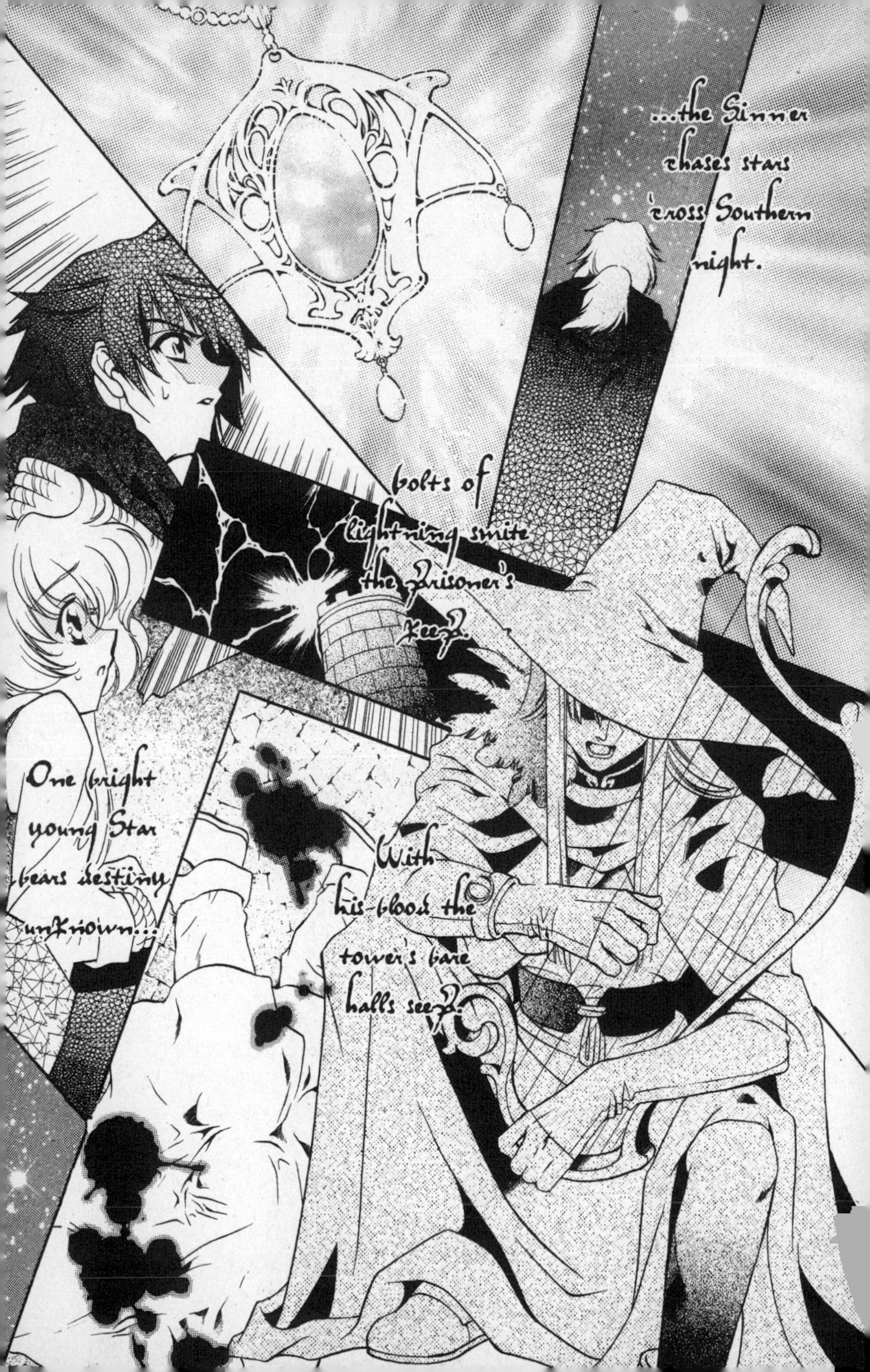
...the Sinner chases stars 'cross Southern night.
bolts of lightning smite the prisoner's keep.
With his blood the tower's bare halls seep.
One bright young Star bears destiny unknown...

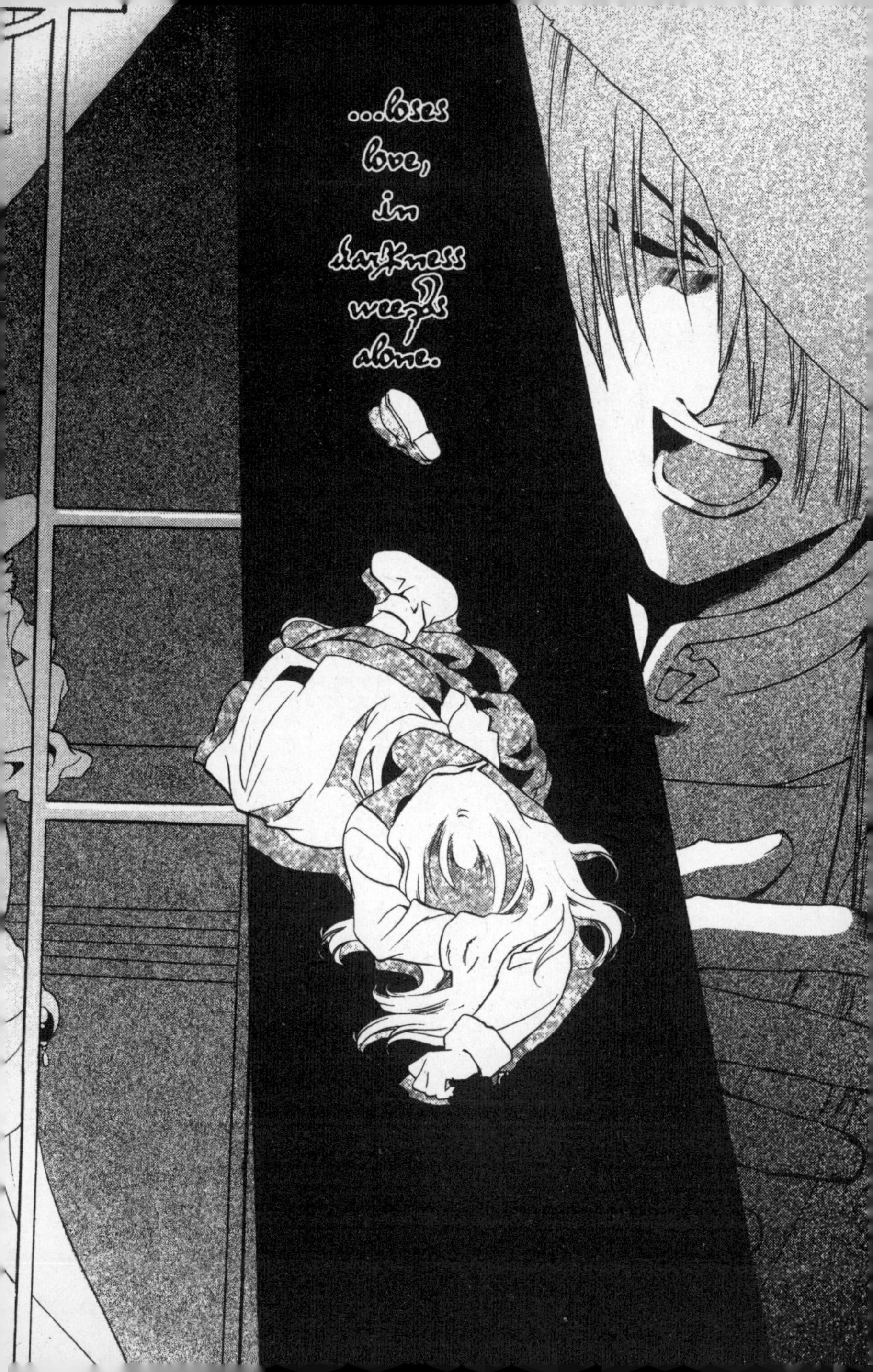
...loses love, in darkness weeps alone.

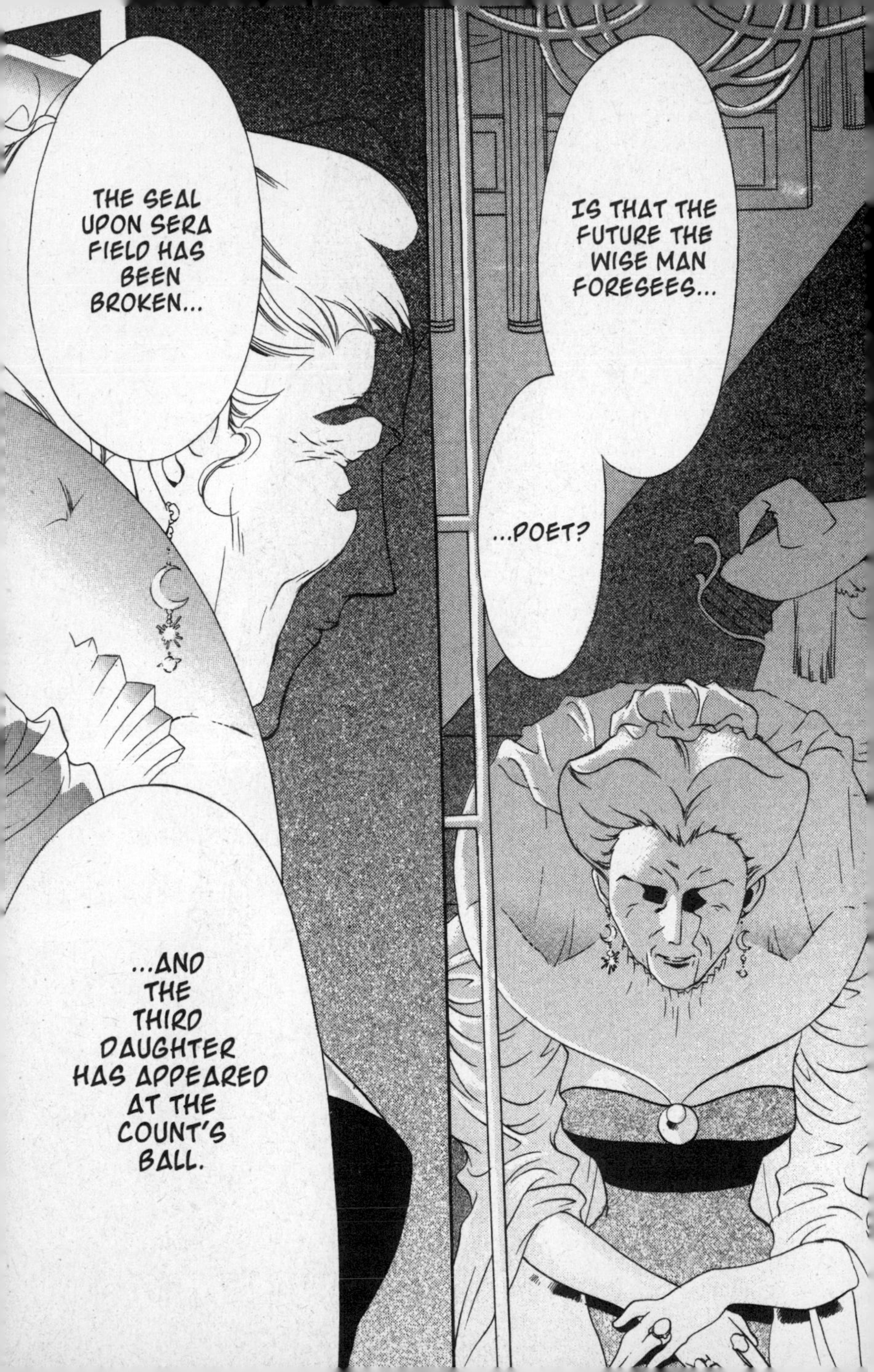
IS THAT THE FUTURE THE WISE MAN FORESEES...
...POET?
THE SEAL UPON SERA FIELD HAS BEEN BROKEN...
...AND THE THIRD DAUGHTER HAS APPEARED AT THE COUNT'S BALL.

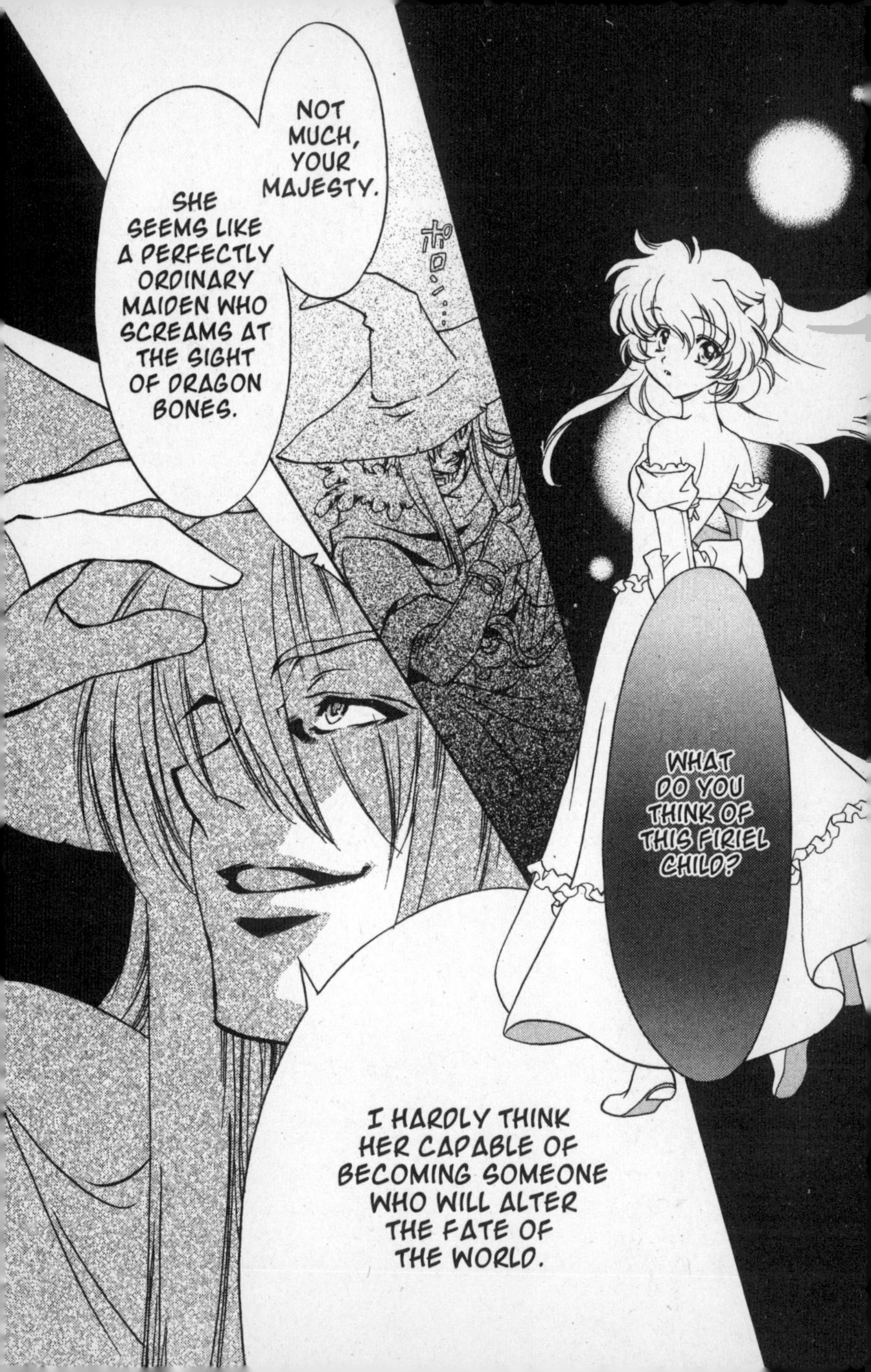
WHAT DO YOU THINK OF THIS FIRIEL CHILD?
NOT MUCH, YOUR MAJESTY.
SHE SEEMS LIKE A PERFECTLY ORDINARY MAIDEN WHO SCREAMS AT THE SIGHT OF DRAGON BONES.
ポロ…
I HARDLY THINK HER CAPABLE OF BECOMING SOMEONE WHO WILL ALTER THE FATE OF THE WORLD.

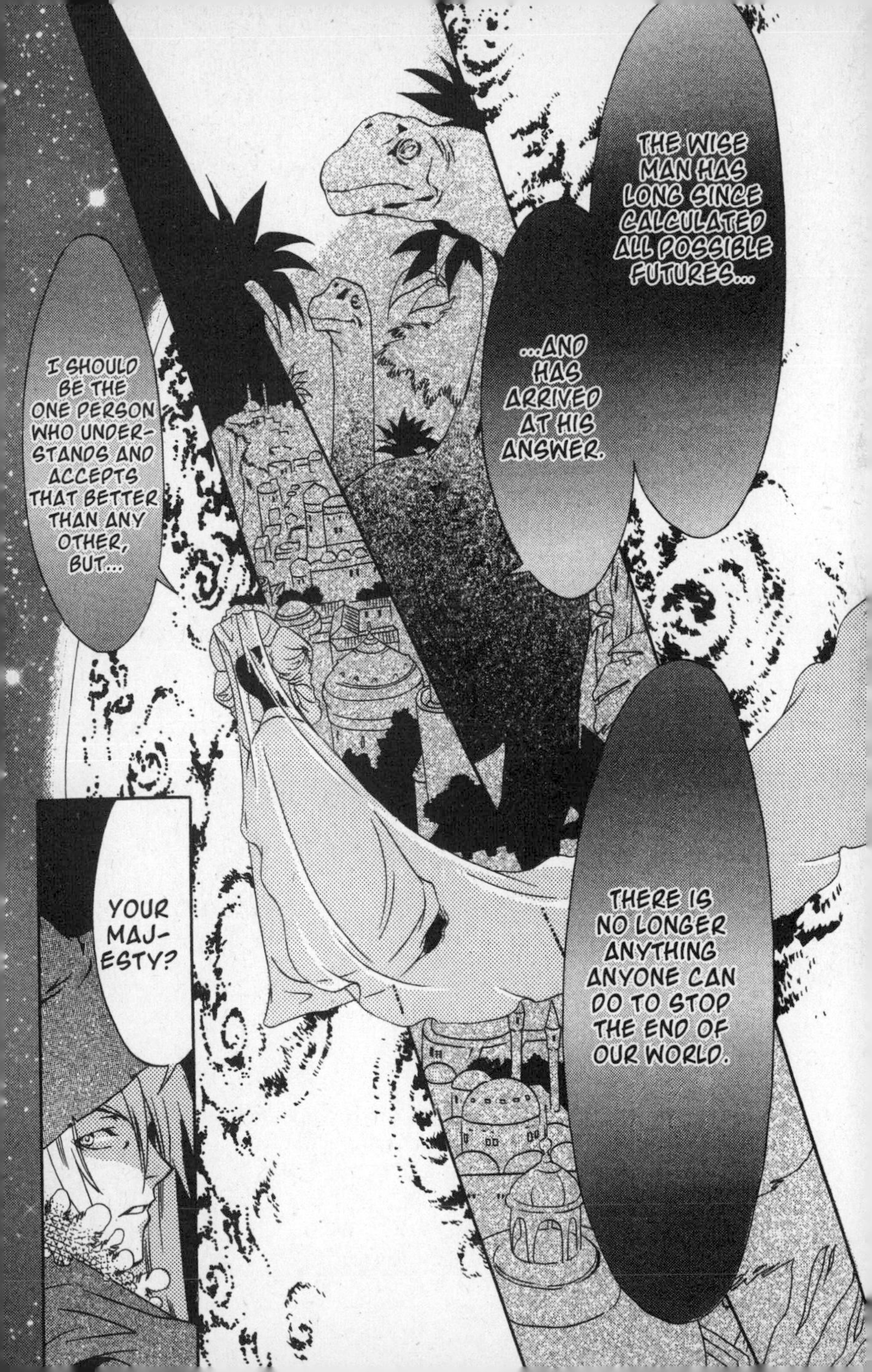
THE WISE MAN HAS LONG SINCE CALCULATED ALL POSSIBLE FUTURES...
...AND HAS ARRIVED AT HIS ANSWER.
I SHOULD BE THE ONE PERSON WHO UNDER-STANDS AND ACCEPTS THAT BETTER THAN ANY OTHER, BUT...
THERE IS NO LONGER ANYTHING ANYONE CAN DO TO STOP THE END OF OUR WORLD.
YOUR MAJ-ESTY?

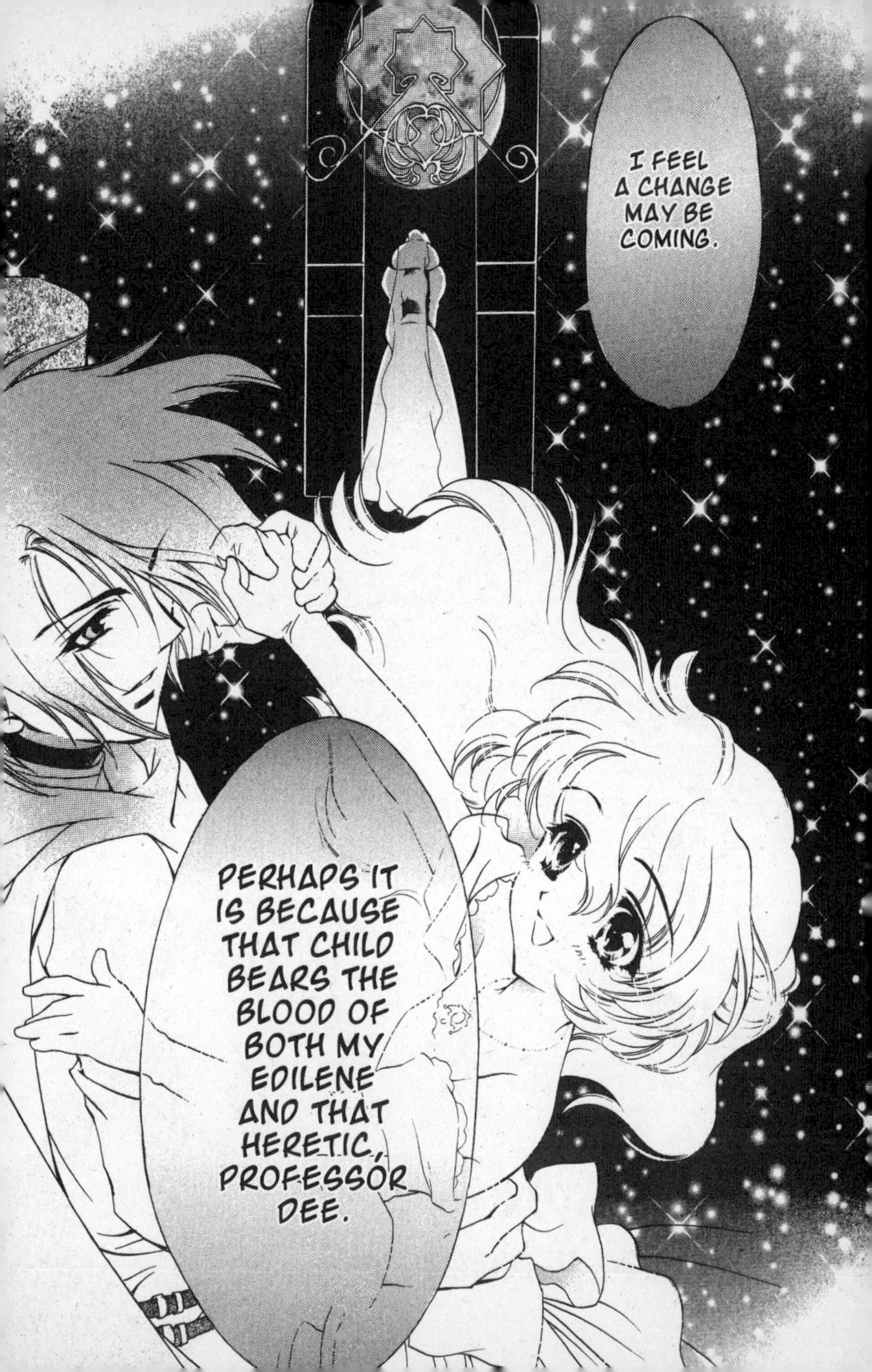
I FEEL A CHANGE MAY BE COMING.
PERHAPS IT IS BECAUSE THAT CHILD BEARS THE BLOOD OF BOTH MY EDILENE AND THAT HERETIC, PROFESSOR DEE.

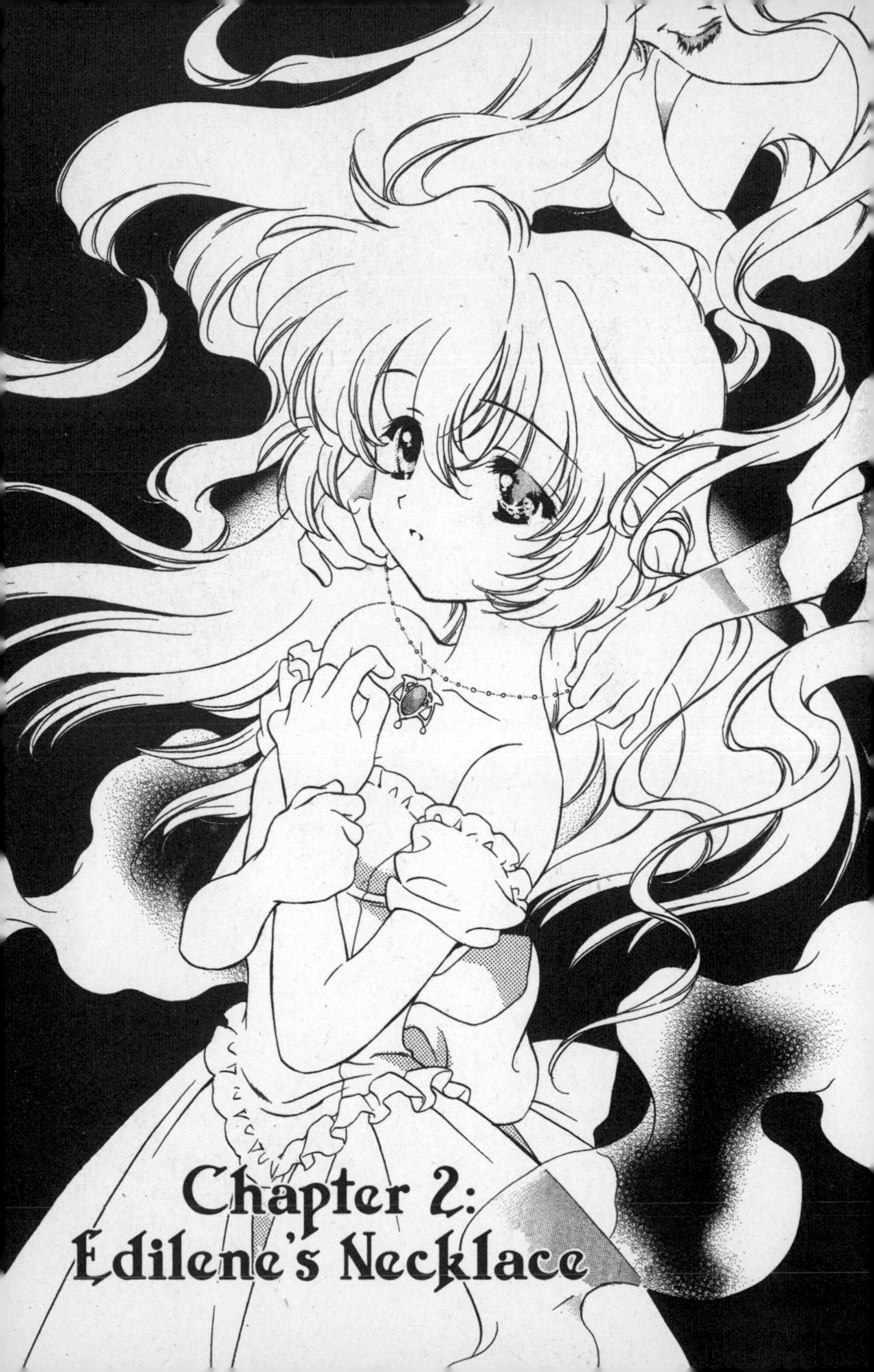

Chapter 2: Edilene's Necklace

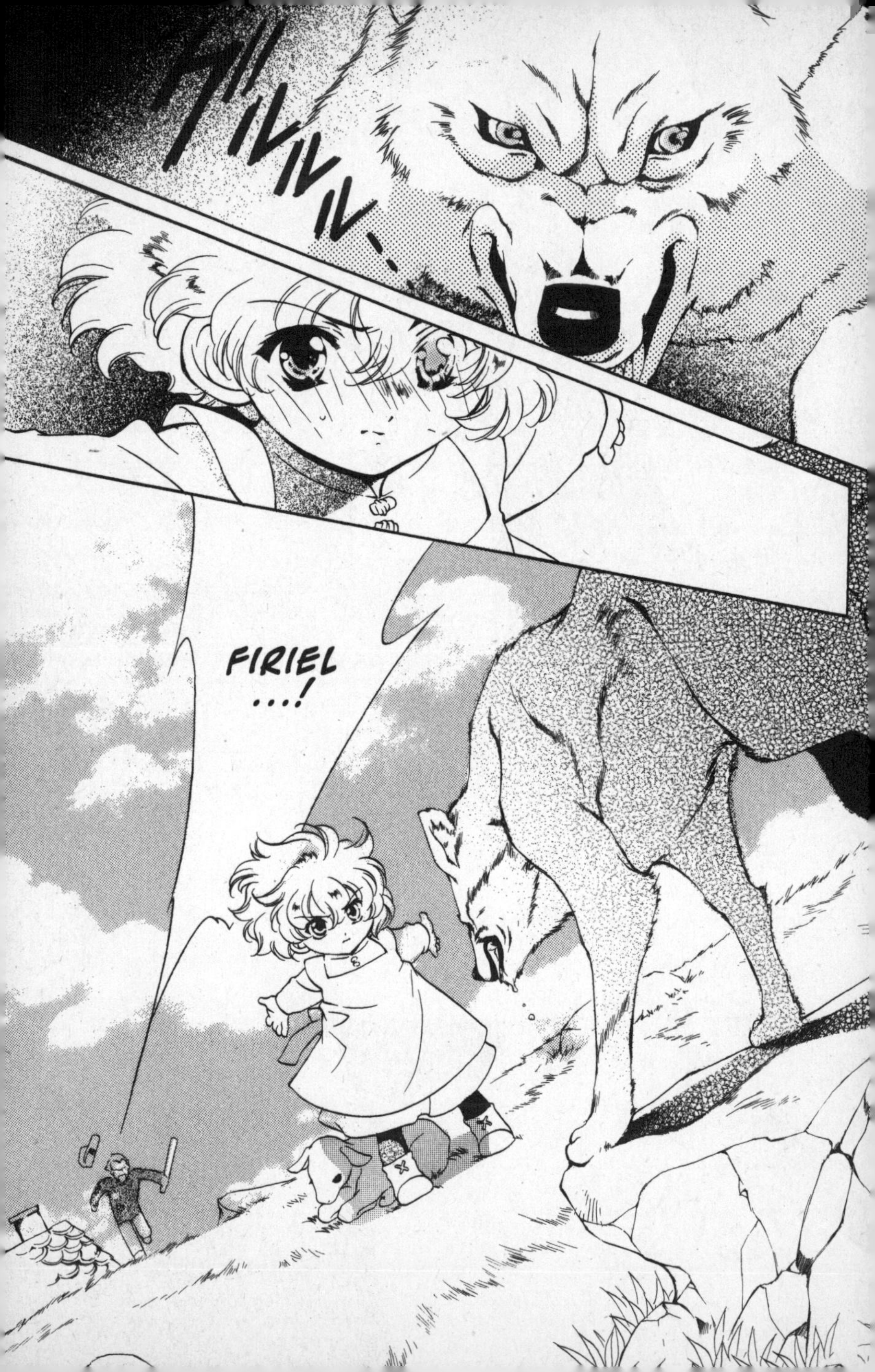
FIRIEL
...!

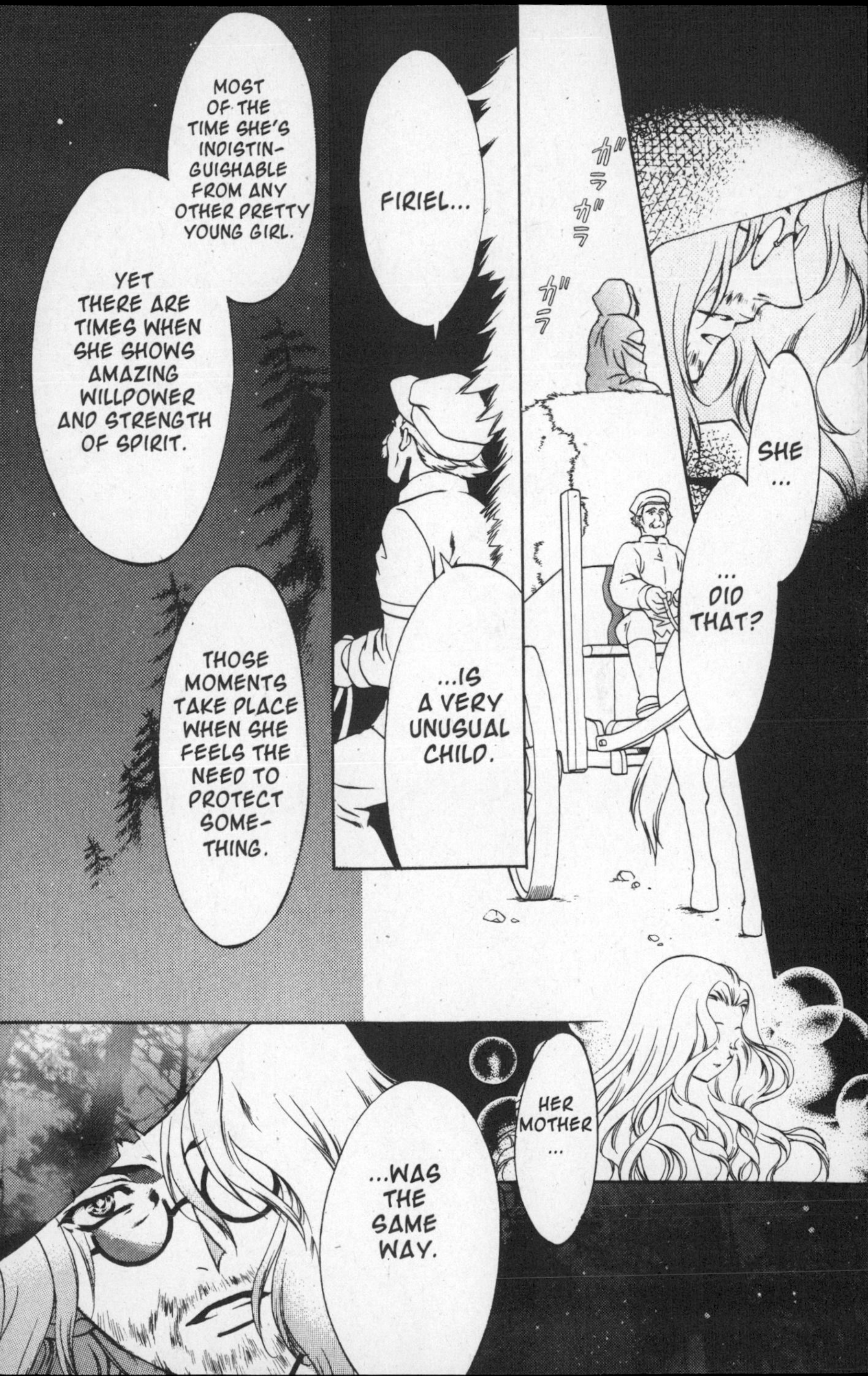
SHE ...
... DID THAT?
ガラガラ
ガラ
FIRIEL...
...IS A VERY UNUSUAL CHILD.
MOST OF THE TIME SHE'S INDISTIN-GUISHABLE FROM ANY OTHER PRETTY YOUNG GIRL.
YET THERE ARE TIMES WHEN SHE SHOWS AMAZING WILLPOWER AND STRENGTH OF SPIRIT.
THOSE MOMENTS TAKE PLACE WHEN SHE FEELS THE NEED TO PROTECT SOME-THING.
HER MOTHER ...
...WAS THE SAME WAY.

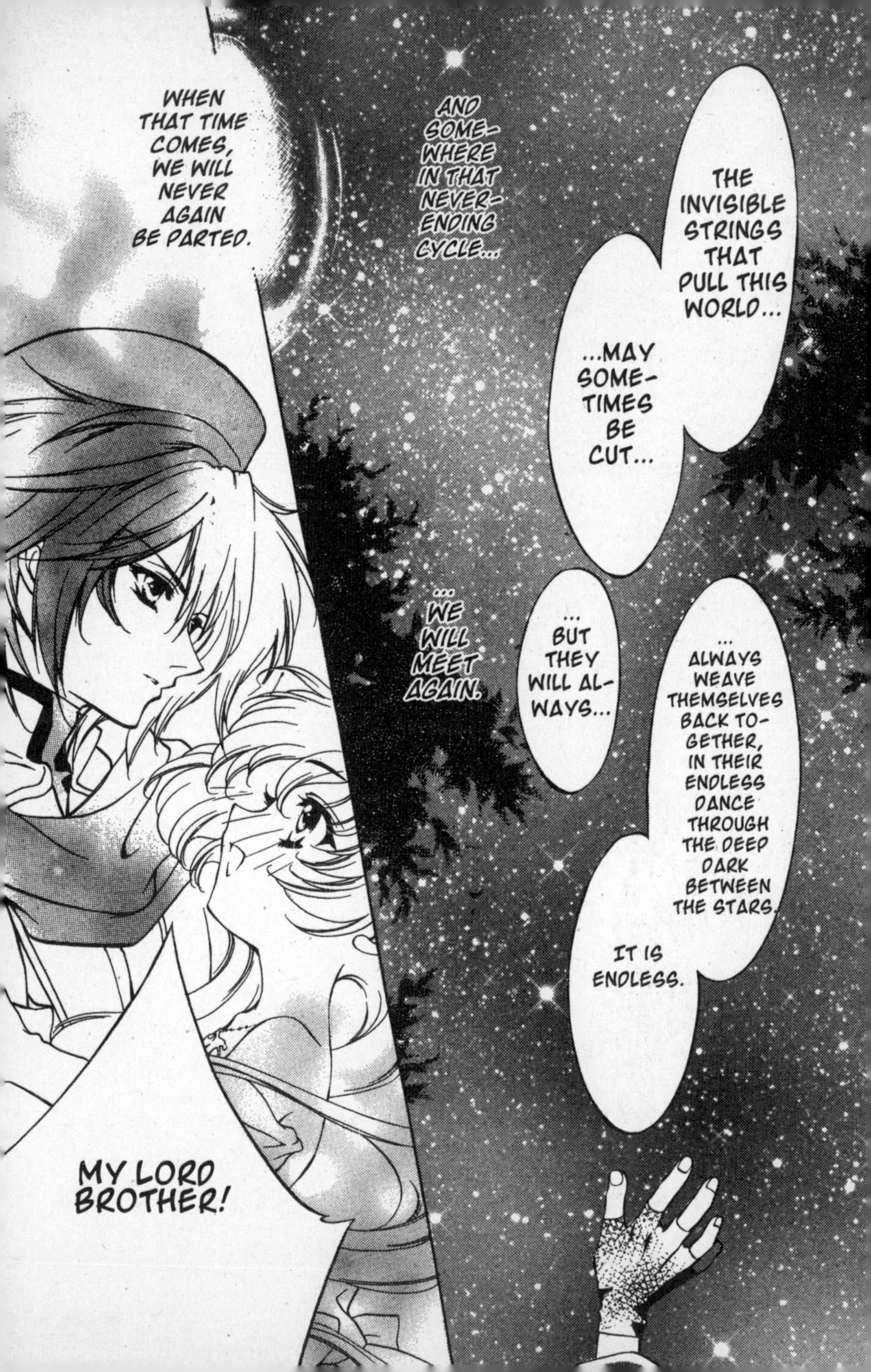
THE INVISIBLE STRINGS THAT PULL THIS WORLD...
...MAY SOME-TIMES BE CUT...
... BUT THEY WILL AL-WAYS...
... ALWAYS WEAVE THEMSELVES BACK TO-GETHER, IN THEIR ENDLESS DANCE THROUGH THE DEEP DARK BETWEEN THE STARS.
IT IS ENDLESS.
AND SOME-WHERE IN THAT NEVER-ENDING CYCLE...
... WE WILL MEET AGAIN.
WHEN THAT TIME COMES, WE WILL NEVER AGAIN BE PARTED.
MY LORD BROTHER!

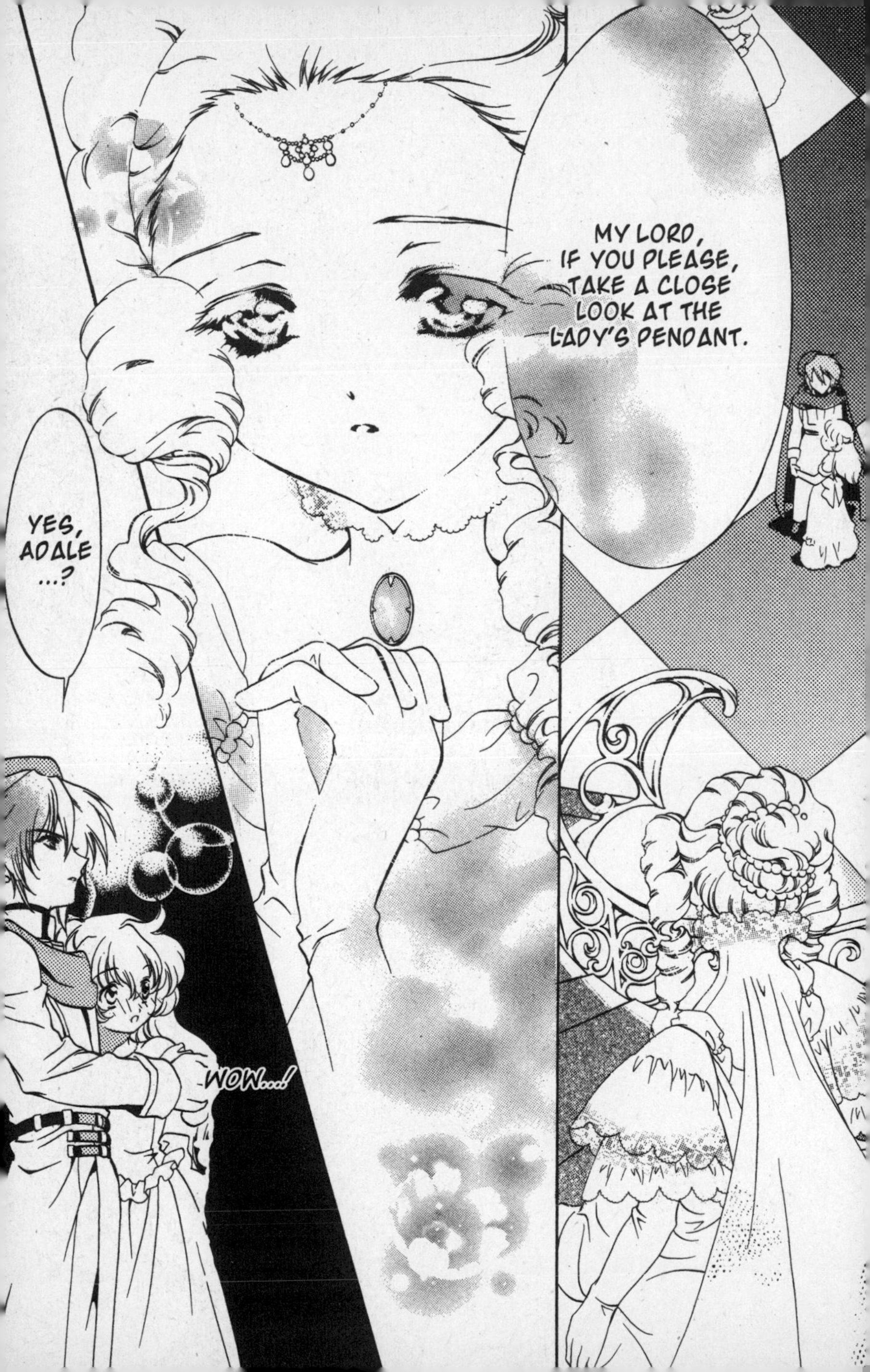
MY LORD, IF YOU PLEASE, TAKE A CLOSE LOOK AT THE LADY'S PENDANT.
YES, ADALE ...?
WOW...!

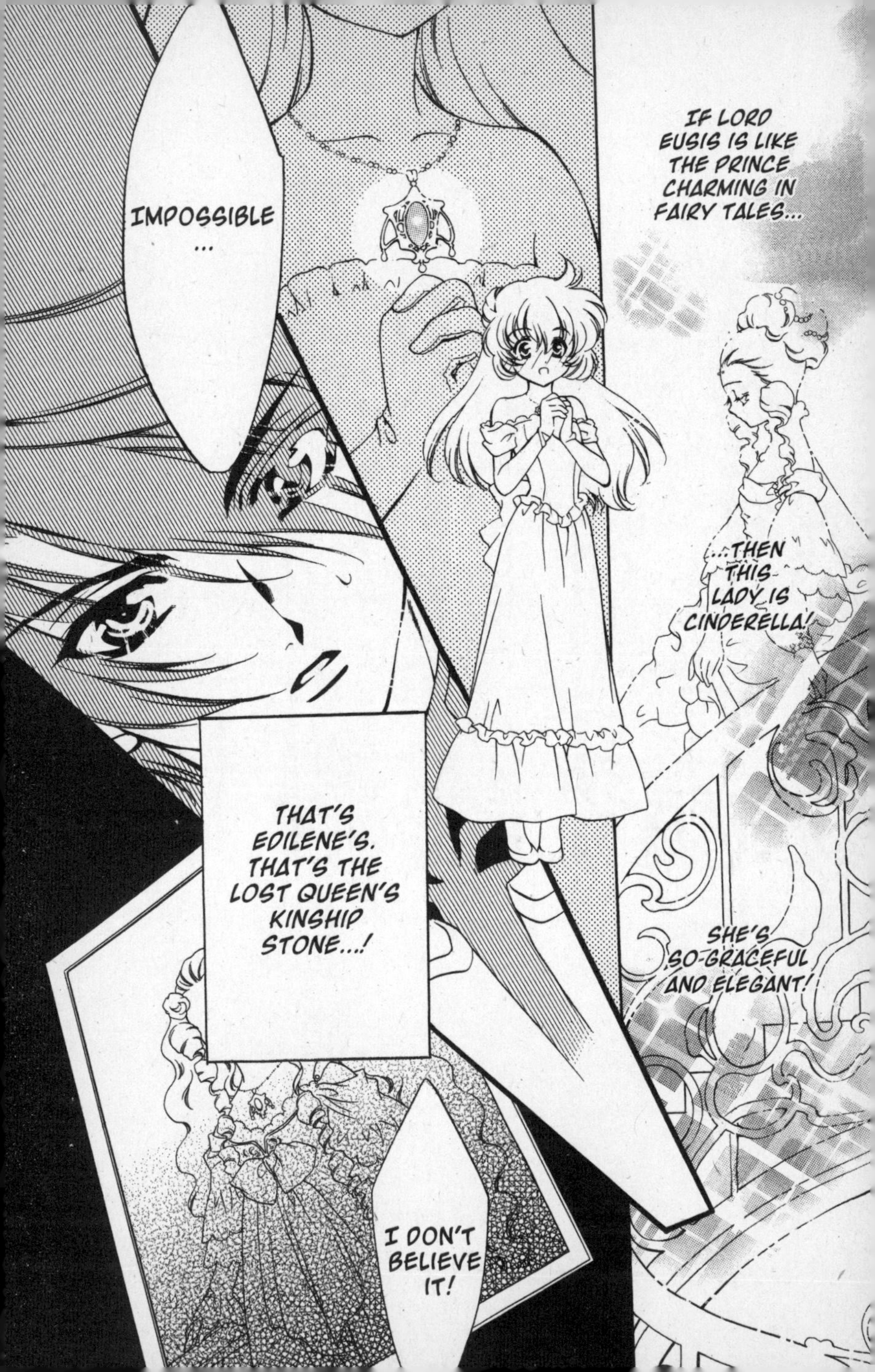
IF LORD EUSIS IS LIKE THE PRINCE CHARMING IN FAIRY TALES...
...THEN THIS LADY IS CINDERELLA!
SHE'S SO GRACEFUL AND ELEGANT!
IMPOSSIBLE...
THAT'S EDILENE'S. THAT'S THE LOST QUEEN'S KINSHIP STONE...!
I DON'T BELIEVE IT!

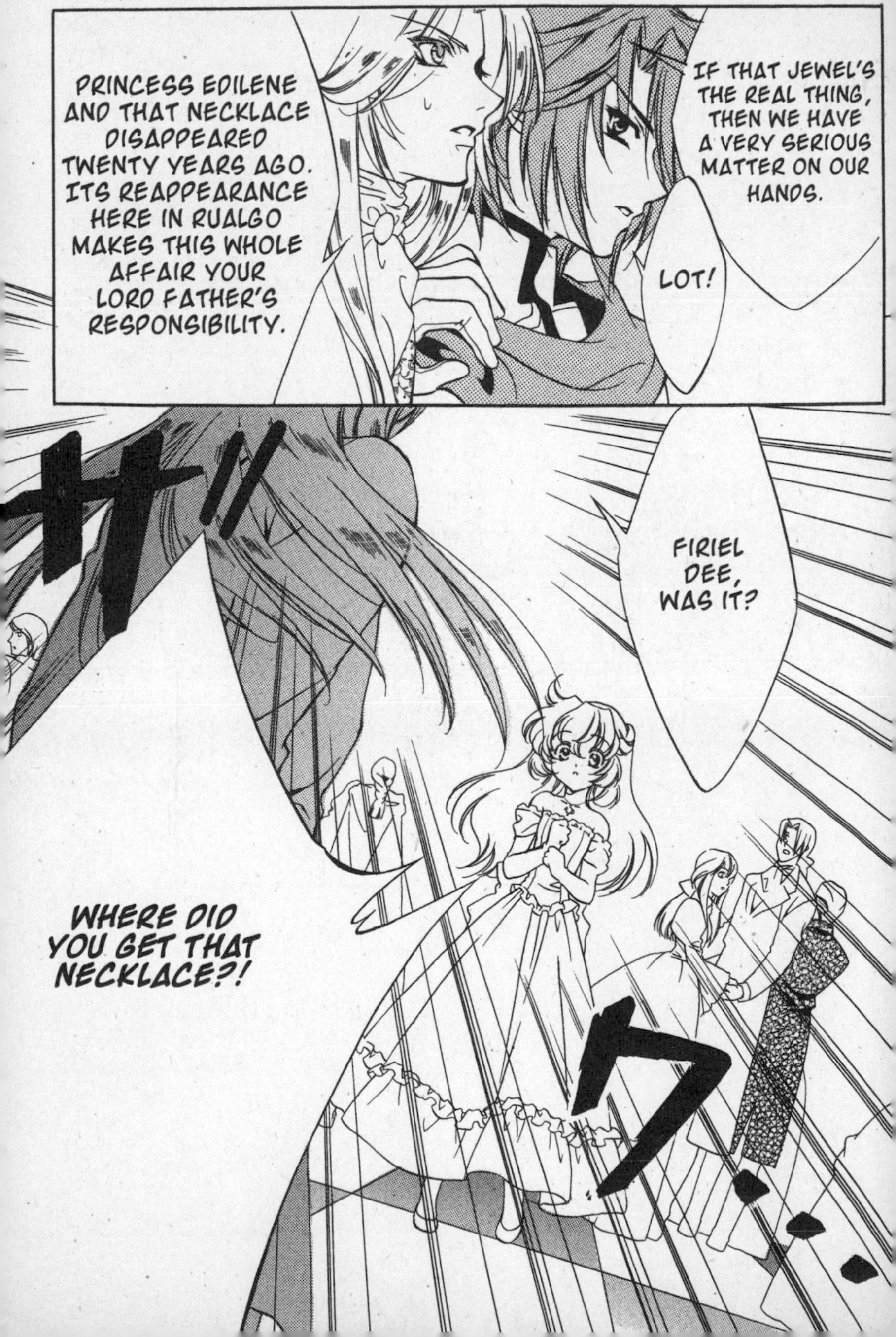
IF THAT JEWEL'S THE REAL THING, THEN WE HAVE A VERY SERIOUS MATTER ON OUR HANDS.
PRINCESS EDILENE AND THAT NECKLACE DISAPPEARED TWENTY YEARS AGO. ITS REAPPEARANCE HERE IN RUALGO MAKES THIS WHOLE AFFAIR YOUR LORD FATHER'S RESPONSIBILITY.
LOT!
FIRIEL DEE, WAS IT?
WHERE DID YOU GET THAT NECKLACE?!

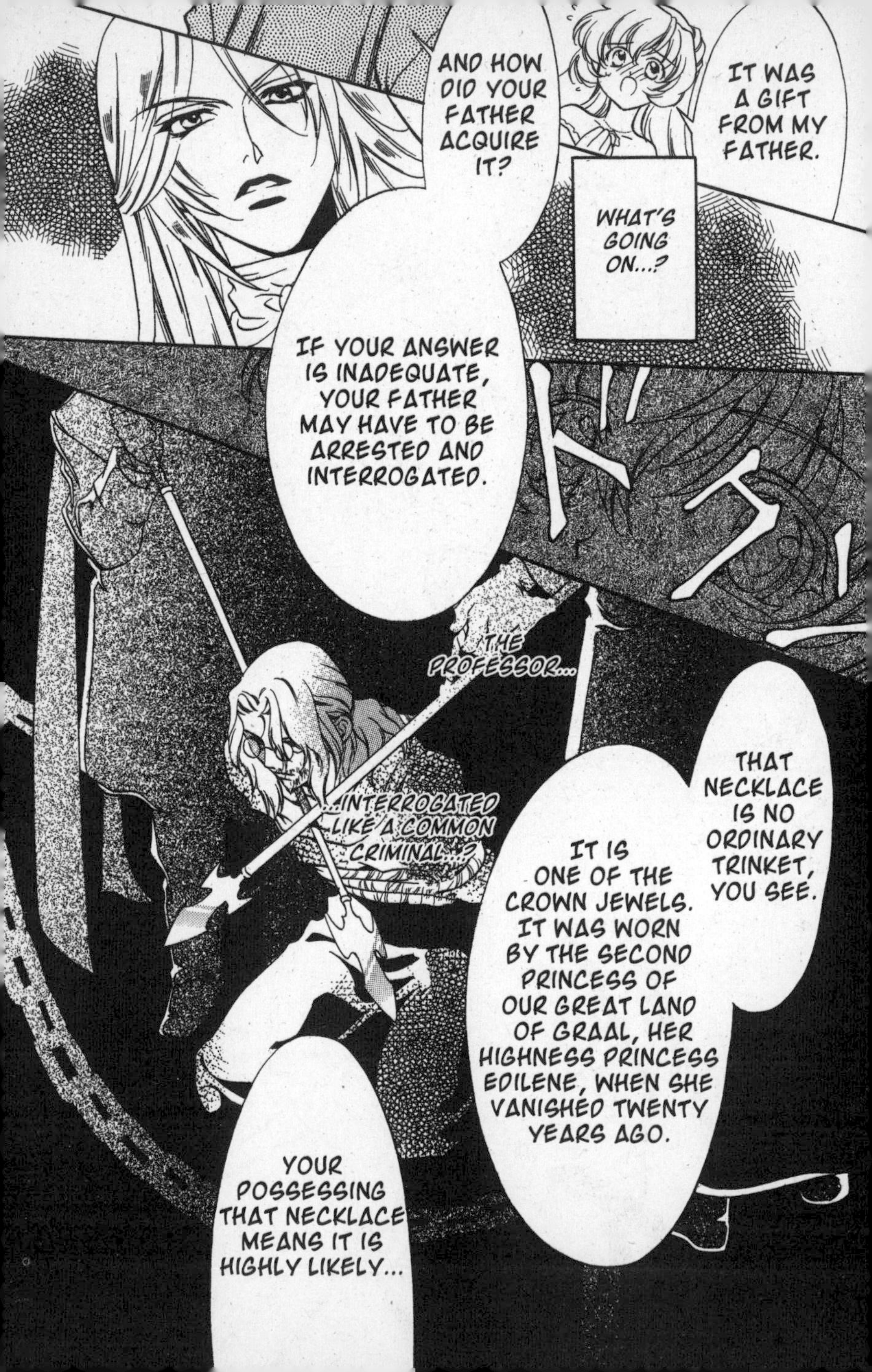
IT WAS A GIFT FROM MY FATHER.
WHAT'S GOING ON...?
AND HOW DID YOUR FATHER ACQUIRE IT?
IF YOUR ANSWER IS INADEQUATE, YOUR FATHER MAY HAVE TO BE ARRESTED AND INTERROGATED.
THE PROFESSOR...
...INTERROGATED LIKE A COMMON CRIMINAL...?
THAT NECKLACE IS NO ORDINARY TRINKET, YOU SEE.
IT IS ONE OF THE CROWN JEWELS. IT WAS WORN BY THE SECOND PRINCESS OF OUR GREAT LAND OF GRAAL, HER HIGHNESS PRINCESS EDILENE, WHEN SHE VANISHED TWENTY YEARS AGO.
YOUR POSSESSING THAT NECKLACE MEANS IT IS HIGHLY LIKELY...

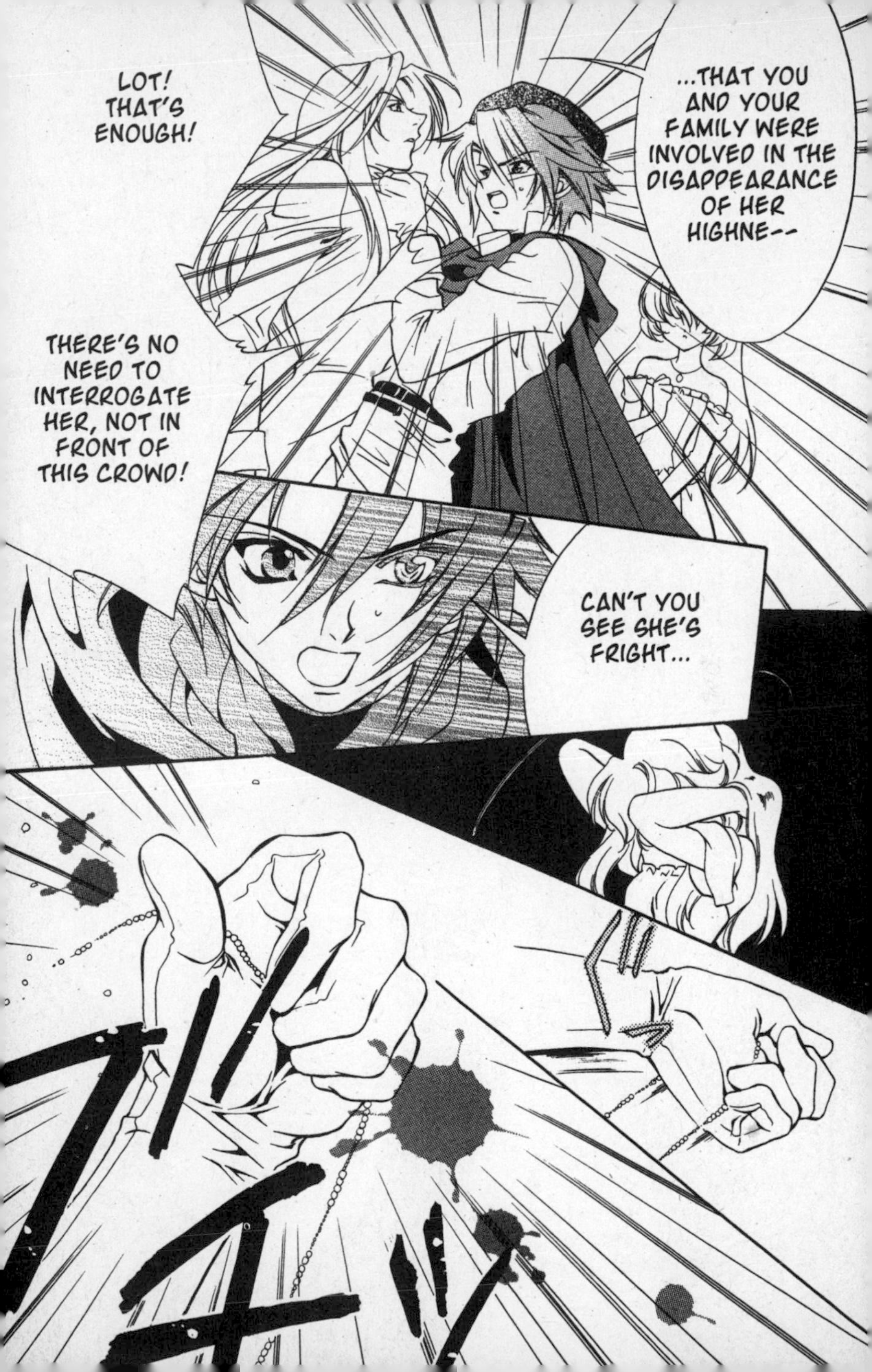
...THAT YOU AND YOUR FAMILY WERE INVOLVED IN THE DISAPPEARANCE OF HER HIGHNE--
LOT! THAT'S ENOUGH!
THERE'S NO NEED TO INTERROGATE HER, NOT IN FRONT OF THIS CROWD!
CAN'T YOU SEE SHE'S FRIGHT...

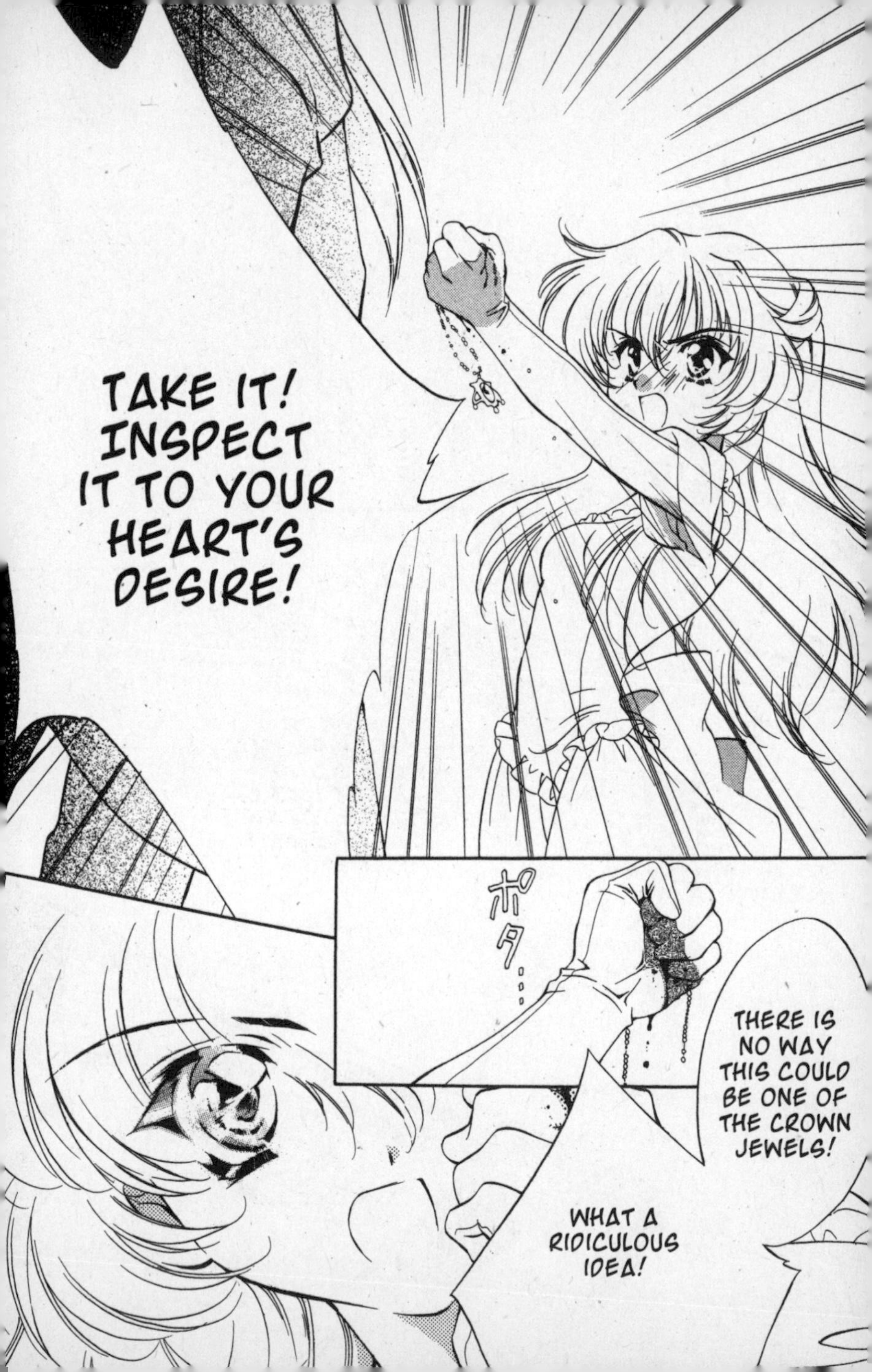
TAKE IT! INSPECT IT TO YOUR HEART'S DESIRE!
ポタ…
THERE IS NO WAY THIS COULD BE ONE OF THE CROWN JEWELS!
WHAT A RIDICULOUS IDEA!

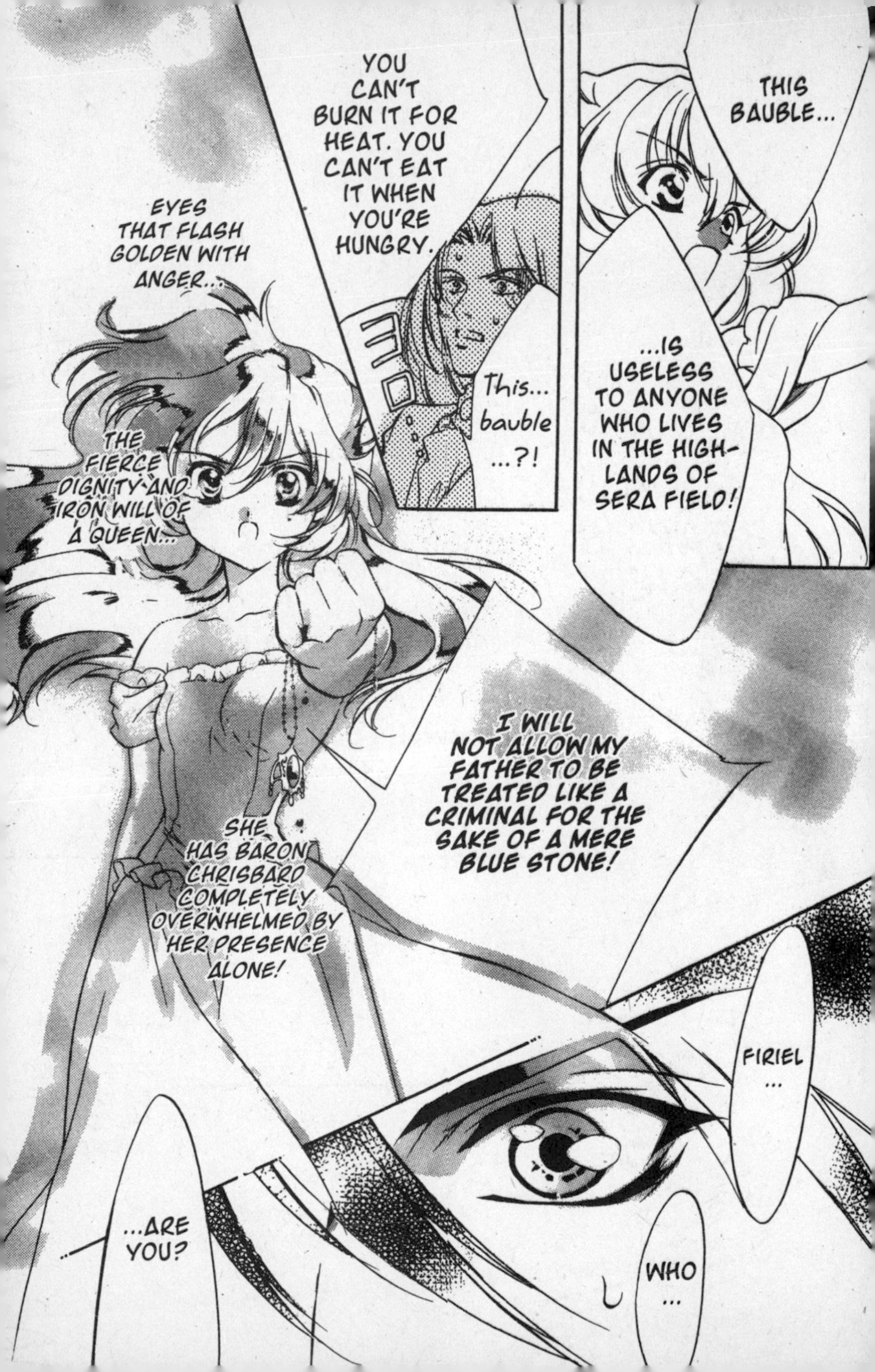
THIS BAUBLE...
...IS USELESS TO ANYONE WHO LIVES IN THE HIGH-LANDS OF SERA FIELD!
YOU CAN'T BURN IT FOR HEAT. YOU CAN'T EAT IT WHEN YOU'RE HUNGRY.
This... bauble ...?!
EYES THAT FLASH GOLDEN WITH ANGER...
THE FIERCE DIGNITY AND IRON WILL OF A QUEEN...
I WILL NOT ALLOW MY FATHER TO BE TREATED LIKE A CRIMINAL FOR THE SAKE OF A MERE BLUE STONE!
SHE HAS BARON CHRISBARD COMPLETELY OVERWHELMED BY HER PRESENCE ALONE!
FIRIEL ...
WHO ...
...ARE YOU?

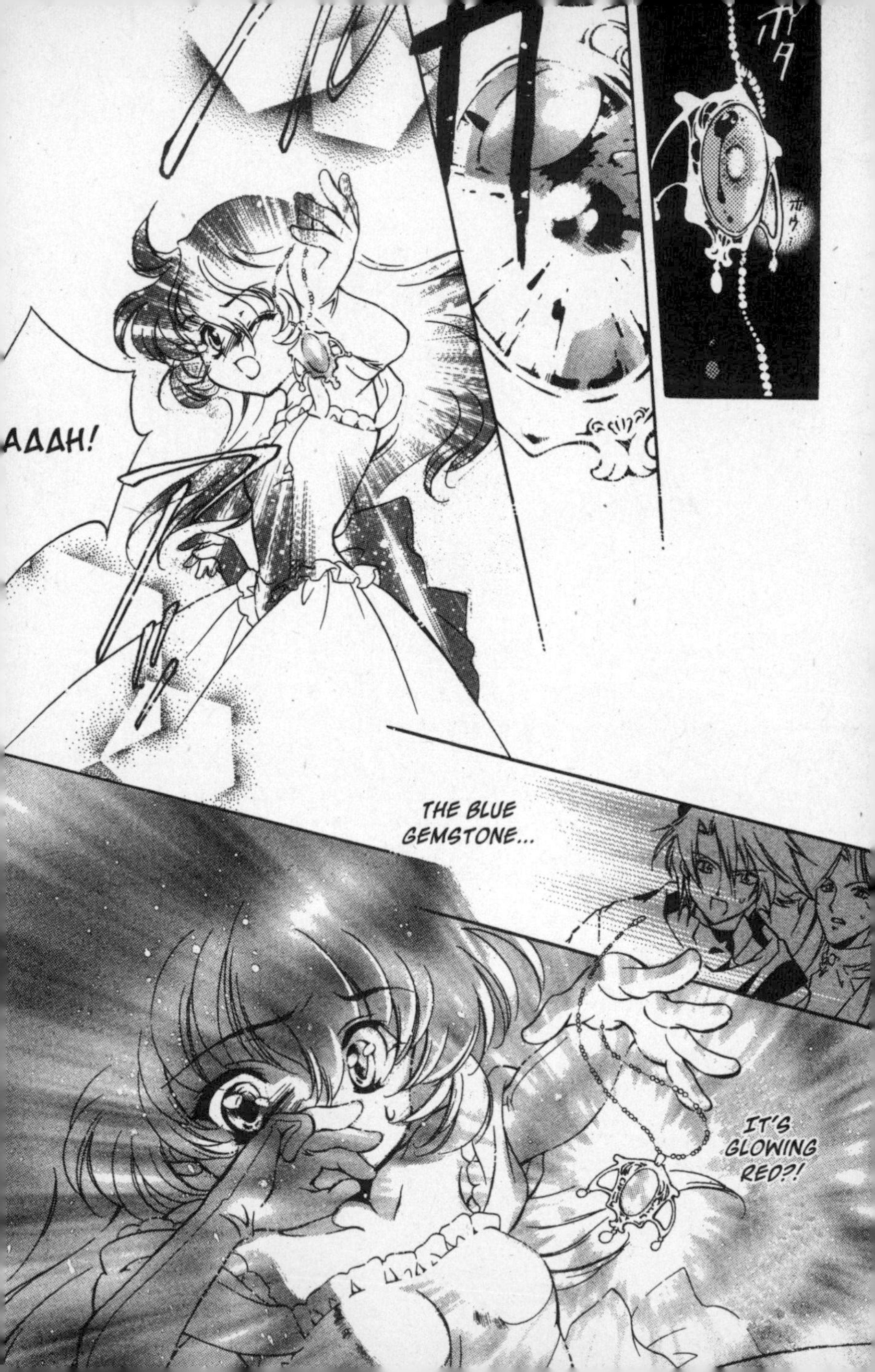
AAAH!
THE BLUE GEMSTONE...
IT'S GLOWING RED?!

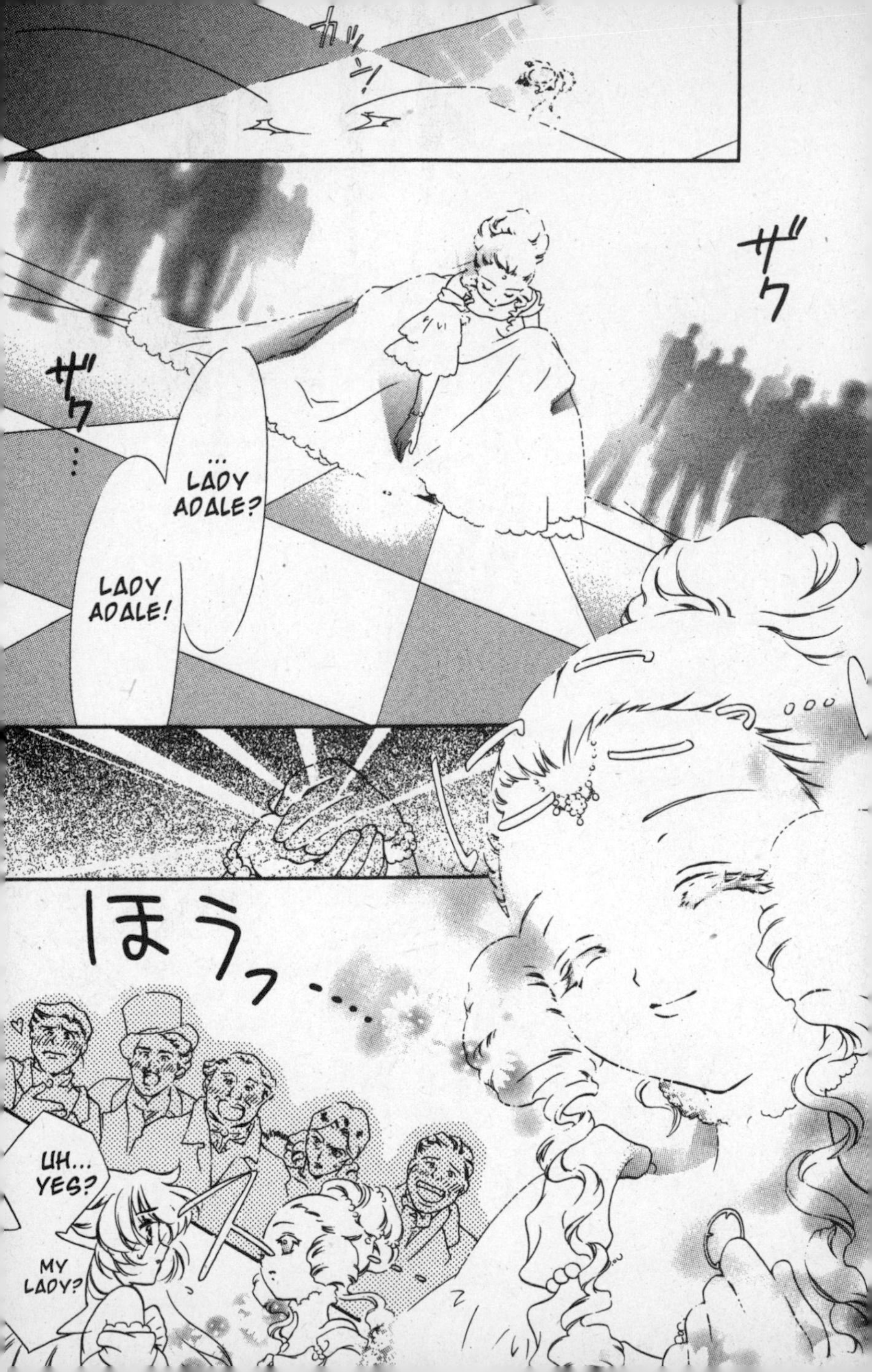
カッッ!
ザク
ザク...
... LADY ADALE?
LADY ADALE!
...
ほうっ...
UH... YES?
MY LADY?

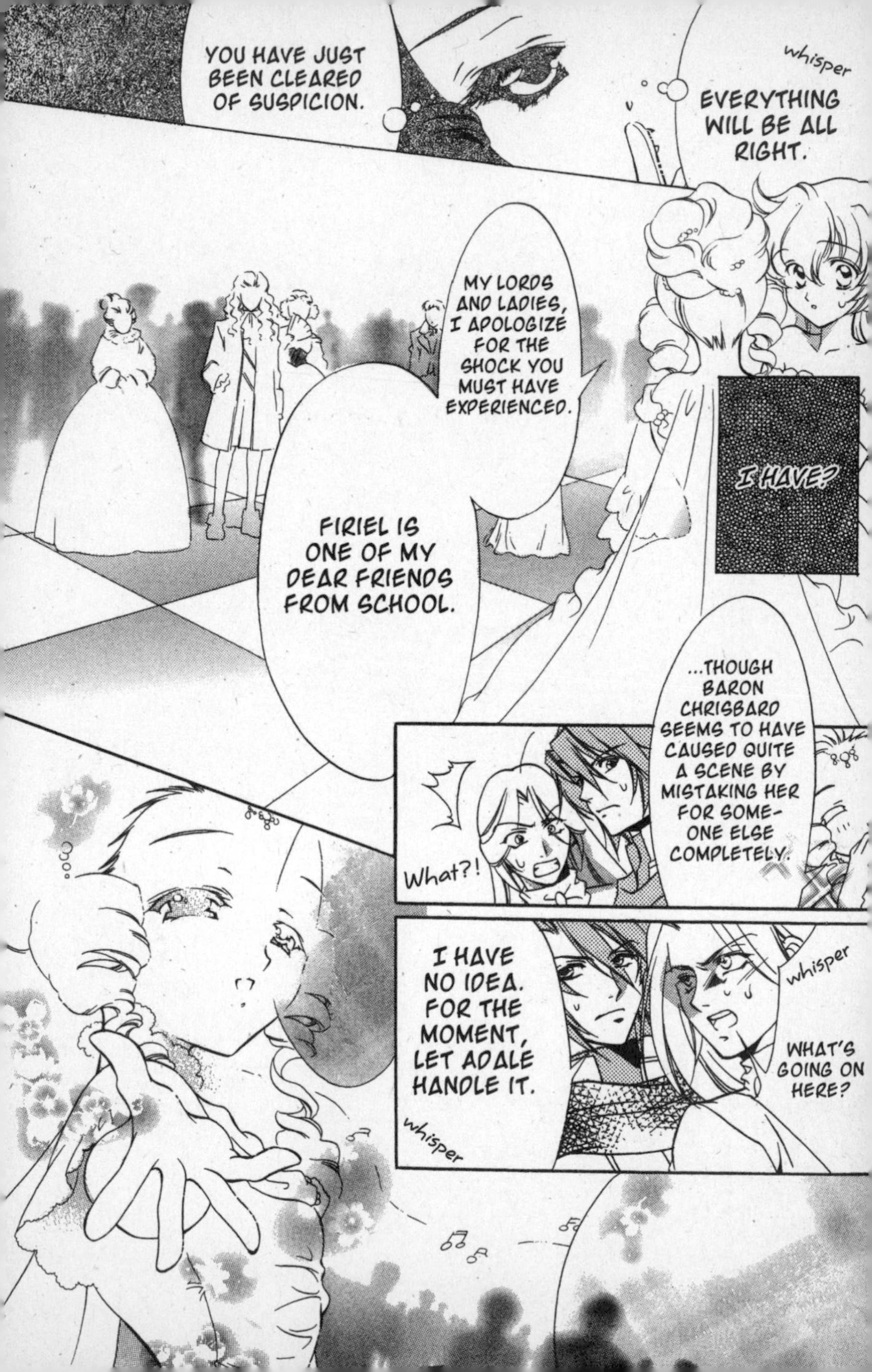
whisper
EVERYTHING WILL BE ALL RIGHT.
YOU HAVE JUST BEEN CLEARED OF SUSPICION.
I HAVE?
MY LORDS AND LADIES, I APOLOGIZE FOR THE SHOCK YOU MUST HAVE EXPERIENCED.
FIRIEL IS ONE OF MY DEAR FRIENDS FROM SCHOOL.
...THOUGH BARON CHRISBARD SEEMS TO HAVE CAUSED QUITE A SCENE BY MISTAKING HER FOR SOME-ONE ELSE COMPLETELY.
What?!
whisper
WHAT'S GOING ON HERE?
I HAVE NO IDEA. FOR THE MOMENT, LET ADALE HANDLE IT.
whisper

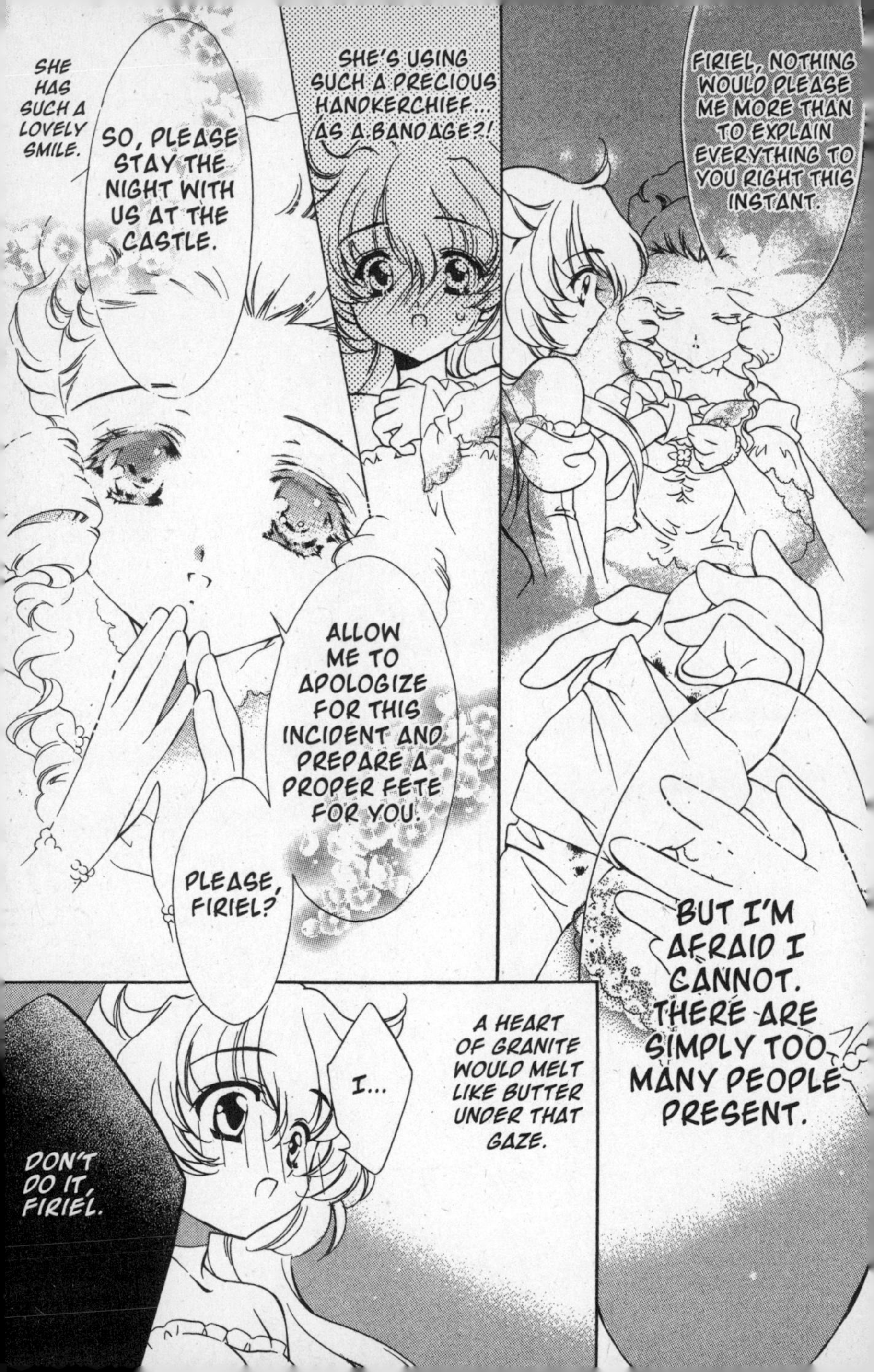
FIRIEL, NOTHING WOULD PLEASE ME MORE THAN TO EXPLAIN EVERYTHING TO YOU RIGHT THIS INSTANT.
BUT I'M AFRAID I CANNOT. THERE ARE SIMPLY TOO MANY PEOPLE PRESENT.
SHE'S USING SUCH A PRECIOUS HANDKERCHIEF... AS A BANDAGE?!
SO, PLEASE STAY THE NIGHT WITH US AT THE CASTLE.
SHE HAS SUCH A LOVELY SMILE.
ALLOW ME TO APOLOGIZE FOR THIS INCIDENT AND PREPARE A PROPER FETE FOR YOU.
PLEASE, FIRIEL?
A HEART OF GRANITE WOULD MELT LIKE BUTTER UNDER THAT GAZE.
I...
DON'T DO IT, FIRIEL.

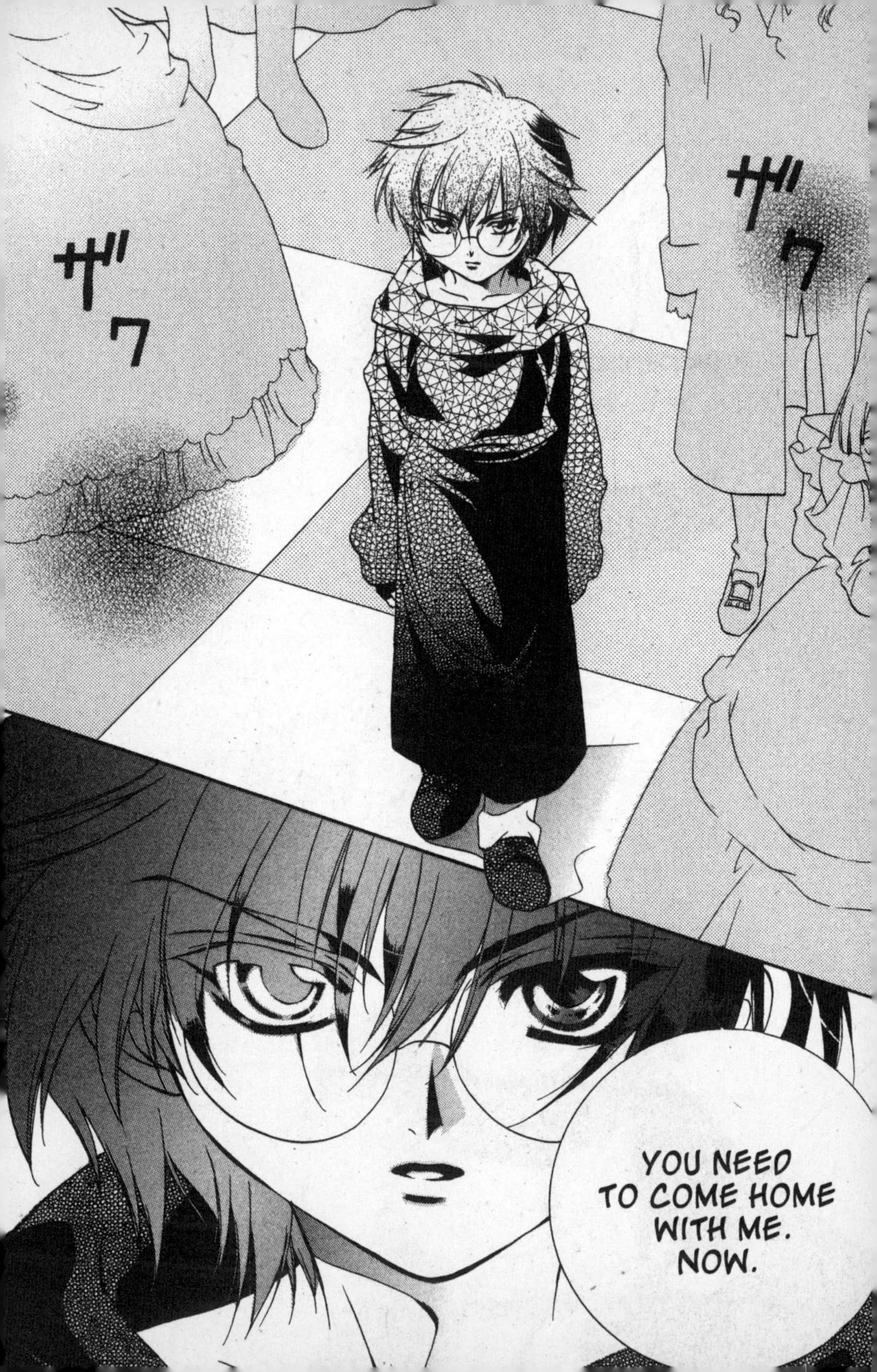
ザワ
ザワ
YOU NEED TO COME HOME WITH ME. NOW.

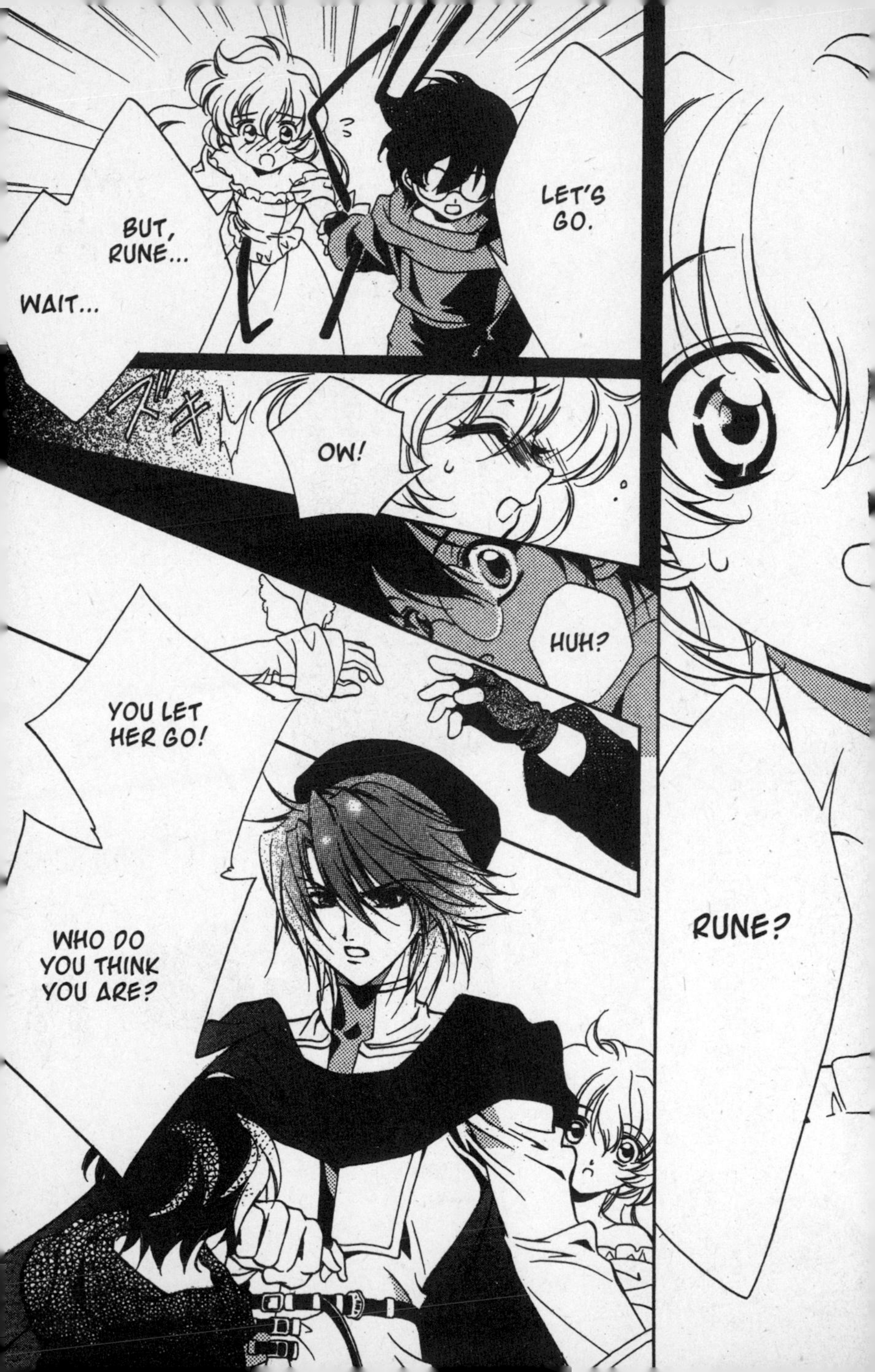
RUNE?
LET'S GO.
BUT, RUNE...
WAIT...
ズキ
OW!
HUH?
YOU LET HER GO!
WHO DO YOU THINK YOU ARE?

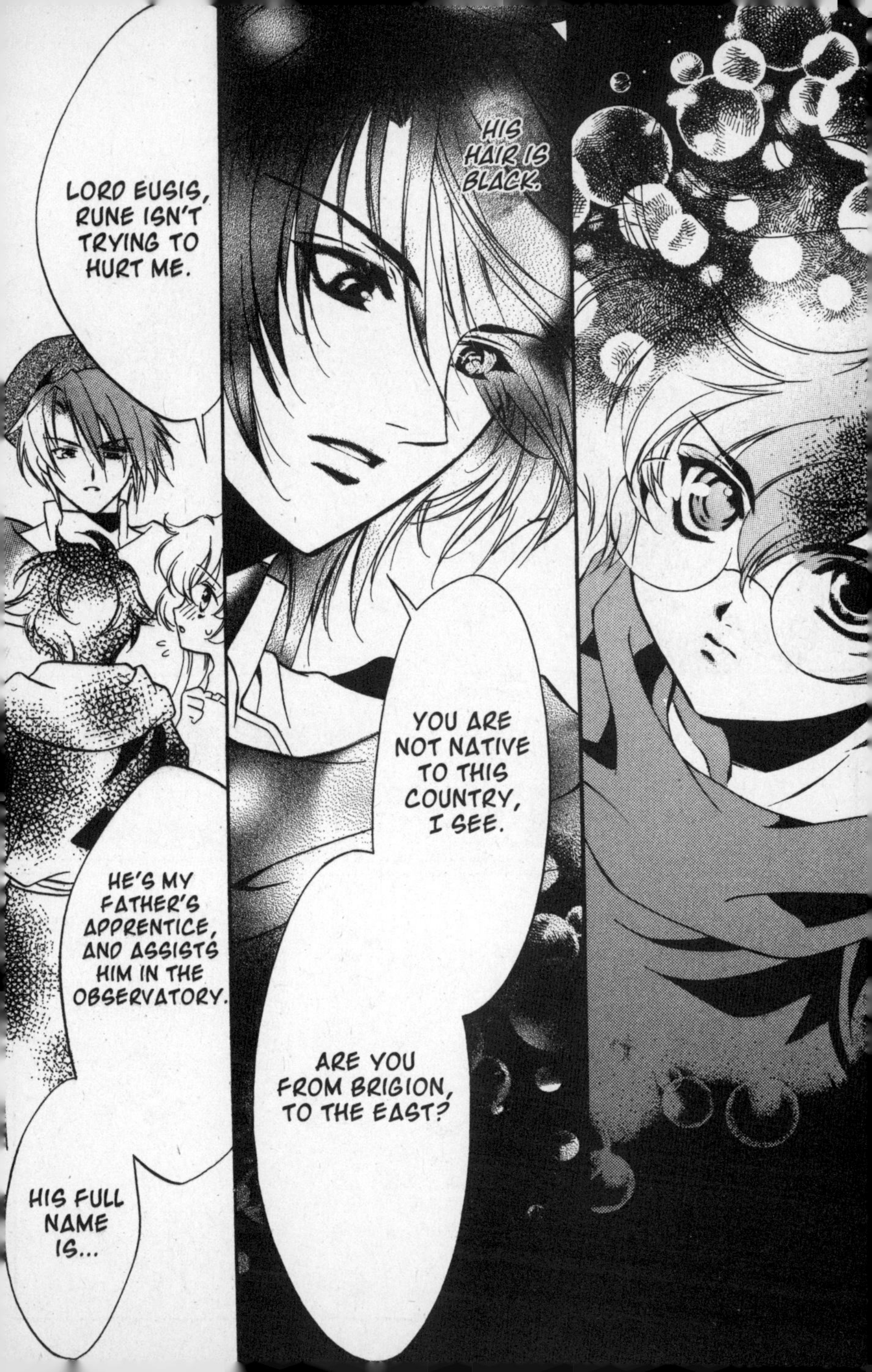
HIS HAIR IS BLACK.
YOU ARE NOT NATIVE TO THIS COUNTRY, I SEE.
ARE YOU FROM BRIGION, TO THE EAST?
LORD EUSIS, RUNE ISN'T TRYING TO HURT ME.
HE'S MY FATHER'S APPRENTICE, AND ASSISTS HIM IN THE OBSERVATORY.
HIS FULL NAME IS...

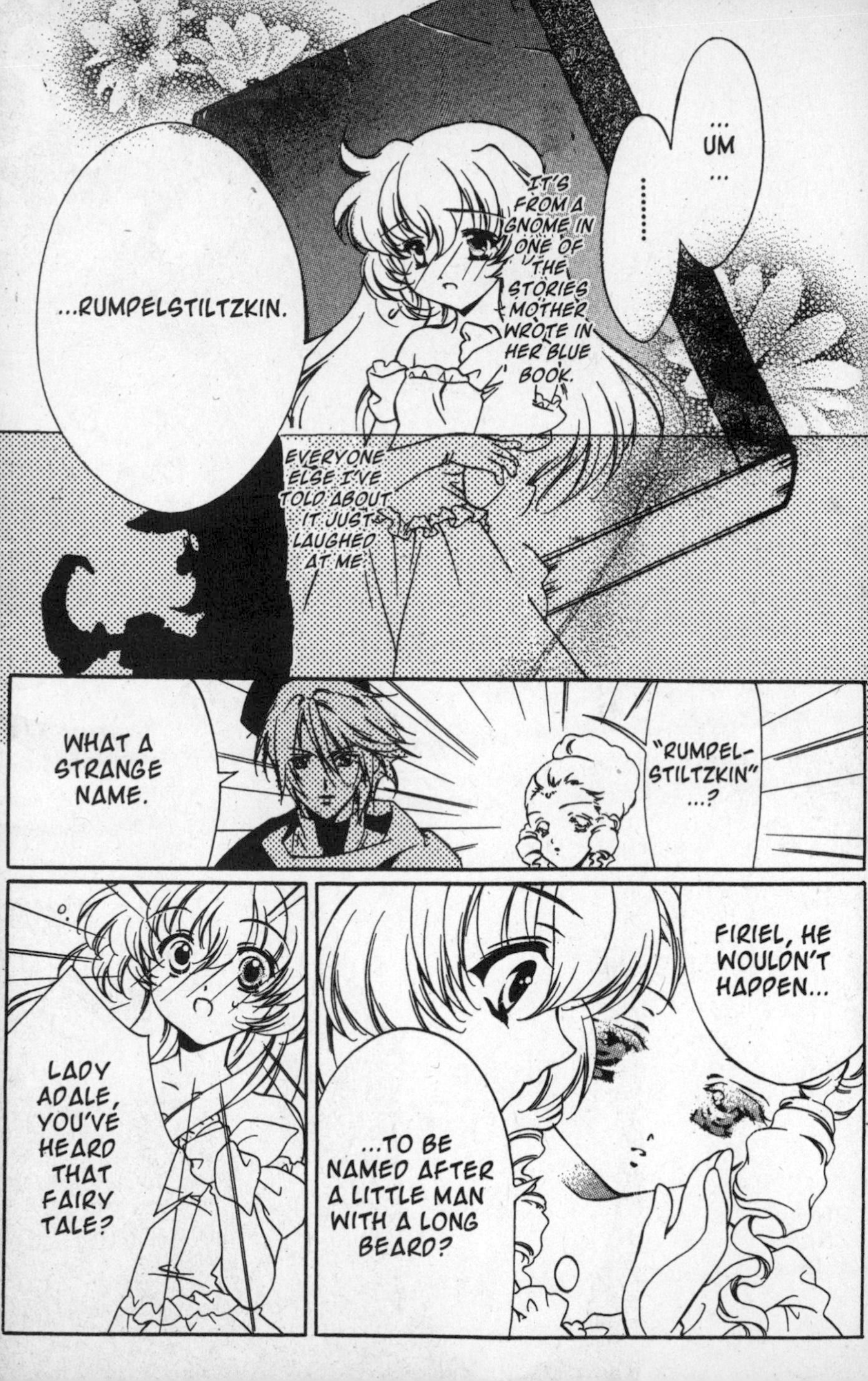
... UM ... .
IT'S FROM A GNOME IN ONE OF THE STORIES MOTHER WROTE IN HER BLUE BOOK.
...RUMPELSTILTZKIN.
EVERYONE ELSE I'VE TOLD ABOUT IT JUST LAUGHED AT ME.
"RUMPEL-STILTZKIN" ...?
WHAT A STRANGE NAME.
FIRIEL, HE WOULDN'T HAPPEN...
...TO BE NAMED AFTER A LITTLE MAN WITH A LONG BEARD?
LADY ADALE, YOU'VE HEARD THAT FAIRY TALE?

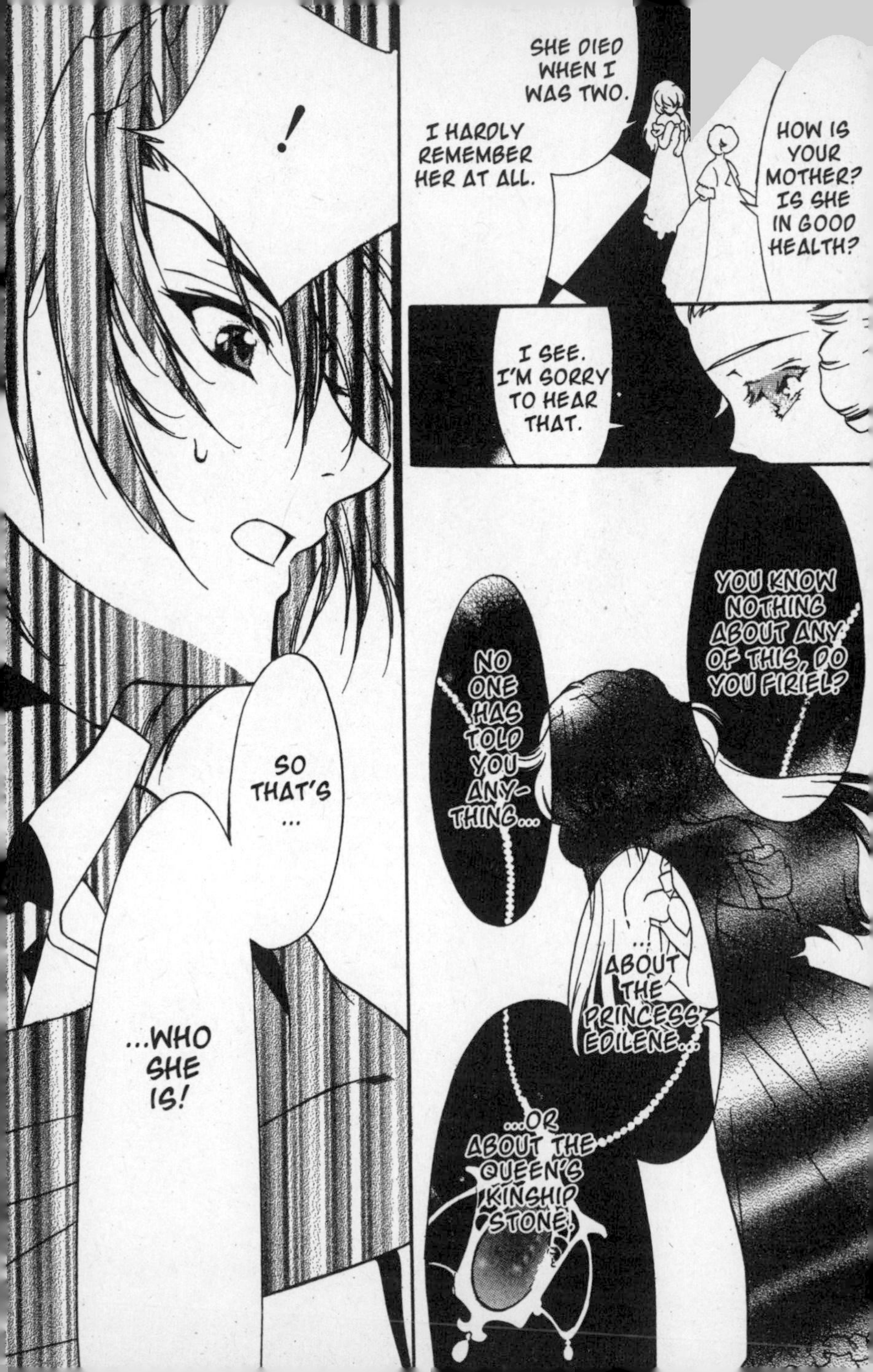
HOW IS YOUR MOTHER? IS SHE IN GOOD HEALTH?
SHE DIED WHEN I WAS TWO.
I HARDLY REMEMBER HER AT ALL.
I SEE. I'M SORRY TO HEAR THAT.
YOU KNOW NOTHING ABOUT ANY OF THIS, DO YOU FIRIEL?
NO ONE HAS TOLD YOU ANY-THING...
...ABOUT THE PRINCESS EDILENE...
...OR ABOUT THE QUEEN'S KINSHIP STONE.
!
SO THAT'S...
...WHO SHE IS!

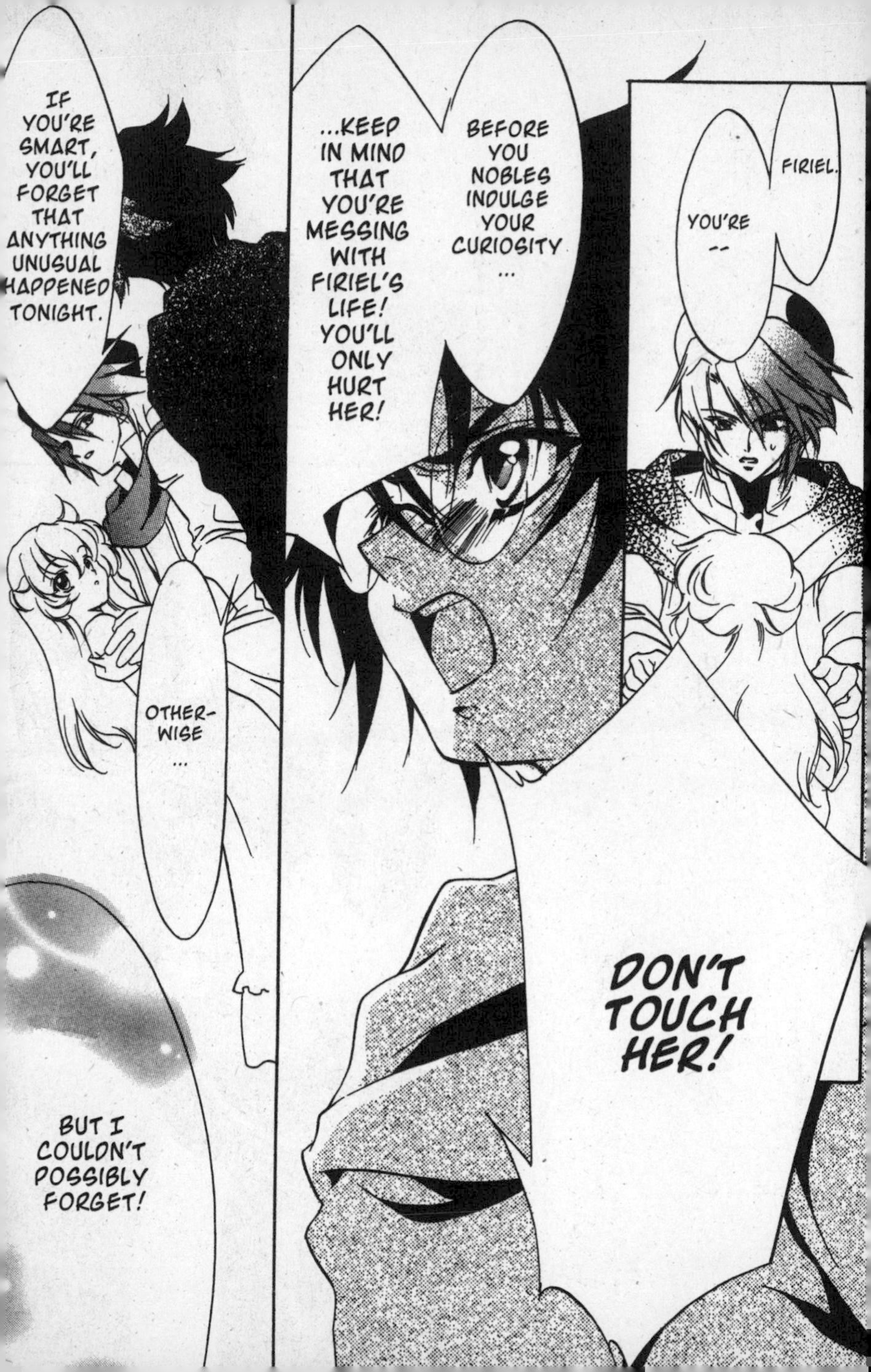
FIRIEL.
YOU'RE --
BEFORE YOU NOBLES INDULGE YOUR CURIOSITY ...
...KEEP IN MIND THAT YOU'RE MESSING WITH FIRIEL'S LIFE! YOU'LL ONLY HURT HER!
DON'T TOUCH HER!
IF YOU'RE SMART, YOU'LL FORGET THAT ANYTHING UNUSUAL HAPPENED TONIGHT.
OTHER-WISE ...
BUT I COULDN'T POSSIBLY FORGET!

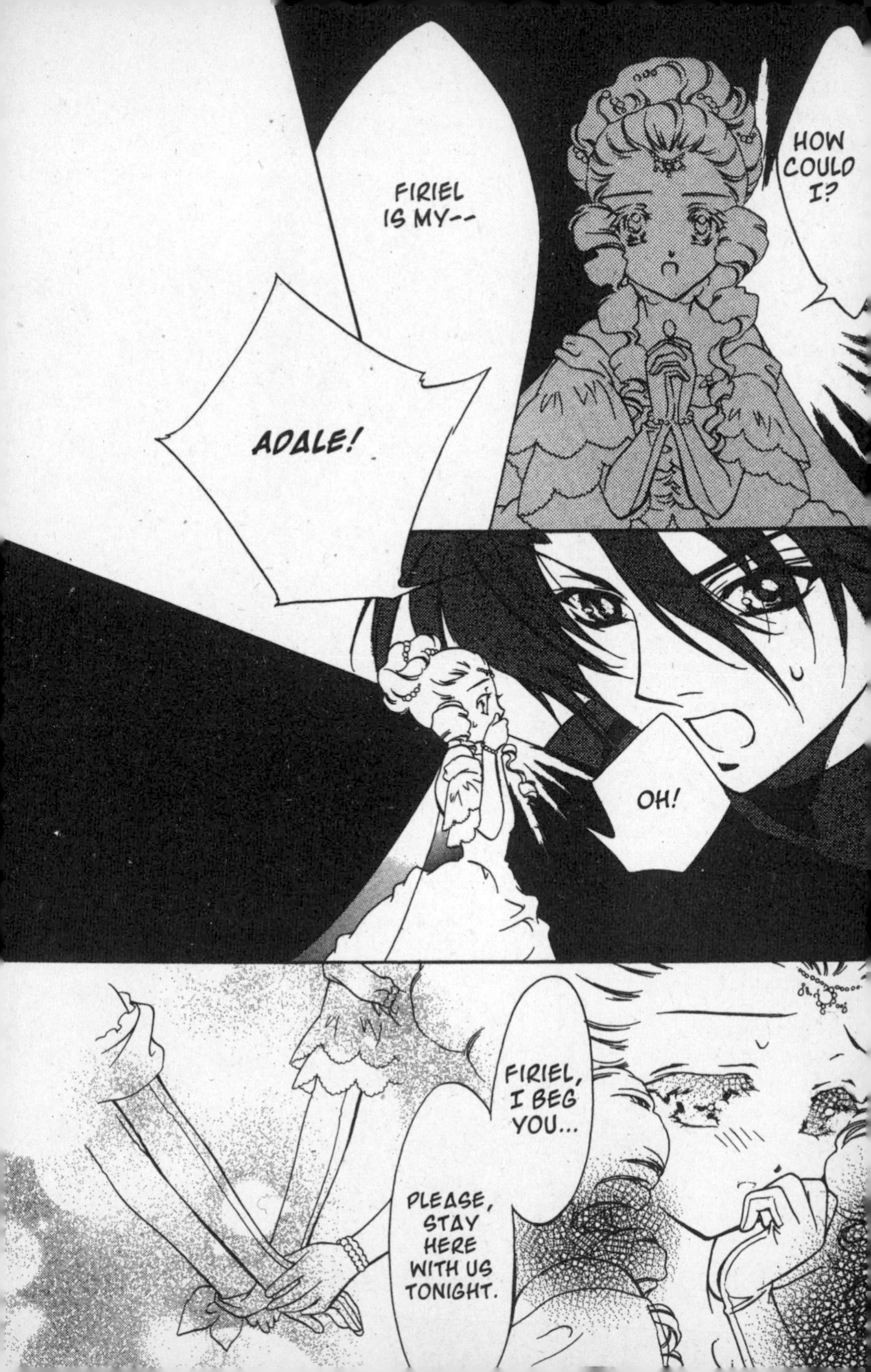
HOW COULD I?
FIRIEL IS MY--
ADALE!
OH!
FIRIEL, I BEG YOU...
PLEASE, STAY HERE WITH US TONIGHT.

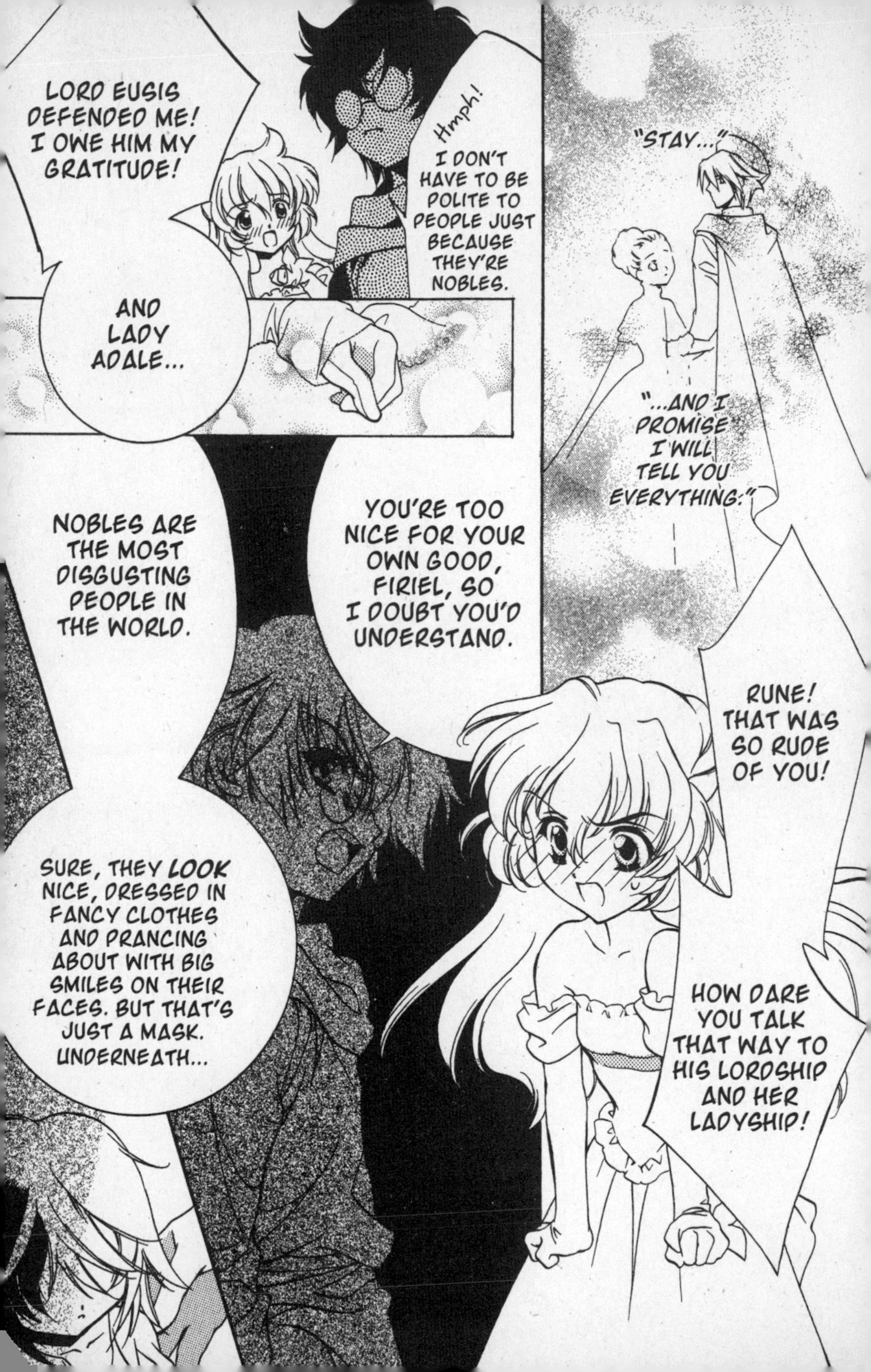
"STAY..."
"...AND I PROMISE I WILL TELL YOU EVERYTHING."
LORD EUSIS DEFENDED ME! I OWE HIM MY GRATITUDE!
Hmph!
I DON'T HAVE TO BE POLITE TO PEOPLE JUST BECAUSE THEY'RE NOBLES.
AND LADY ADALE...
RUNE! THAT WAS SO RUDE OF YOU!
HOW DARE YOU TALK THAT WAY TO HIS LORDSHIP AND HER LADYSHIP!
YOU'RE TOO NICE FOR YOUR OWN GOOD, FIRIEL, SO I DOUBT YOU'D UNDERSTAND.
NOBLES ARE THE MOST DISGUSTING PEOPLE IN THE WORLD.
SURE, THEY LOOK NICE, DRESSED IN FANCY CLOTHES AND PRANCING ABOUT WITH BIG SMILES ON THEIR FACES. BUT THAT'S JUST A MASK. UNDERNEATH...

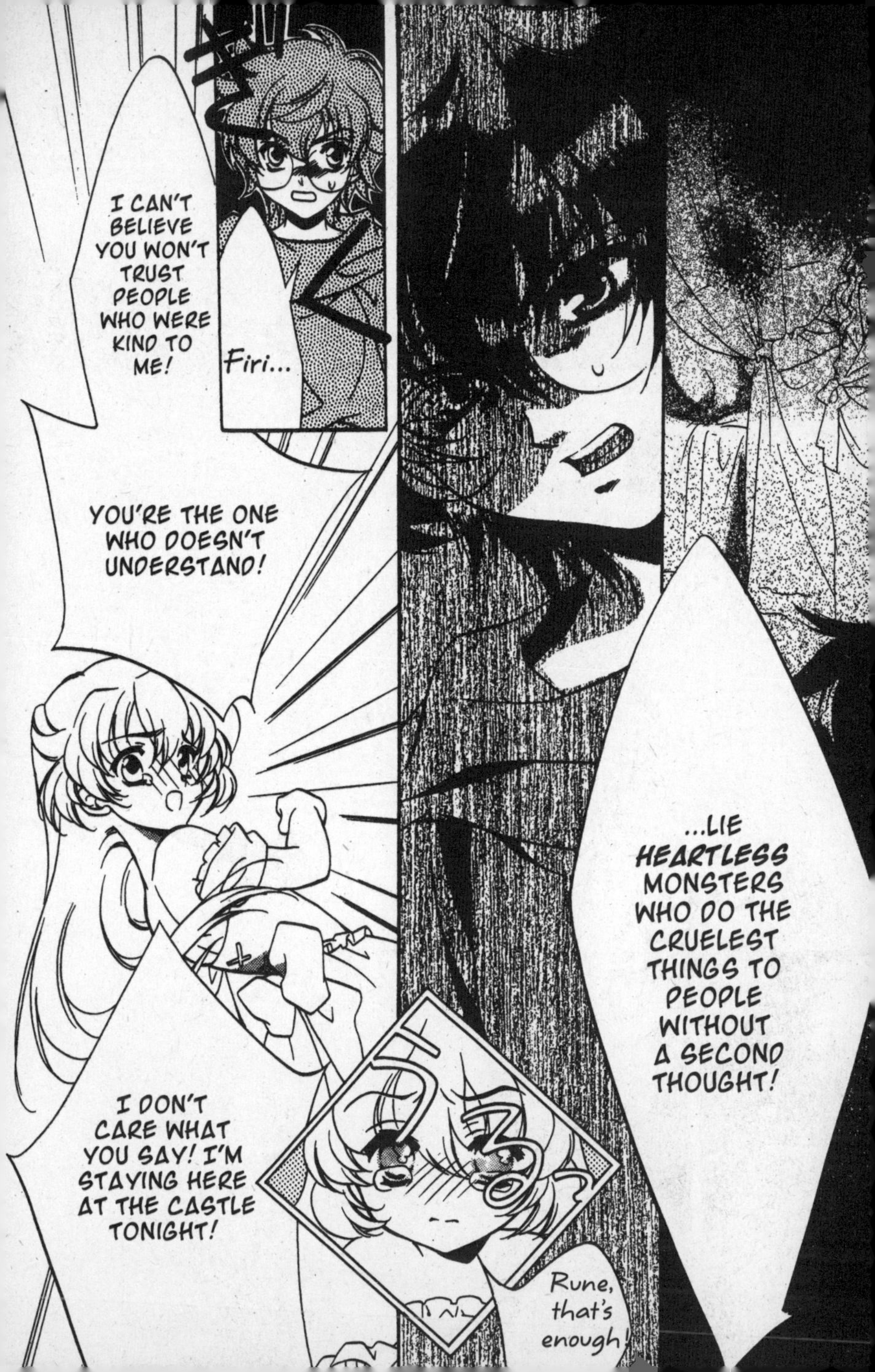
...LIE HEARTLESS MONSTERS WHO DO THE CRUELEST THINGS TO PEOPLE WITHOUT A SECOND THOUGHT!
I CAN'T BELIEVE YOU WON'T TRUST PEOPLE WHO WERE KIND TO ME!
Firi...
YOU'RE THE ONE WHO DOESN'T UNDERSTAND!
I DON'T CARE WHAT YOU SAY! I'M STAYING HERE AT THE CASTLE TONIGHT!
Rune, that's enough!

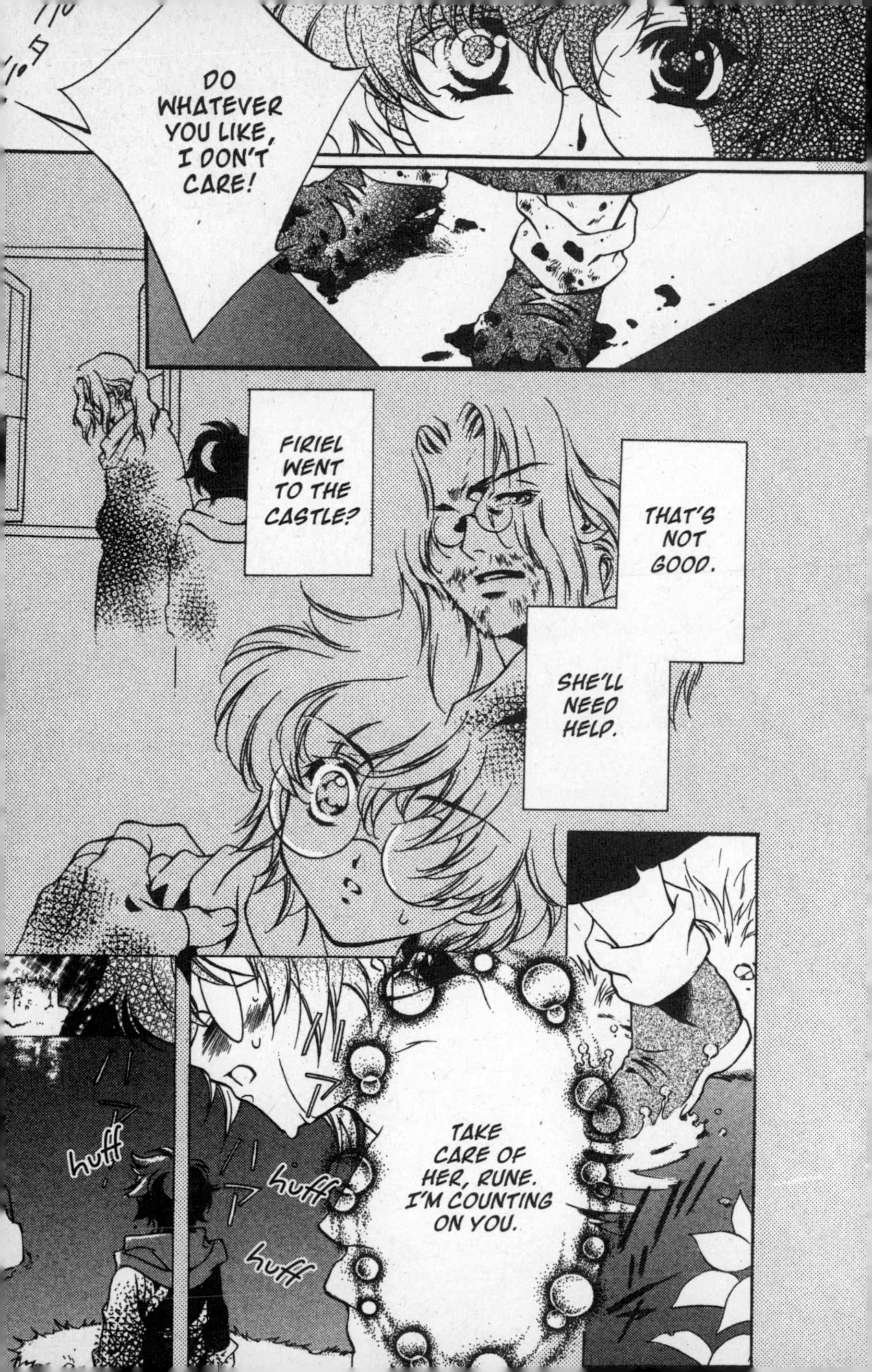
DO WHATEVER YOU LIKE, I DON'T CARE!
FIRIEL WENT TO THE CASTLE?
THAT'S NOT GOOD.
SHE'LL NEED HELP.
TAKE CARE OF HER, RUNE. I'M COUNTING ON YOU.
huff
huff
huff

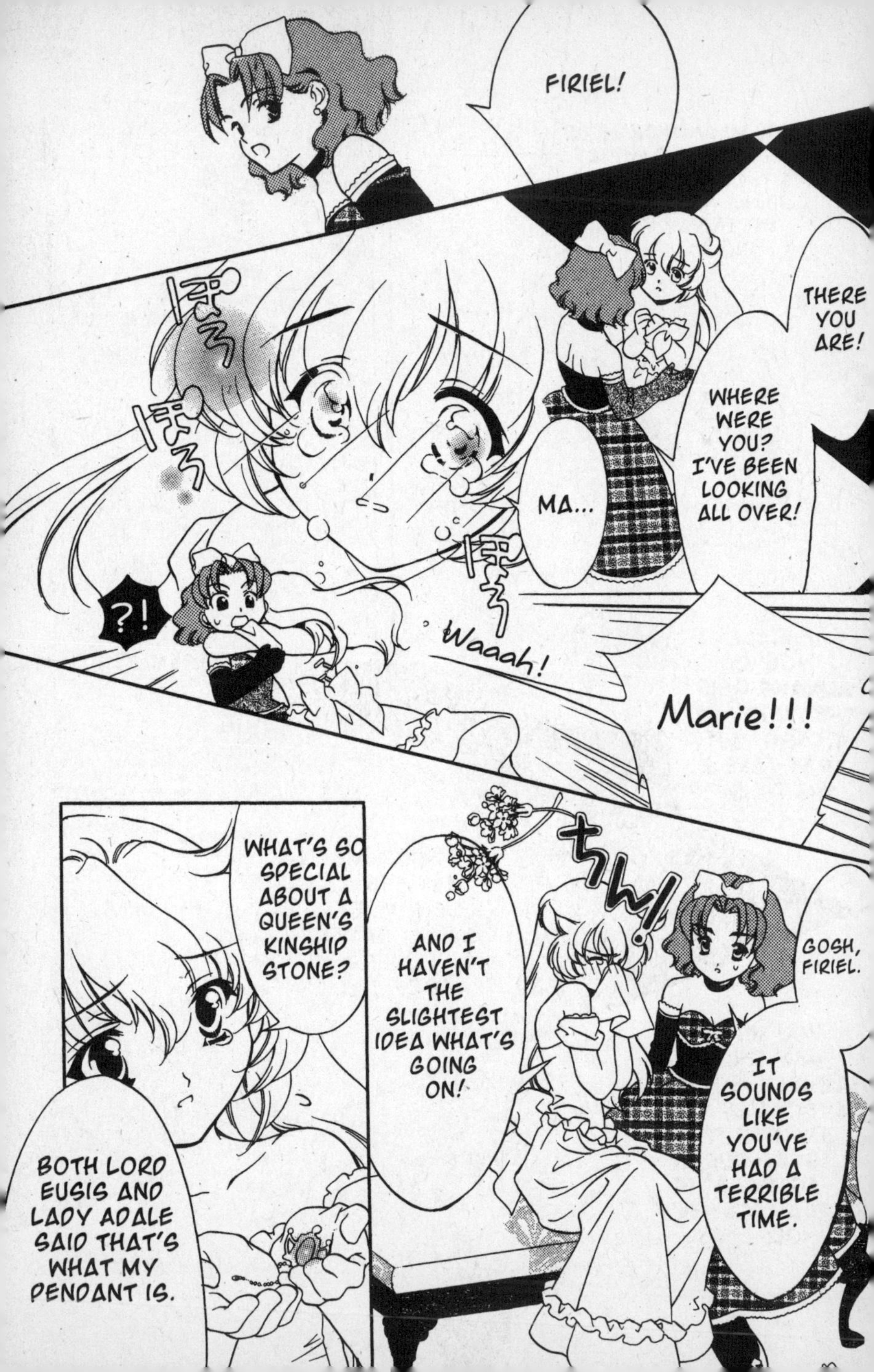
FIRIEL!
THERE YOU ARE!
WHERE WERE YOU? I'VE BEEN LOOKING ALL OVER!
MA...
Marie!!!
Waaah!
?!
GOSH, FIRIEL.
IT SOUNDS LIKE YOU'VE HAD A TERRIBLE TIME.
AND I HAVEN'T THE SLIGHTEST IDEA WHAT'S GOING ON!
WHAT'S SO SPECIAL ABOUT A QUEEN'S KINSHIP STONE?
BOTH LORD EUSIS AND LADY ADALE SAID THAT'S WHAT MY PENDANT IS.

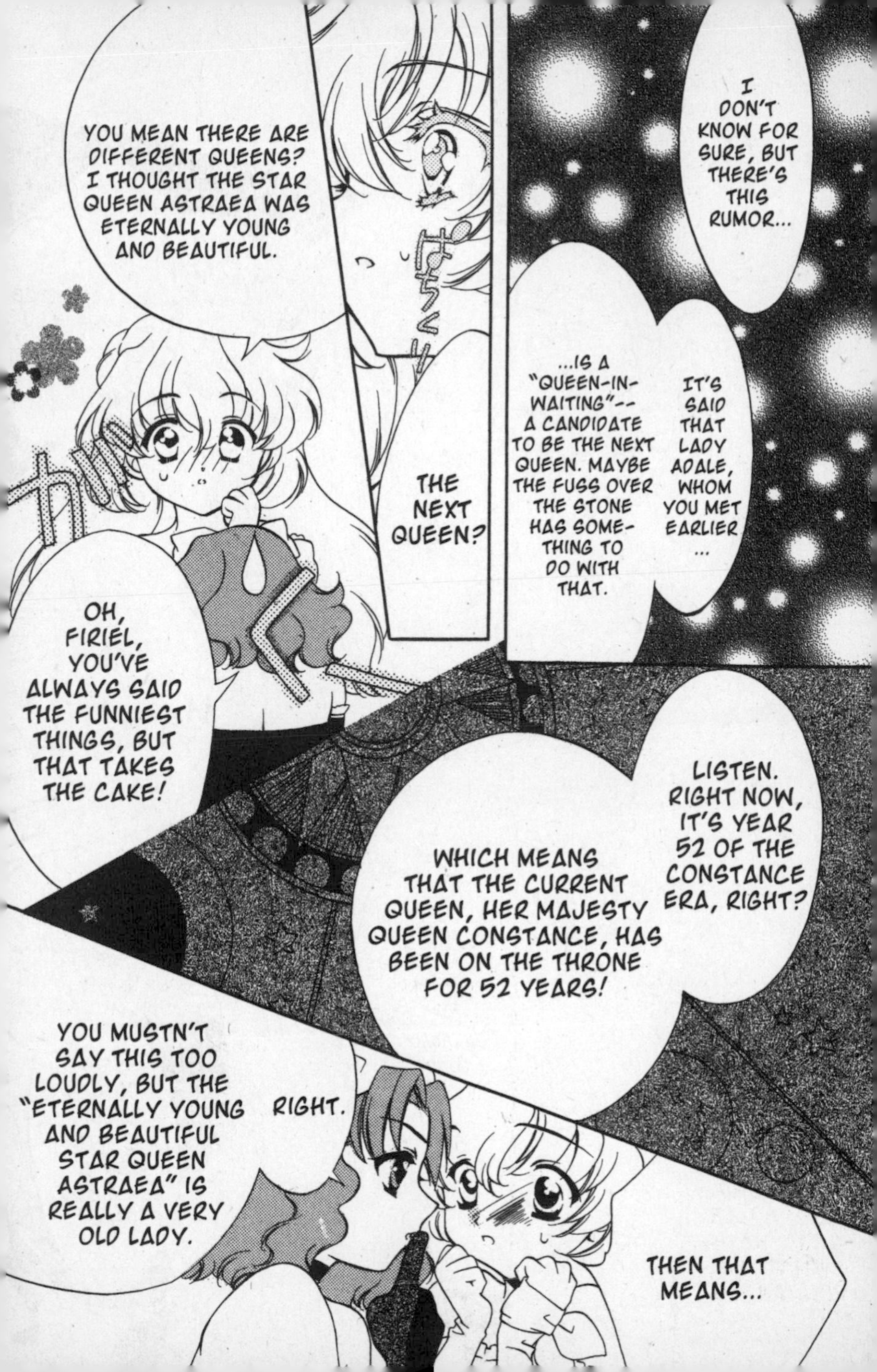
I DON'T KNOW FOR SURE, BUT THERE'S THIS RUMOR...
IT'S SAID THAT LADY ADALE, WHOM YOU MET EARLIER...
...IS A "QUEEN-IN-WAITING"--A CANDIDATE TO BE THE NEXT QUEEN. MAYBE THE FUSS OVER THE STONE HAS SOMETHING TO DO WITH THAT.
THE NEXT QUEEN?
YOU MEAN THERE ARE DIFFERENT QUEENS? I THOUGHT THE STAR QUEEN ASTRAEA WAS ETERNALLY YOUNG AND BEAUTIFUL.
OH, FIRIEL, YOU'VE ALWAYS SAID THE FUNNIEST THINGS, BUT THAT TAKES THE CAKE!
LISTEN. RIGHT NOW, IT'S YEAR 52 OF THE CONSTANCE ERA, RIGHT?
WHICH MEANS THAT THE CURRENT QUEEN, HER MAJESTY QUEEN CONSTANCE, HAS BEEN ON THE THRONE FOR 52 YEARS!
THEN THAT MEANS...
RIGHT.
YOU MUSTN'T SAY THIS TOO LOUDLY, BUT THE "ETERNALLY YOUNG AND BEAUTIFUL STAR QUEEN ASTRAEA" IS REALLY A VERY OLD LADY.

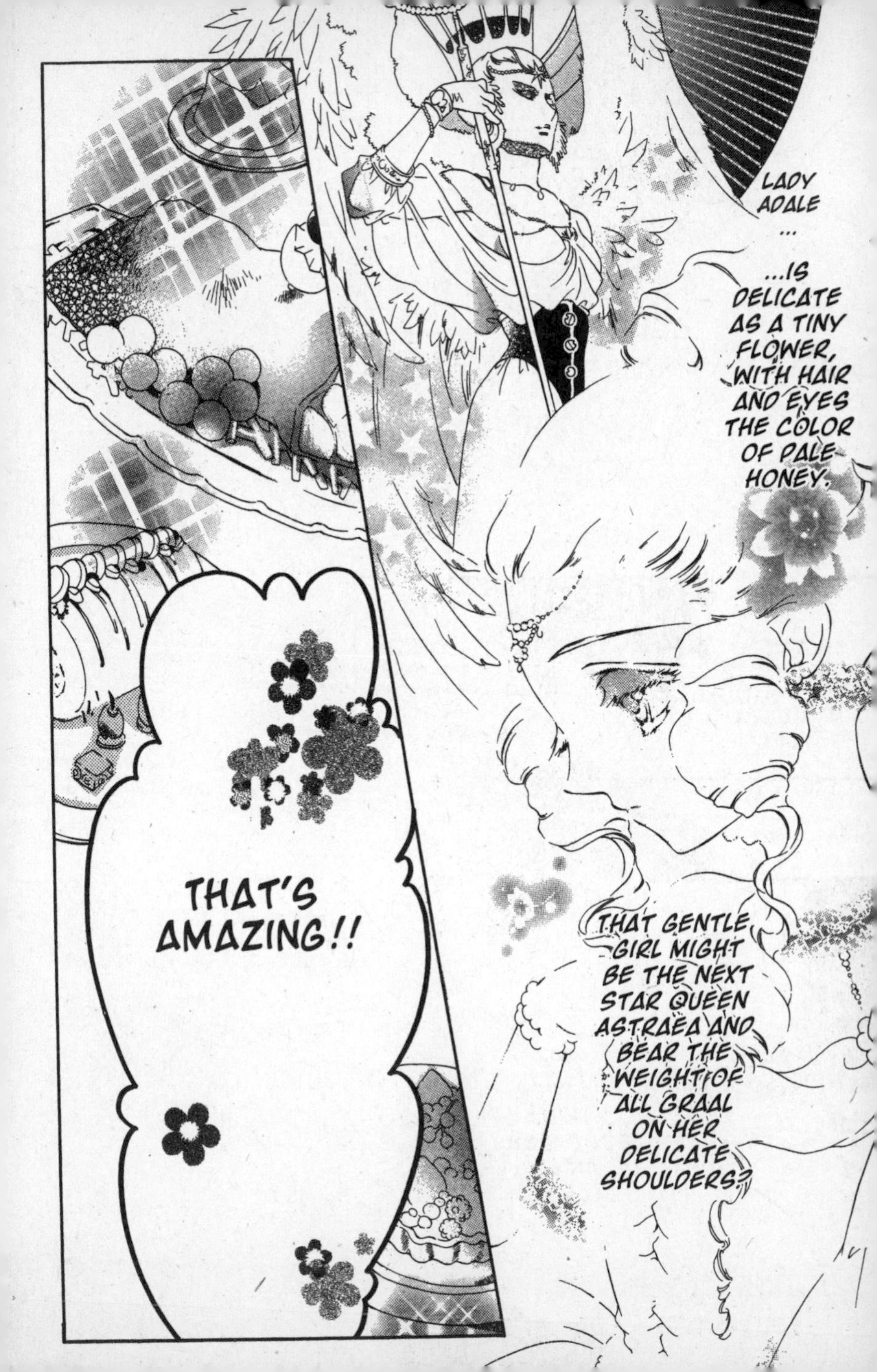
LADY ADALE ...
...IS DELICATE AS A TINY FLOWER, WITH HAIR AND EYES THE COLOR OF PALE HONEY.
THAT GENTLE GIRL MIGHT BE THE NEXT STAR QUEEN ASTRAEA AND BEAR THE WEIGHT OF ALL GRAAL ON HER DELICATE SHOULDERS?
THAT'S AMAZING!!

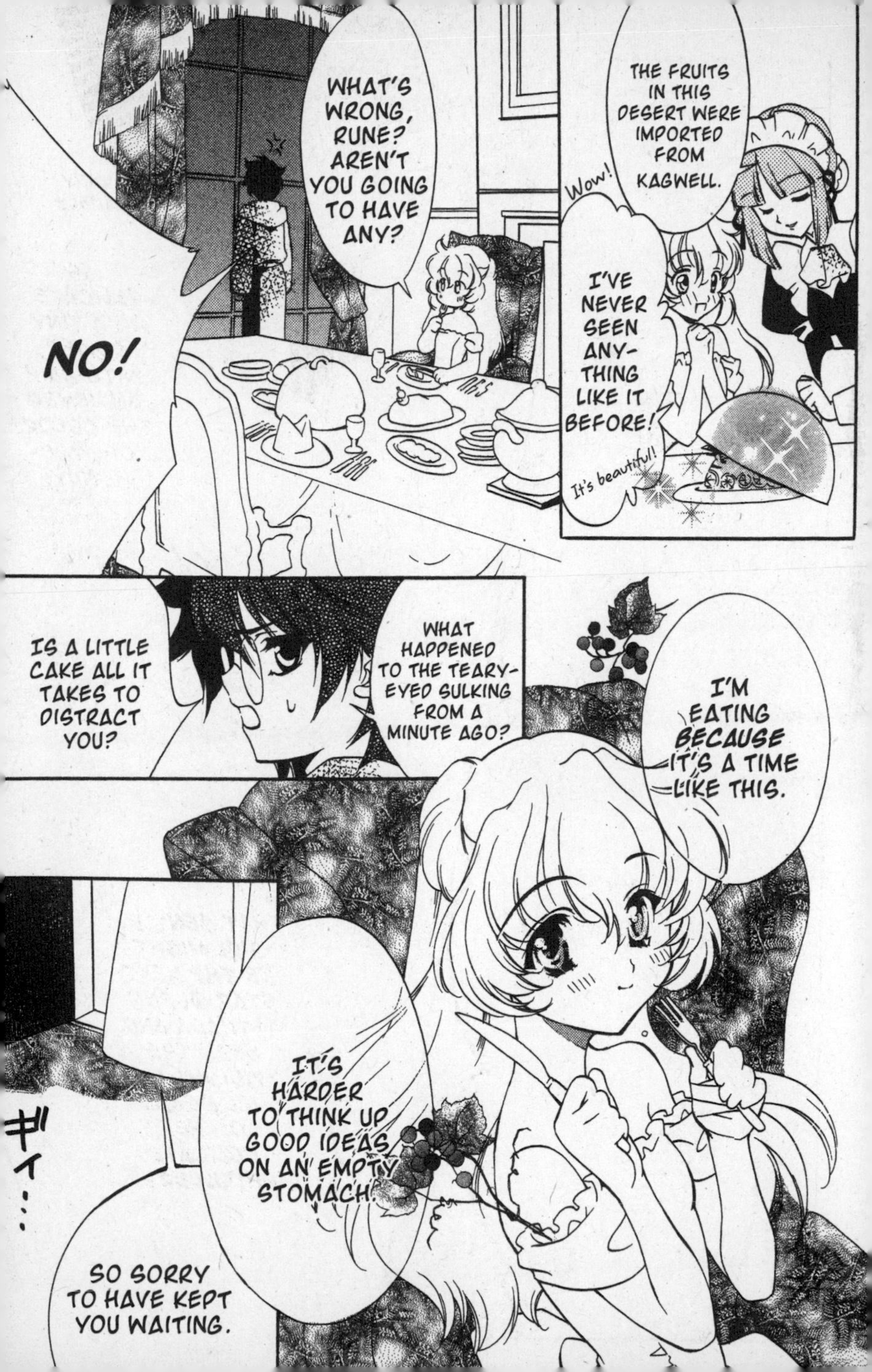
THE FRUITS IN THIS DESERT WERE IMPORTED FROM KAGWELL.
Wow!
I'VE NEVER SEEN ANYTHING LIKE IT BEFORE!
It's beautiful!
WHAT'S WRONG, RUNE? AREN'T YOU GOING TO HAVE ANY?
NO!
WHAT HAPPENED TO THE TEARY-EYED SULKING FROM A MINUTE AGO?
IS A LITTLE CAKE ALL IT TAKES TO DISTRACT YOU?
I'M EATING BECAUSE IT'S A TIME LIKE THIS.
IT'S HARDER TO THINK UP GOOD IDEAS ON AN EMPTY STOMACH.
ギィ…
SO SORRY TO HAVE KEPT YOU WAITING.

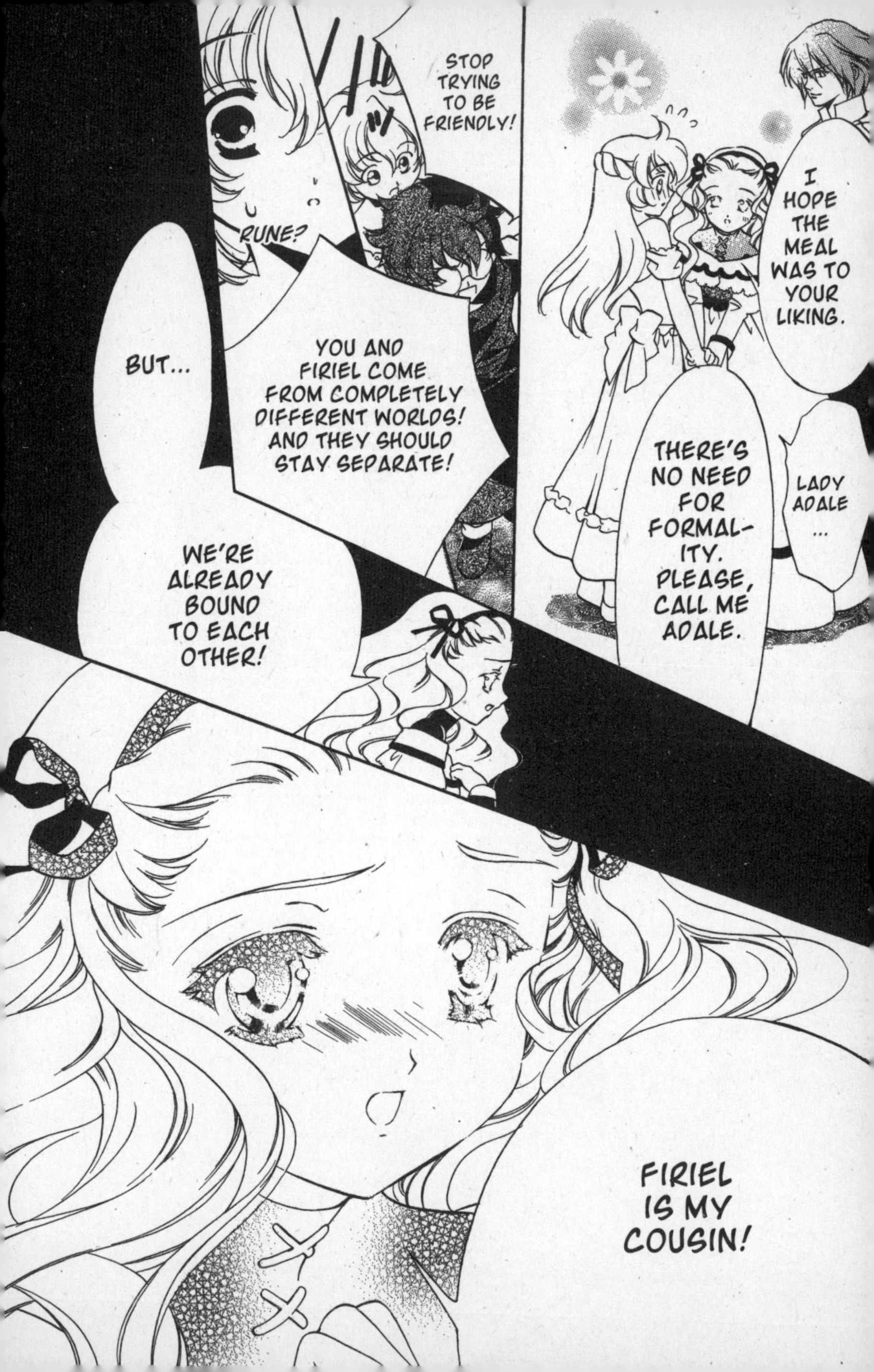
I HOPE THE MEAL WAS TO YOUR LIKING.
LADY ADALE ...
THERE'S NO NEED FOR FORMALITY. PLEASE, CALL ME ADALE.
STOP TRYING TO BE FRIENDLY!
RUNE?
YOU AND FIRIEL COME FROM COMPLETELY DIFFERENT WORLDS! AND THEY SHOULD STAY SEPARATE!
BUT...
WE'RE ALREADY BOUND TO EACH OTHER!
FIRIEL IS MY COUSIN!

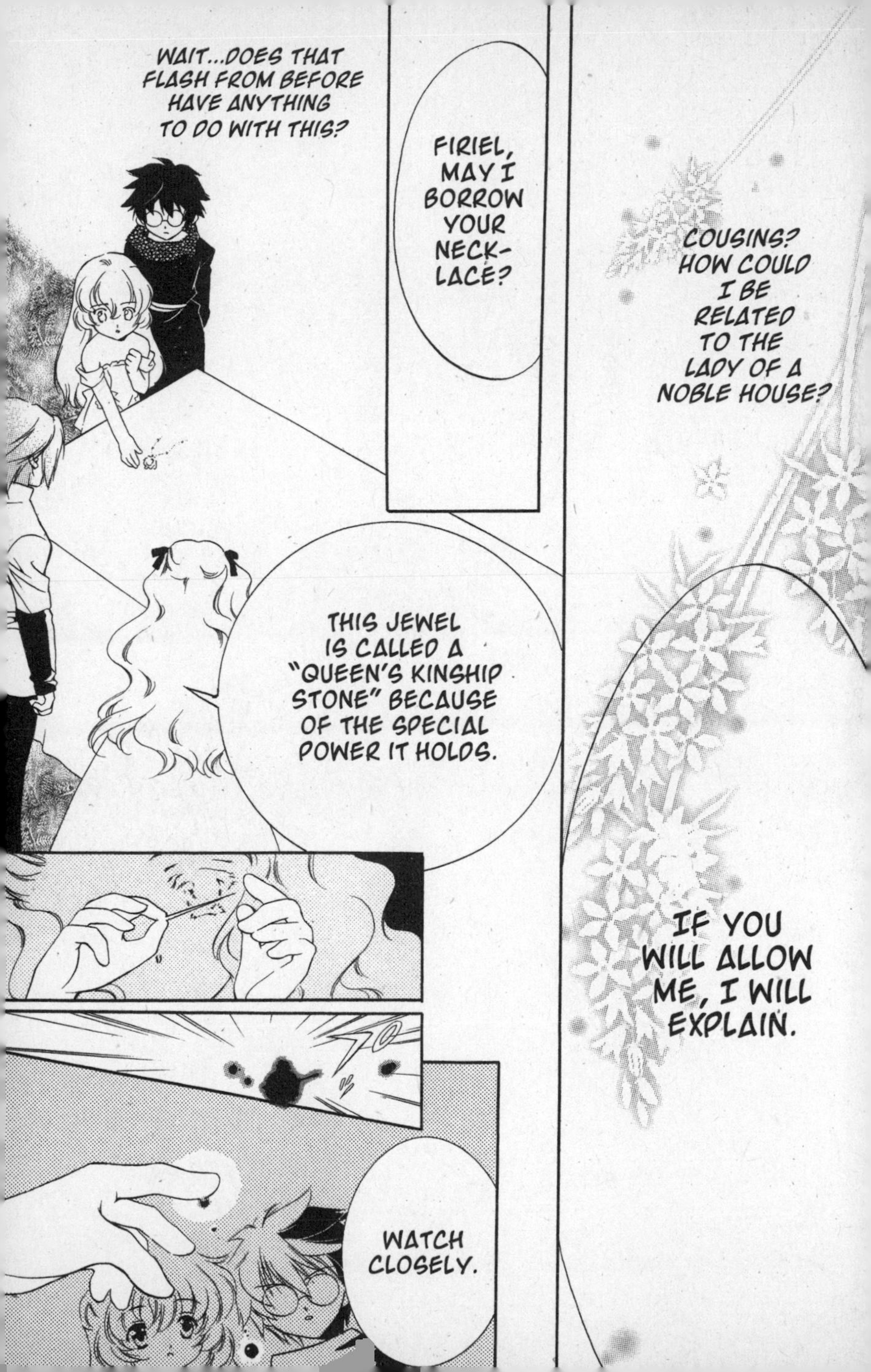
COUSINS? HOW COULD I BE RELATED TO THE LADY OF A NOBLE HOUSE?
IF YOU WILL ALLOW ME, I WILL EXPLAIN.
FIRIEL, MAY I BORROW YOUR NECK-LACE?
WAIT...DOES THAT FLASH FROM BEFORE HAVE ANYTHING TO DO WITH THIS?
THIS JEWEL IS CALLED A "QUEEN'S KINSHIP STONE" BECAUSE OF THE SPECIAL POWER IT HOLDS.
WATCH CLOSELY.

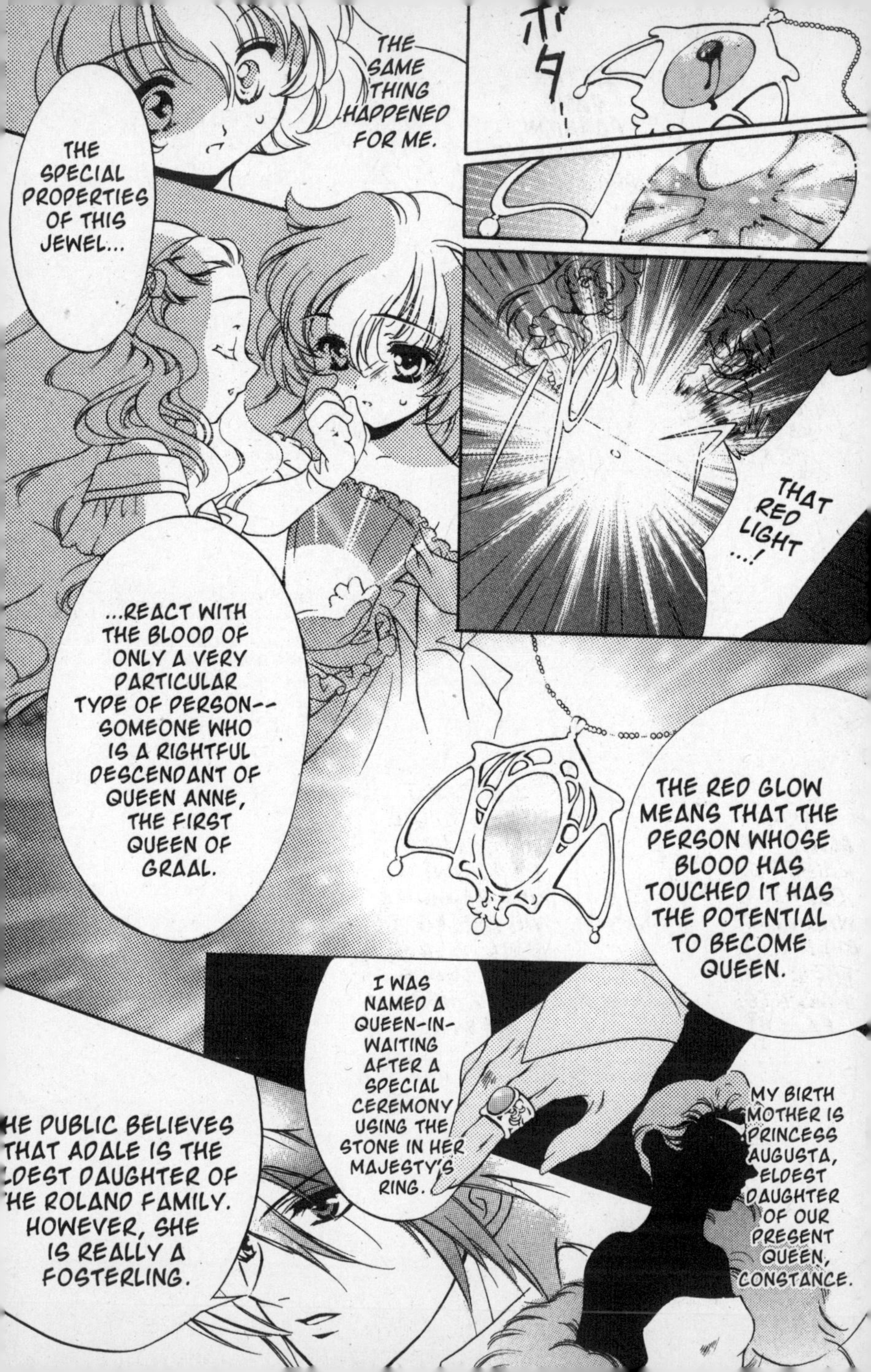
ポタ
THAT RED LIGHT...!
THE SAME THING HAPPENED FOR ME.
THE SPECIAL PROPERTIES OF THIS JEWEL...
...REACT WITH THE BLOOD OF ONLY A VERY PARTICULAR TYPE OF PERSON--SOMEONE WHO IS A RIGHTFUL DESCENDANT OF QUEEN ANNE, THE FIRST QUEEN OF GRAAL.
THE RED GLOW MEANS THAT THE PERSON WHOSE BLOOD HAS TOUCHED IT HAS THE POTENTIAL TO BECOME QUEEN.
MY BIRTH MOTHER IS PRINCESS AUGUSTA, ELDEST DAUGHTER OF OUR PRESENT QUEEN, CONSTANCE.
I WAS NAMED A QUEEN-IN-WAITING AFTER A SPECIAL CEREMONY USING THE STONE IN HER MAJESTY'S RING.
HE PUBLIC BELIEVES HAT ADALE IS THE LDEST DAUGHTER OF HE ROLAND FAMILY. HOWEVER, SHE IS REALLY A FOSTERLING.

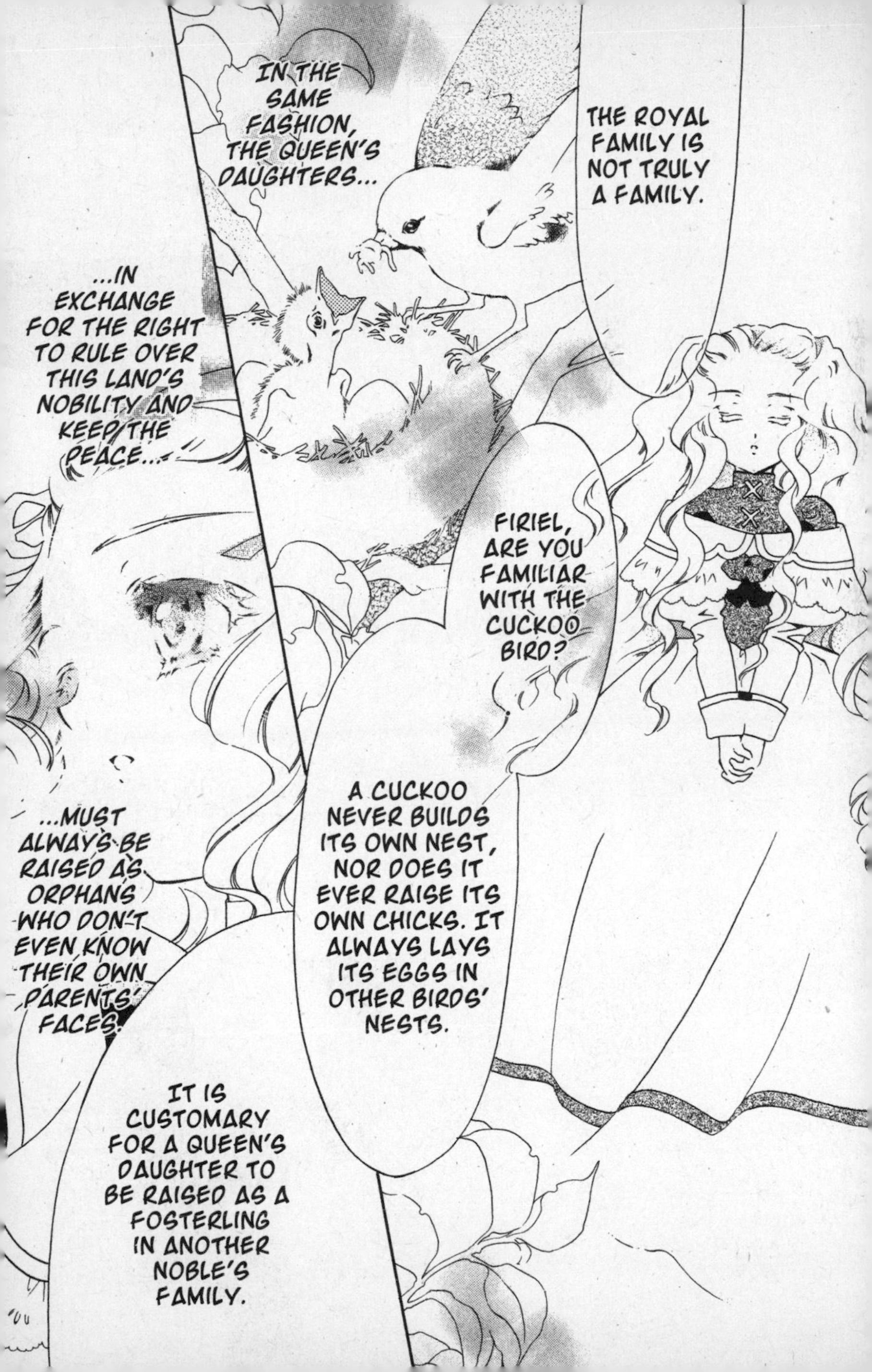
THE ROYAL FAMILY IS NOT TRULY A FAMILY.
FIRIEL, ARE YOU FAMILIAR WITH THE CUCKOO BIRD?
A CUCKOO NEVER BUILDS ITS OWN NEST, NOR DOES IT EVER RAISE ITS OWN CHICKS. IT ALWAYS LAYS ITS EGGS IN OTHER BIRDS' NESTS.
IT IS CUSTOMARY FOR A QUEEN'S DAUGHTER TO BE RAISED AS A FOSTERLING IN ANOTHER NOBLE'S FAMILY.
IN THE SAME FASHION, THE QUEEN'S DAUGHTERS...
...IN EXCHANGE FOR THE RIGHT TO RULE OVER THIS LAND'S NOBILITY AND KEEP THE PEACE...
...MUST ALWAYS BE RAISED AS ORPHANS WHO DON'T EVEN KNOW THEIR OWN PARENTS' FACES.

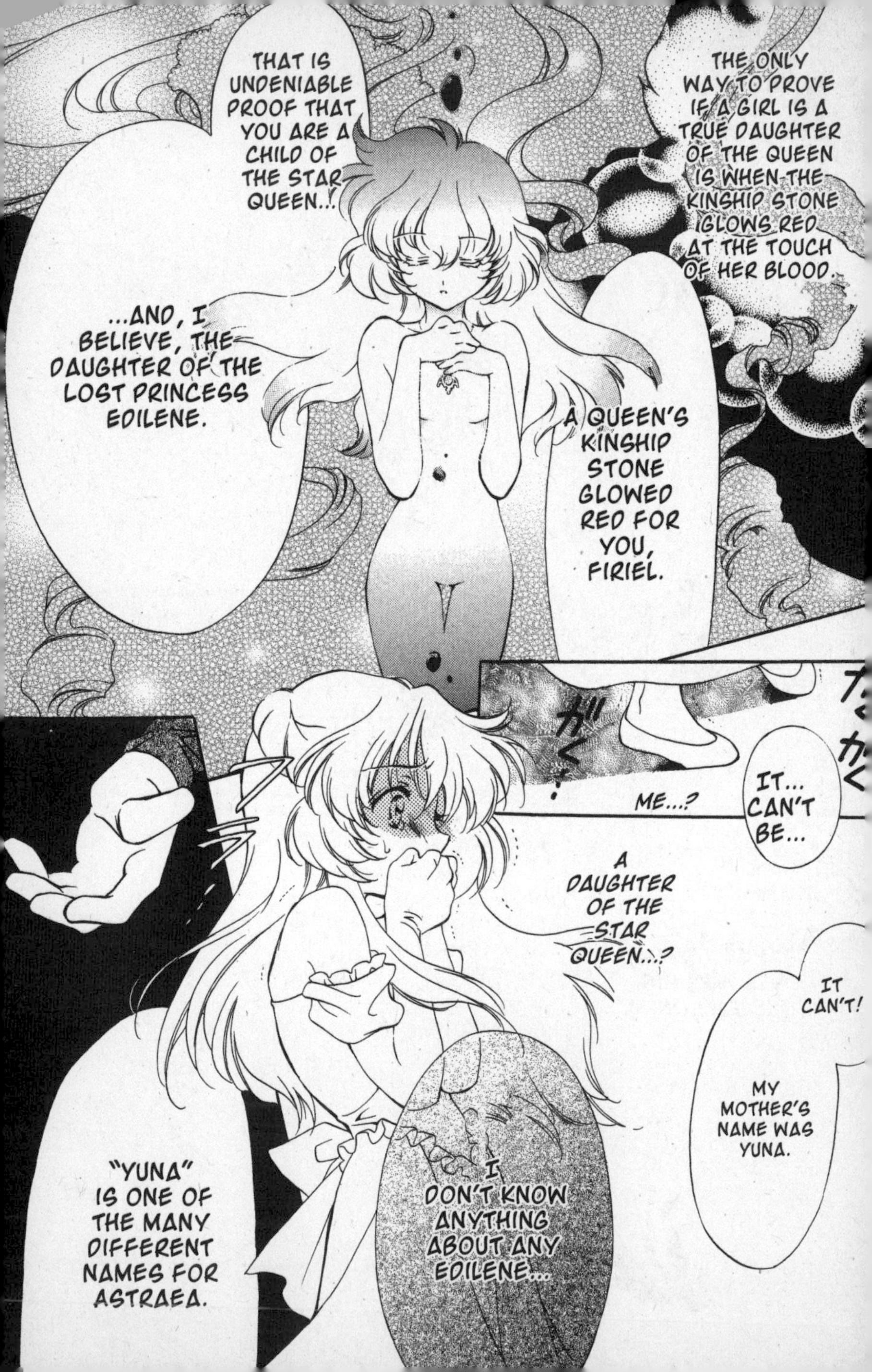
THE ONLY WAY TO PROVE IF A GIRL IS A TRUE DAUGHTER OF THE QUEEN IS WHEN THE KINSHIP STONE GLOWS RED AT THE TOUCH OF HER BLOOD.
A QUEEN'S KINSHIP STONE GLOWED RED FOR YOU, FIRIEL.
THAT IS UNDENIABLE PROOF THAT YOU ARE A CHILD OF THE STAR QUEEN...
...AND, I BELIEVE, THE DAUGHTER OF THE LOST PRINCESS EDILENE.
がく
IT... CAN'T BE...
ME...?
がく
A DAUGHTER OF THE STAR QUEEN...?
IT CAN'T!
MY MOTHER'S NAME WAS YUNA.
I DON'T KNOW ANYTHING ABOUT ANY EDILENE...
"YUNA" IS ONE OF THE MANY DIFFERENT NAMES FOR ASTRAEA.

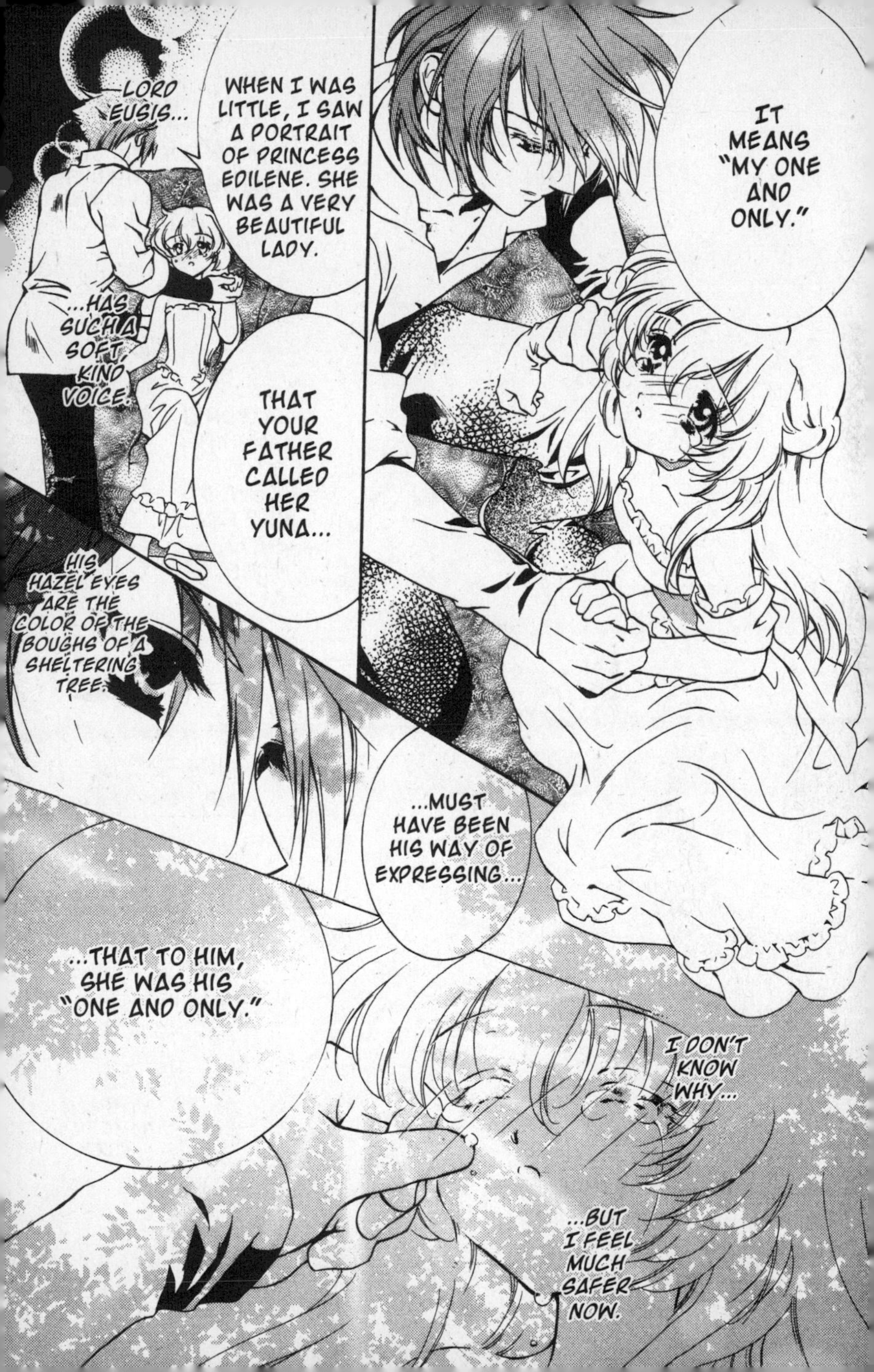
IT MEANS "MY ONE AND ONLY."
WHEN I WAS LITTLE, I SAW A PORTRAIT OF PRINCESS EDILENE. SHE WAS A VERY BEAUTIFUL LADY.
LORD EUSIS...
...HAS SUCH A SOFT, KIND VOICE.
THAT YOUR FATHER CALLED HER YUNA...
HIS HAZEL EYES ARE THE COLOR OF THE BOUGHS OF A SHELTERING TREE.
...MUST HAVE BEEN HIS WAY OF EXPRESSING...
...THAT TO HIM, SHE WAS HIS "ONE AND ONLY."
I DON'T KNOW WHY...
...BUT I FEEL MUCH SAFER NOW.

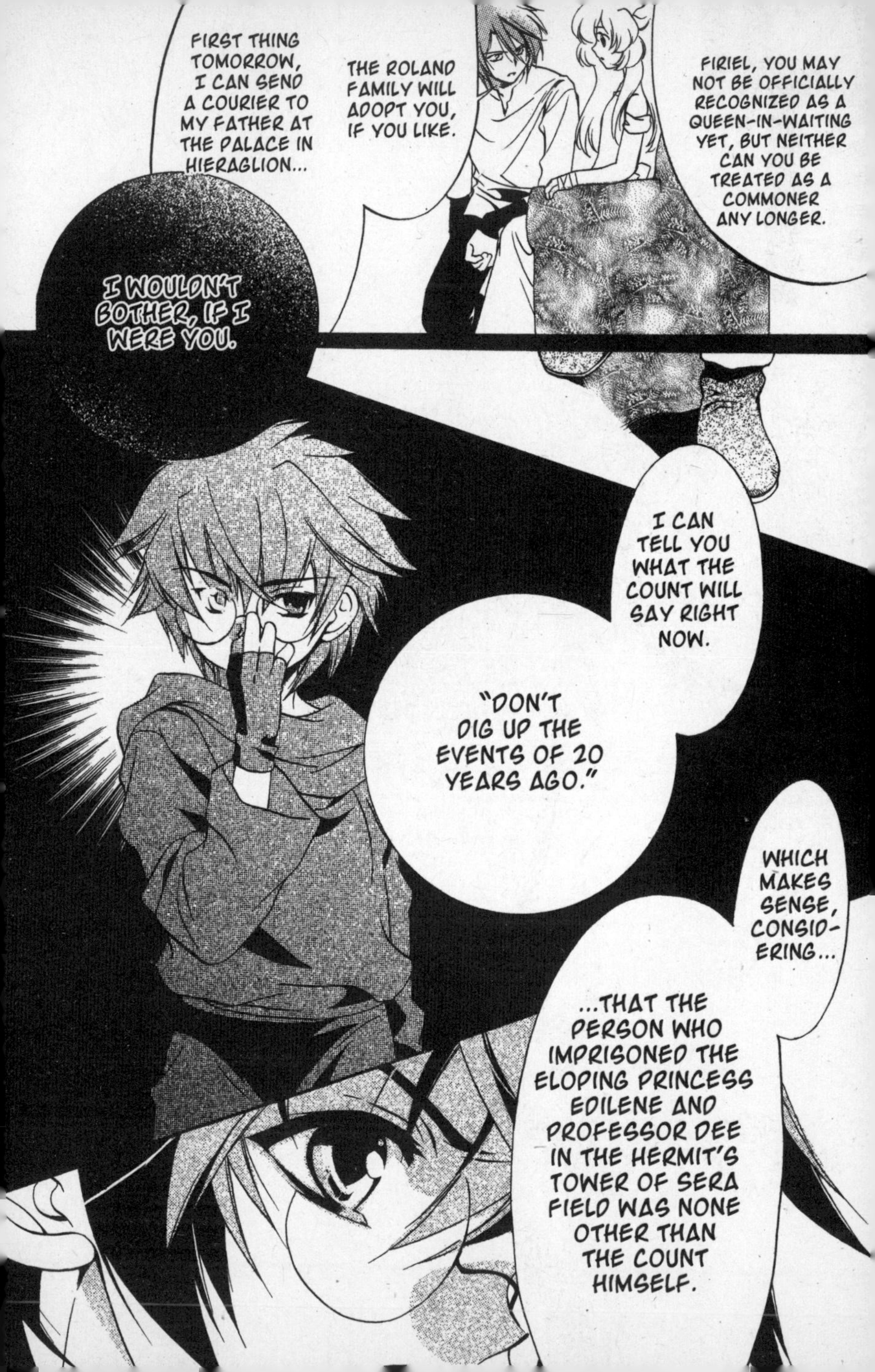
FIRIEL, YOU MAY NOT BE OFFICIALLY RECOGNIZED AS A QUEEN-IN-WAITING YET, BUT NEITHER CAN YOU BE TREATED AS A COMMONER ANY LONGER.
THE ROLAND FAMILY WILL ADOPT YOU, IF YOU LIKE.
FIRST THING TOMORROW, I CAN SEND A COURIER TO MY FATHER AT THE PALACE IN HIERAGLION...
I WOULDN'T BOTHER, IF I WERE YOU.
I CAN TELL YOU WHAT THE COUNT WILL SAY RIGHT NOW.
"DON'T DIG UP THE EVENTS OF 20 YEARS AGO."
WHICH MAKES SENSE, CONSID-ERING...
...THAT THE PERSON WHO IMPRISONED THE ELOPING PRINCESS EDILENE AND PROFESSOR DEE IN THE HERMIT'S TOWER OF SERA FIELD WAS NONE OTHER THAN THE COUNT HIMSELF.

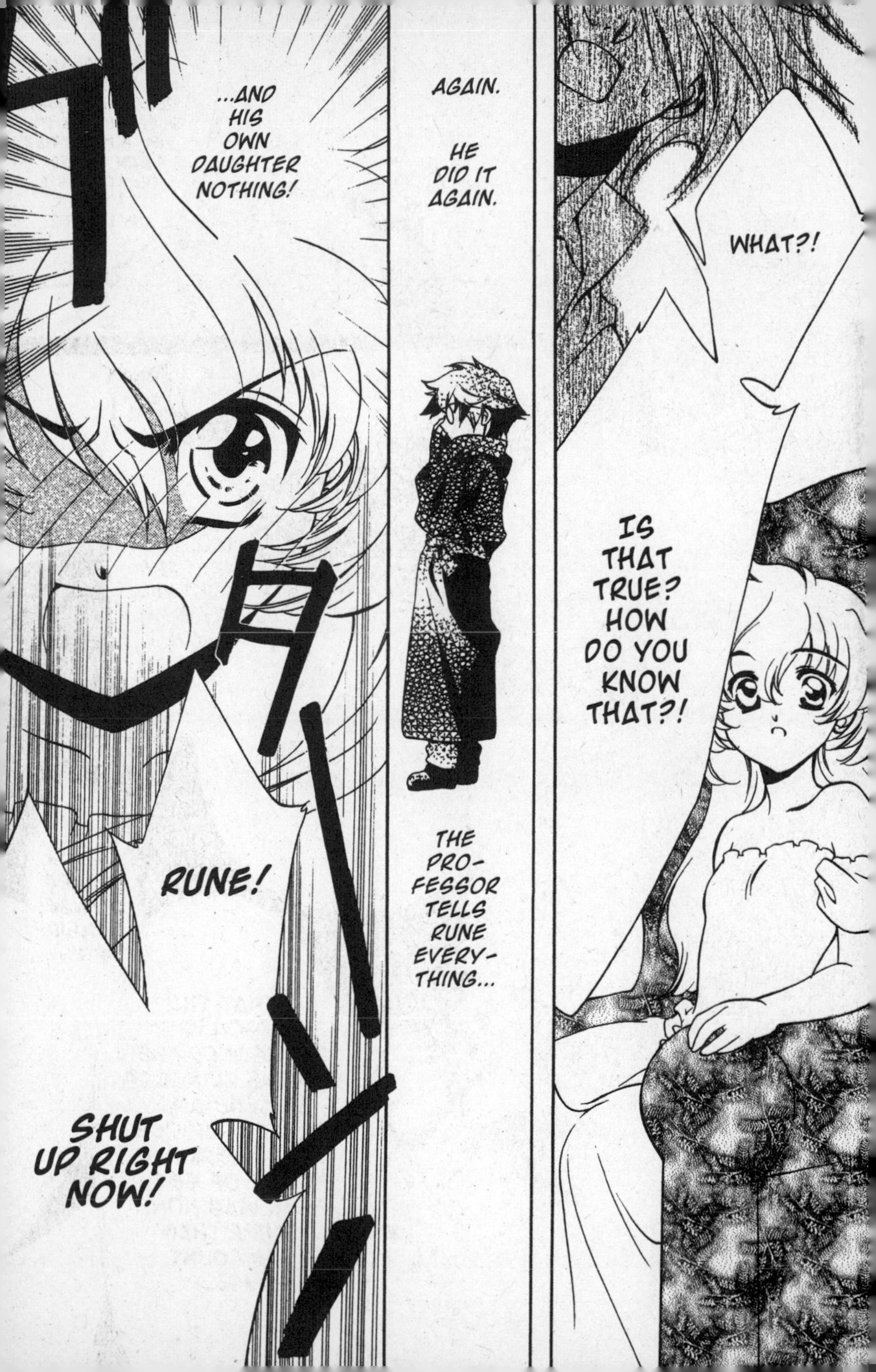
WHAT?!
IS THAT TRUE? HOW DO YOU KNOW THAT?!
AGAIN.
HE DID IT AGAIN.
THE PROFESSOR TELLS RUNE EVERYTHING...
...AND HIS OWN DAUGHTER NOTHING!
RUNE!
SHUT UP RIGHT NOW!

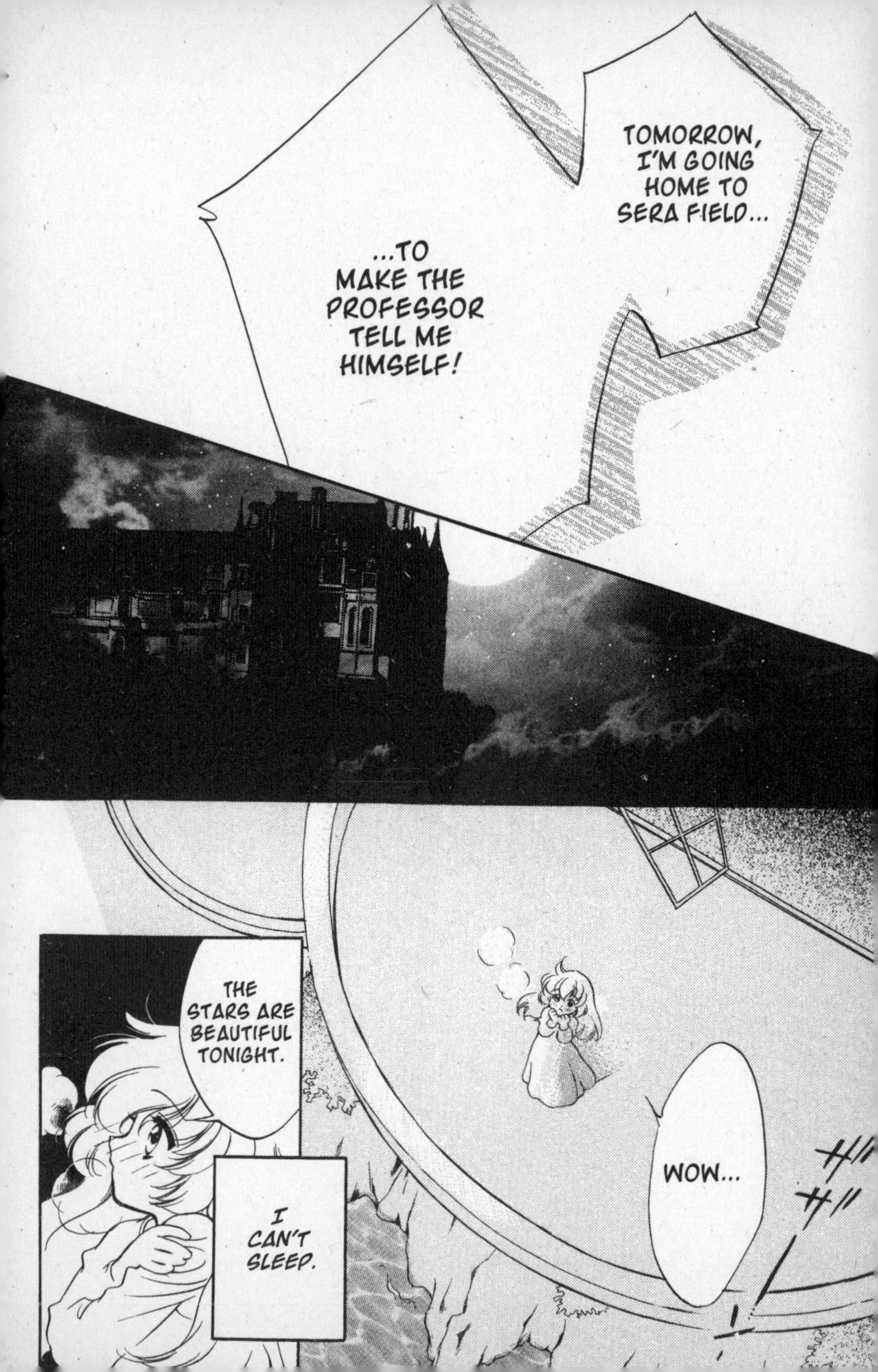
TOMORROW, I'M GOING HOME TO SERA FIELD...
...TO MAKE THE PROFESSOR TELL ME HIMSELF!
WOW...
THE STARS ARE BEAUTIFUL TONIGHT.
I CAN'T SLEEP.

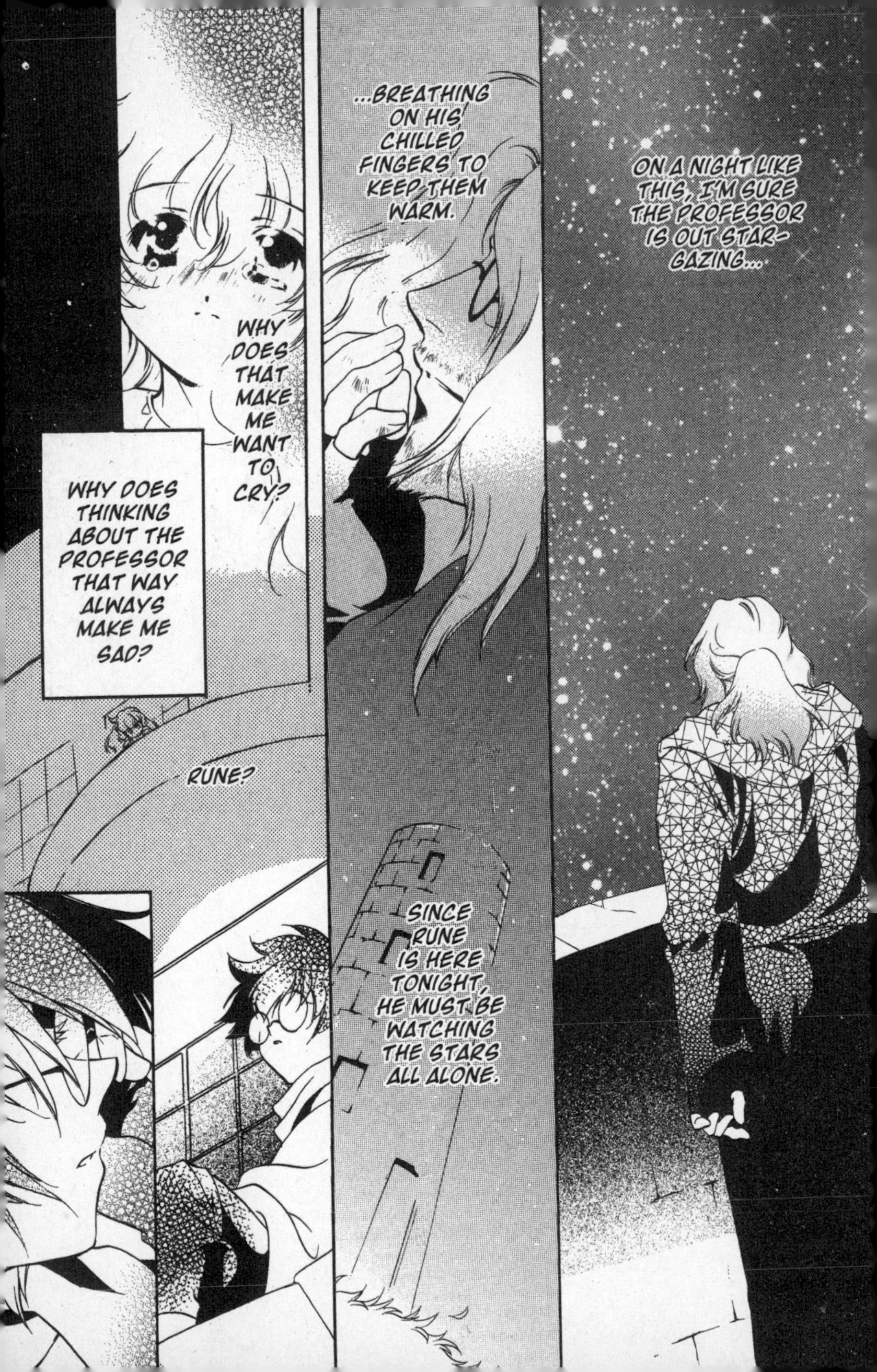
ON A NIGHT LIKE THIS, I'M SURE THE PROFESSOR IS OUT STAR-GAZING...
...BREATHING ON HIS CHILLED FINGERS TO KEEP THEM WARM.
SINCE RUNE IS HERE TONIGHT, HE MUST BE WATCHING THE STARS ALL ALONE.
WHY DOES THAT MAKE ME WANT TO CRY?
WHY DOES THINKING ABOUT THE PROFESSOR THAT WAY ALWAYS MAKE ME SAD?
RUNE?

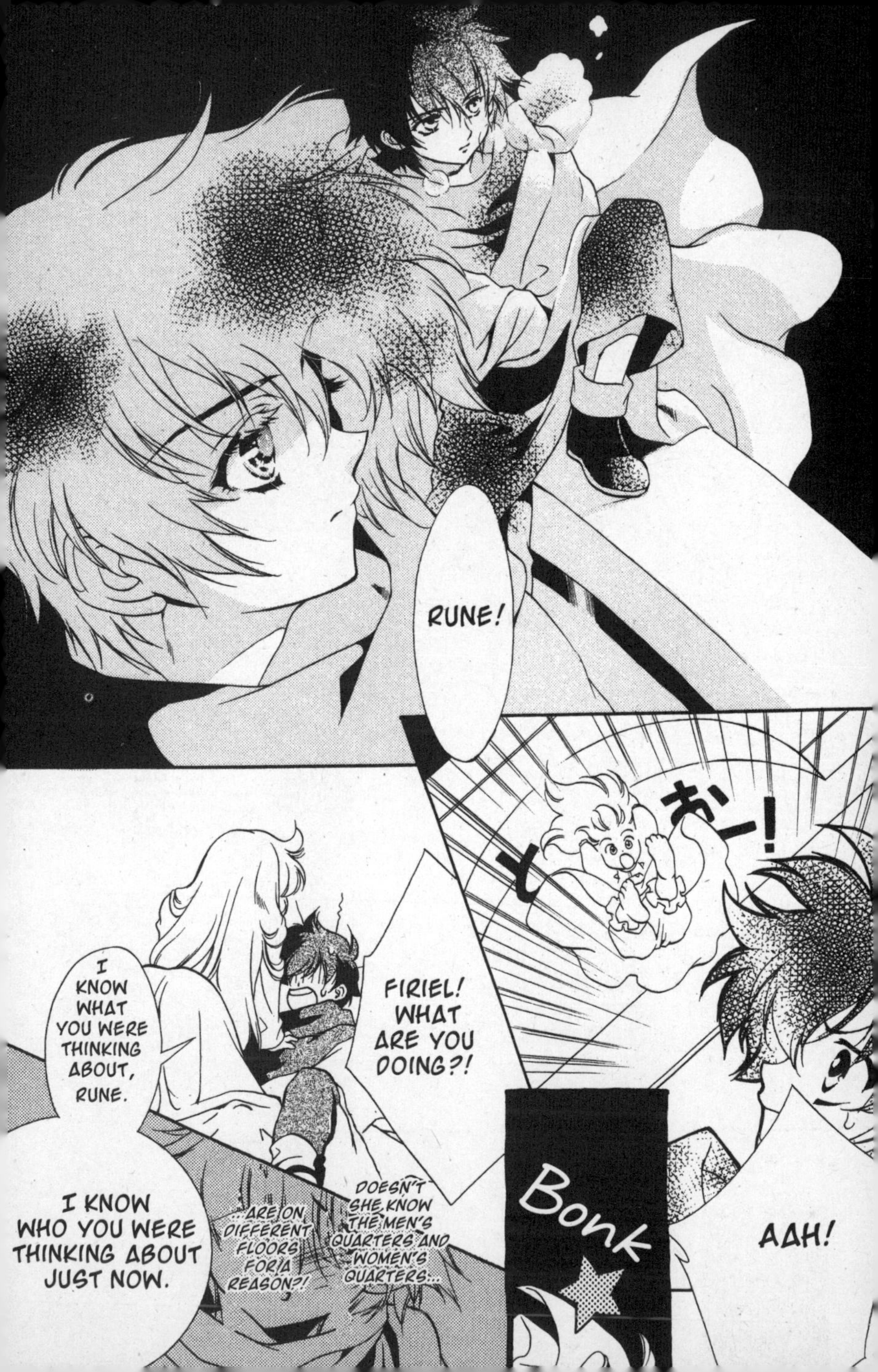
RUNE!
とお〜!
AAH!
Bonk
FIRIEL! WHAT ARE YOU DOING?!
I KNOW WHAT YOU WERE THINKING ABOUT, RUNE.
I KNOW WHO YOU WERE THINKING ABOUT JUST NOW.
DOESN'T SHE KNOW THE MEN'S QUARTERS AND WOMEN'S QUARTERS...
...ARE ON DIFFERENT FLOORS FOR A REASON?!

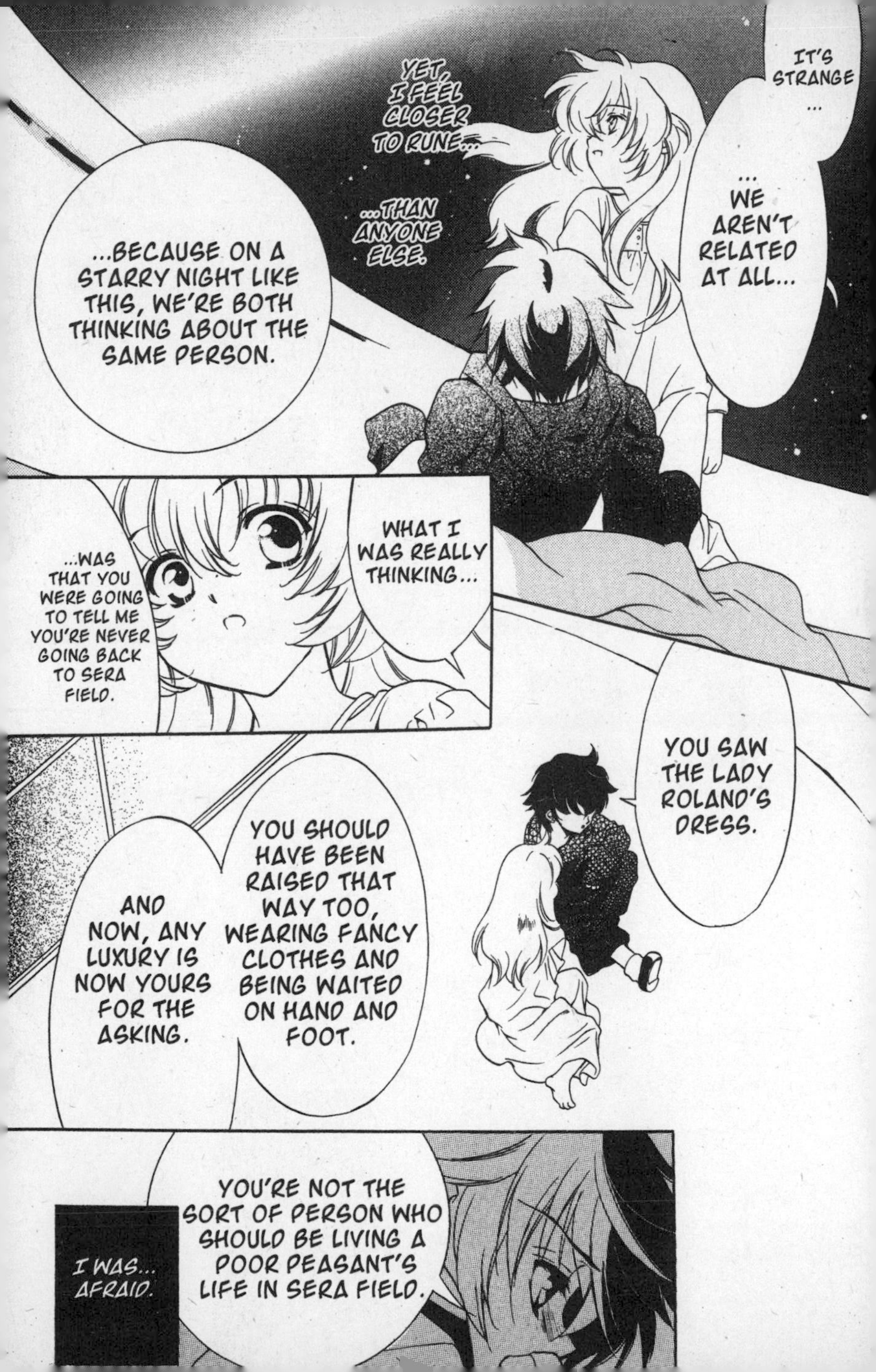
IT'S STRANGE...
...WE AREN'T RELATED AT ALL...
YET, I FEEL CLOSER TO RUNE...
...THAN ANYONE ELSE.
...BECAUSE ON A STARRY NIGHT LIKE THIS, WE'RE BOTH THINKING ABOUT THE SAME PERSON.
WHAT I WAS REALLY THINKING...
...WAS THAT YOU WERE GOING TO TELL ME YOU'RE NEVER GOING BACK TO SERA FIELD.
YOU SAW THE LADY ROLAND'S DRESS.
YOU SHOULD HAVE BEEN RAISED THAT WAY TOO, WEARING FANCY CLOTHES AND BEING WAITED ON HAND AND FOOT.
AND NOW, ANY LUXURY IS NOW YOURS FOR THE ASKING.
YOU'RE NOT THE SORT OF PERSON WHO SHOULD BE LIVING A POOR PEASANT'S LIFE IN SERA FIELD.
I WAS... AFRAID.

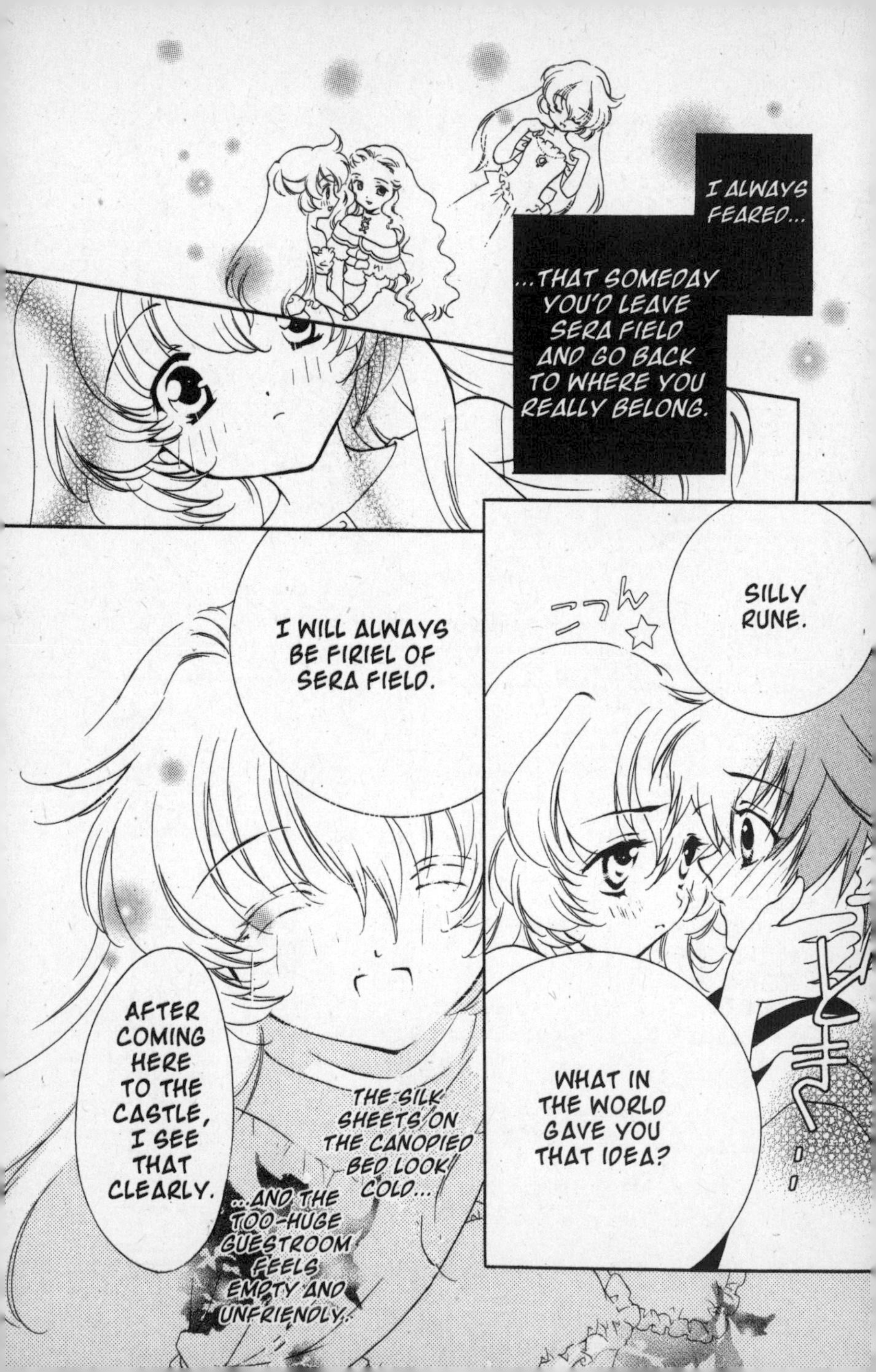
I ALWAYS FEARED...
...THAT SOMEDAY YOU'D LEAVE SERA FIELD AND GO BACK TO WHERE YOU REALLY BELONG.
SILLY RUNE.
こつん
WHAT IN THE WORLD GAVE YOU THAT IDEA?
I WILL ALWAYS BE FIRIEL OF SERA FIELD.
AFTER COMING HERE TO THE CASTLE, I SEE THAT CLEARLY.
THE SILK SHEETS ON THE CANOPIED BED LOOK COLD...
...AND THE TOO-HUGE GUESTROOM FEELS EMPTY AND UNFRIENDLY.

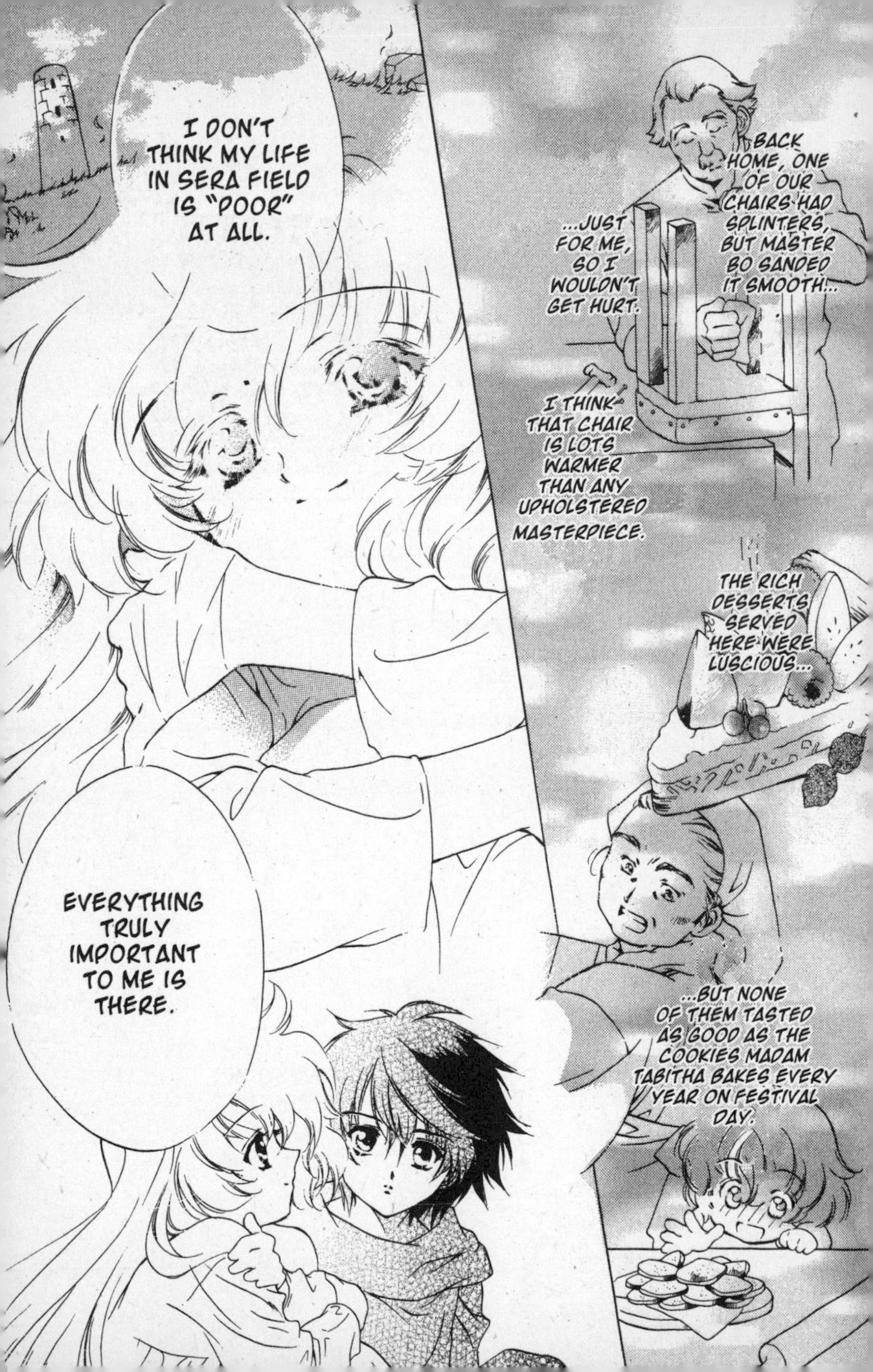
BACK HOME, ONE OF OUR CHAIRS HAD SPLINTERS, BUT MASTER BO SANDED IT SMOOTH...
...JUST FOR ME, SO I WOULDN'T GET HURT.
I THINK THAT CHAIR IS LOTS WARMER THAN ANY UPHOLSTERED MASTERPIECE.
THE RICH DESSERTS SERVED HERE WERE LUSCIOUS...
...BUT NONE OF THEM TASTED AS GOOD AS THE COOKIES MADAM TABITHA BAKES EVERY YEAR ON FESTIVAL DAY.
I DON'T THINK MY LIFE IN SERA FIELD IS "POOR" AT ALL.
EVERYTHING TRULY IMPORTANT TO ME IS THERE.

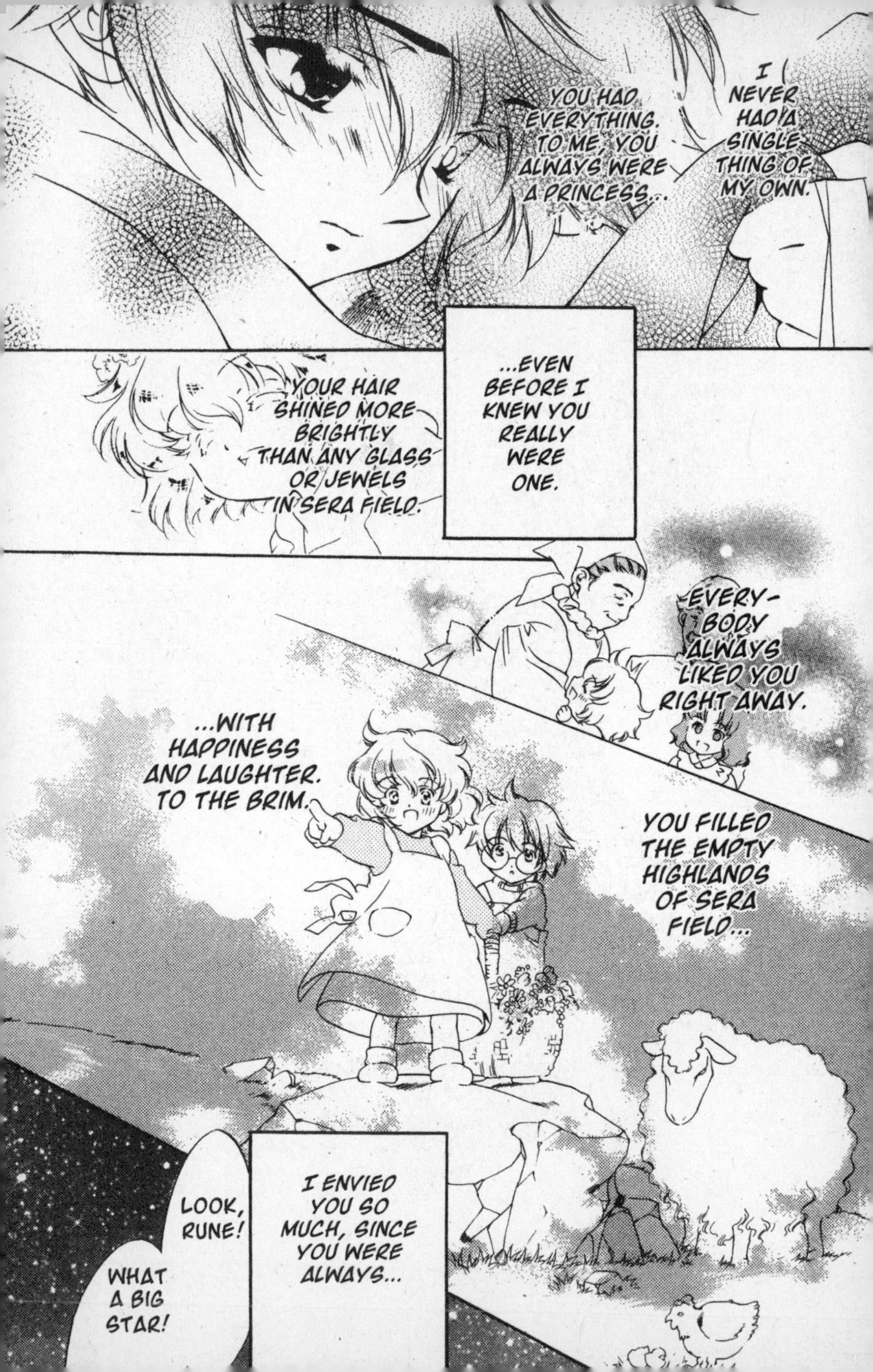
I NEVER HAD A SINGLE THING OF MY OWN.
YOU HAD EVERYTHING. TO ME, YOU ALWAYS WERE A PRINCESS...
...EVEN BEFORE I KNEW YOU REALLY WERE ONE.
YOUR HAIR SHINED MORE BRIGHTLY THAN ANY GLASS OR JEWELS IN SERA FIELD.
EVERY-BODY ALWAYS LIKED YOU RIGHT AWAY.
YOU FILLED THE EMPTY HIGHLANDS OF SERA FIELD...
...WITH HAPPINESS AND LAUGHTER. TO THE BRIM.
I ENVIED YOU SO MUCH, SINCE YOU WERE ALWAYS...
LOOK, RUNE!
WHAT A BIG STAR!

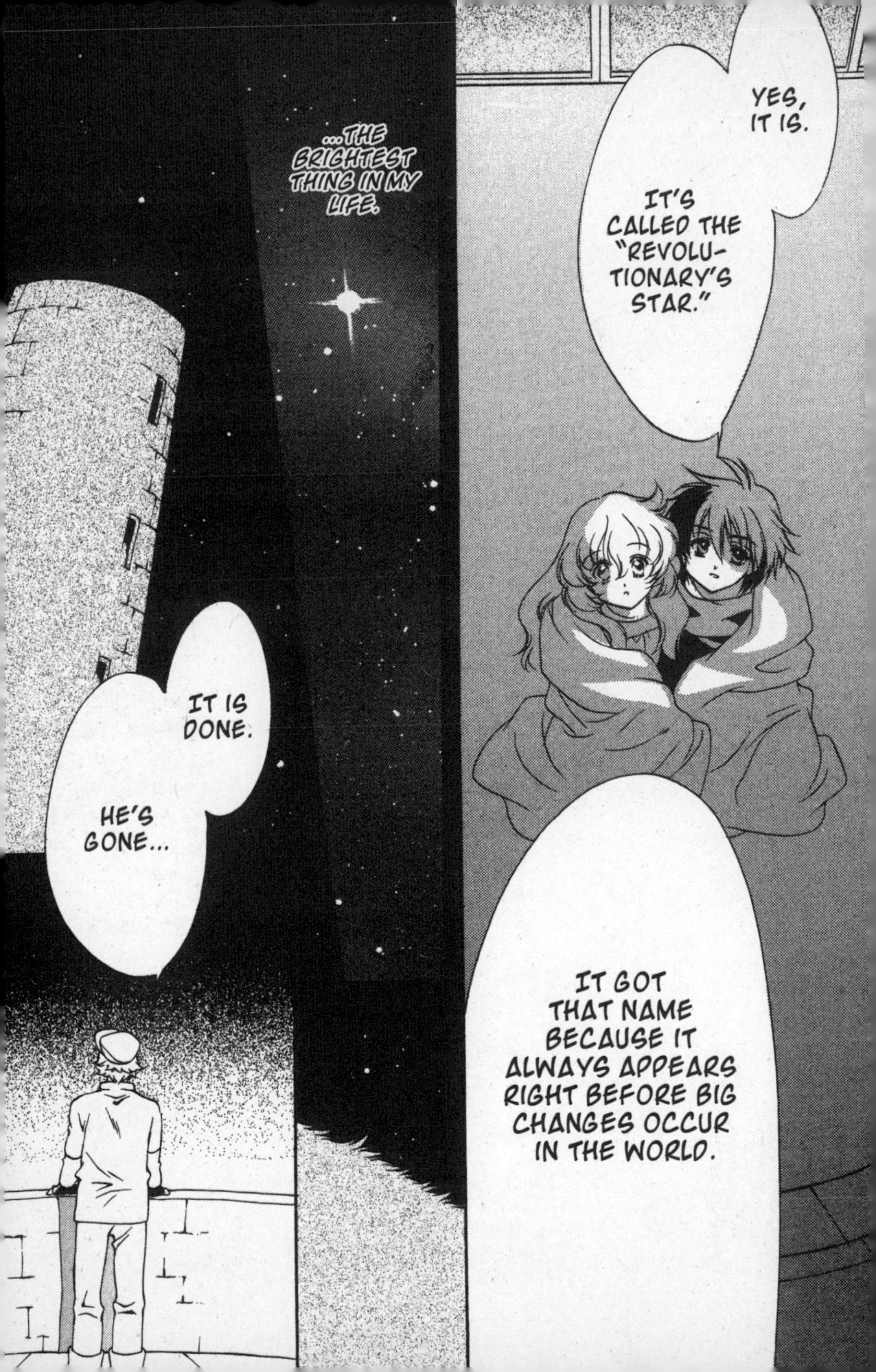
YES, IT IS.
IT'S CALLED THE "REVOLUTIONARY'S STAR."
IT GOT THAT NAME BECAUSE IT ALWAYS APPEARS RIGHT BEFORE BIG CHANGES OCCUR IN THE WORLD.
...THE BRIGHTEST THING IN MY LIFE.
IT IS DONE.
HE'S GONE...

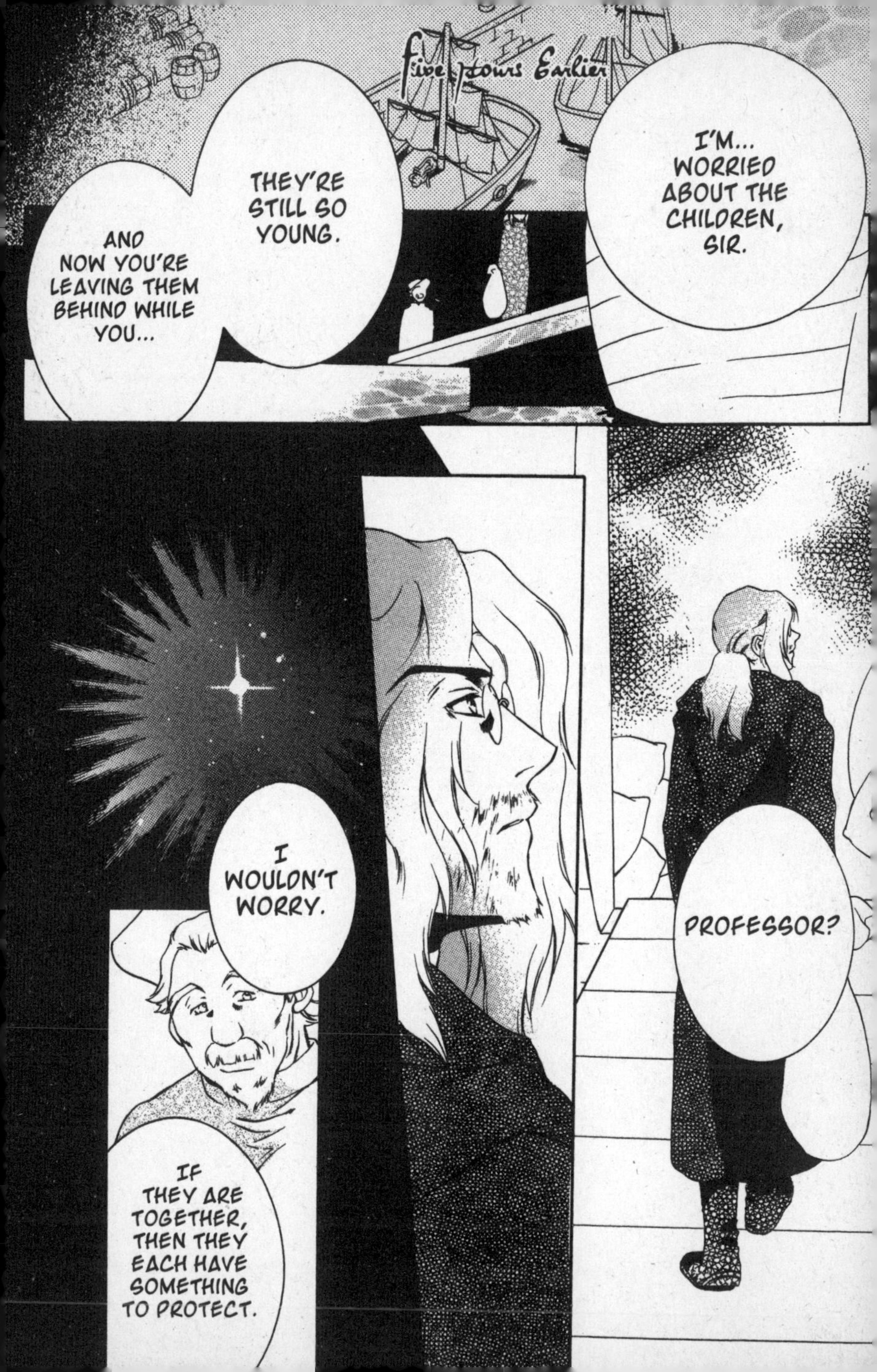
five Hours Earlier
I'M... WORRIED ABOUT THE CHILDREN, SIR.
THEY'RE STILL SO YOUNG.
AND NOW YOU'RE LEAVING THEM BEHIND WHILE YOU...
PROFESSOR?
I WOULDN'T WORRY.
IF THEY ARE TOGETHER, THEN THEY EACH HAVE SOMETHING TO PROTECT.

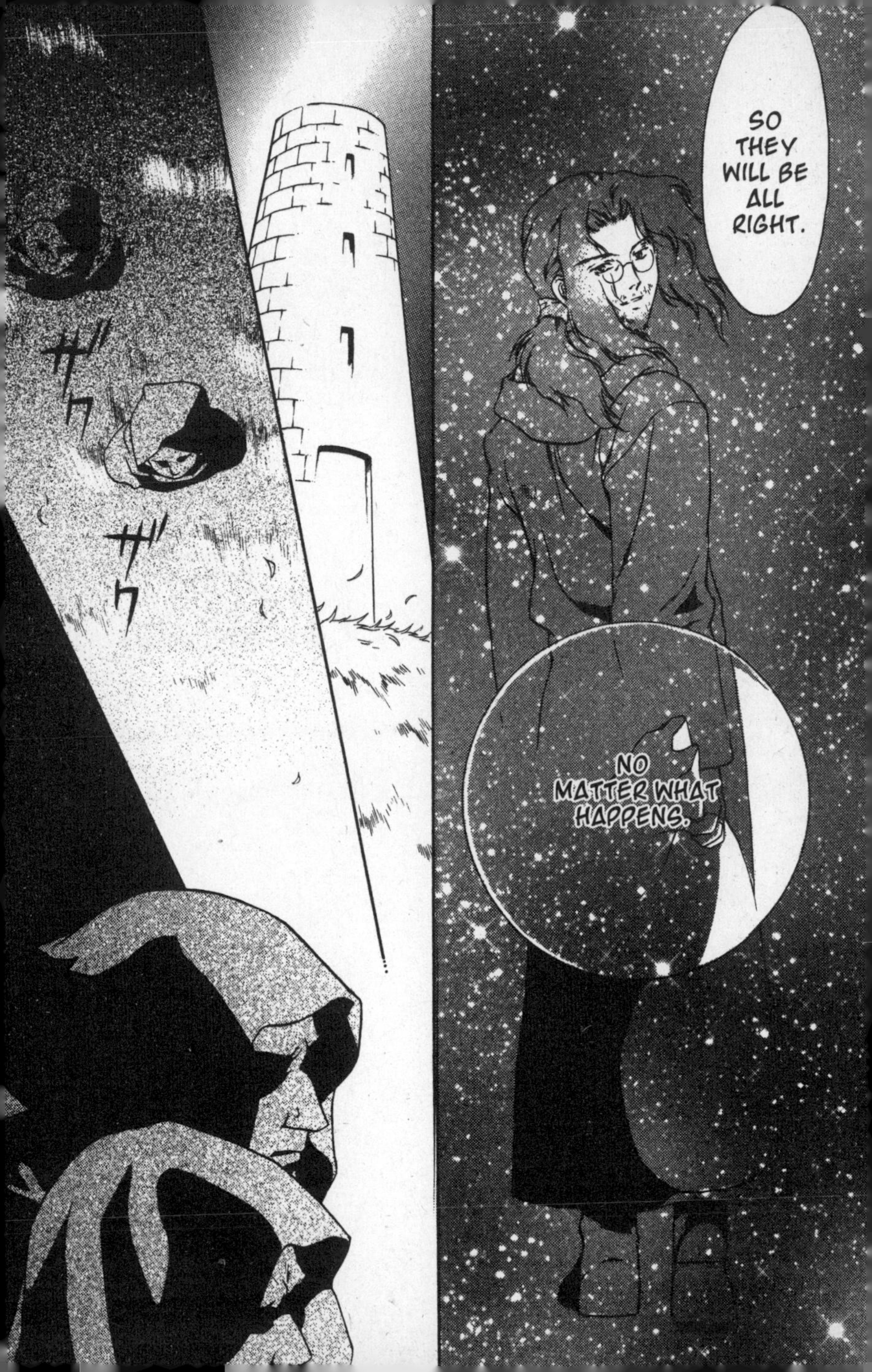
SO THEY WILL BE ALL RIGHT.
NO MATTER WHAT HAPPENS.

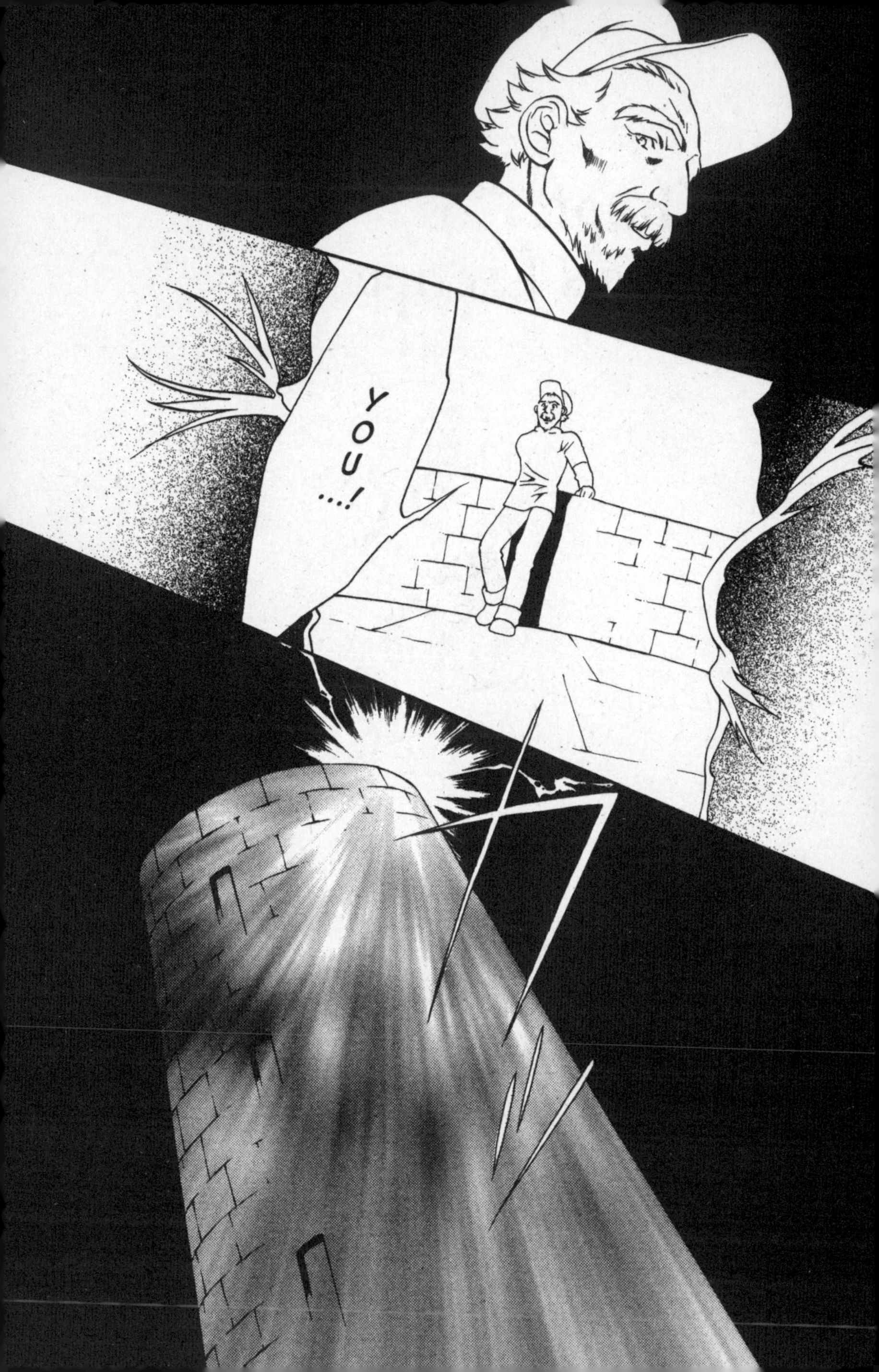
YOU...!

Chapter 3: Gideon's Escape

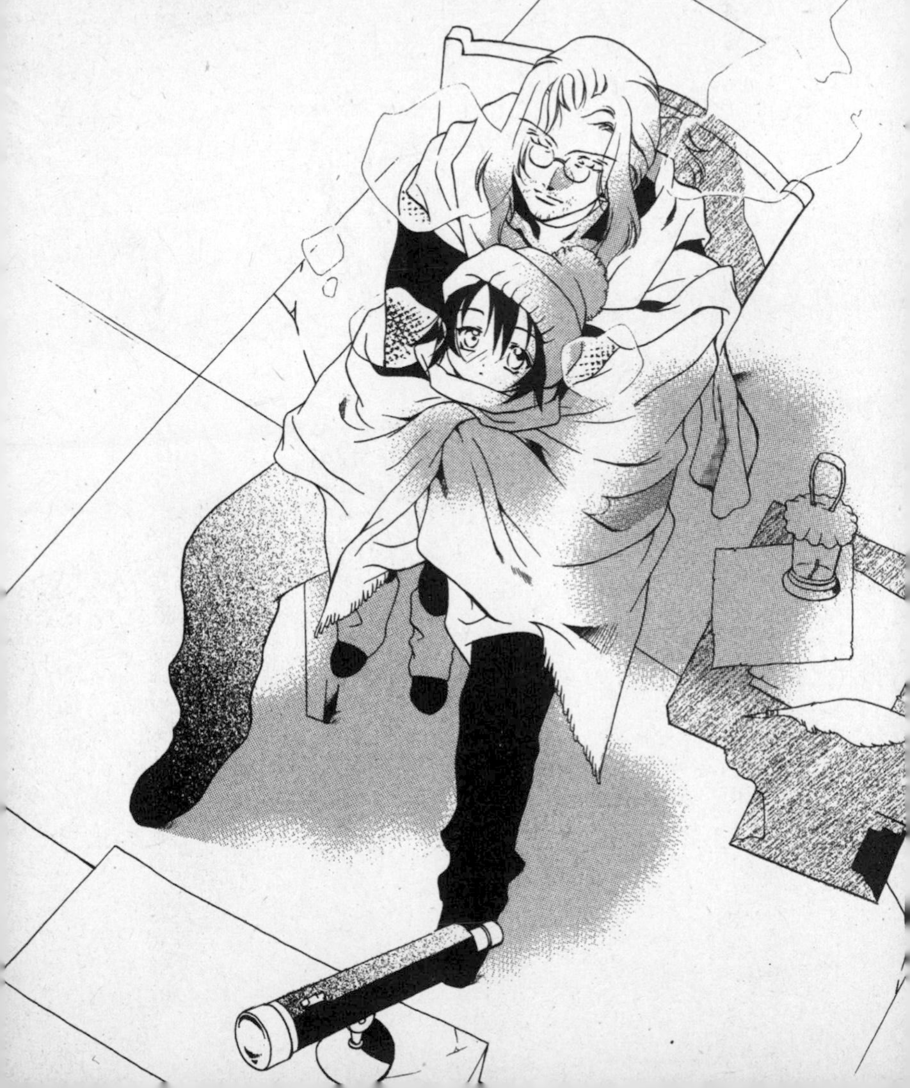

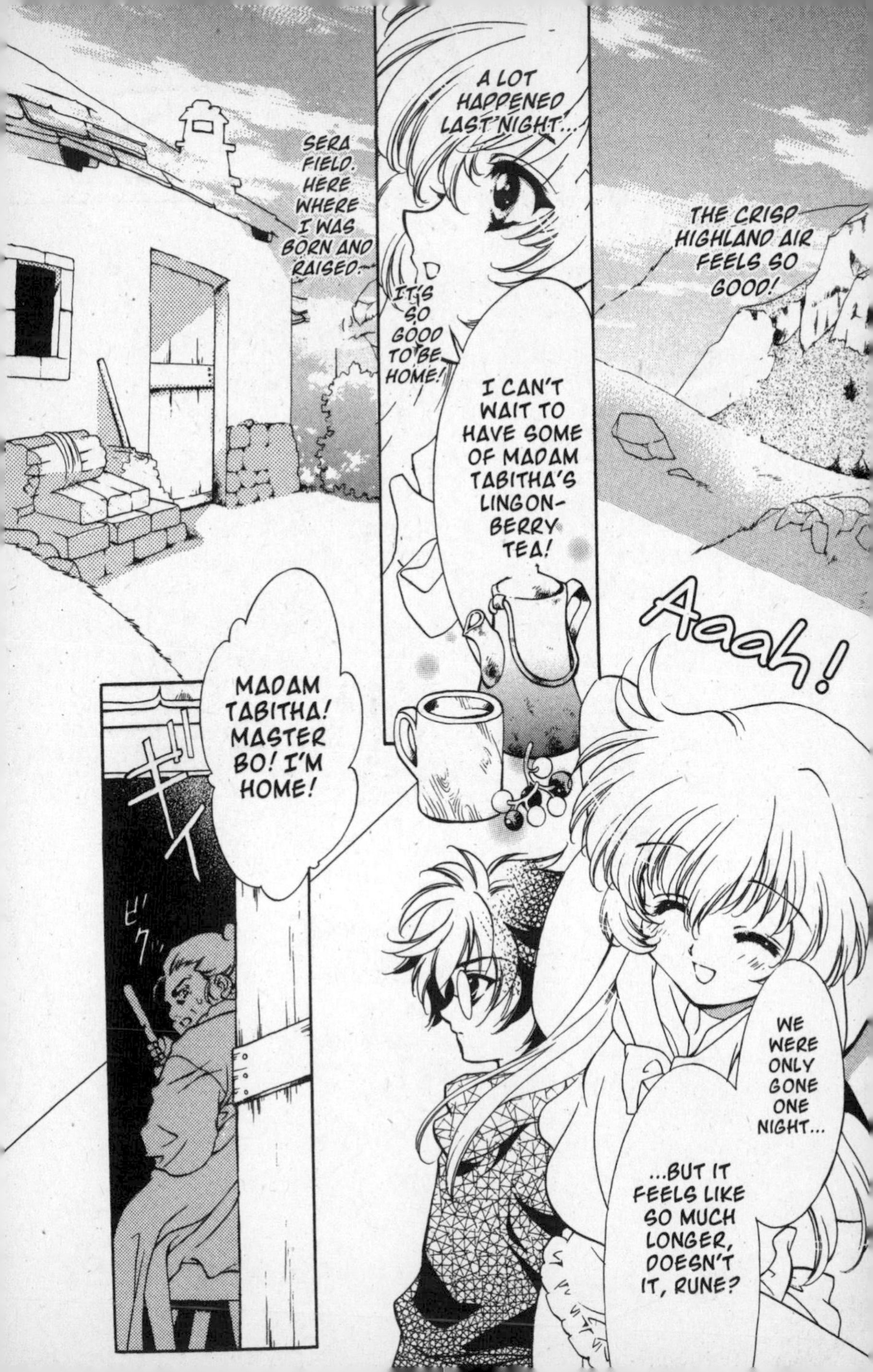
THE CRISP HIGHLAND AIR FEELS SO GOOD!
A LOT HAPPENED LAST NIGHT...
IT'S SO GOOD TO BE HOME!
I CAN'T WAIT TO HAVE SOME OF MADAM TABITHA'S LINGON-BERRY TEA!
SERA FIELD. HERE WHERE I WAS BORN AND RAISED.
Aaah!
WE WERE ONLY GONE ONE NIGHT...
...BUT IT FEELS LIKE SO MUCH LONGER, DOESN'T IT, RUNE?
MADAM TABITHA! MASTER BO! I'M HOME!
ギイ
ビクッ

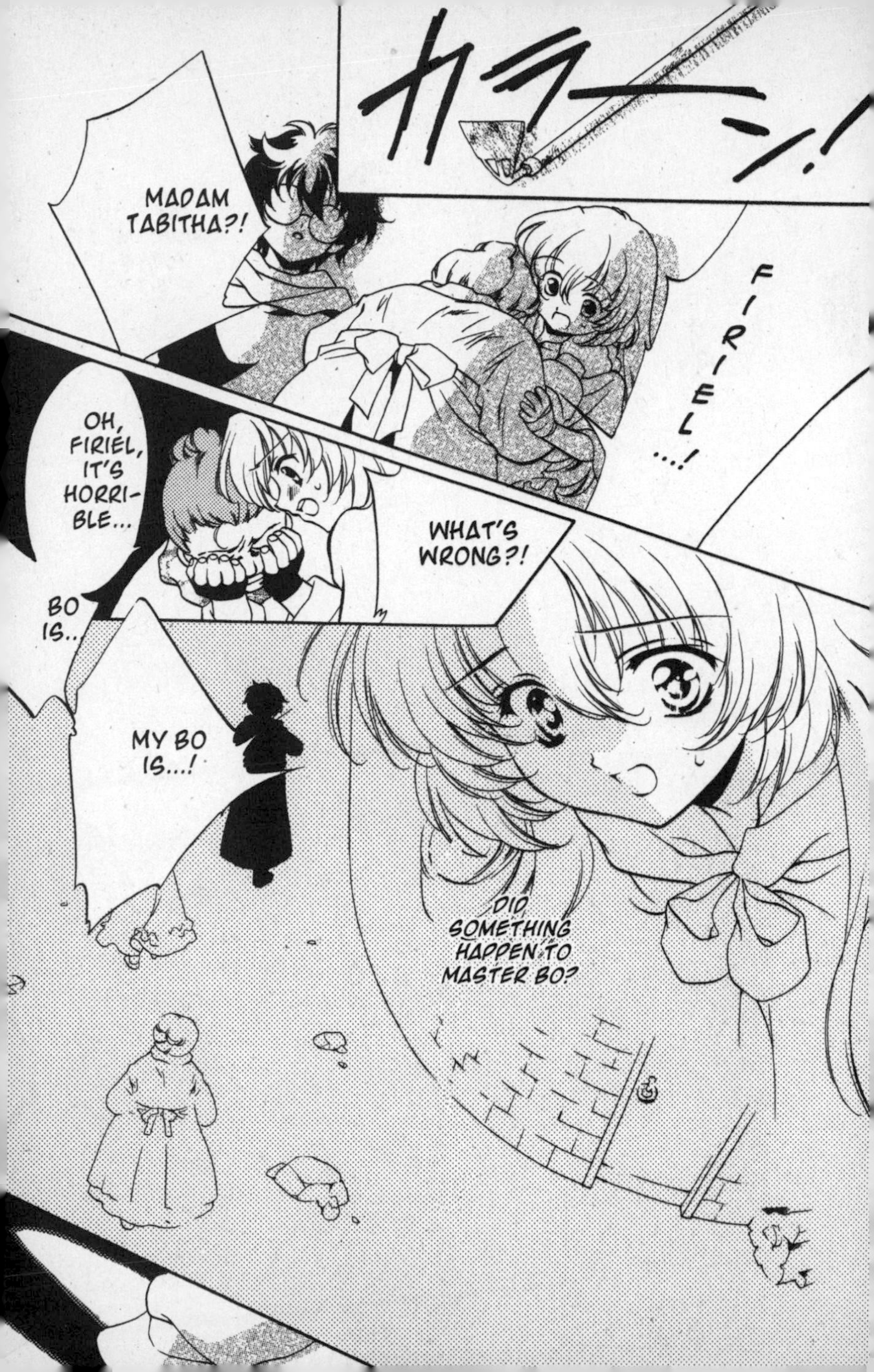

カラーン!
MADAM TABITHA?!
FIRIEL...!
WHAT'S WRONG?!
OH, FIRIEL, IT'S HORRIBLE...
BO IS...
MY BO IS...!
DID SOMETHING HAPPEN TO MASTER BO?

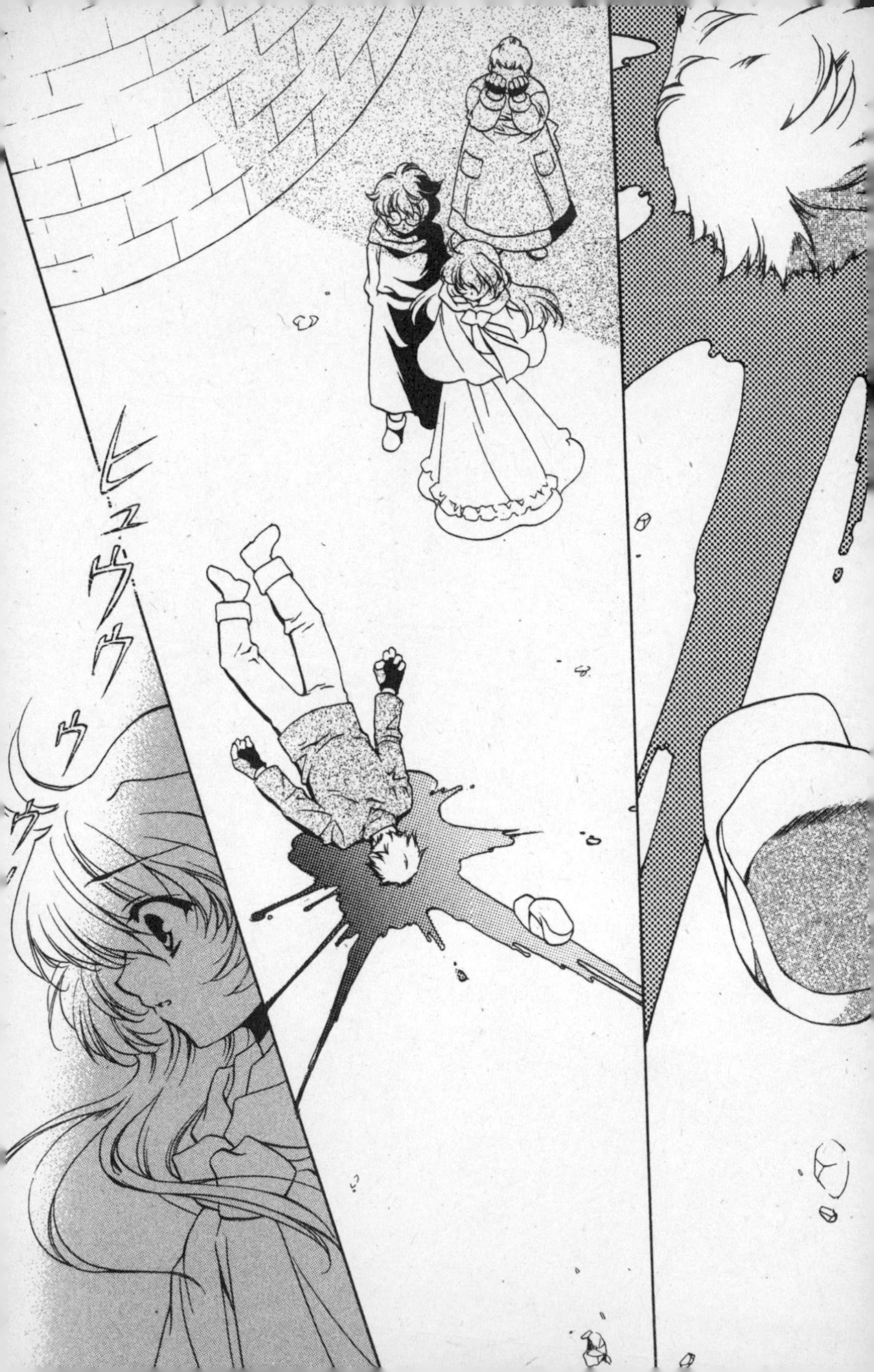
ヒュウウウウ…

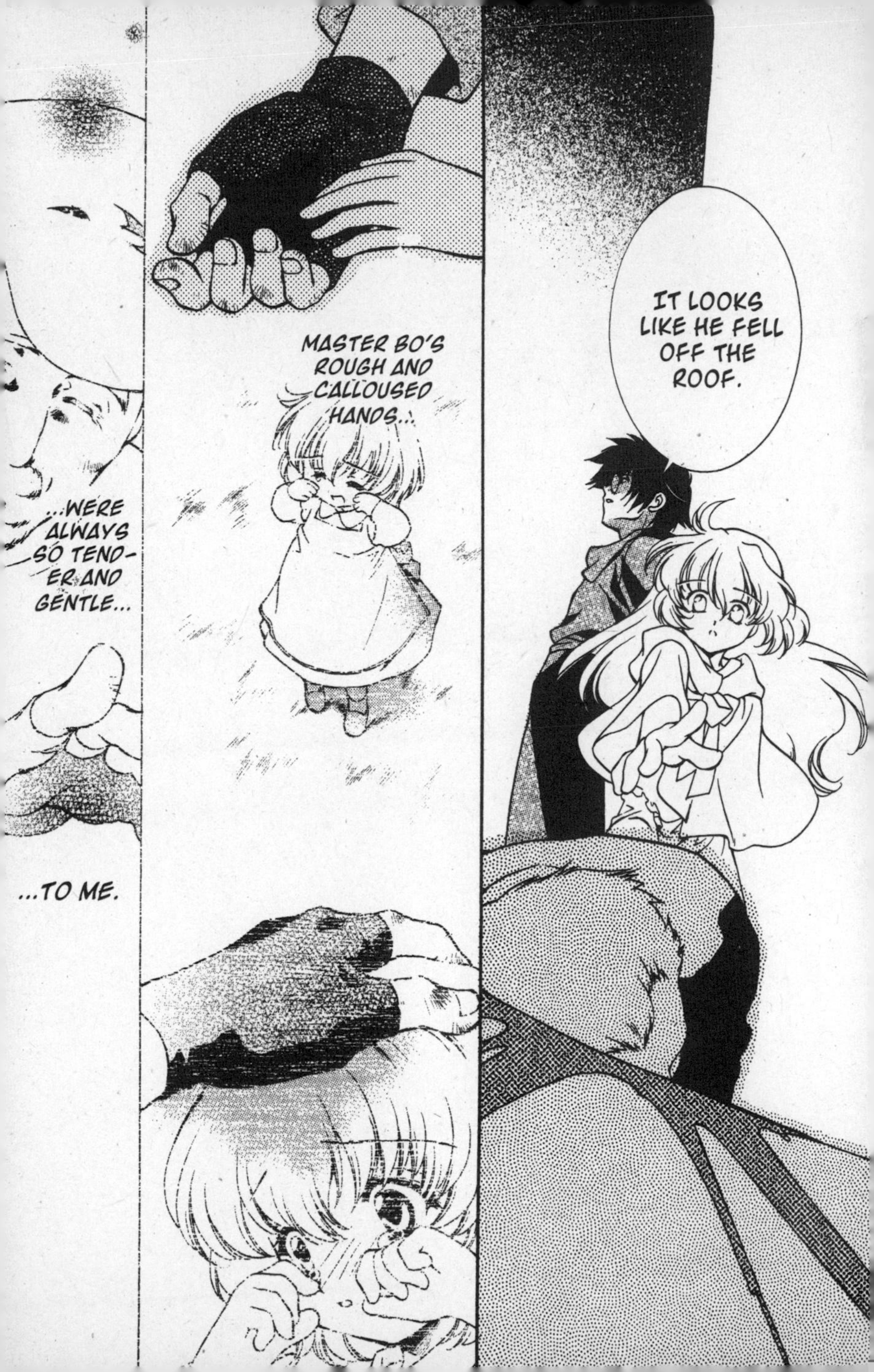
IT LOOKS LIKE HE FELL OFF THE ROOF.
MASTER BO'S ROUGH AND CALLOUSED HANDS...
...WERE ALWAYS SO TEND-ER AND GENTLE...
...TO ME.

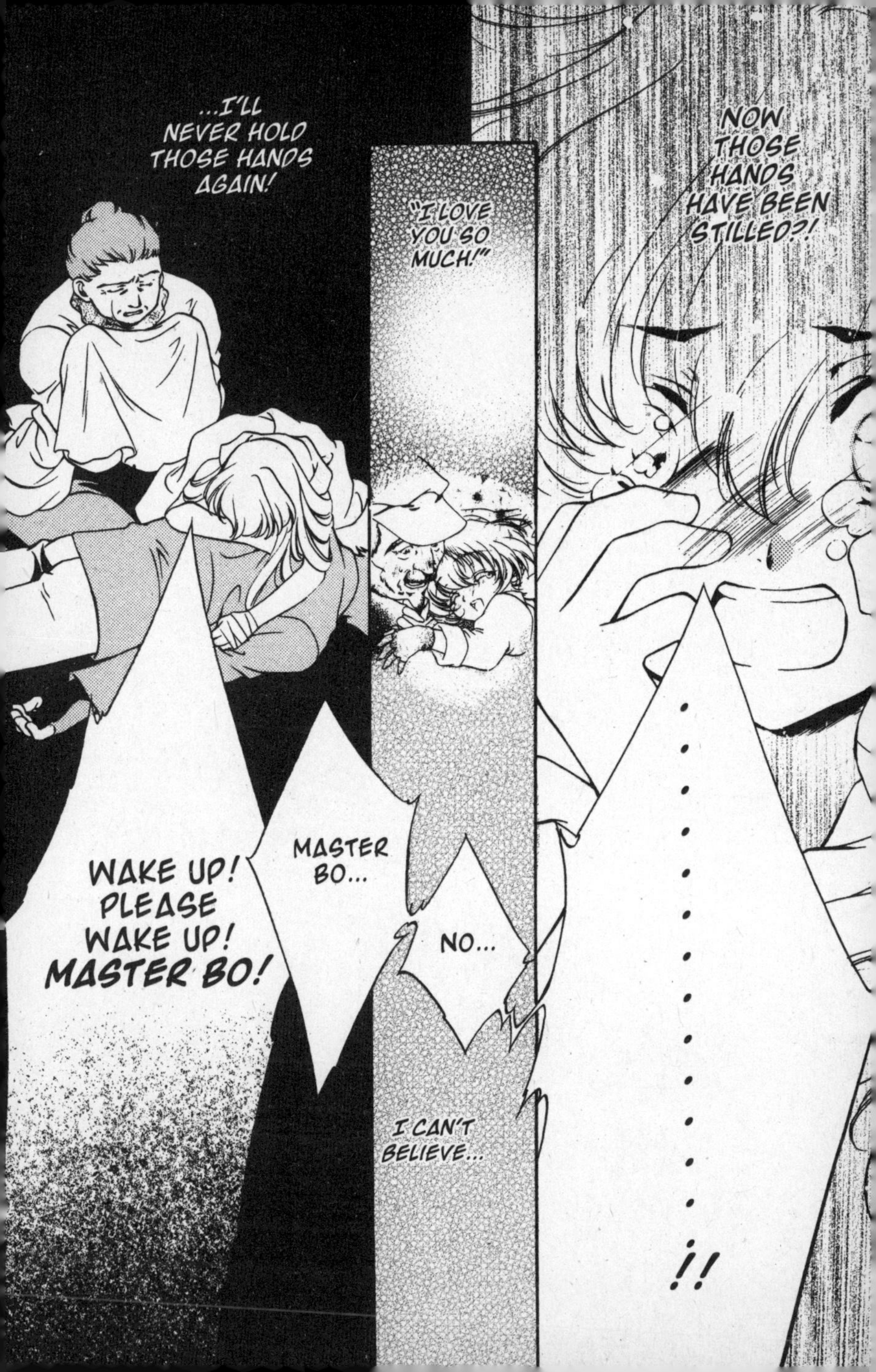
NOW THOSE HANDS HAVE BEEN STILLED?!
...........!!
"I LOVE YOU SO MUCH!"
NO...
I CAN'T BELIEVE...
...I'LL NEVER HOLD THOSE HANDS AGAIN!
MASTER BO...
WAKE UP! PLEASE WAKE UP! MASTER BO!

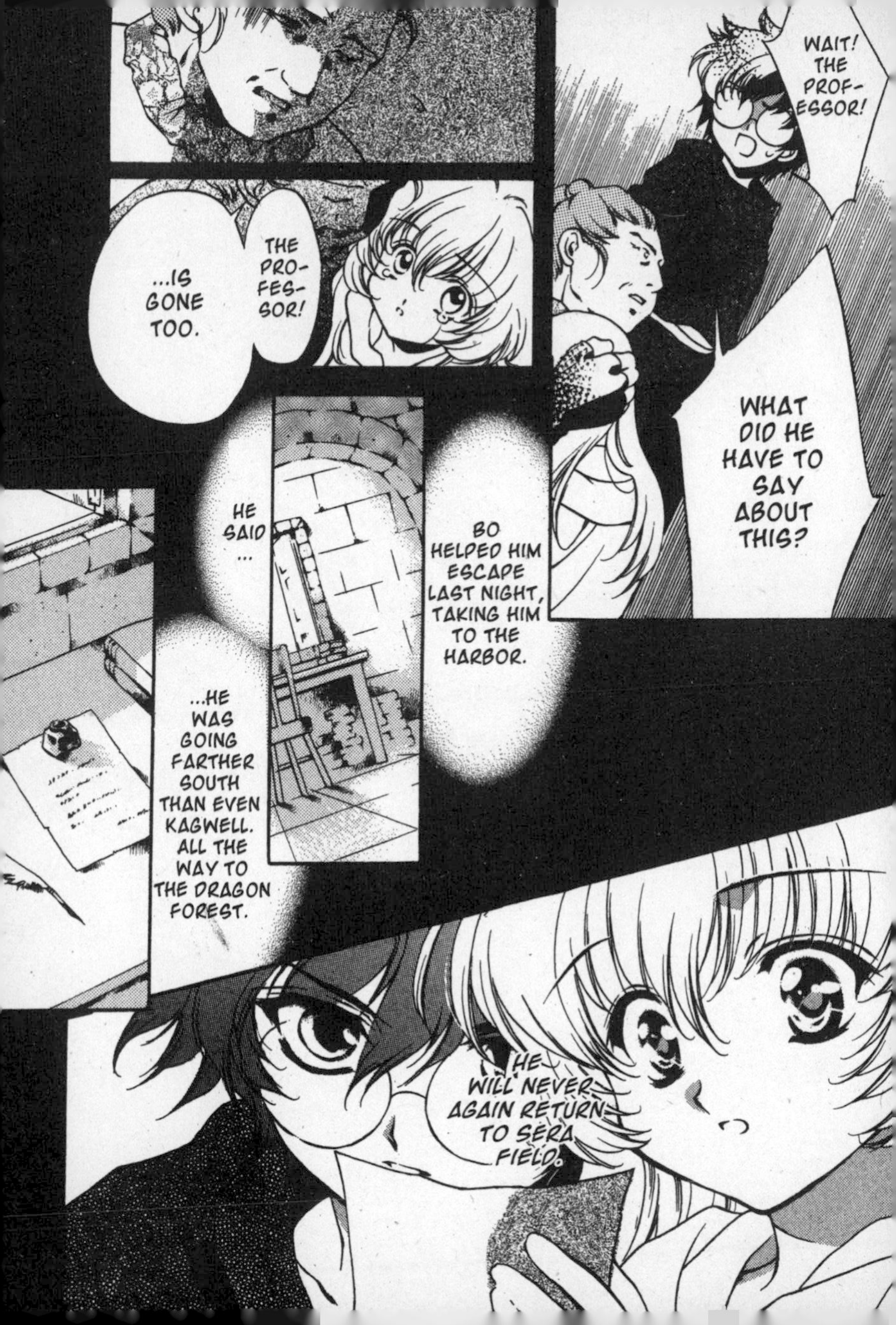
WAIT! THE PROF-ESSOR!
WHAT DID HE HAVE TO SAY ABOUT THIS?
THE PRO-FES-SOR!
...IS GONE TOO.
BO HELPED HIM ESCAPE LAST NIGHT, TAKING HIM TO THE HARBOR.
HE SAID ...
...HE WAS GOING FARTHER SOUTH THAN EVEN KAGWELL. ALL THE WAY TO THE DRAGON FOREST.
HE WILL NEVER AGAIN RETURN TO SERA FIELD.

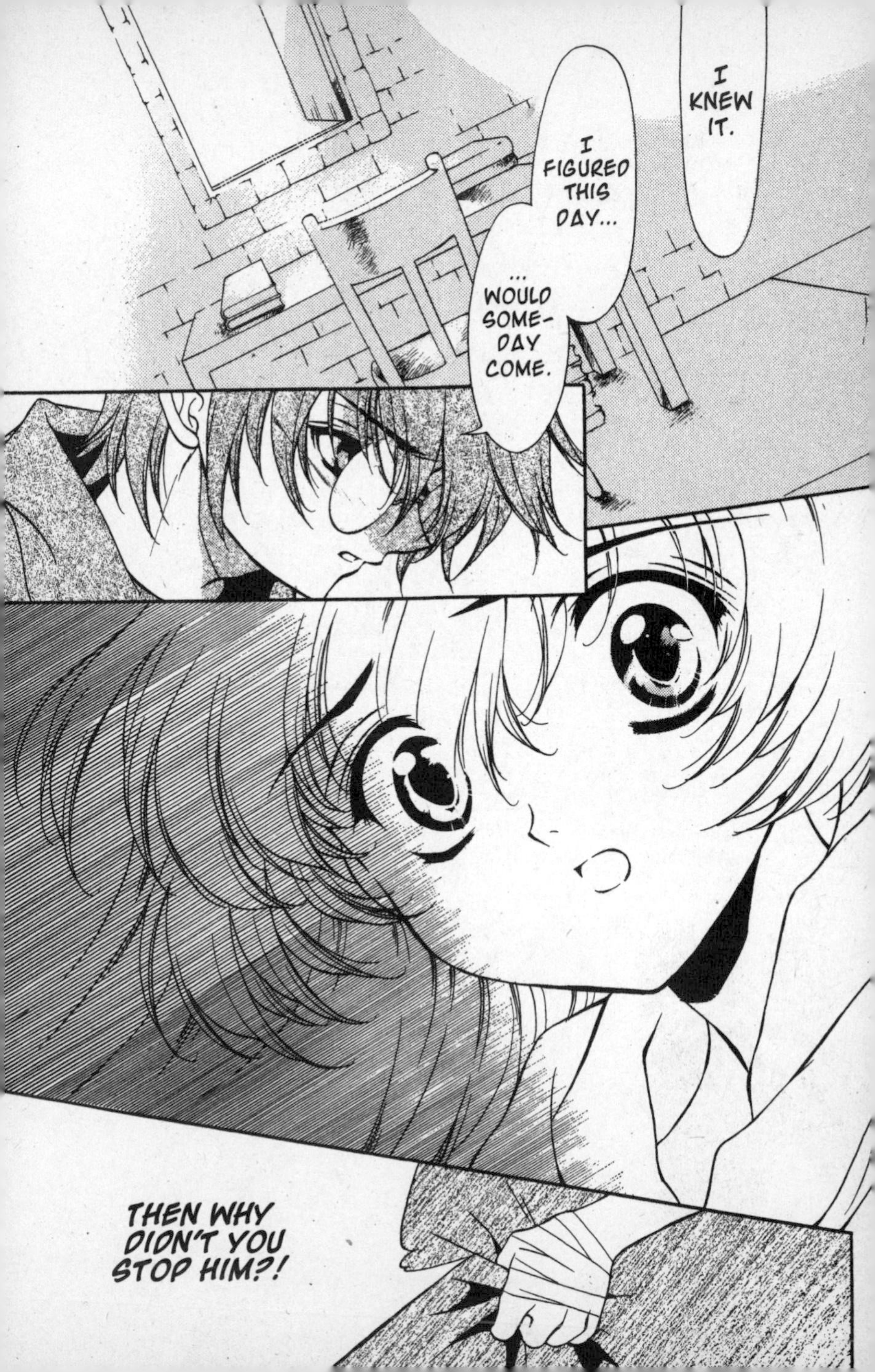
I KNEW IT.
I FIGURED THIS DAY...
... WOULD SOME-DAY COME.
THEN WHY DIDN'T YOU STOP HIM?!

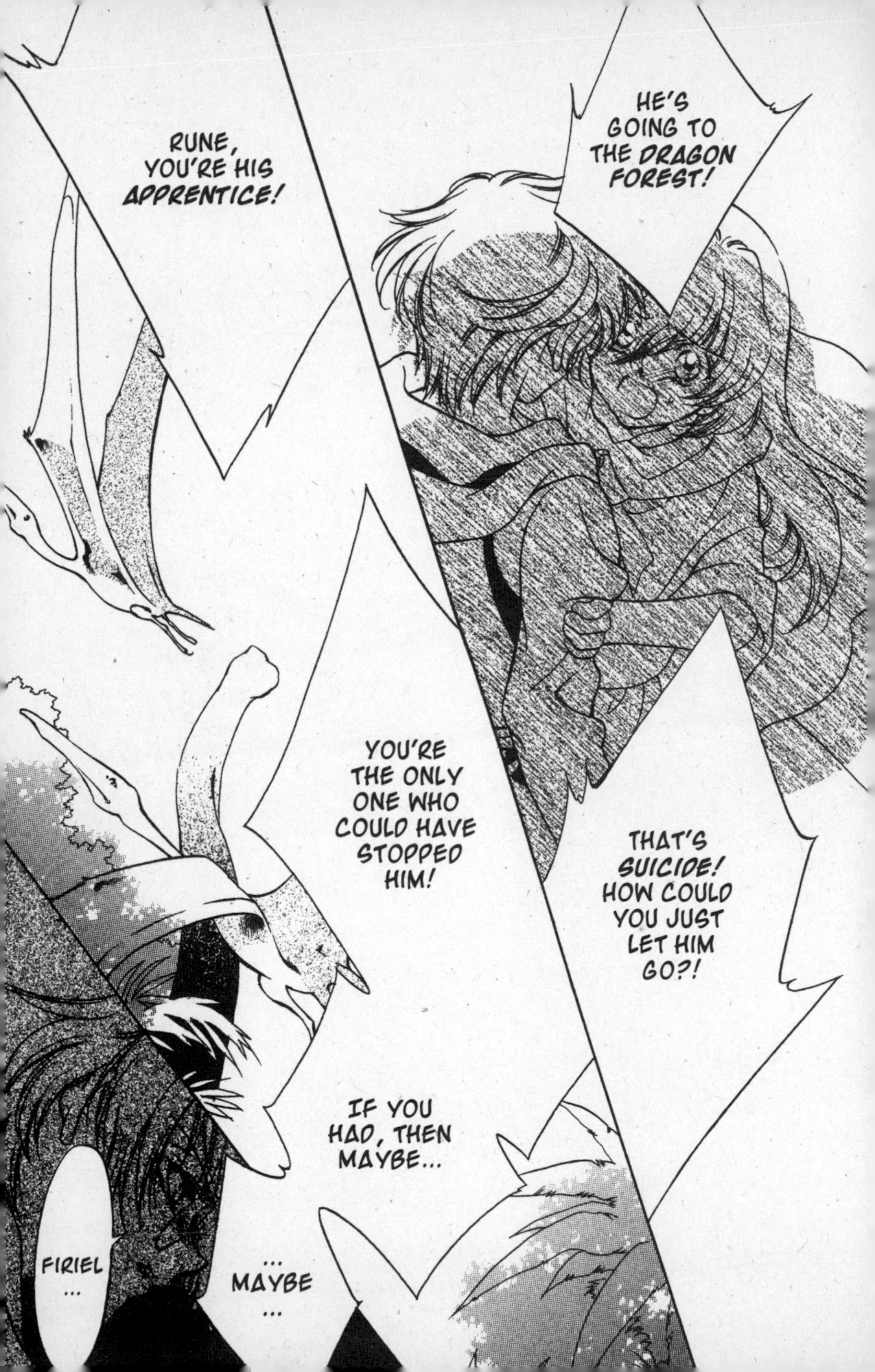
HE'S GOING TO THE DRAGON FOREST!
THAT'S SUICIDE! HOW COULD YOU JUST LET HIM GO?!
RUNE, YOU'RE HIS APPRENTICE!
YOU'RE THE ONLY ONE WHO COULD HAVE STOPPED HIM!
IF YOU HAD, THEN MAYBE...
...MAYBE...
FIRIEL...

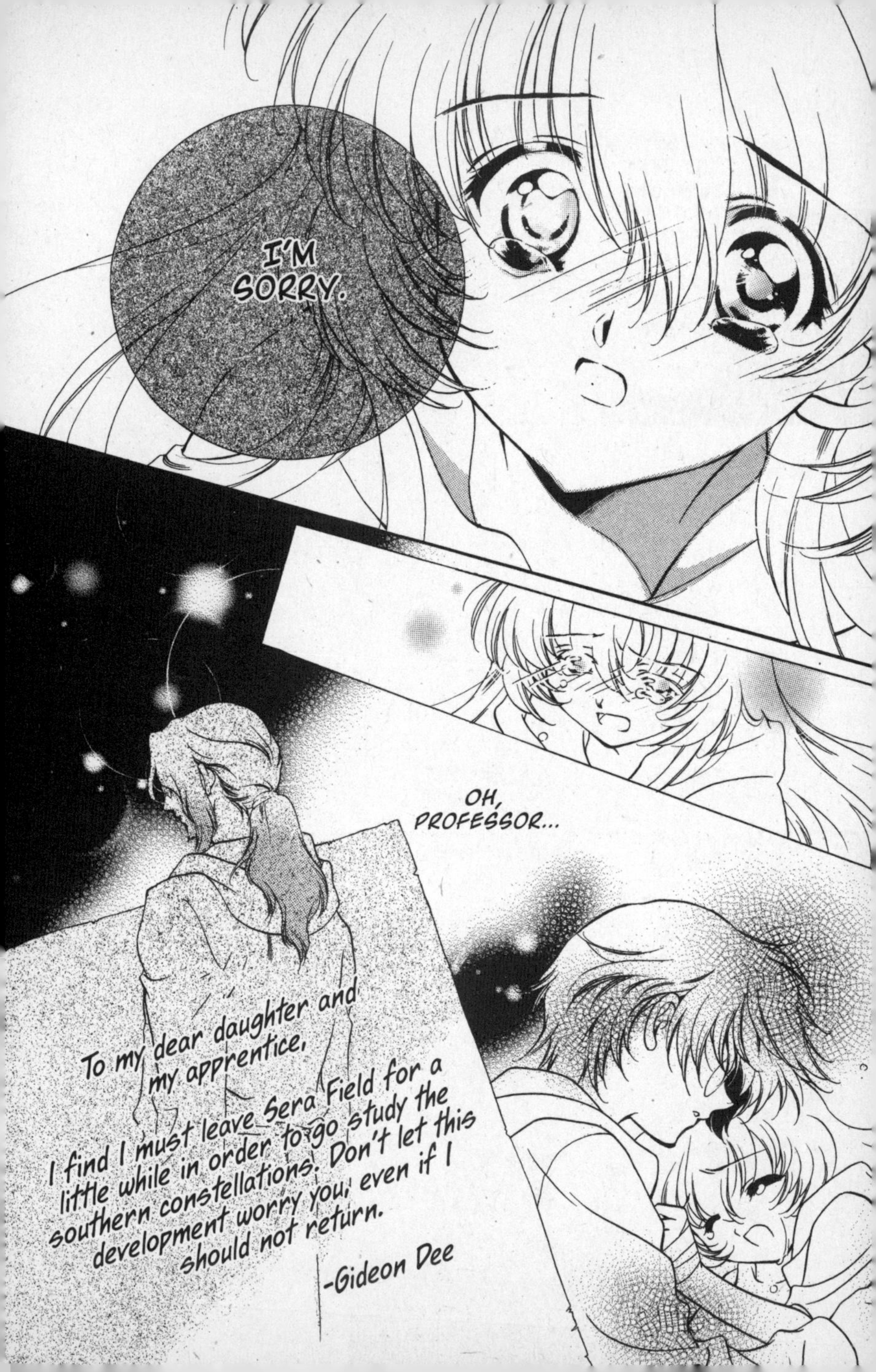

I'M SORRY.
OH, PROFESSOR...
To my dear daughter and my apprentice,
I find I must leave Sera Field for a little while in order to go study the southern constellations. Don't let this development worry you, even if I should not return.
-Gideon Dee

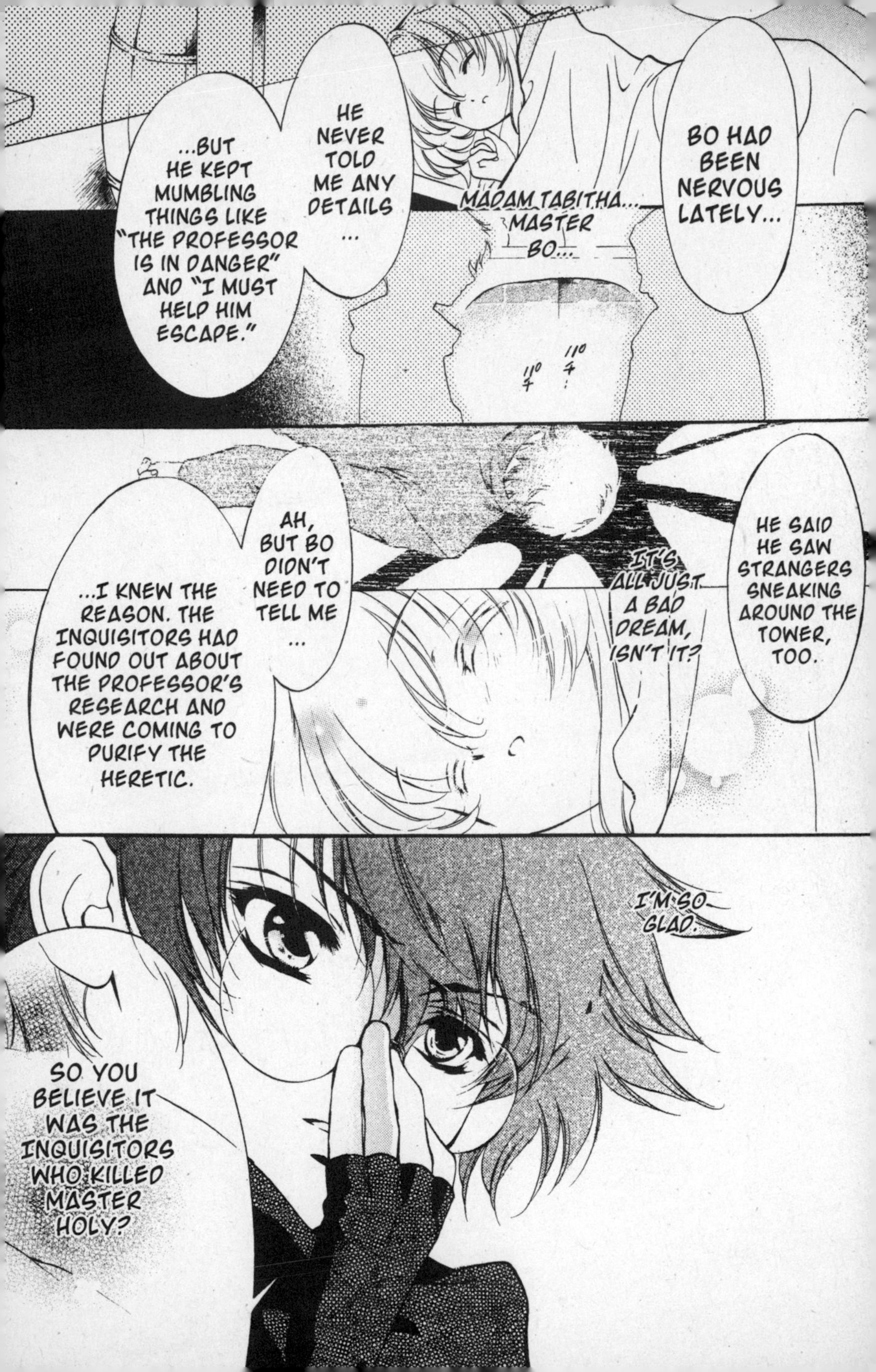
BO HAD BEEN NERVOUS LATELY...
MADAM TABITHA... MASTER BO...
HE NEVER TOLD ME ANY DETAILS ...
...BUT HE KEPT MUMBLING THINGS LIKE "THE PROFESSOR IS IN DANGER" AND "I MUST HELP HIM ESCAPE."
HE SAID HE SAW STRANGERS SNEAKING AROUND THE TOWER, TOO.
IT'S ALL JUST A BAD DREAM, ISN'T IT?
AH, BUT BO DIDN'T NEED TO TELL ME ...
...I KNEW THE REASON. THE INQUISITORS HAD FOUND OUT ABOUT THE PROFESSOR'S RESEARCH AND WERE COMING TO PURIFY THE HERETIC.
I'M SO GLAD.
SO YOU BELIEVE IT WAS THE INQUISITORS WHO KILLED MASTER HOLY?

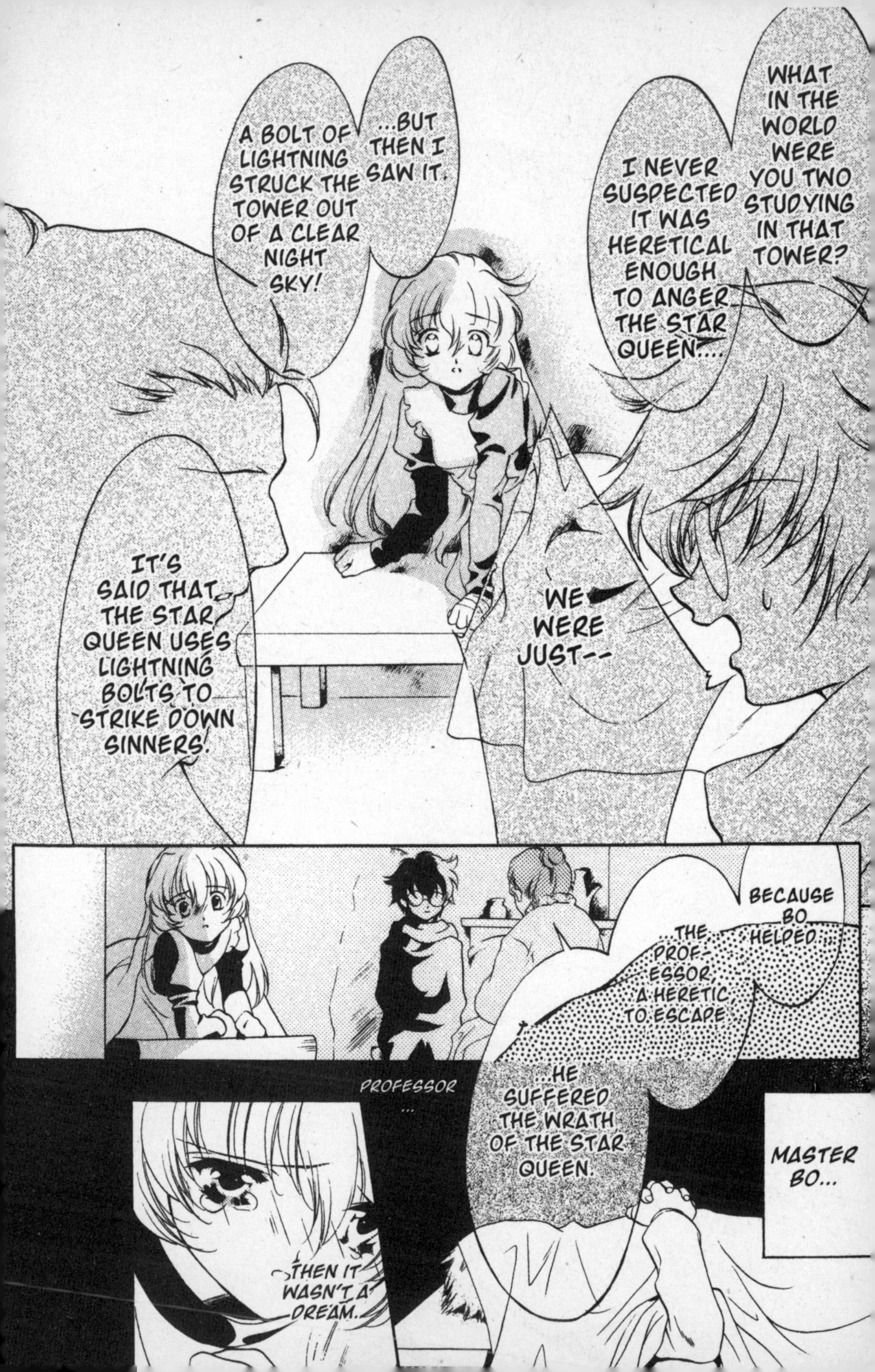
WHAT IN THE WORLD WERE YOU TWO STUDYING IN THAT TOWER?
I NEVER SUSPECTED IT WAS HERETICAL ENOUGH TO ANGER THE STAR QUEEN....
...BUT THEN I SAW IT.
A BOLT OF LIGHTNING STRUCK THE TOWER OUT OF A CLEAR NIGHT SKY!
WE WERE JUST--
IT'S SAID THAT THE STAR QUEEN USES LIGHTNING BOLTS TO STRIKE DOWN SINNERS.
BECAUSE BO HELPED
THE PROFESSOR, A HERETIC, TO ESCAPE
HE SUFFERED THE WRATH OF THE STAR QUEEN.
MASTER BO...
PROFESSOR...
THEN IT WASN'T A DREAM.

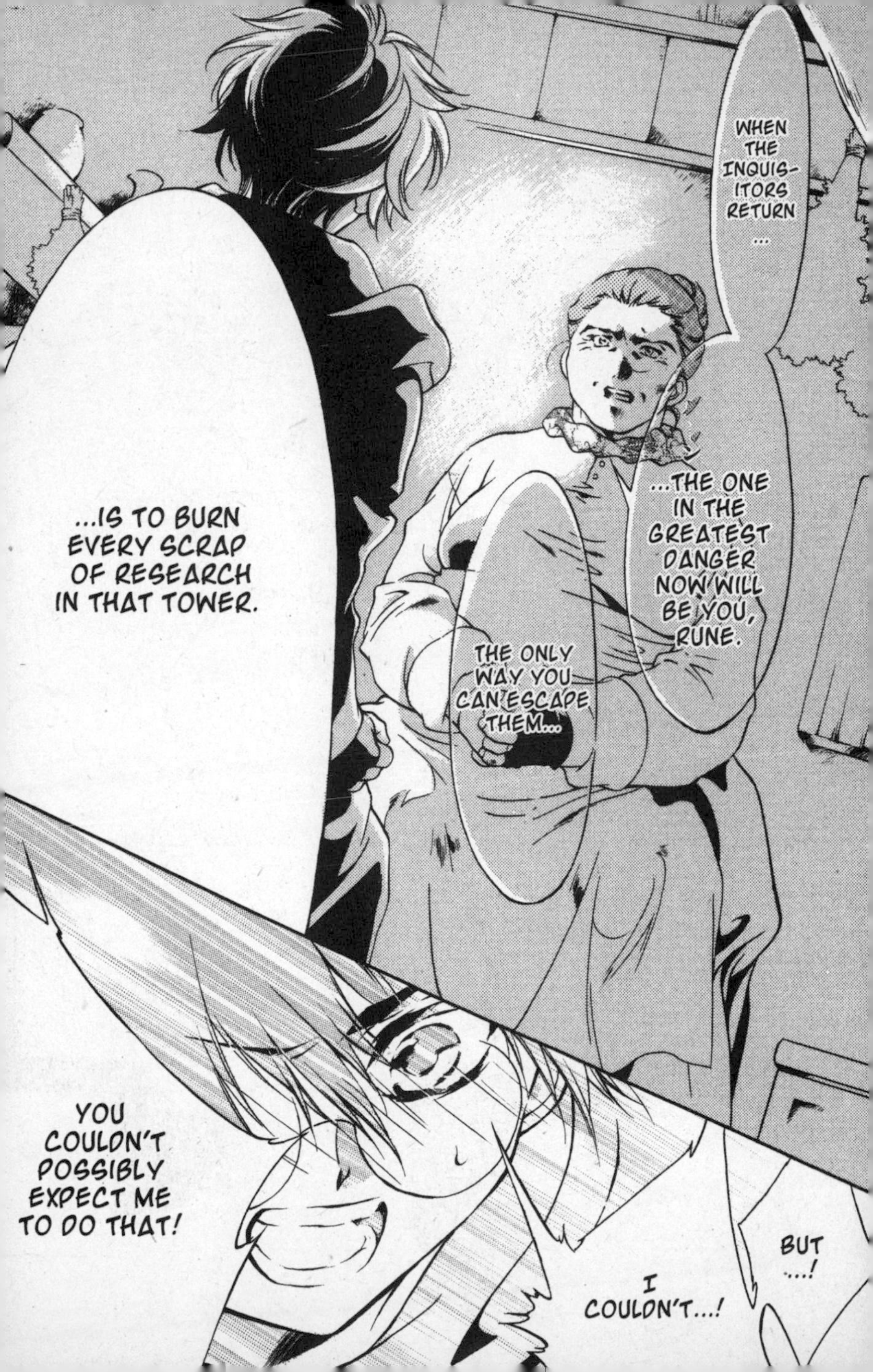
WHEN THE INQUISITORS RETURN...
...THE ONE IN THE GREATEST DANGER NOW WILL BE YOU, RUNE.
THE ONLY WAY YOU CAN ESCAPE THEM...
...IS TO BURN EVERY SCRAP OF RESEARCH IN THAT TOWER.
BUT...!
I COULDN'T...!
YOU COULDN'T POSSIBLY EXPECT ME TO DO THAT!

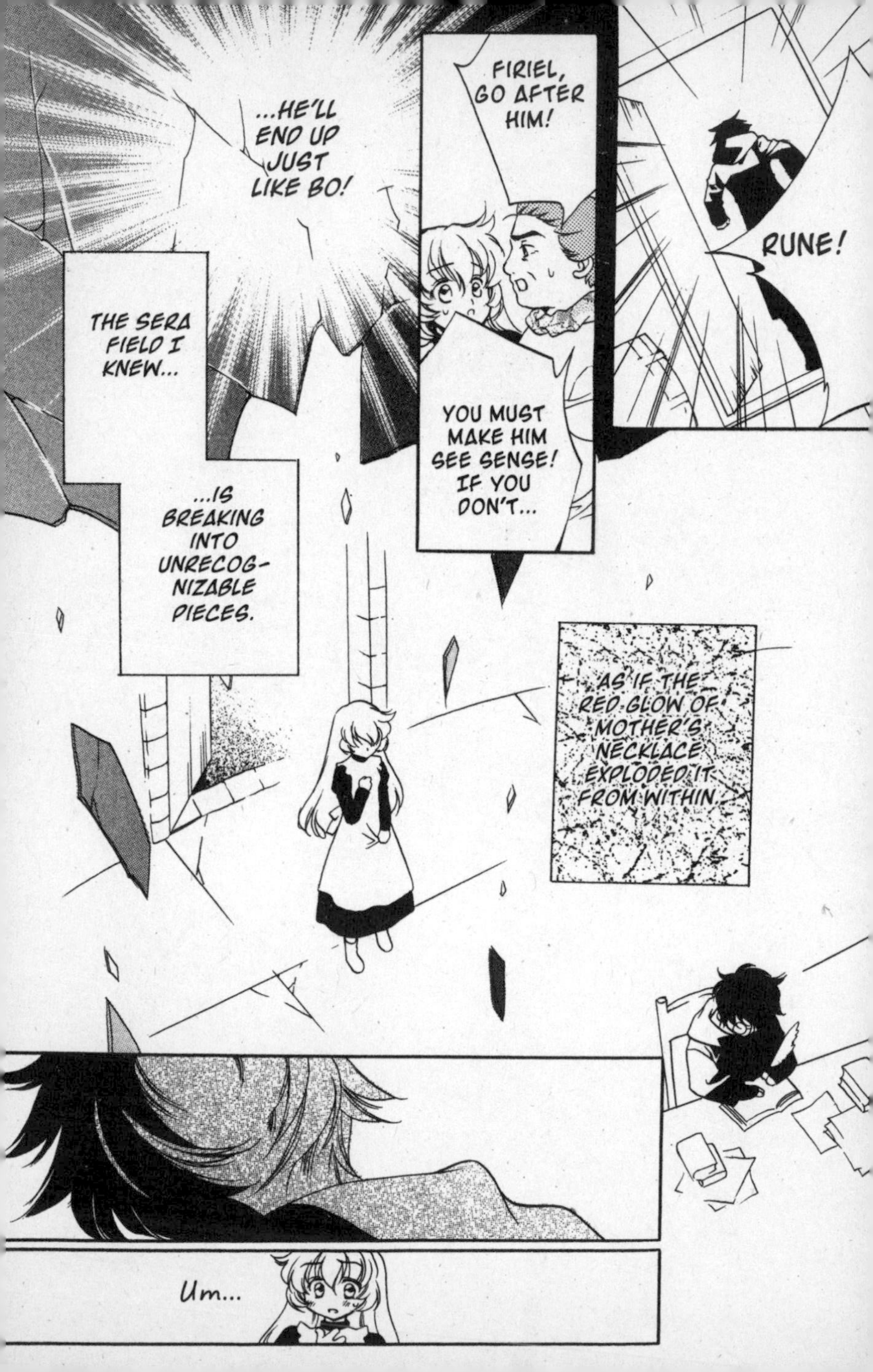
RUNE!
FIRIEL, GO AFTER HIM!
YOU MUST MAKE HIM SEE SENSE! IF YOU DON'T...
...HE'LL END UP JUST LIKE BO!
THE SERA FIELD I KNEW...
...IS BREAKING INTO UNRECOG-NIZABLE PIECES.
AS IF THE RED GLOW OF MOTHER'S NECKLACE EXPLODED IT FROM WITHIN.
Um...

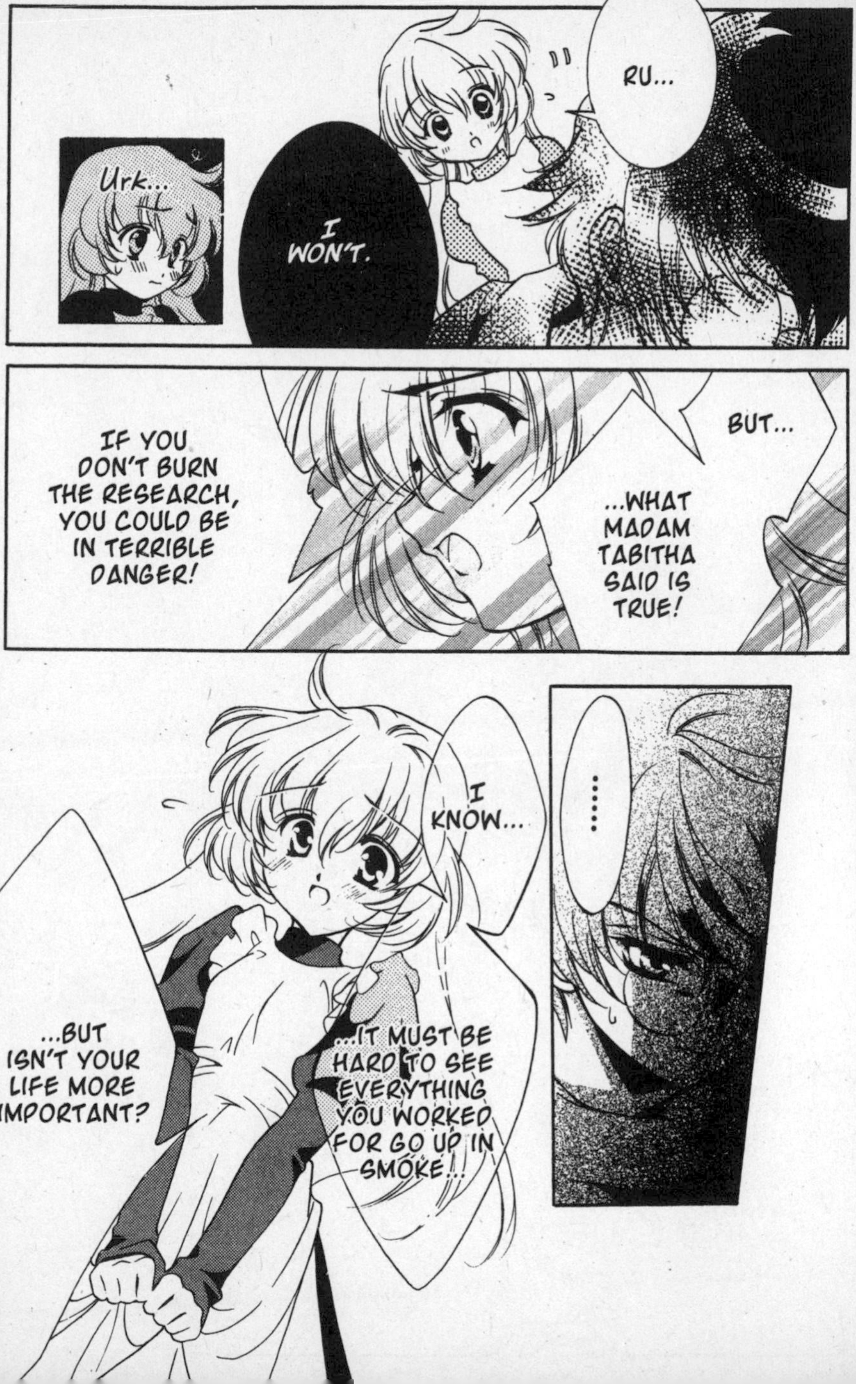
RU...
I WON'T.
Urk...
BUT...
...WHAT MADAM TABITHA SAID IS TRUE!
IF YOU DON'T BURN THE RESEARCH, YOU COULD BE IN TERRIBLE DANGER!
......
I KNOW...
...IT MUST BE HARD TO SEE EVERYTHING YOU WORKED FOR GO UP IN SMOKE...
...BUT ISN'T YOUR LIFE MORE IMPORTANT?

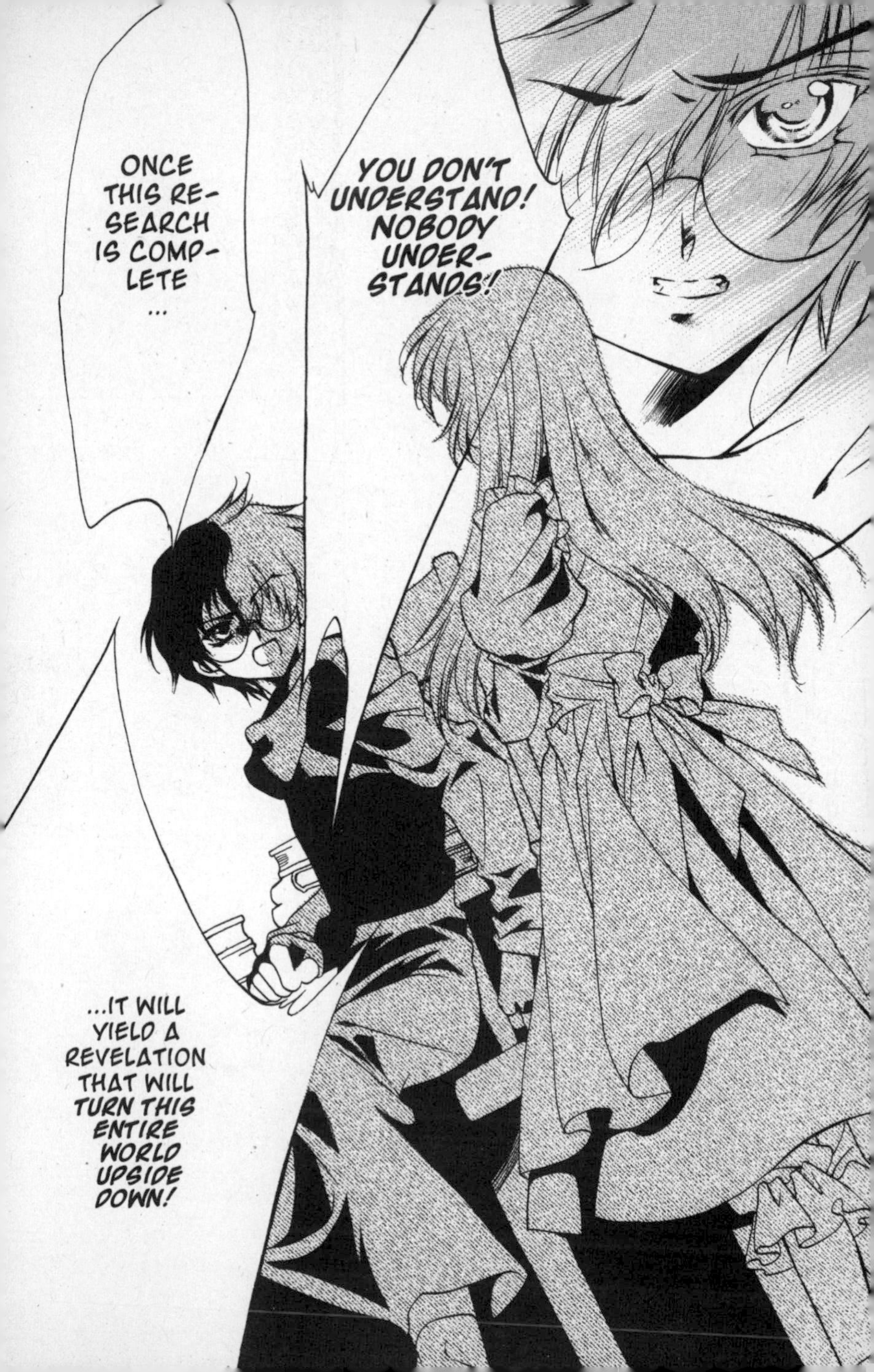
YOU DON'T UNDERSTAND! NOBODY UNDER-STANDS!!
ONCE THIS RE-SEARCH IS COMP-LETE ...
...IT WILL YIELD A REVELATION THAT WILL TURN THIS ENTIRE WORLD UPSIDE DOWN!

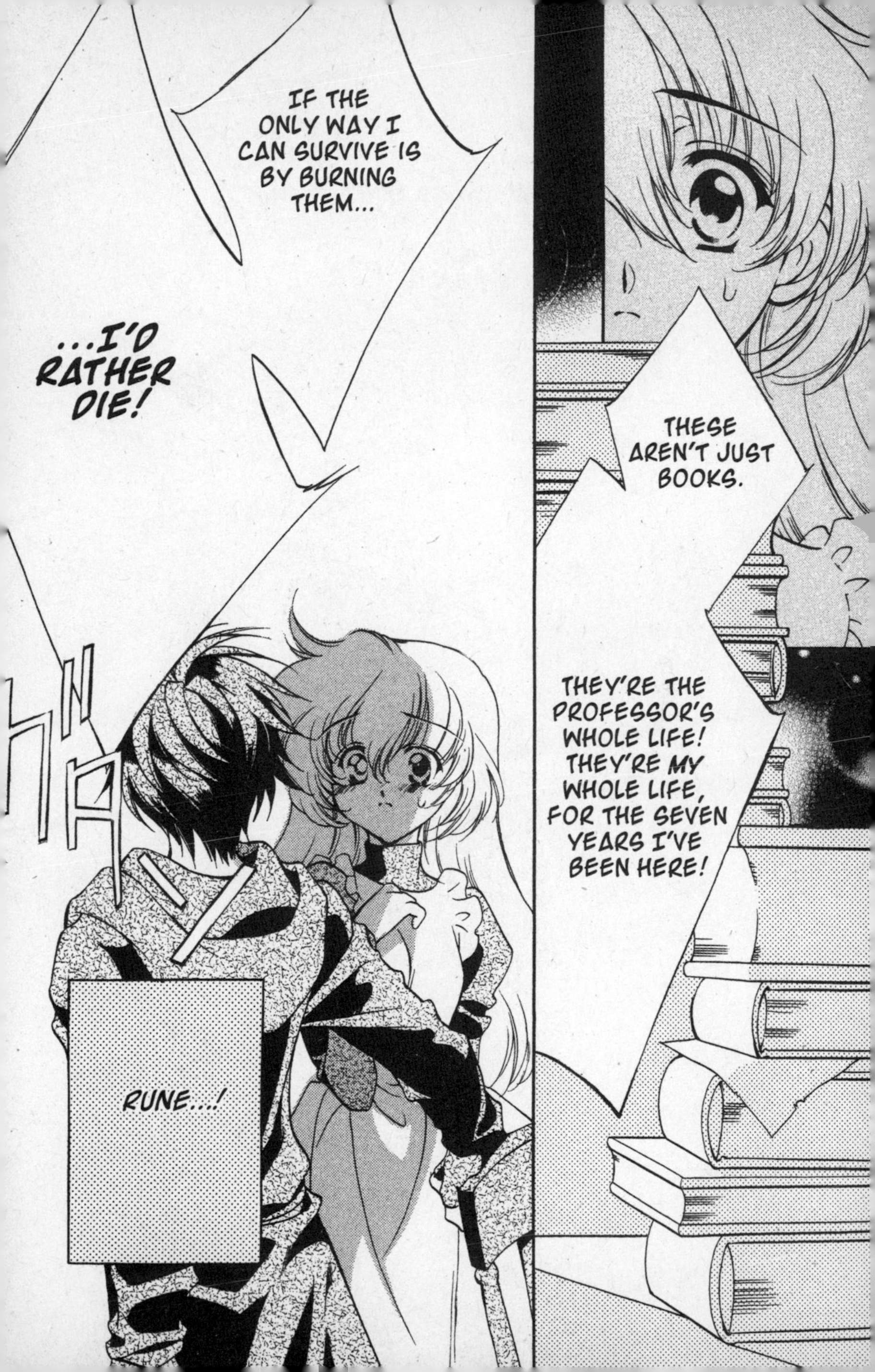
THESE AREN'T JUST BOOKS.
THEY'RE THE PROFESSOR'S WHOLE LIFE! THEY'RE MY WHOLE LIFE, FOR THE SEVEN YEARS I'VE BEEN HERE!
IF THE ONLY WAY I CAN SURVIVE IS BY BURNING THEM...
...I'D RATHER DIE!
RUNE...!

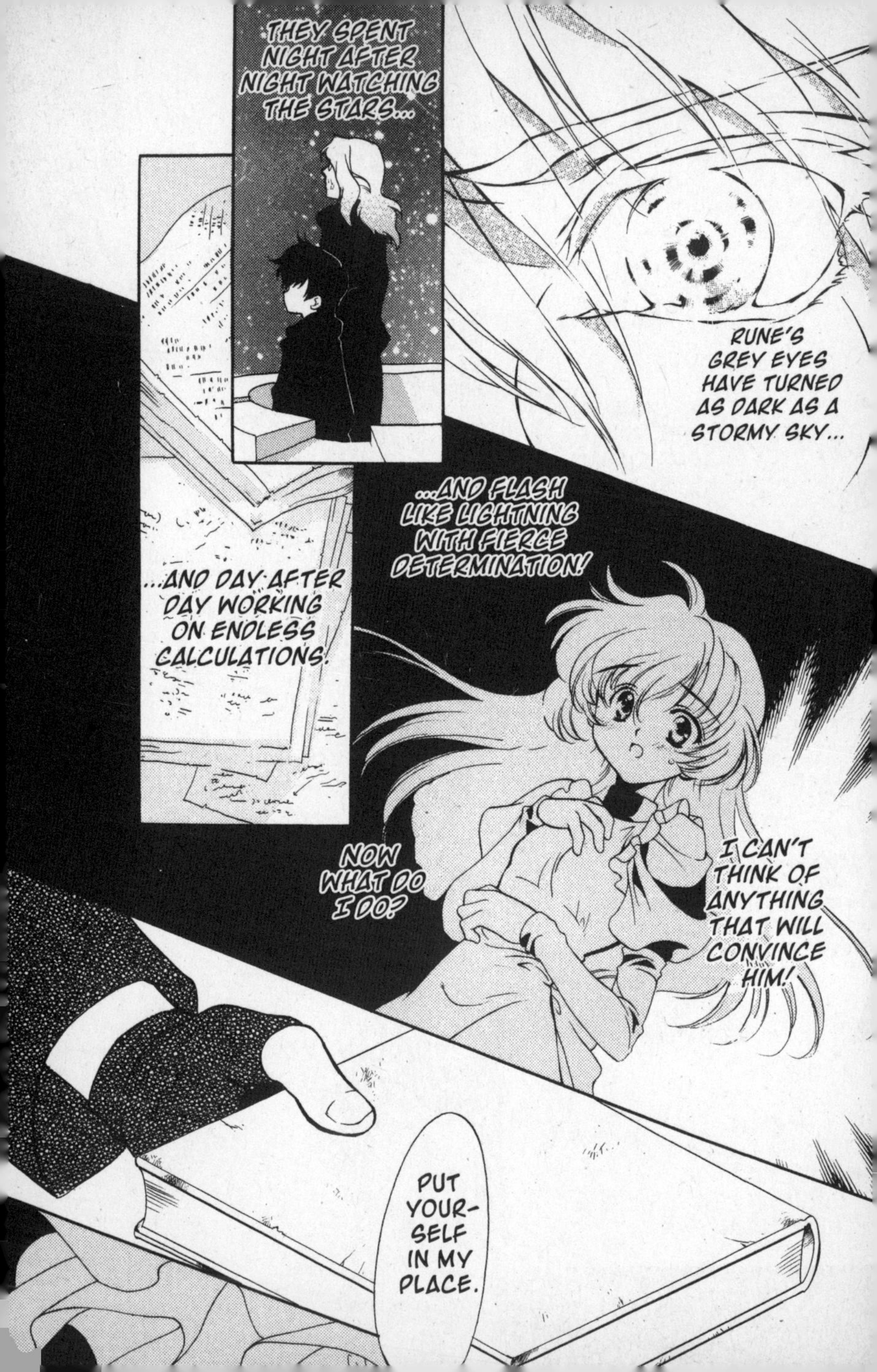
RUNE'S GREY EYES HAVE TURNED AS DARK AS A STORMY SKY...
...AND FLASH LIKE LIGHTNING WITH FIERCE DETERMINATION!
THEY SPENT NIGHT AFTER NIGHT WATCHING THE STARS...
...AND DAY AFTER DAY WORKING ON ENDLESS CALCULATIONS.
I CAN'T THINK OF ANYTHING THAT WILL CONVINCE HIM!
NOW WHAT DO I DO?
PUT YOURSELF IN MY PLACE.

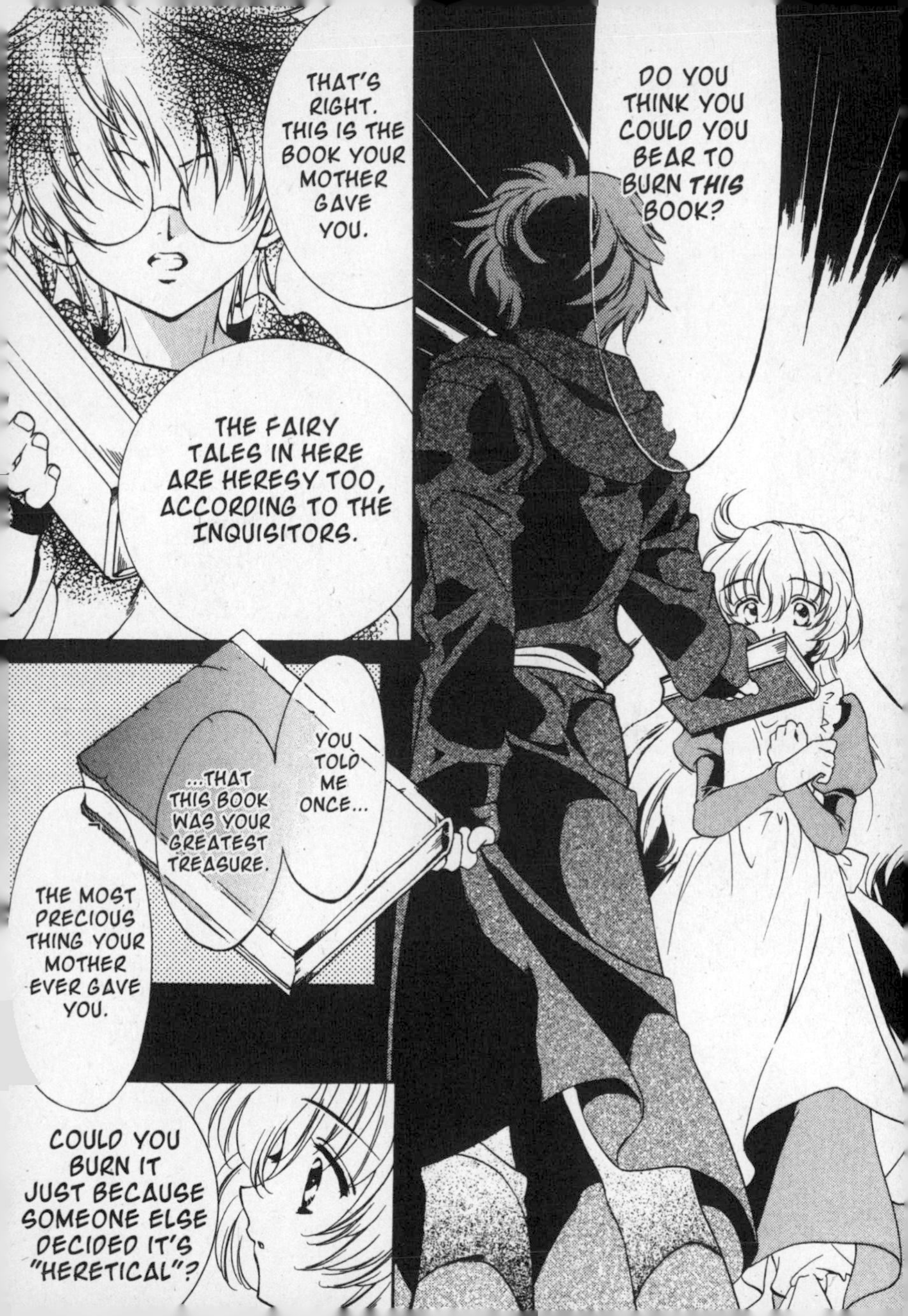
DO YOU THINK YOU COULD YOU BEAR TO BURN *THIS* BOOK?
THAT'S RIGHT. THIS IS THE BOOK YOUR MOTHER GAVE YOU.
THE FAIRY TALES IN HERE ARE HERESY TOO, ACCORDING TO THE INQUISITORS.
YOU TOLD ME ONCE...
...THAT THIS BOOK WAS YOUR GREATEST TREASURE.
THE MOST PRECIOUS THING YOUR MOTHER EVER GAVE YOU.
COULD YOU BURN IT JUST BECAUSE SOMEONE ELSE DECIDED IT'S "HERETICAL"?

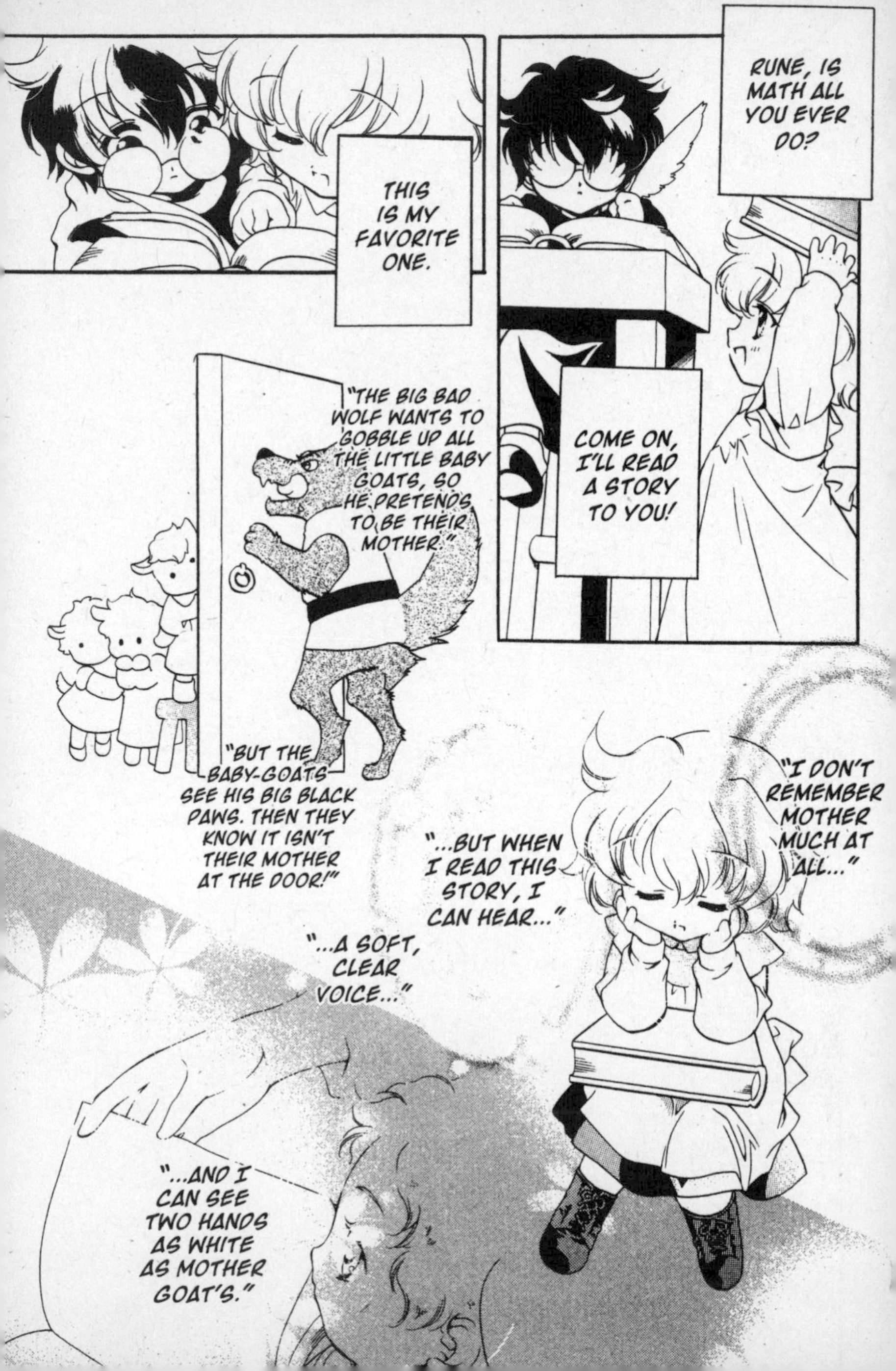
RUNE, IS MATH ALL YOU EVER DO?
COME ON, I'LL READ A STORY TO YOU!
THIS IS MY FAVORITE ONE.
"THE BIG BAD WOLF WANTS TO GOBBLE UP ALL THE LITTLE BABY GOATS, SO HE PRETENDS TO BE THEIR MOTHER."
"BUT THE BABY-GOATS SEE HIS BIG BLACK PAWS. THEN THEY KNOW IT ISN'T THEIR MOTHER AT THE DOOR!"
"I DON'T REMEMBER MOTHER MUCH AT ALL..."
"...BUT WHEN I READ THIS STORY, I CAN HEAR..."
"...A SOFT, CLEAR VOICE..."
"...AND I CAN SEE TWO HANDS AS WHITE AS MOTHER GOAT'S."

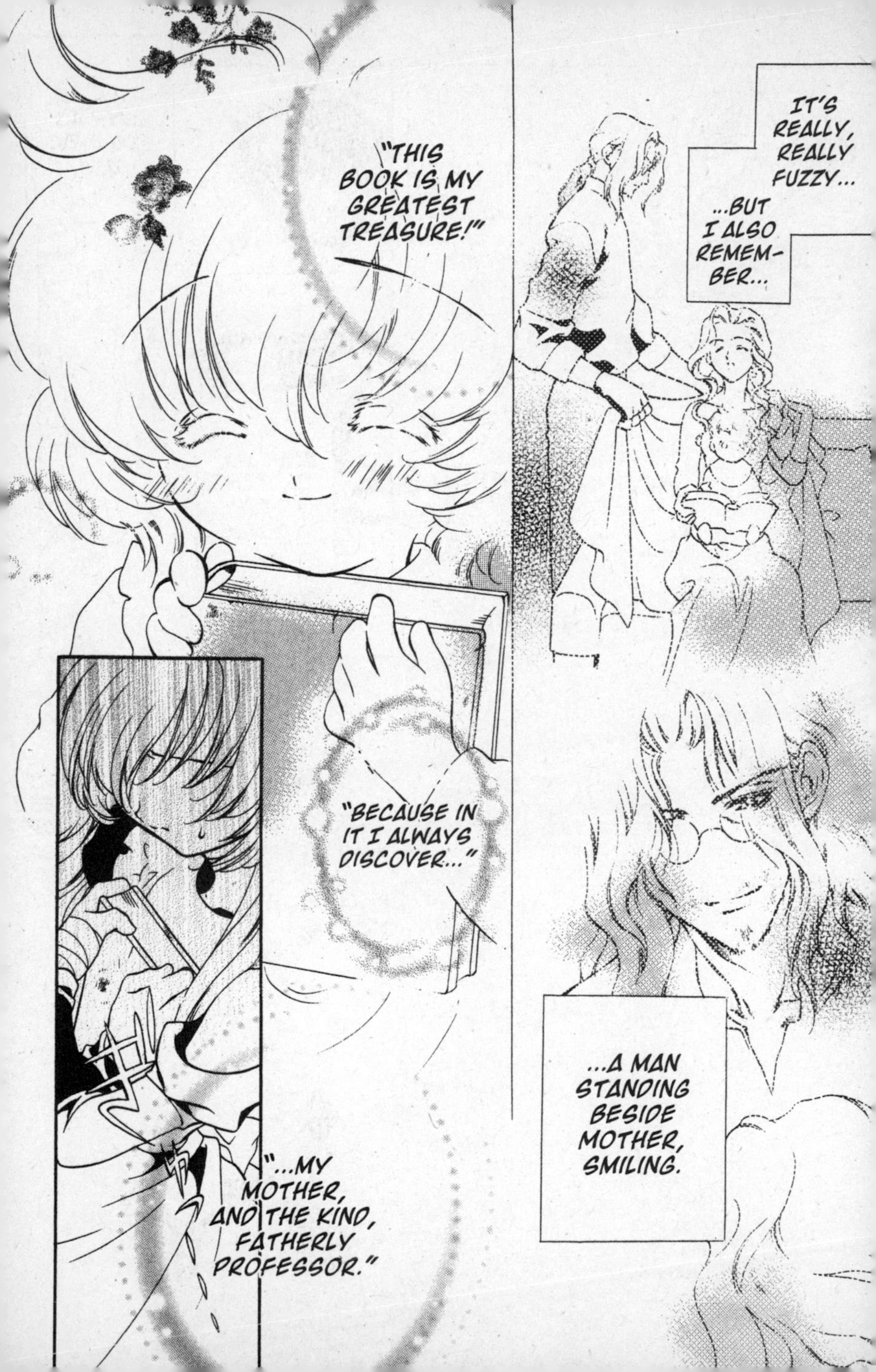
IT'S REALLY, REALLY FUZZY...
...BUT I ALSO REMEMBER...
...A MAN STANDING BESIDE MOTHER, SMILING.
"THIS BOOK IS MY GREATEST TREASURE!"
"BECAUSE IN IT I ALWAYS DISCOVER..."
"...MY MOTHER, AND THE KIND, FATHERLY PROFESSOR."

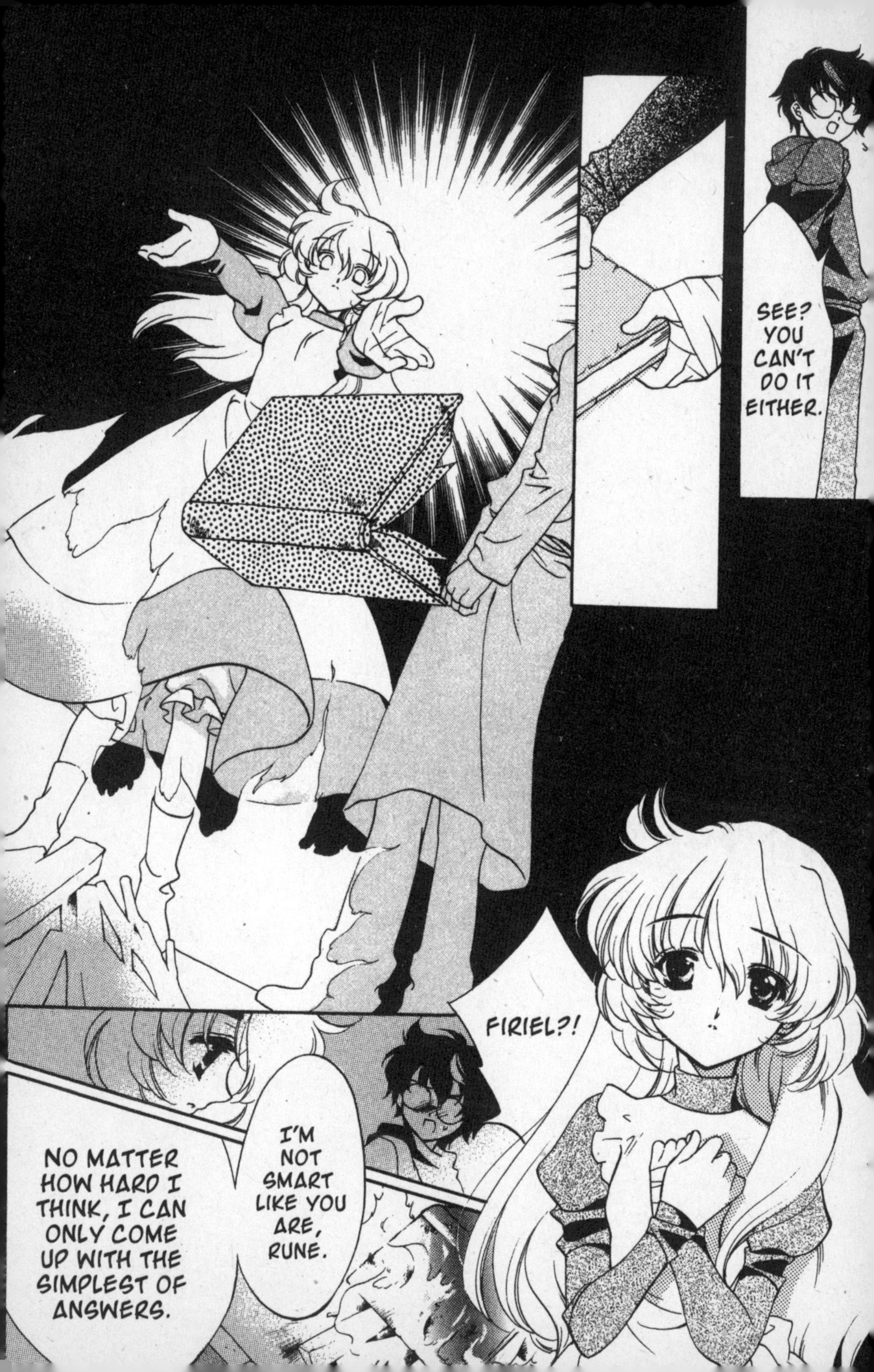
SEE? YOU CAN'T DO IT EITHER.
FIRIEL?!
I'M NOT SMART LIKE YOU ARE, RUNE.
NO MATTER HOW HARD I THINK, I CAN ONLY COME UP WITH THE SIMPLEST OF ANSWERS.

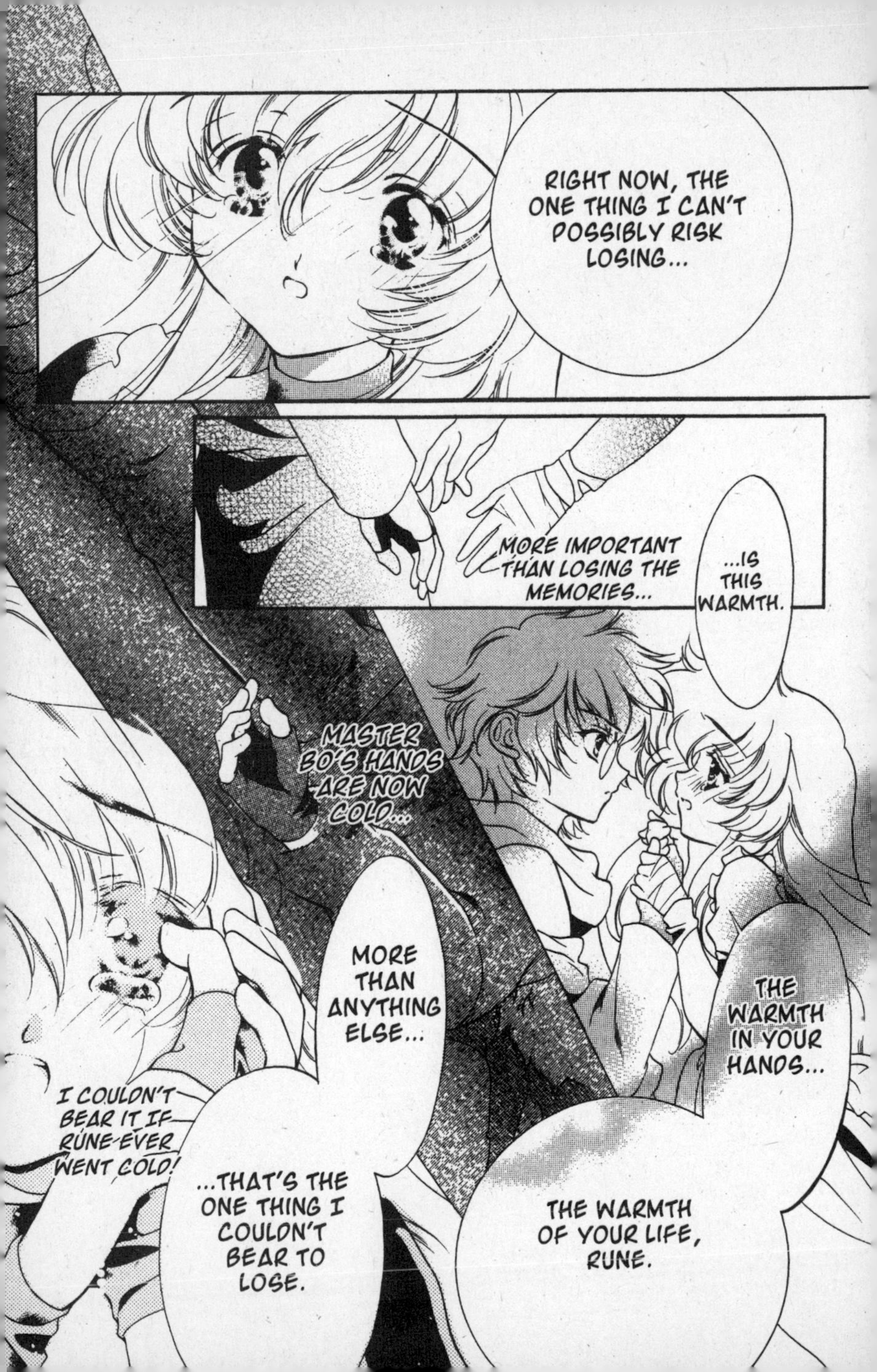
RIGHT NOW, THE ONE THING I CAN'T POSSIBLY RISK LOSING...
MORE IMPORTANT THAN LOSING THE MEMORIES...
...IS THIS WARMTH.
THE WARMTH IN YOUR HANDS...
THE WARMTH OF YOUR LIFE, RUNE.
MASTER BO'S HANDS ARE NOW COLD...
MORE THAN ANYTHING ELSE...
...THAT'S THE ONE THING I COULDN'T BEAR TO LOSE.
I COULDN'T BEAR IT IF RUNE EVER WENT COLD!

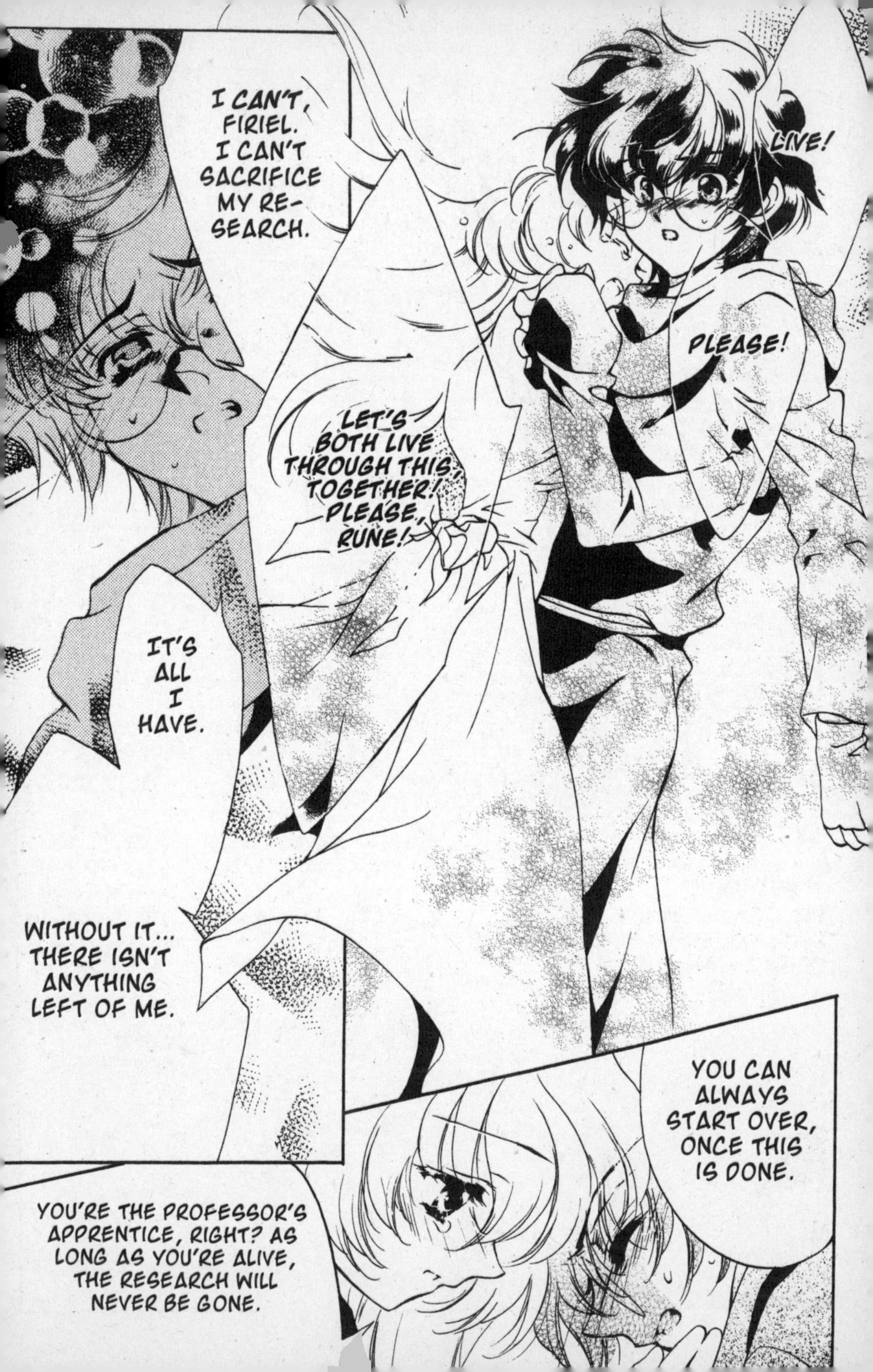
LIVE!
PLEASE!
LET'S BOTH LIVE THROUGH THIS, TOGETHER! PLEASE, RUNE!
I CAN'T, FIRIEL. I CAN'T SACRIFICE MY RE-SEARCH.
IT'S ALL I HAVE.
WITHOUT IT... THERE ISN'T ANYTHING LEFT OF ME.
YOU CAN ALWAYS START OVER, ONCE THIS IS DONE.
YOU'RE THE PROFESSOR'S APPRENTICE, RIGHT? AS LONG AS YOU'RE ALIVE, THE RESEARCH WILL NEVER BE GONE.

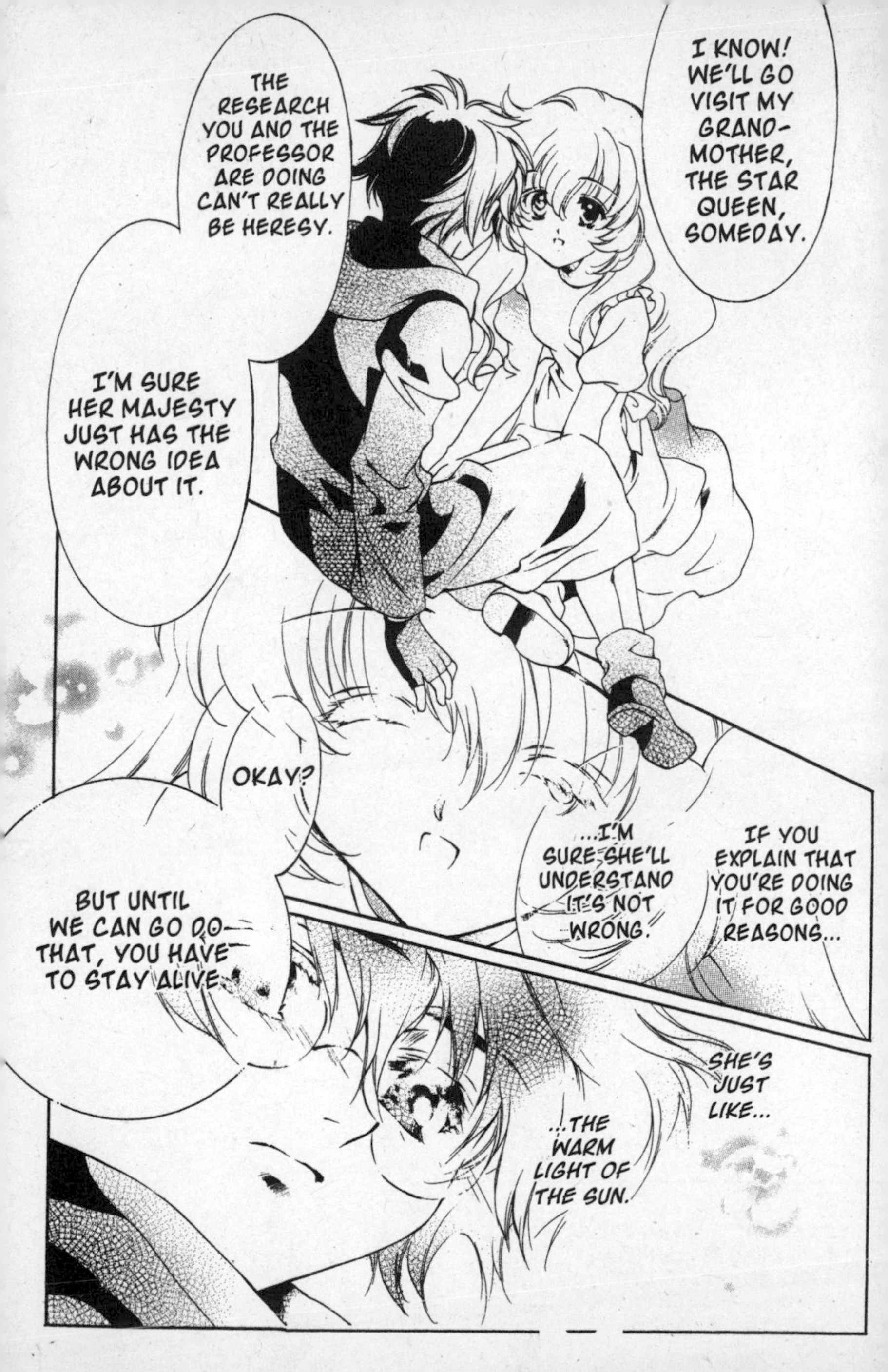
I KNOW! WE'LL GO VISIT MY GRAND-MOTHER, THE STAR QUEEN, SOMEDAY.
THE RESEARCH YOU AND THE PROFESSOR ARE DOING CAN'T REALLY BE HERESY.
I'M SURE HER MAJESTY JUST HAS THE WRONG IDEA ABOUT IT.
OKAY?
IF YOU EXPLAIN THAT YOU'RE DOING IT FOR GOOD REASONS...
...I'M SURE SHE'LL UNDERSTAND IT'S NOT WRONG.
BUT UNTIL WE CAN GO DO THAT, YOU HAVE TO STAY ALIVE.
SHE'S JUST LIKE...
...THE WARM LIGHT OF THE SUN.

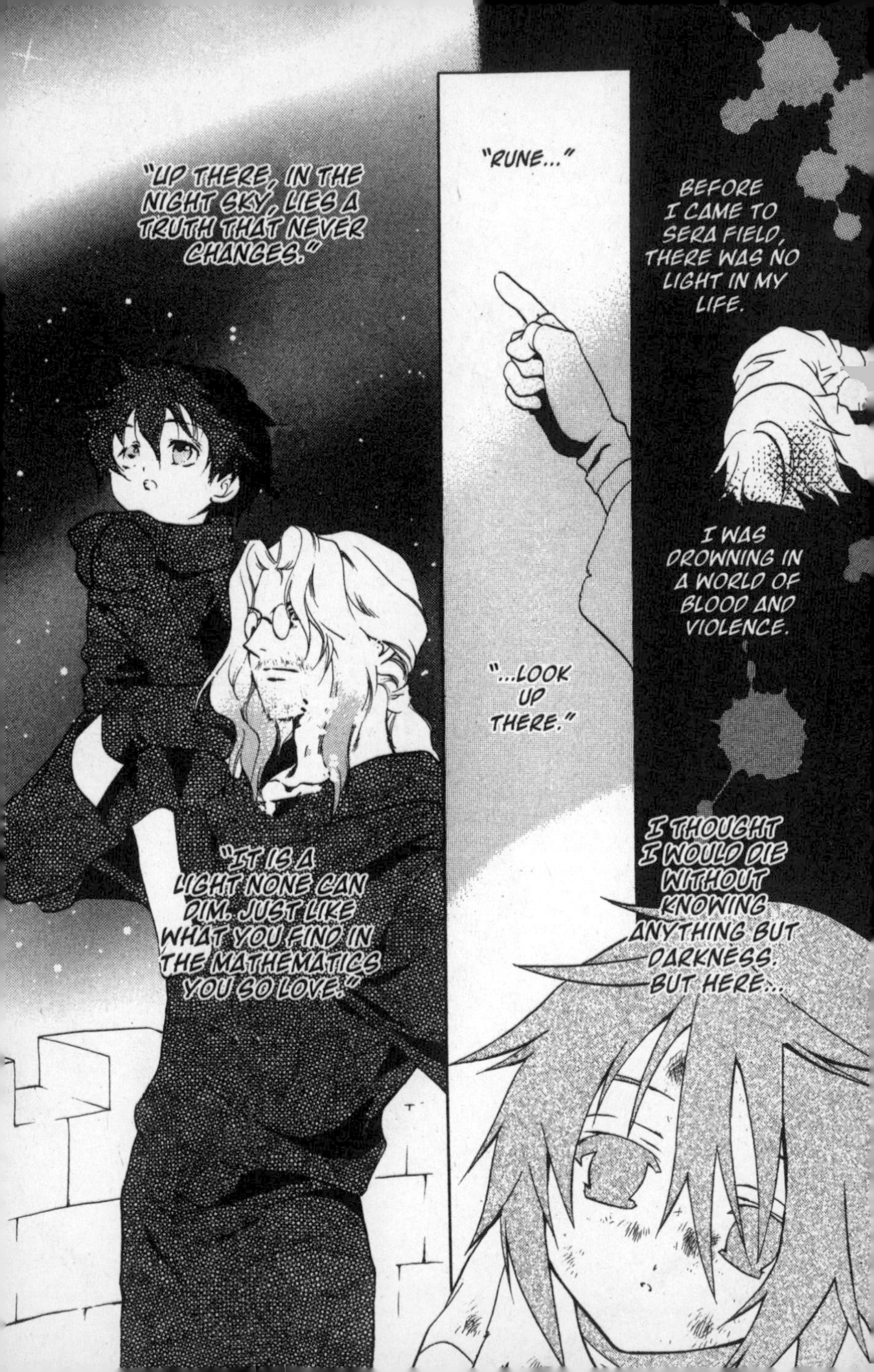
BEFORE I CAME TO SERA FIELD, THERE WAS NO LIGHT IN MY LIFE.
I WAS DROWNING IN A WORLD OF BLOOD AND VIOLENCE.
I THOUGHT I WOULD DIE WITHOUT KNOWING ANYTHING BUT DARKNESS. BUT HERE...
"RUNE..."
"...LOOK UP THERE."
"UP THERE, IN THE NIGHT SKY, LIES A TRUTH THAT NEVER CHANGES."
"IT IS A LIGHT NONE CAN DIM. JUST LIKE WHAT YOU FIND IN THE MATHEMATICS YOU SO LOVE."

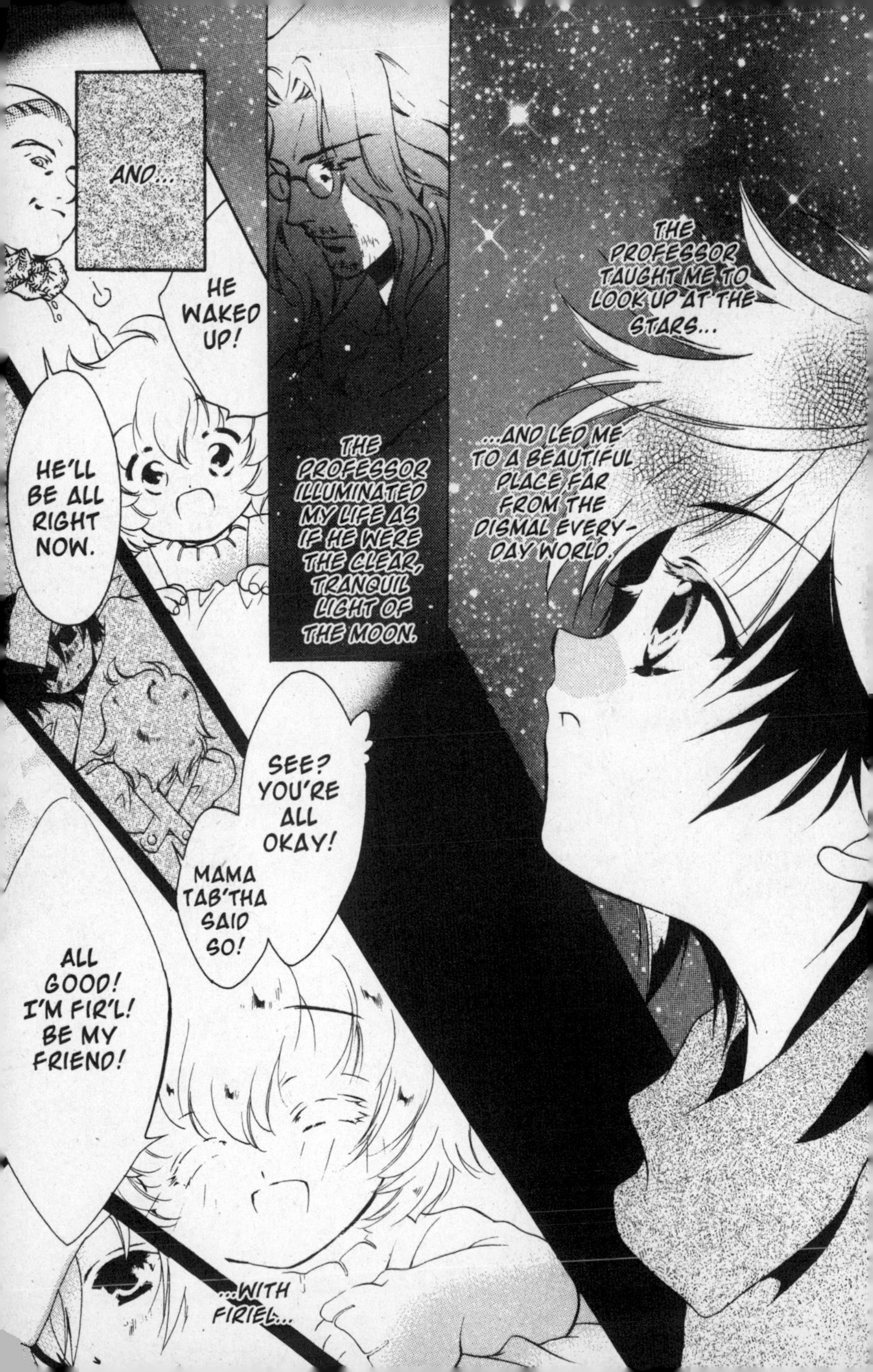
THE PROFESSOR TAUGHT ME TO LOOK UP AT THE STARS...
...AND LED ME TO A BEAUTIFUL PLACE FAR FROM THE DISMAL EVERY-DAY WORLD.
THE PROFESSOR ILLUMINATED MY LIFE AS IF HE WERE THE CLEAR, TRANQUIL LIGHT OF THE MOON.
AND...
HE WAKED UP!
HE'LL BE ALL RIGHT NOW.
SEE? YOU'RE ALL OKAY!
MAMA TAB'THA SAID SO!
ALL GOOD! I'M FIR'L! BE MY FRIEND!
...WITH FIRIEL...

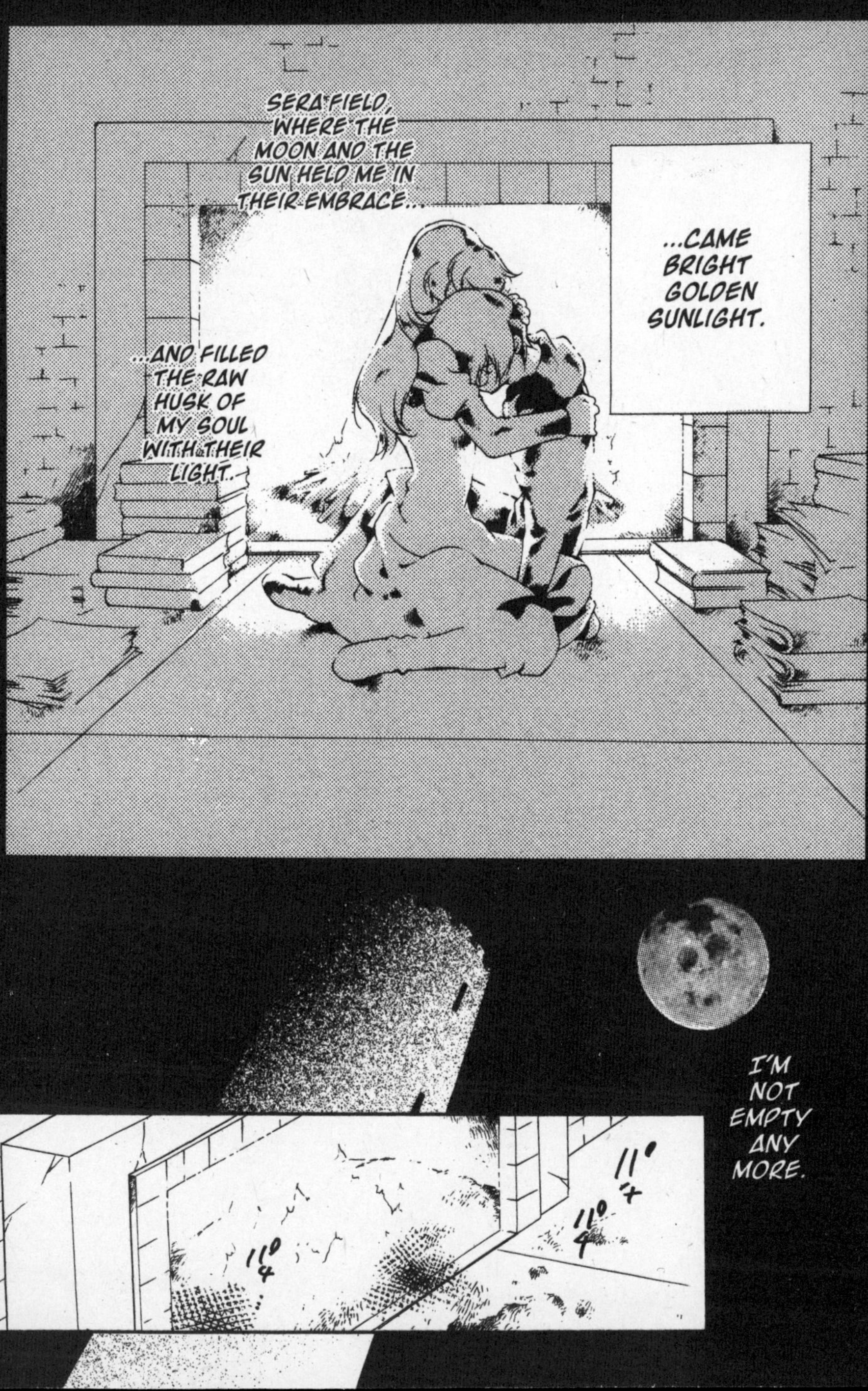
SERA FIELD, WHERE THE MOON AND THE SUN HELD ME IN THEIR EMBRACE...
...CAME BRIGHT GOLDEN SUNLIGHT.
...AND FILLED THE RAW HUSK OF MY SOUL WITH THEIR LIGHT.
I'M NOT EMPTY ANY MORE.

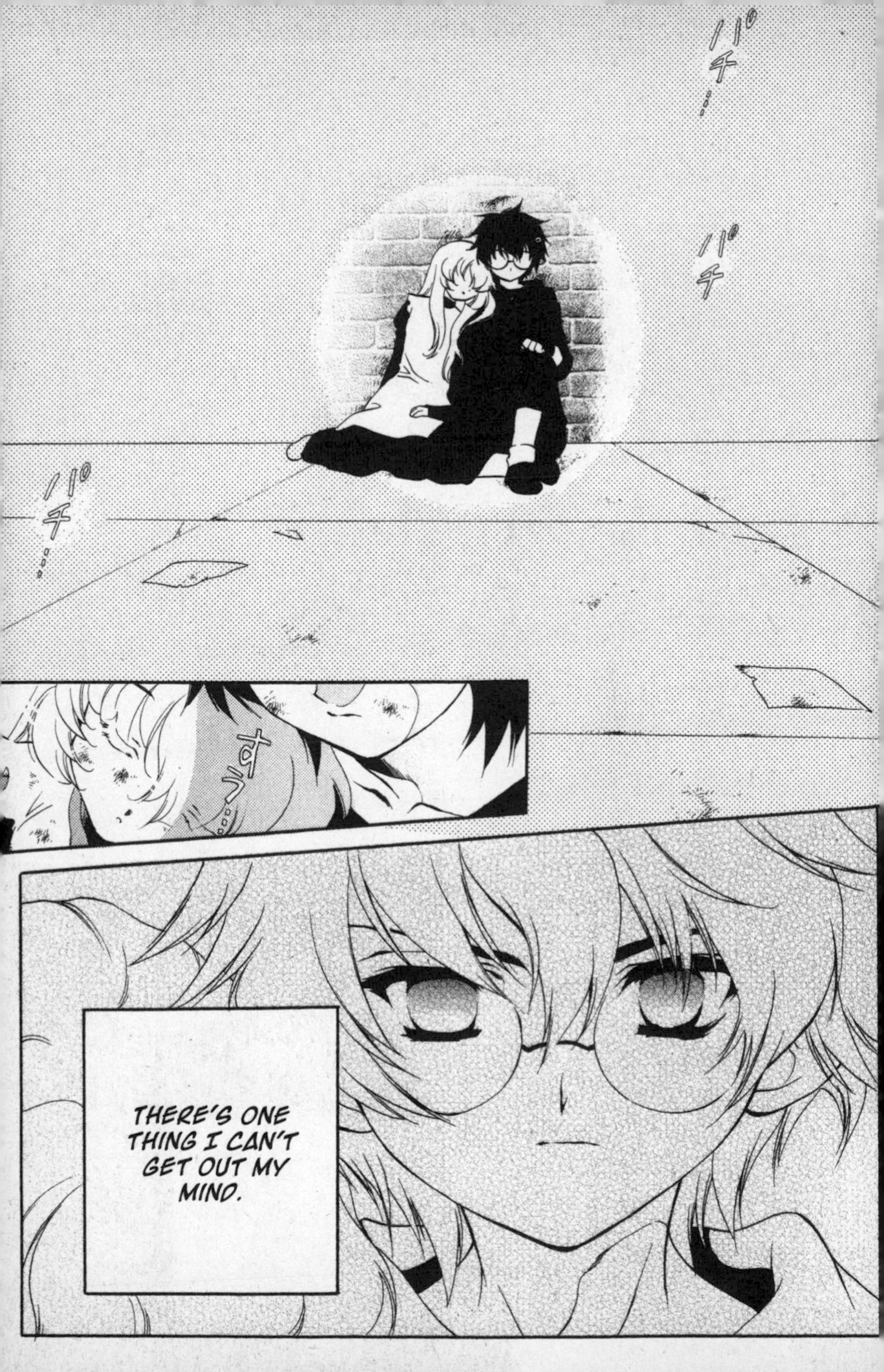
パチ…
パチ
パチ…
すぅ…
THERE'S ONE THING I CAN'T GET OUT MY MIND.

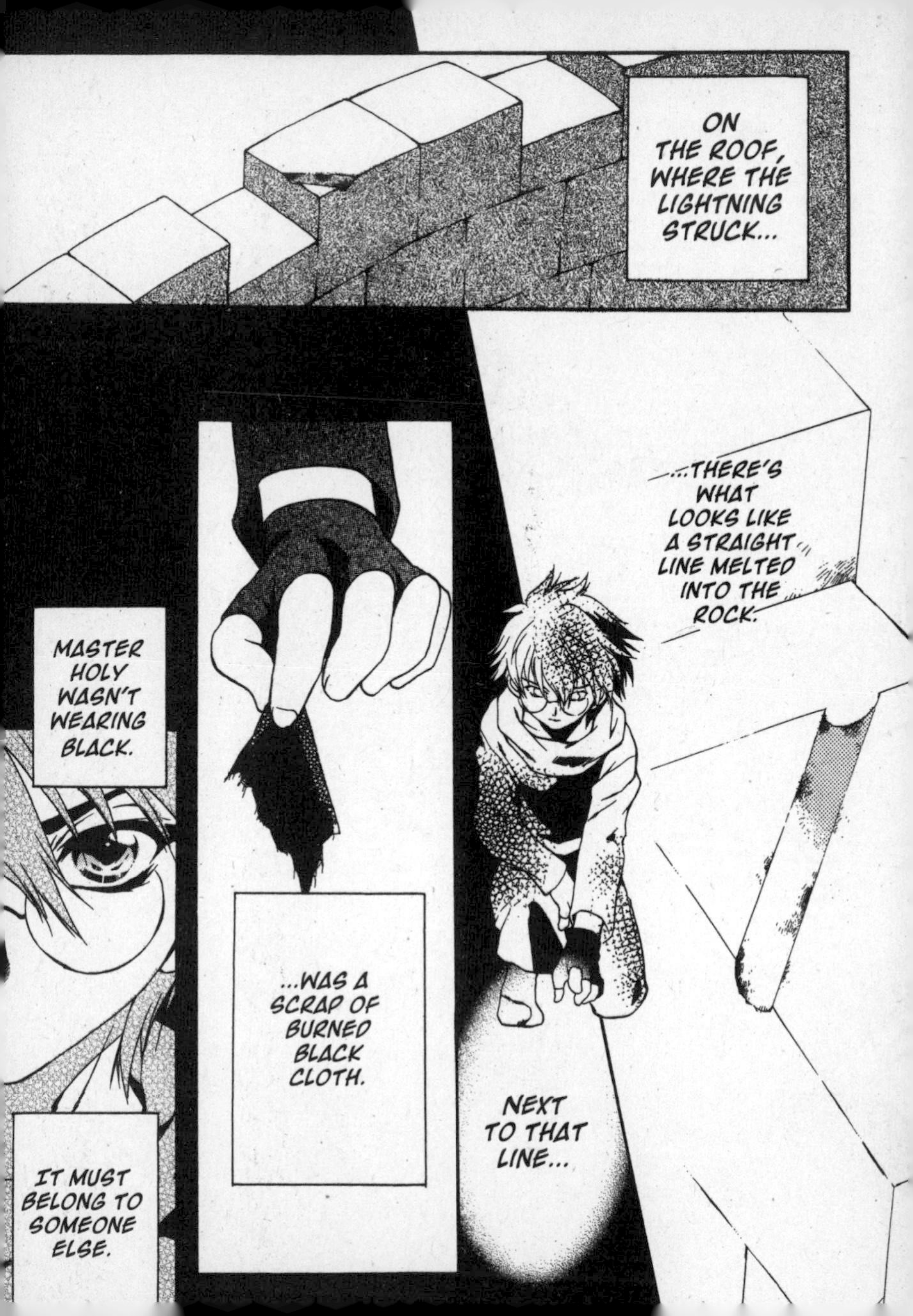
ON THE ROOF, WHERE THE LIGHTNING STRUCK...
...THERE'S WHAT LOOKS LIKE A STRAIGHT LINE MELTED INTO THE ROCK.
NEXT TO THAT LINE...
...WAS A SCRAP OF BURNED BLACK CLOTH.
MASTER HOLY WASN'T WEARING BLACK.
IT MUST BELONG TO SOMEONE ELSE.

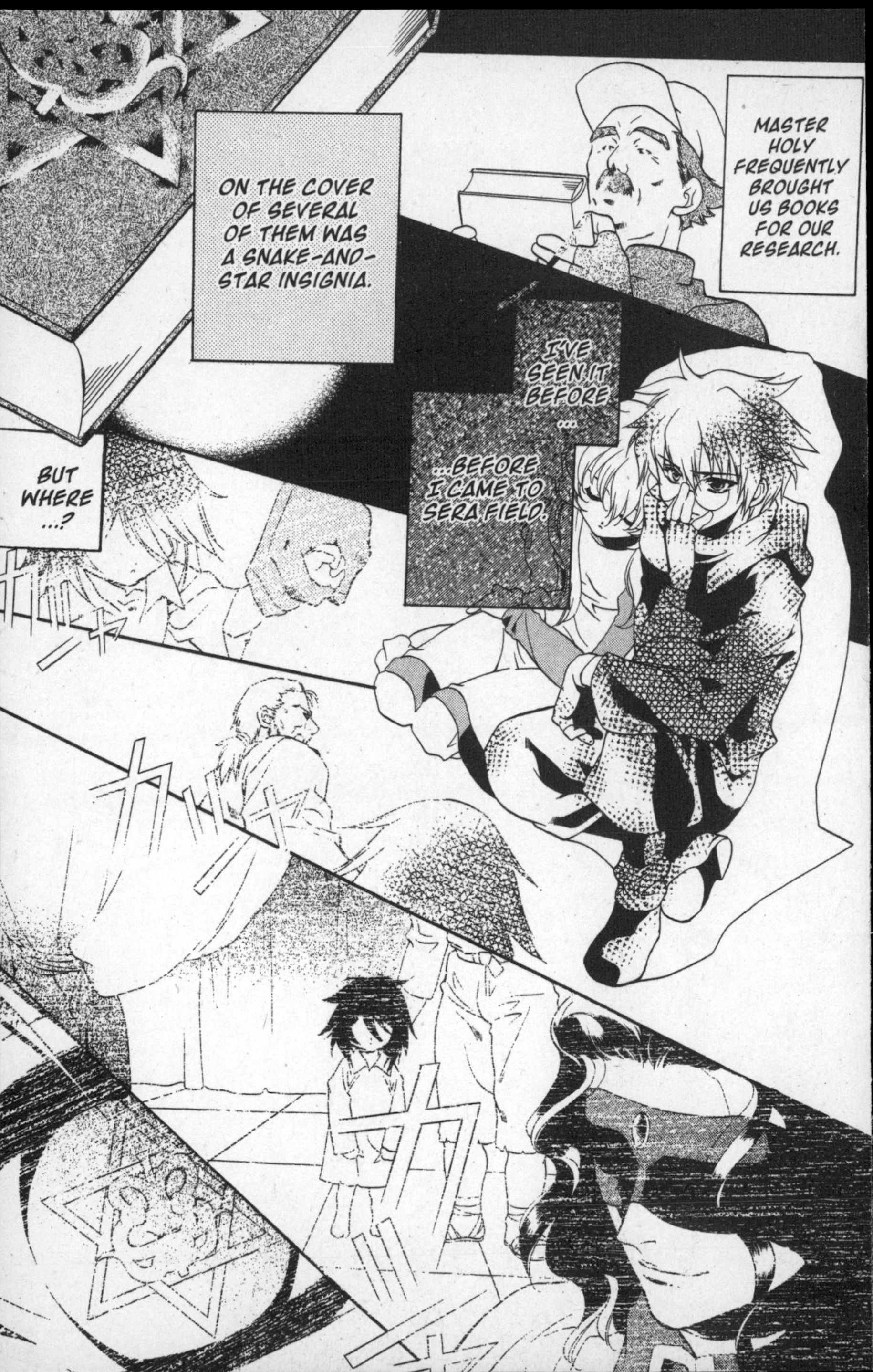
MASTER HOLY FREQUENTLY BROUGHT US BOOKS FOR OUR RESEARCH.
ON THE COVER OF SEVERAL OF THEM WAS A SNAKE-AND-STAR INSIGNIA.
I'VE SEEN IT BEFORE...
...BEFORE I CAME TO SERA FIELD.
BUT WHERE...?

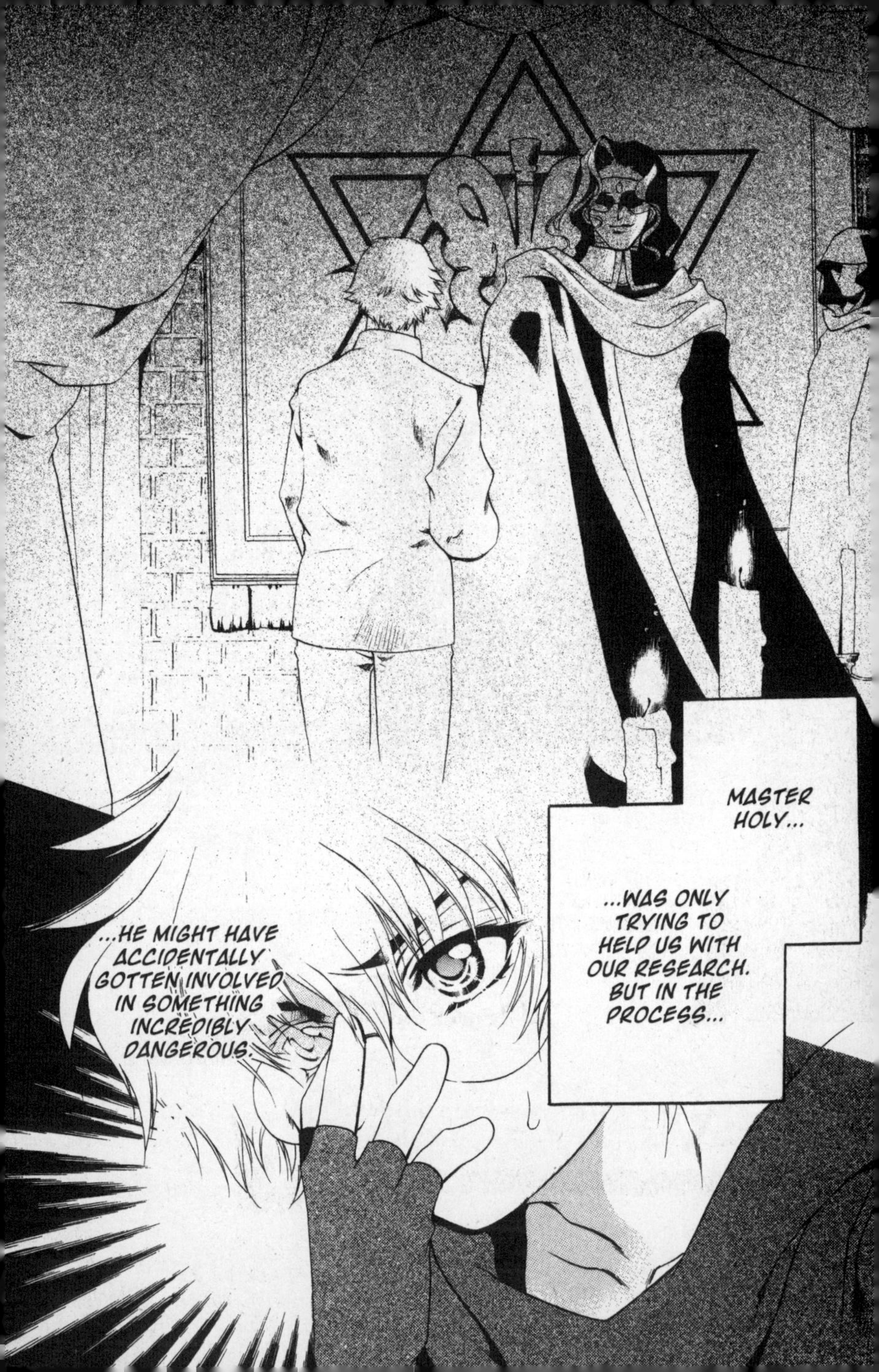
MASTER HOLY...
...WAS ONLY TRYING TO HELP US WITH OUR RESEARCH. BUT IN THE PROCESS...
...HE MIGHT HAVE ACCIDENTALLY GOTTEN INVOLVED IN SOMETHING INCREDIBLY DANGEROUS.

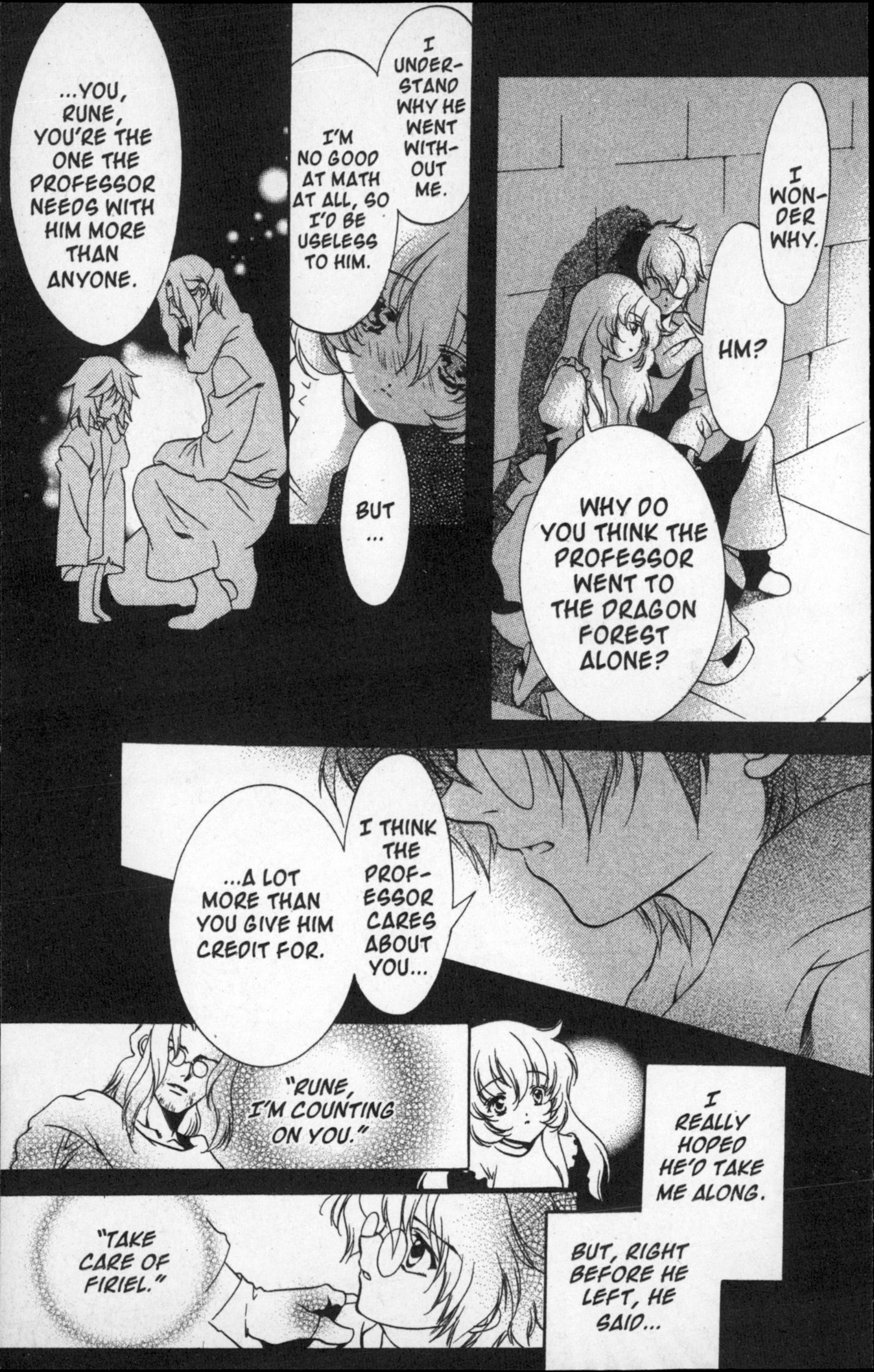
I WONDER WHY.
HM?
WHY DO YOU THINK THE PROFESSOR WENT TO THE DRAGON FOREST ALONE?
I UNDERSTAND WHY HE WENT WITHOUT ME.
I'M NO GOOD AT MATH AT ALL, SO I'D BE USELESS TO HIM.
BUT...
...YOU, RUNE, YOU'RE THE ONE THE PROFESSOR NEEDS WITH HIM MORE THAN ANYONE.
I THINK THE PROFESSOR CARES ABOUT YOU...
...A LOT MORE THAN YOU GIVE HIM CREDIT FOR.
I REALLY HOPED HE'D TAKE ME ALONG.
"RUNE, I'M COUNTING ON YOU."
BUT, RIGHT BEFORE HE LEFT, HE SAID...
"TAKE CARE OF FIRIEL."

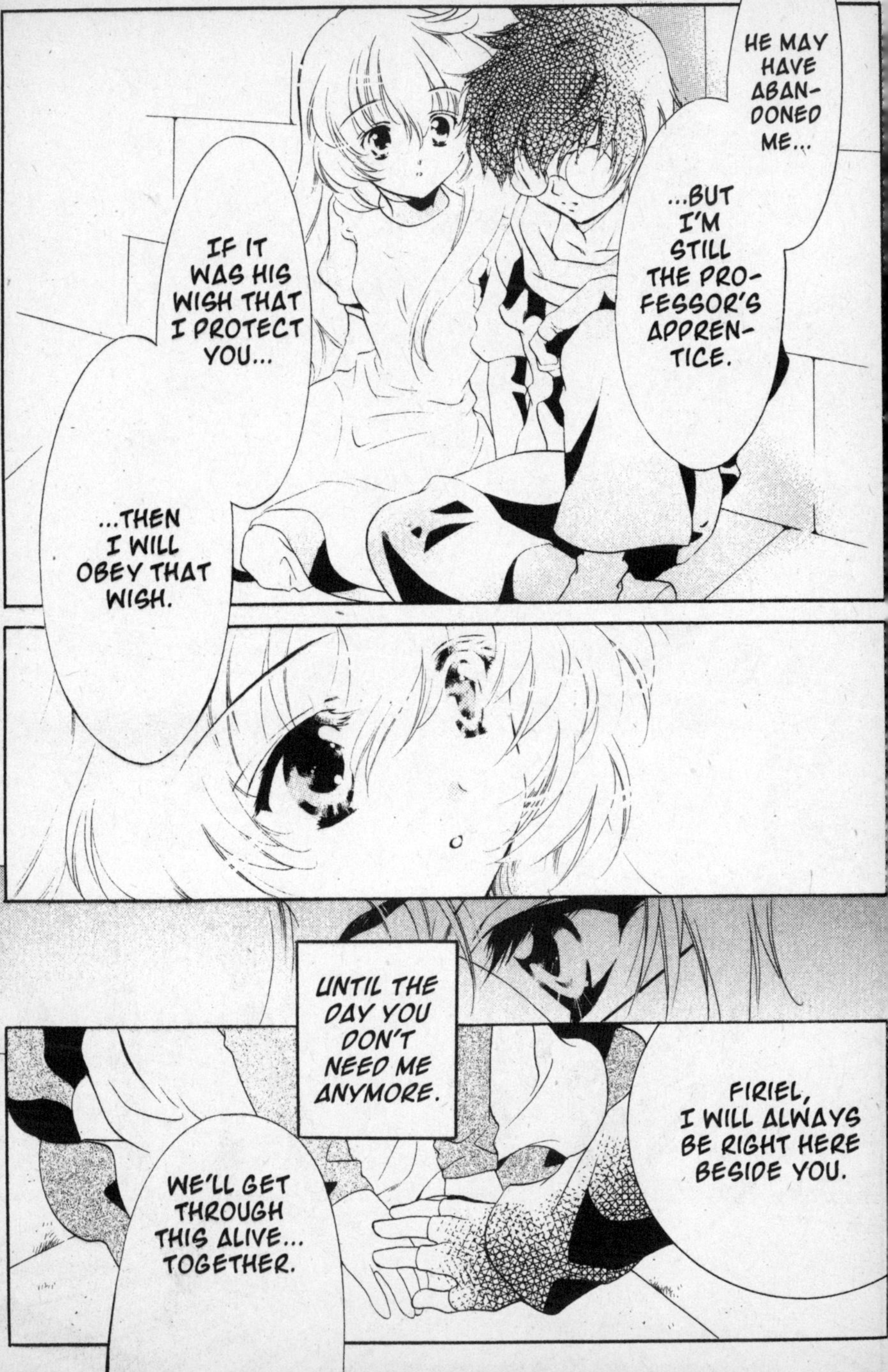
HE MAY HAVE ABAN-DONED ME...
...BUT I'M STILL THE PRO-FESSOR'S APPREN-TICE.
IF IT WAS HIS WISH THAT I PROTECT YOU...
...THEN I WILL OBEY THAT WISH.
FIRIEL, I WILL ALWAYS BE RIGHT HERE BESIDE YOU.
UNTIL THE DAY YOU DON'T NEED ME ANYMORE.
WE'LL GET THROUGH THIS ALIVE... TOGETHER.

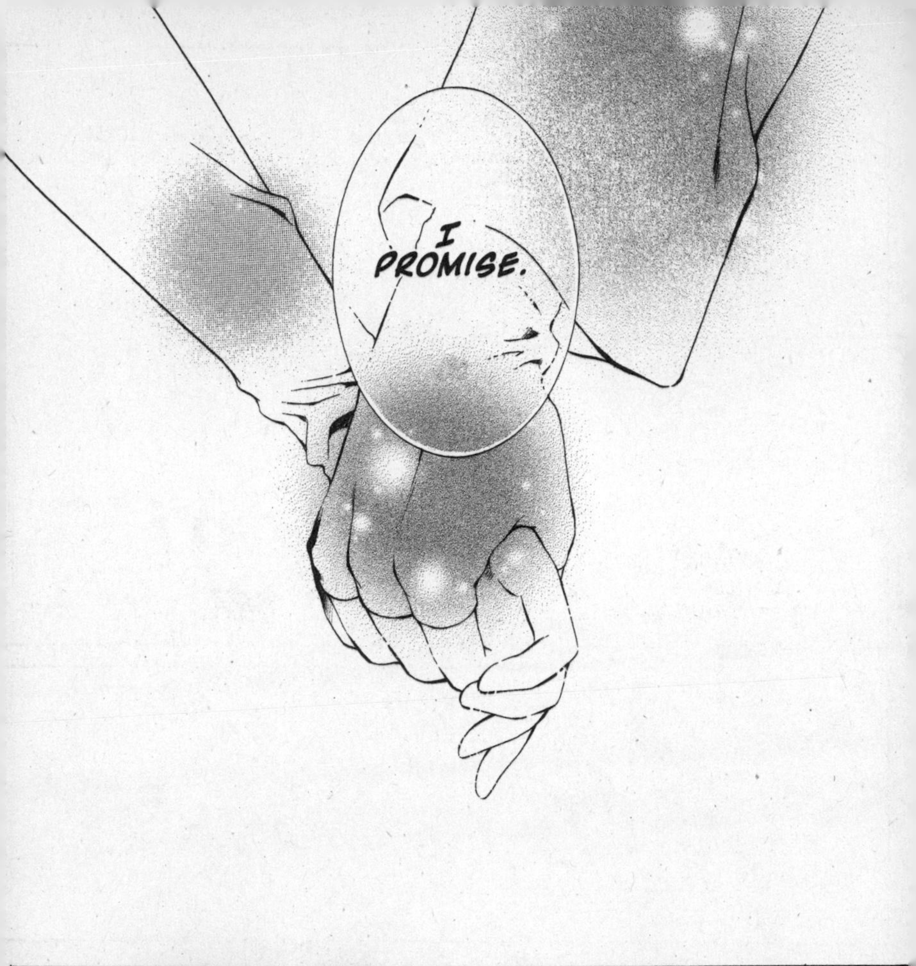
I PROMISE.
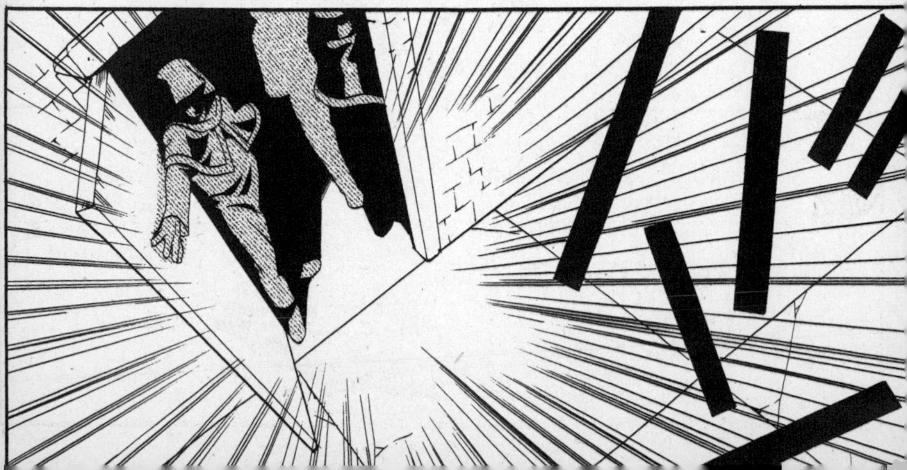

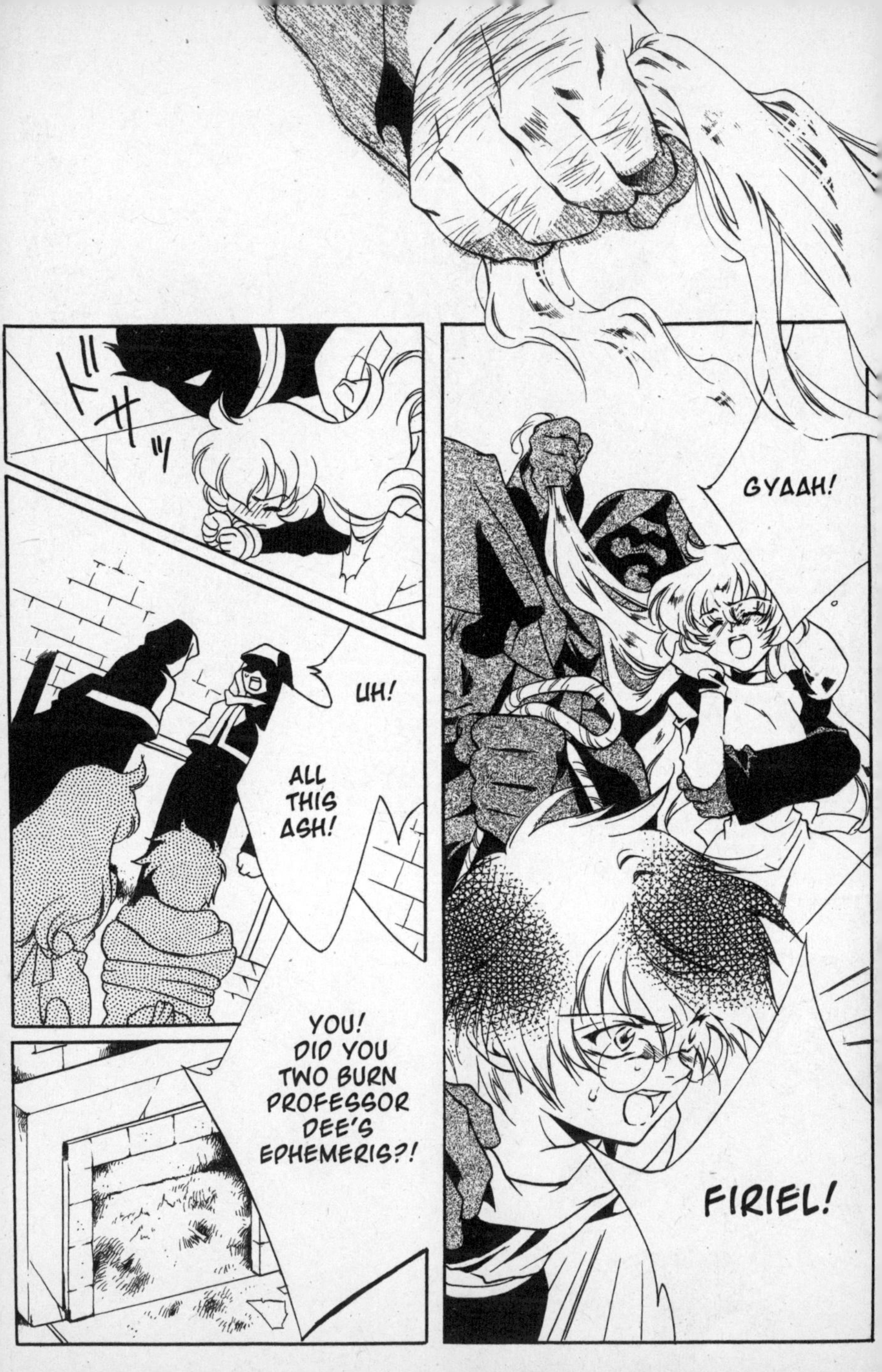
GYAAH!
FIRIEL!
ドサッ
UH!
ALL THIS ASH!
YOU! DID YOU TWO BURN PROFESSOR DEE'S EPHEMERIS?!

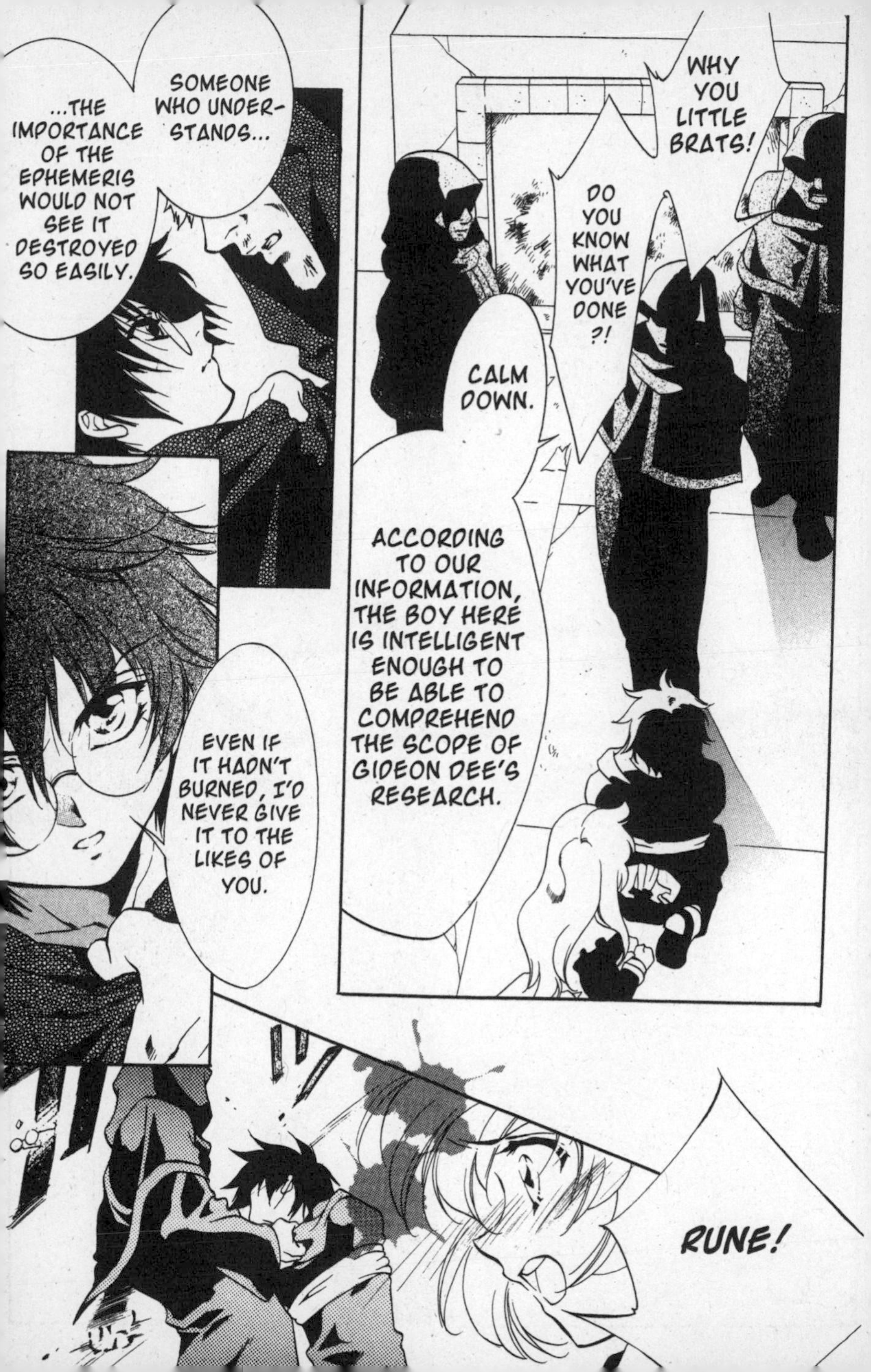
WHY YOU LITTLE BRATS!
DO YOU KNOW WHAT YOU'VE DONE?!
CALM DOWN.
ACCORDING TO OUR INFORMATION, THE BOY HERE IS INTELLIGENT ENOUGH TO BE ABLE TO COMPREHEND THE SCOPE OF GIDEON DEE'S RESEARCH.
SOMEONE WHO UNDERSTANDS...
...THE IMPORTANCE OF THE EPHEMERIS WOULD NOT SEE IT DESTROYED SO EASILY.
EVEN IF IT HADN'T BURNED, I'D NEVER GIVE IT TO THE LIKES OF YOU.
RUNE!

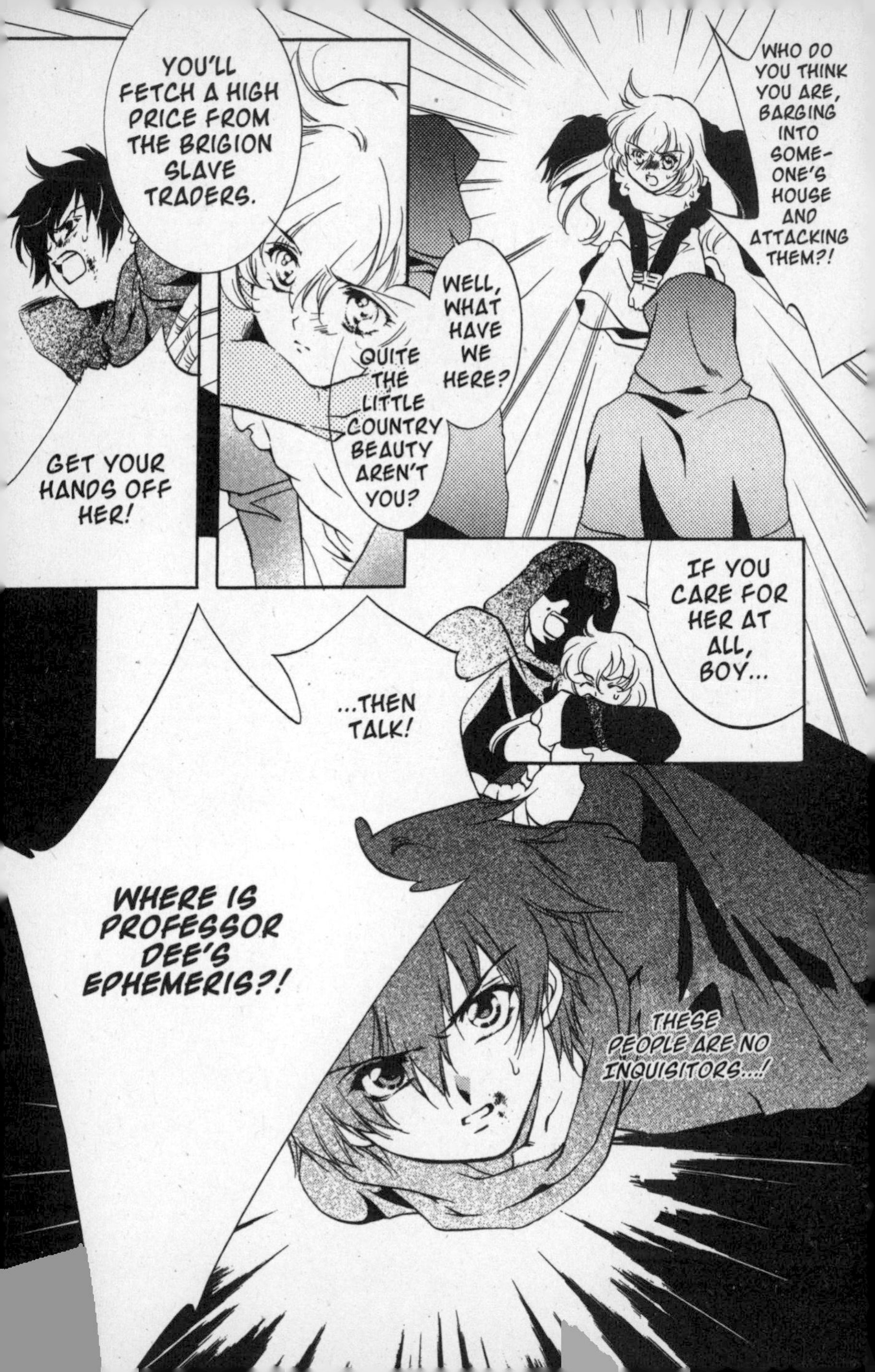
WHO DO YOU THINK YOU ARE, BARGING INTO SOME-ONE'S HOUSE AND ATTACKING THEM?!
WELL, WHAT HAVE WE HERE?
QUITE THE LITTLE COUNTRY BEAUTY AREN'T YOU?
YOU'LL FETCH A HIGH PRICE FROM THE BRIGION SLAVE TRADERS.
GET YOUR HANDS OFF HER!
IF YOU CARE FOR HER AT ALL, BOY...
...THEN TALK!
WHERE IS PROFESSOR DEE'S EPHEMERIS?!
THESE PEOPLE ARE NO INQUISITORS...!

Chapter 4: Where Have All the Little Goats Gone? (Part 1)

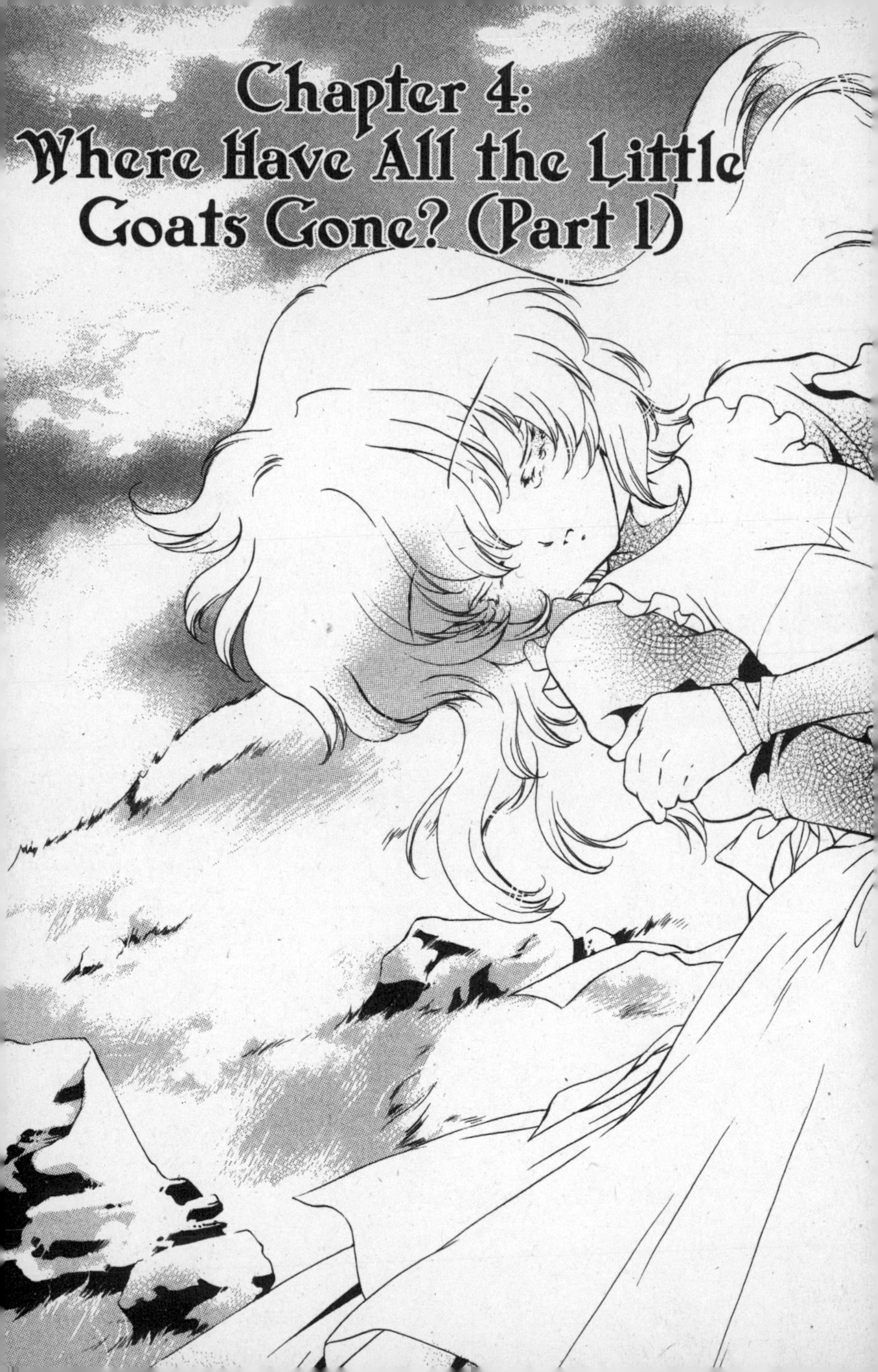

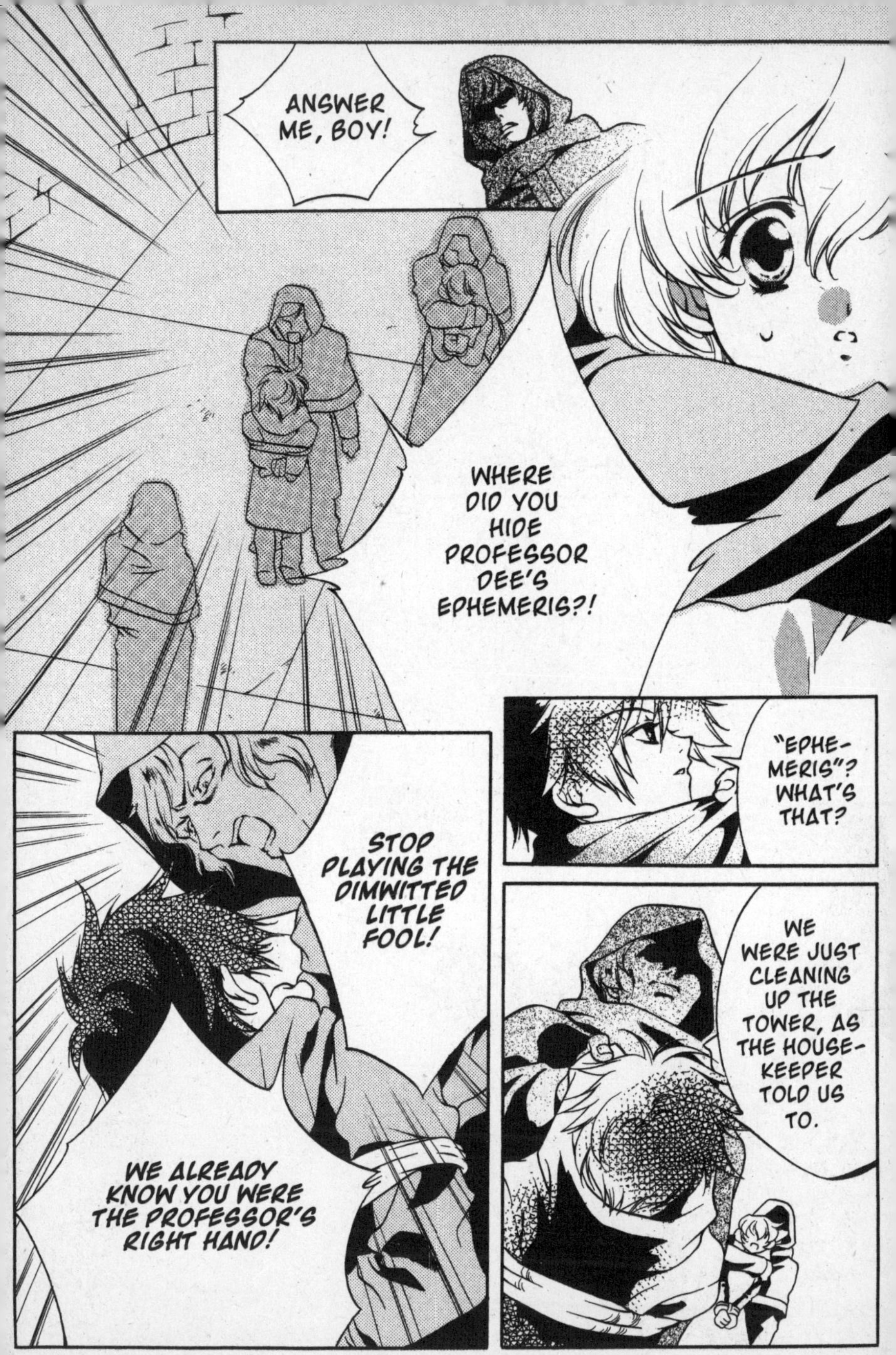
ANSWER ME, BOY!
WHERE DID YOU HIDE PROFESSOR DEE'S EPHEMERIS?!
"EPHE-MERIS"? WHAT'S THAT?
WE WERE JUST CLEANING UP THE TOWER, AS THE HOUSE-KEEPER TOLD US TO.
STOP PLAYING THE DIMWITTED LITTLE FOOL!
WE ALREADY KNOW YOU WERE THE PROFESSOR'S RIGHT HAND!

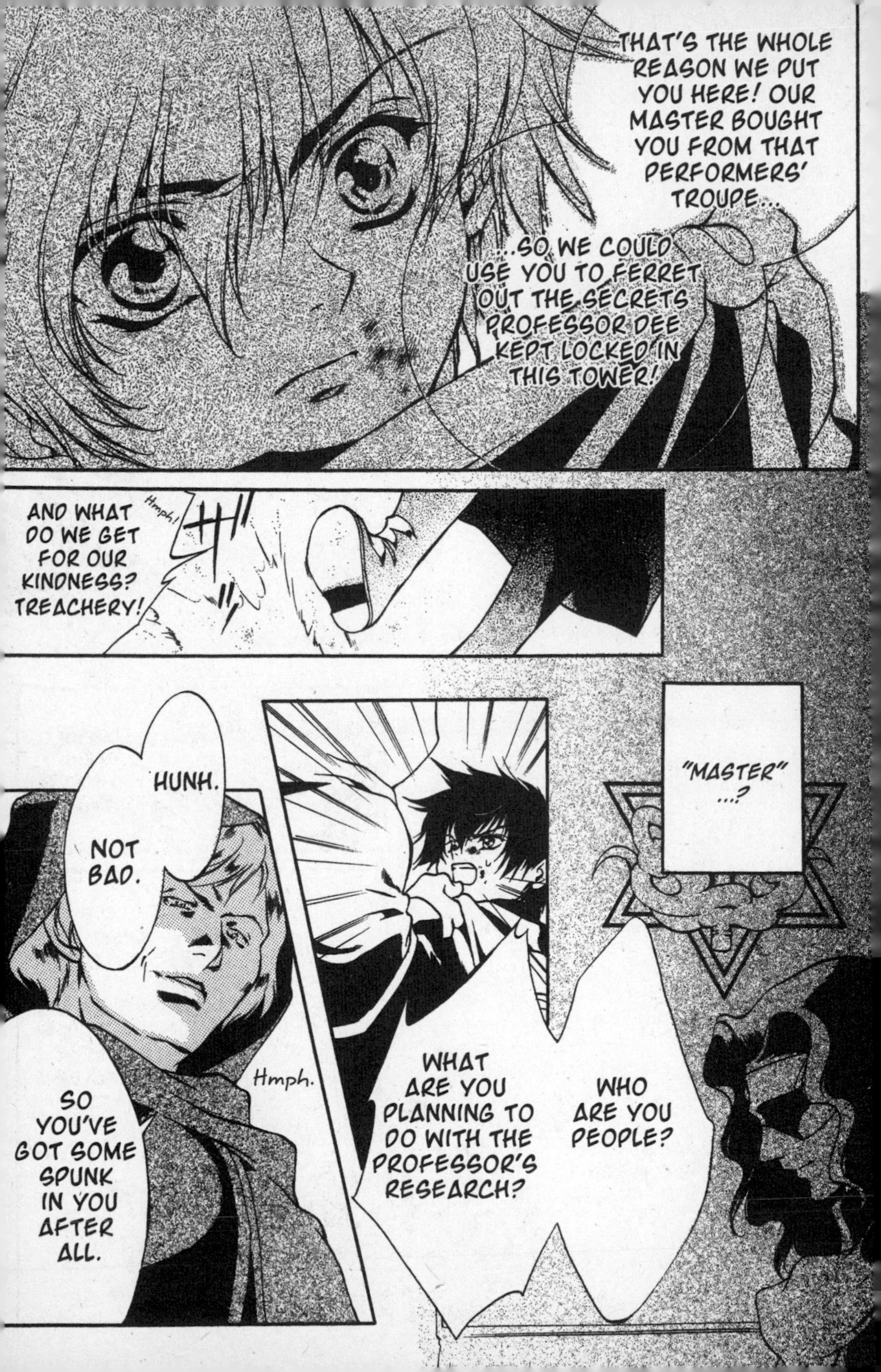
THAT'S THE WHOLE REASON WE PUT YOU HERE! OUR MASTER BOUGHT YOU FROM THAT PERFORMERS' TROUPE...
...SO WE COULD USE YOU TO FERRET OUT THE SECRETS PROFESSOR DEE KEPT LOCKED IN THIS TOWER!
Hmph!
AND WHAT DO WE GET FOR OUR KINDNESS? TREACHERY!
"MASTER" ...?
WHO ARE YOU PEOPLE?
WHAT ARE YOU PLANNING TO DO WITH THE PROFESSOR'S RESEARCH?
HUNH.
NOT BAD.
Hmph.
SO YOU'VE GOT SOME SPUNK IN YOU AFTER ALL.

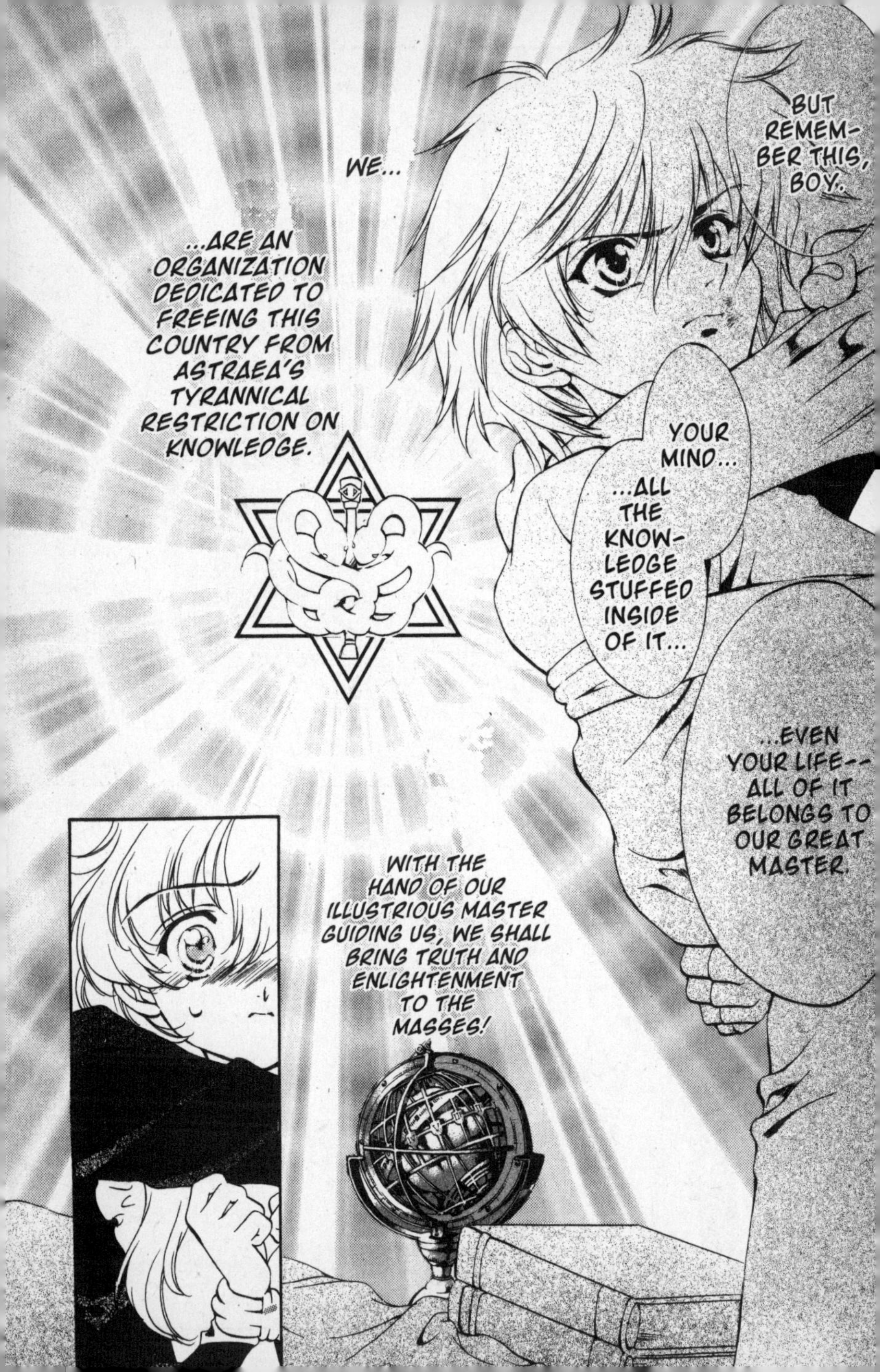
BUT REMEMBER THIS, BOY.
WE...
...ARE AN ORGANIZATION DEDICATED TO FREEING THIS COUNTRY FROM ASTRAEA'S TYRANNICAL RESTRICTION ON KNOWLEDGE.
YOUR MIND...
...ALL THE KNOWLEDGE STUFFED INSIDE OF IT...
...EVEN YOUR LIFE--ALL OF IT BELONGS TO OUR GREAT MASTER.
WITH THE HAND OF OUR ILLUSTRIOUS MASTER GUIDING US, WE SHALL BRING TRUTH AND ENLIGHTENMENT TO THE MASSES!

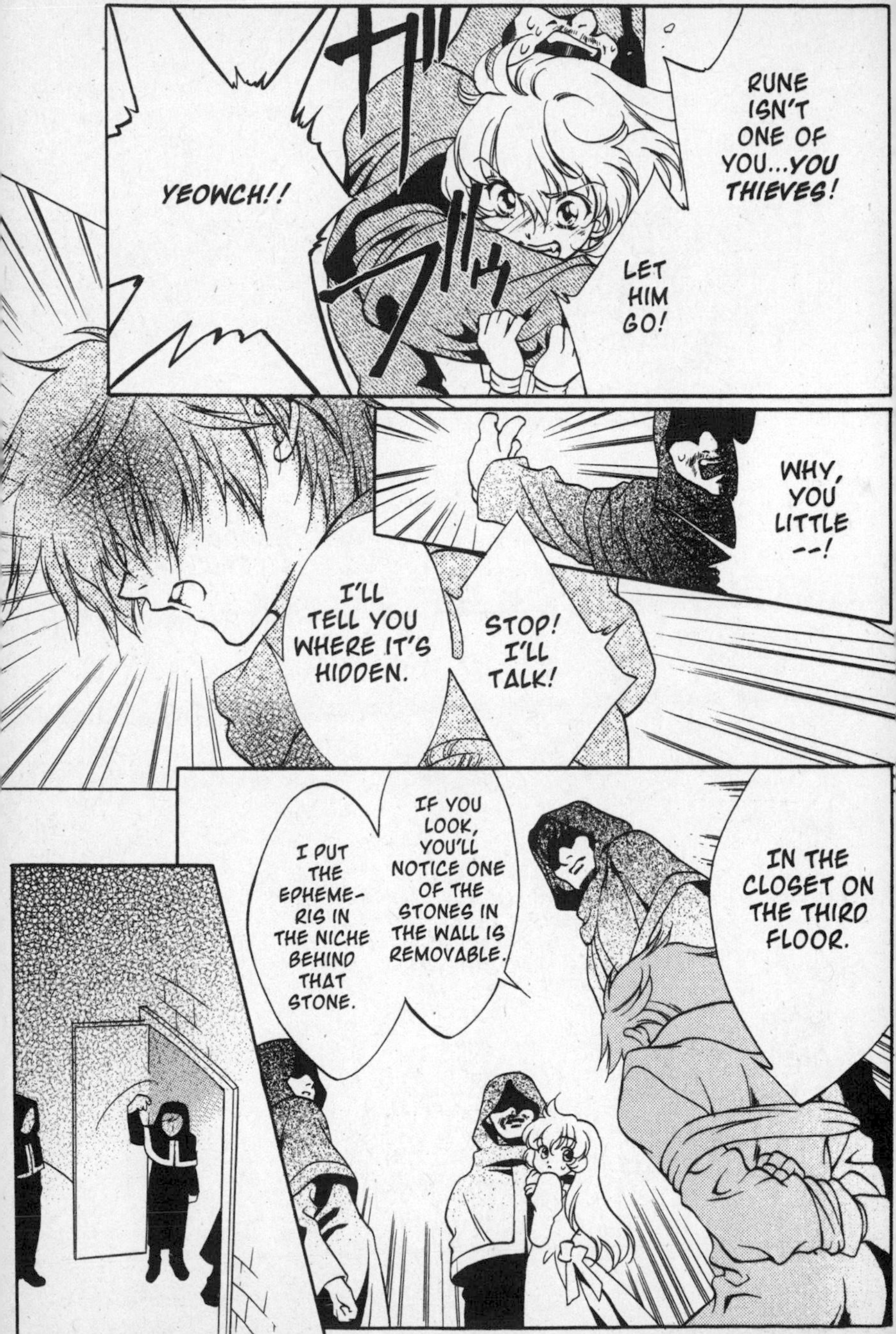
RUNE ISN'T ONE OF YOU...YOU THIEVES!
LET HIM GO!
YEOWCH!!
WHY, YOU LITTLE --!
STOP! I'LL TALK!
I'LL TELL YOU WHERE IT'S HIDDEN.
IN THE CLOSET ON THE THIRD FLOOR.
IF YOU LOOK, YOU'LL NOTICE ONE OF THE STONES IN THE WALL IS REMOVABLE.
I PUT THE EPHEME-RIS IN THE NICHE BEHIND THAT STONE.

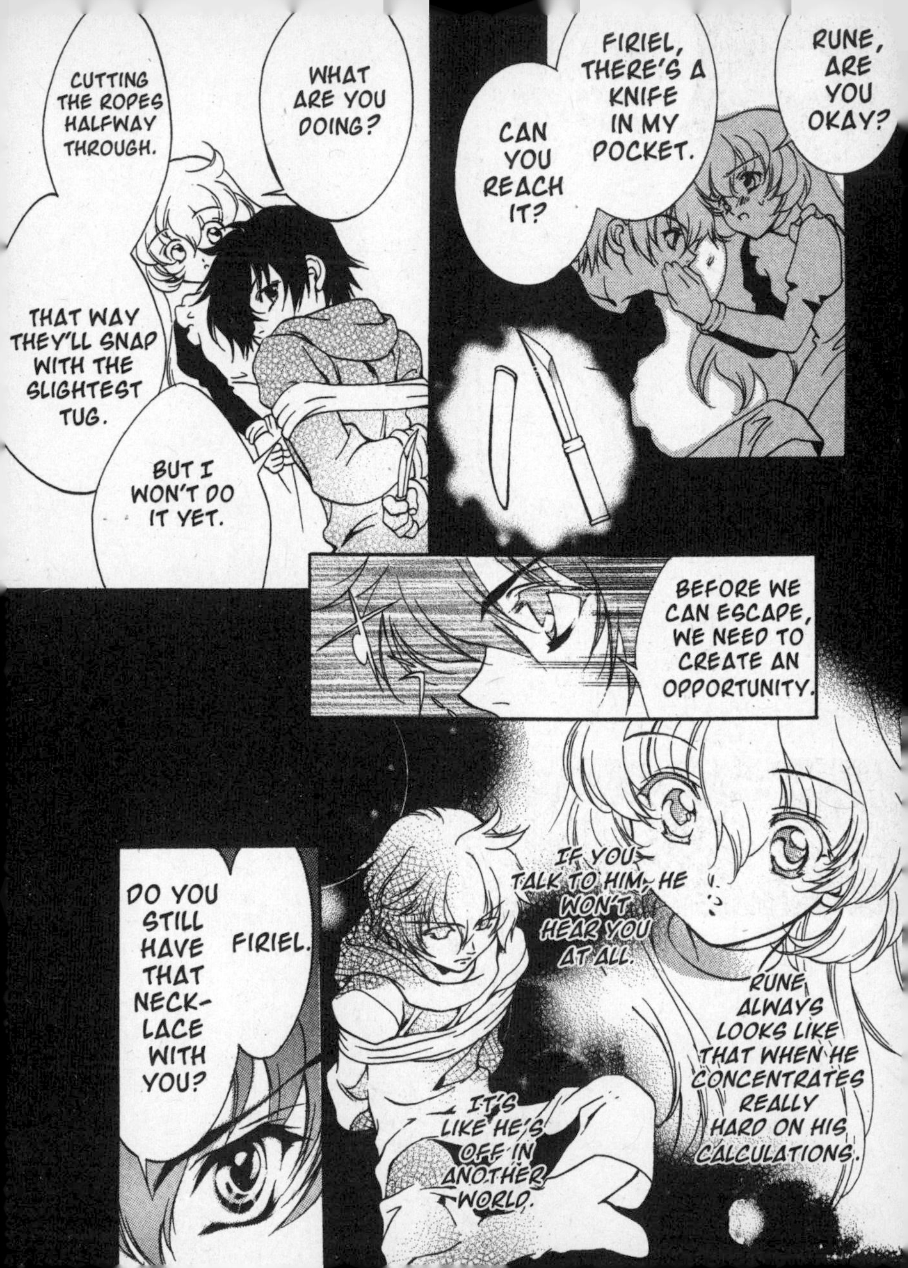
RUNE, ARE YOU OKAY?
FIRIEL, THERE'S A KNIFE IN MY POCKET.
CAN YOU REACH IT?
WHAT ARE YOU DOING?
CUTTING THE ROPES HALFWAY THROUGH.
THAT WAY THEY'LL SNAP WITH THE SLIGHTEST TUG.
BUT I WON'T DO IT YET.
BEFORE WE CAN ESCAPE, WE NEED TO CREATE AN OPPORTUNITY.
IF YOU TALK TO HIM, HE WON'T HEAR YOU AT ALL.
RUNE ALWAYS LOOKS LIKE THAT WHEN HE CONCENTRATES REALLY HARD ON HIS CALCULATIONS.
IT'S LIKE HE'S OFF IN ANOTHER WORLD.
FIRIEL.
DO YOU STILL HAVE THAT NECKLACE WITH YOU?

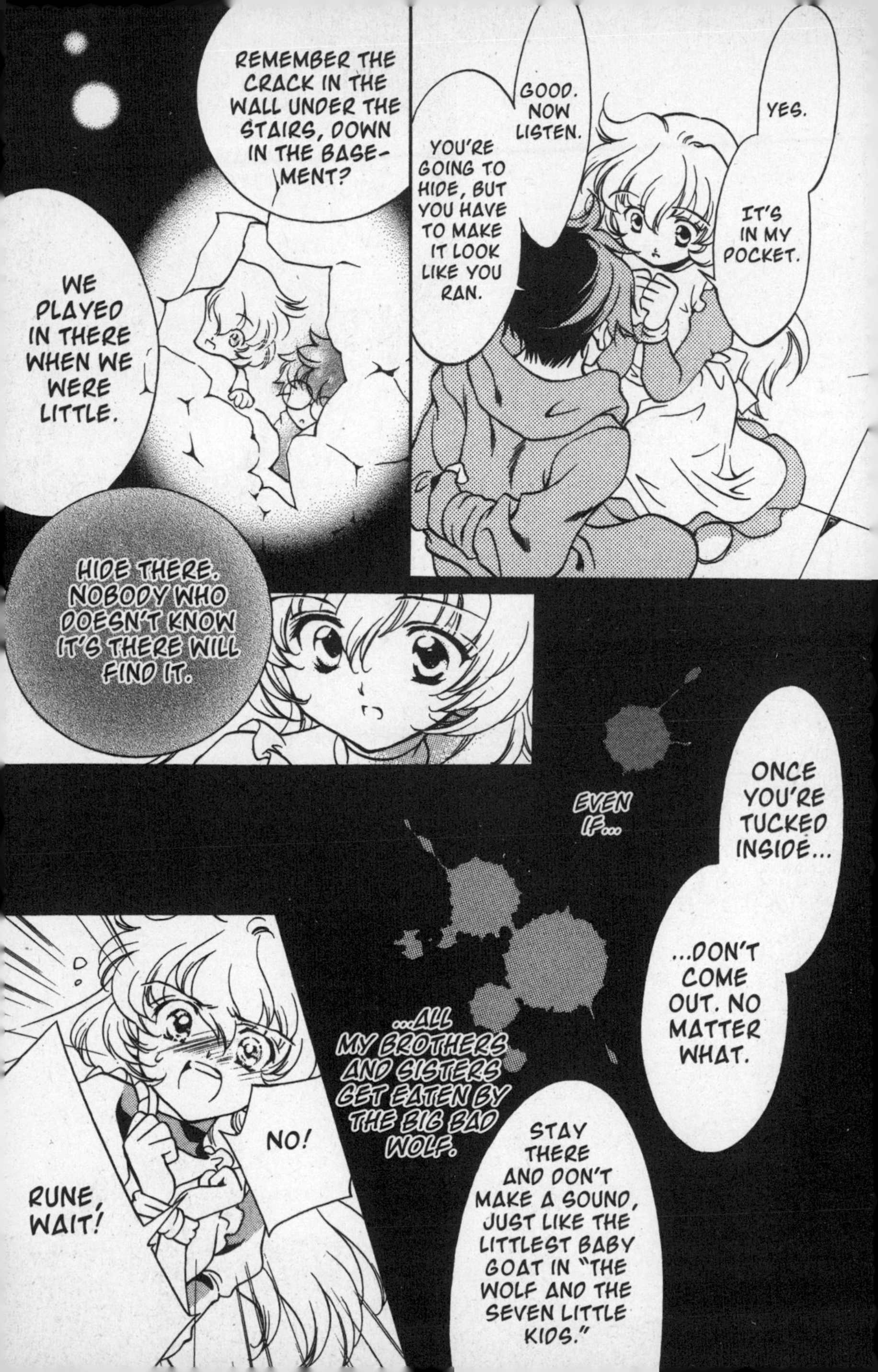
YES.
IT'S IN MY POCKET.
GOOD. NOW LISTEN.
YOU'RE GOING TO HIDE, BUT YOU HAVE TO MAKE IT LOOK LIKE YOU RAN.
REMEMBER THE CRACK IN THE WALL UNDER THE STAIRS, DOWN IN THE BASE-MENT?
WE PLAYED IN THERE WHEN WE WERE LITTLE.
HIDE THERE. NOBODY WHO DOESN'T KNOW IT'S THERE WILL FIND IT.
ONCE YOU'RE TUCKED INSIDE...
EVEN IF...
...DON'T COME OUT. NO MATTER WHAT.
...ALL MY BROTHERS AND SISTERS GET EATEN BY THE BIG BAD WOLF.
STAY THERE AND DON'T MAKE A SOUND, JUST LIKE THE LITTLEST BABY GOAT IN "THE WOLF AND THE SEVEN LITTLE KIDS."
NO!
RUNE, WAIT!

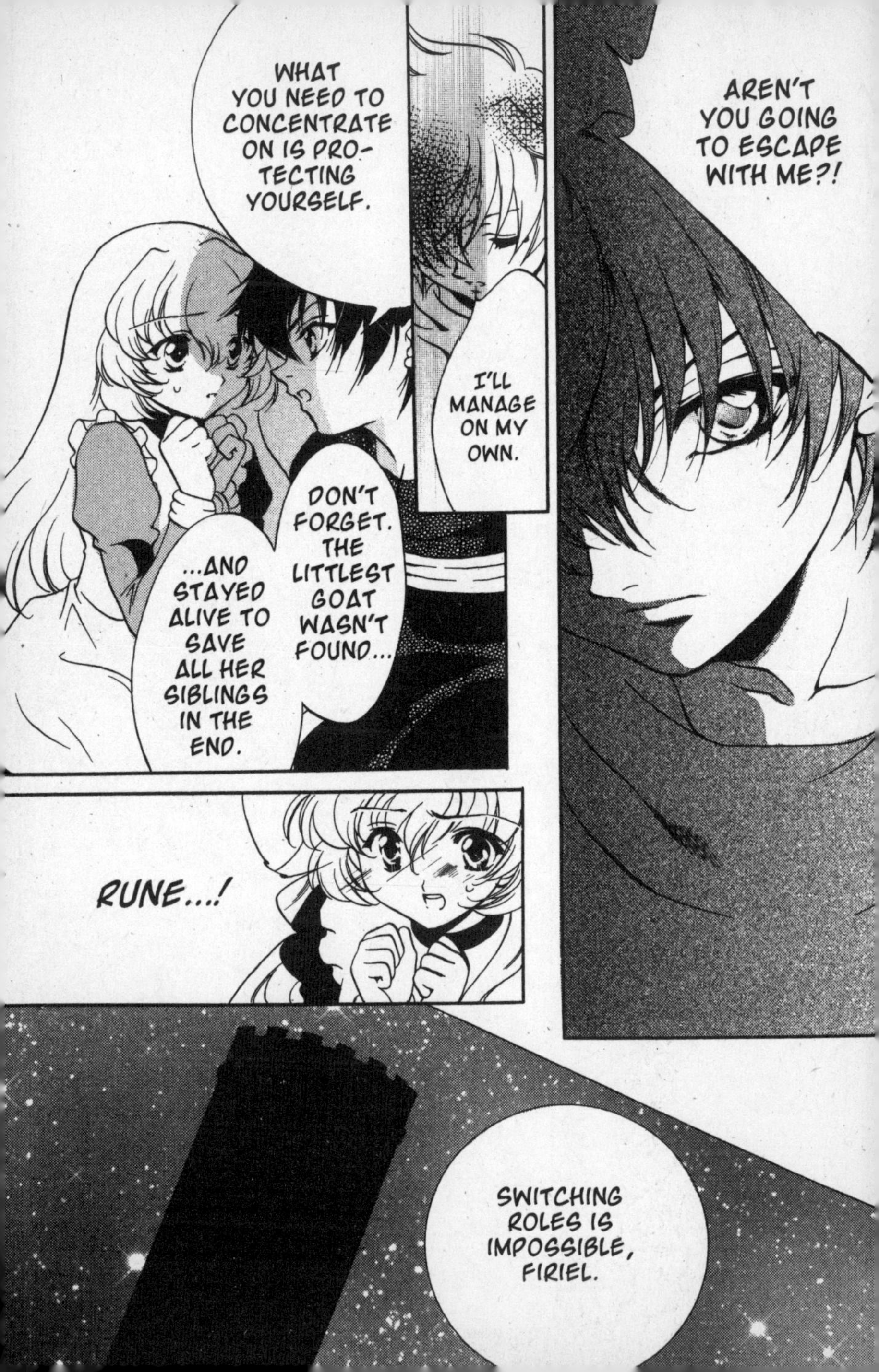
AREN'T YOU GOING TO ESCAPE WITH ME?!
WHAT YOU NEED TO CONCENTRATE ON IS PRO-TECTING YOURSELF.
I'LL MANAGE ON MY OWN.
DON'T FORGET. THE LITTLEST GOAT WASN'T FOUND...
...AND STAYED ALIVE TO SAVE ALL HER SIBLINGS IN THE END.
RUNE...!
SWITCHING ROLES IS IMPOSSIBLE, FIRIEL.

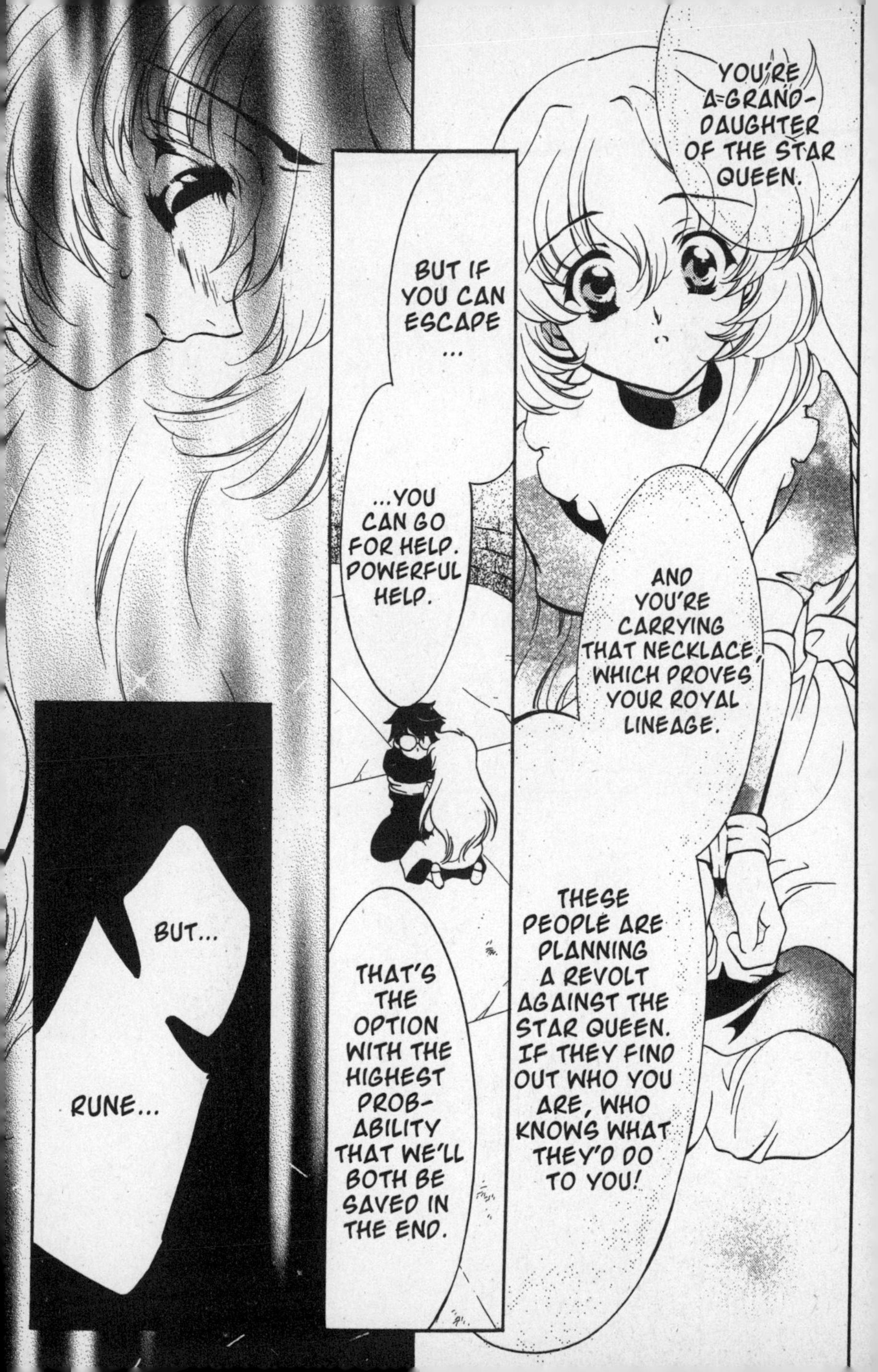
YOU'RE A GRAND-DAUGHTER OF THE STAR QUEEN.
AND YOU'RE CARRYING THAT NECKLACE, WHICH PROVES YOUR ROYAL LINEAGE.
THESE PEOPLE ARE PLANNING A REVOLT AGAINST THE STAR QUEEN. IF THEY FIND OUT WHO YOU ARE, WHO KNOWS WHAT THEY'D DO TO YOU!
BUT IF YOU CAN ESCAPE ...
...YOU CAN GO FOR HELP. POWERFUL HELP.
THAT'S THE OPTION WITH THE HIGHEST PROB-ABILITY THAT WE'LL BOTH BE SAVED IN THE END.
BUT...
RUNE...

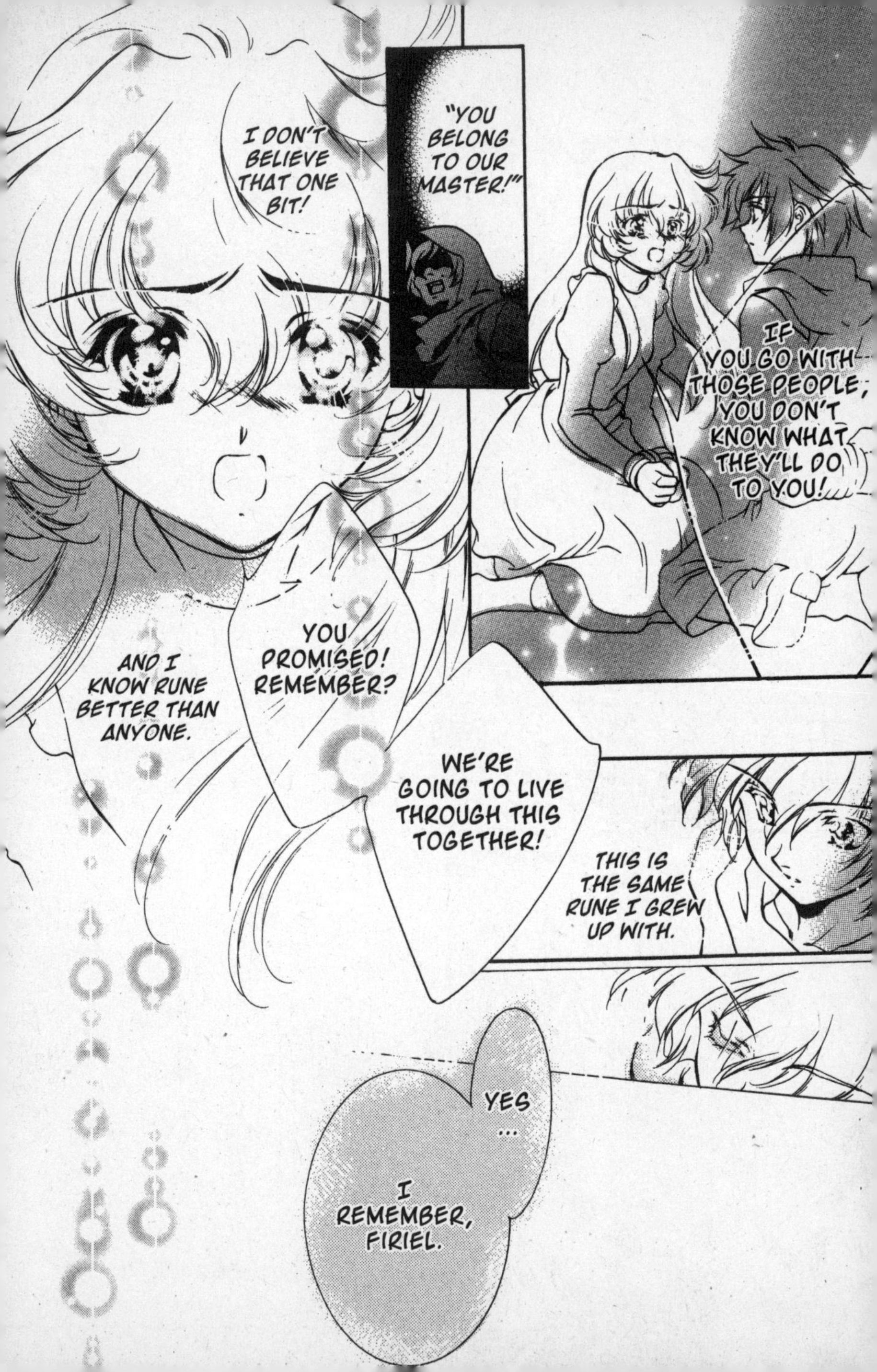
IF YOU GO WITH THOSE PEOPLE, YOU DON'T KNOW WHAT THEY'LL DO TO YOU!
"YOU BELONG TO OUR MASTER!"
I DON'T BELIEVE THAT ONE BIT!
AND I KNOW RUNE BETTER THAN ANYONE.
YOU PROMISED! REMEMBER?
WE'RE GOING TO LIVE THROUGH THIS TOGETHER!
THIS IS THE SAME RUNE I GREW UP WITH.
YES...
I REMEMBER, FIRIEL.

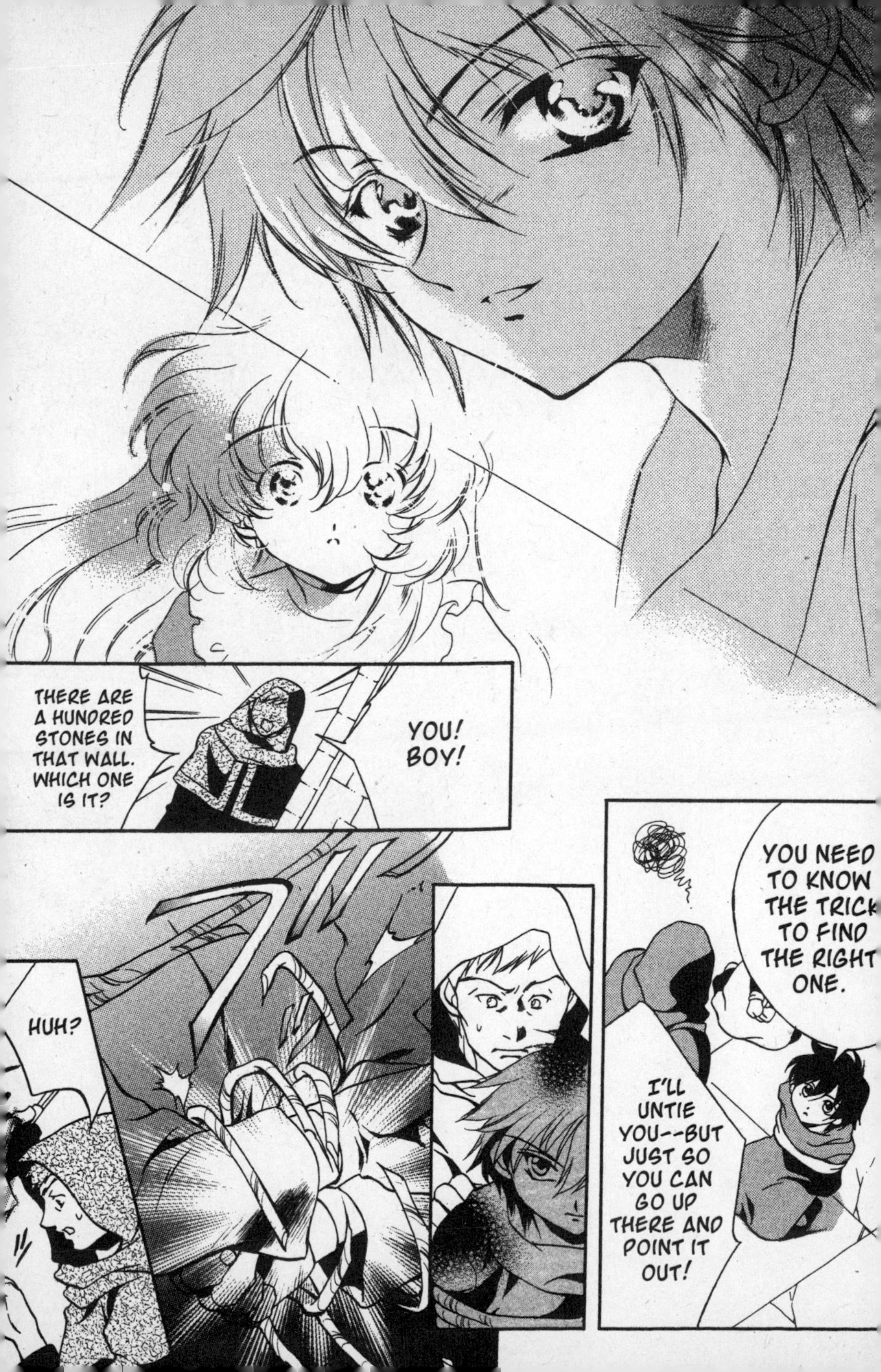
YOU! BOY!
THERE ARE A HUNDRED STONES IN THAT WALL. WHICH ONE IS IT?
YOU NEED TO KNOW THE TRICK TO FIND THE RIGHT ONE.
I'LL UNTIE YOU--BUT JUST SO YOU CAN GO UP THERE AND POINT IT OUT!
HUH?

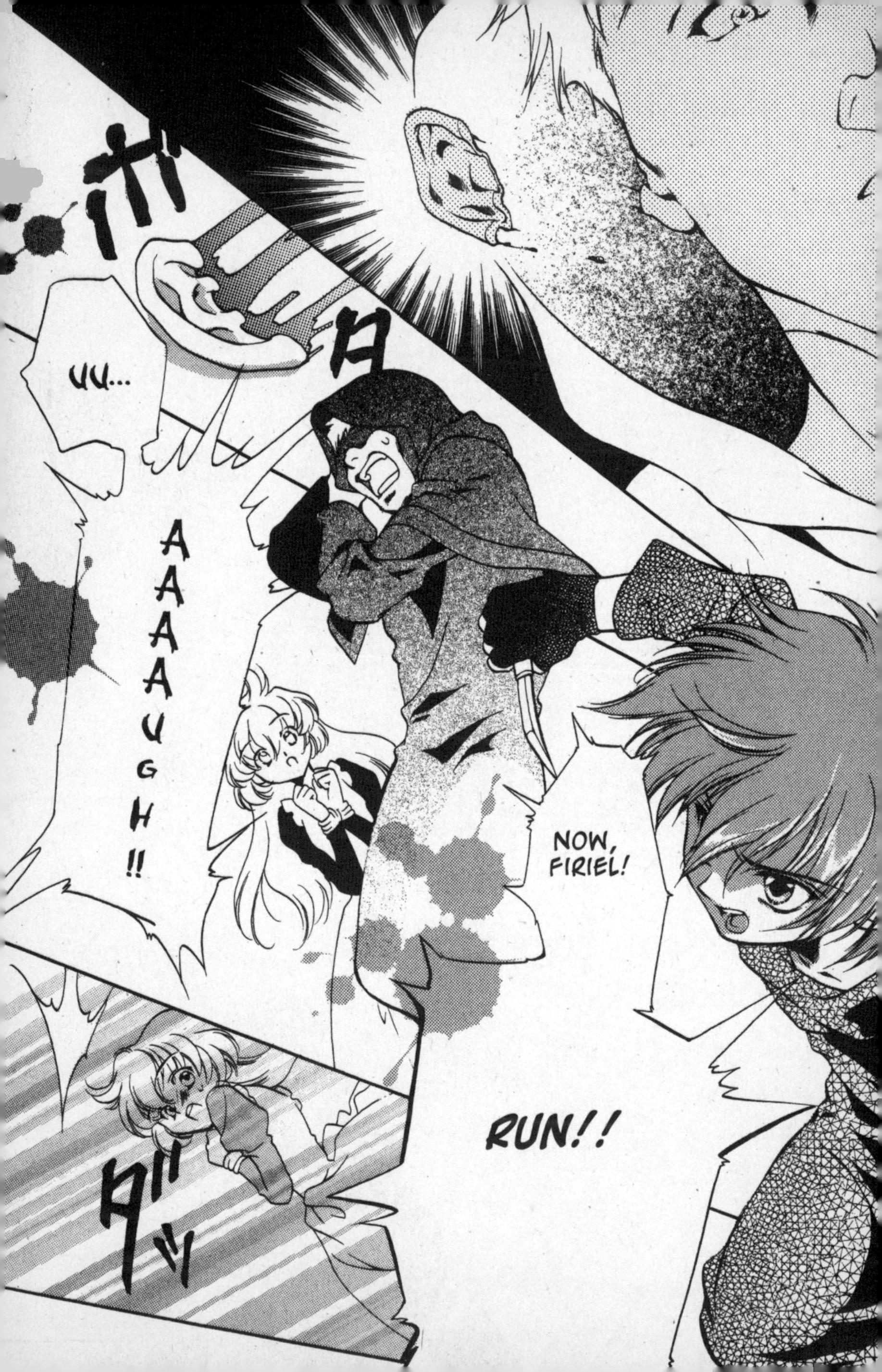
UU...
AAAAUGH!!
NOW, FIRIEL!
RUN!!

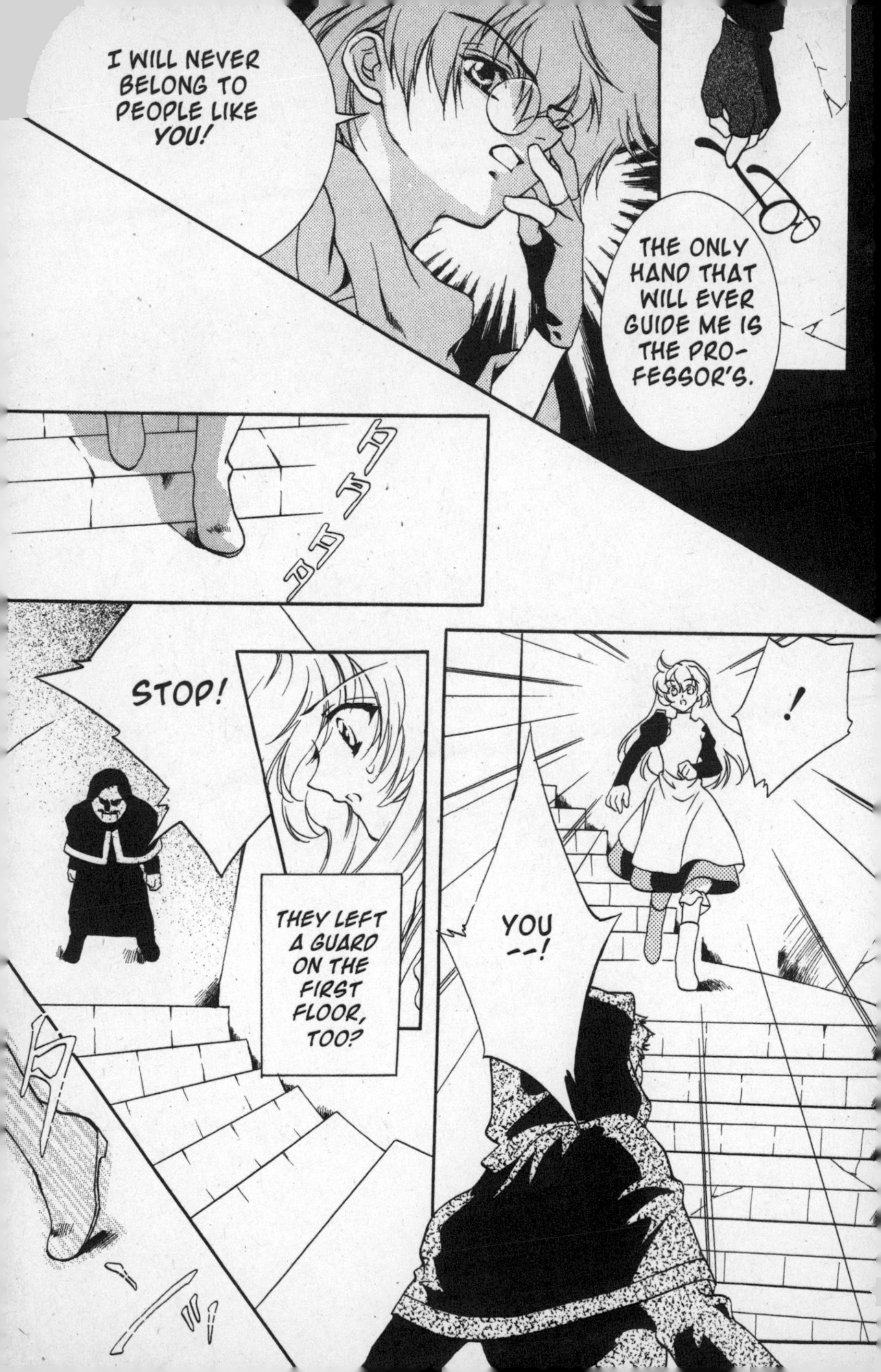
THE ONLY HAND THAT WILL EVER GUIDE ME IS THE PRO-FESSOR'S.
I WILL NEVER BELONG TO PEOPLE LIKE YOU!
タタタタ
!
YOU --!
THEY LEFT A GUARD ON THE FIRST FLOOR, TOO?
STOP!

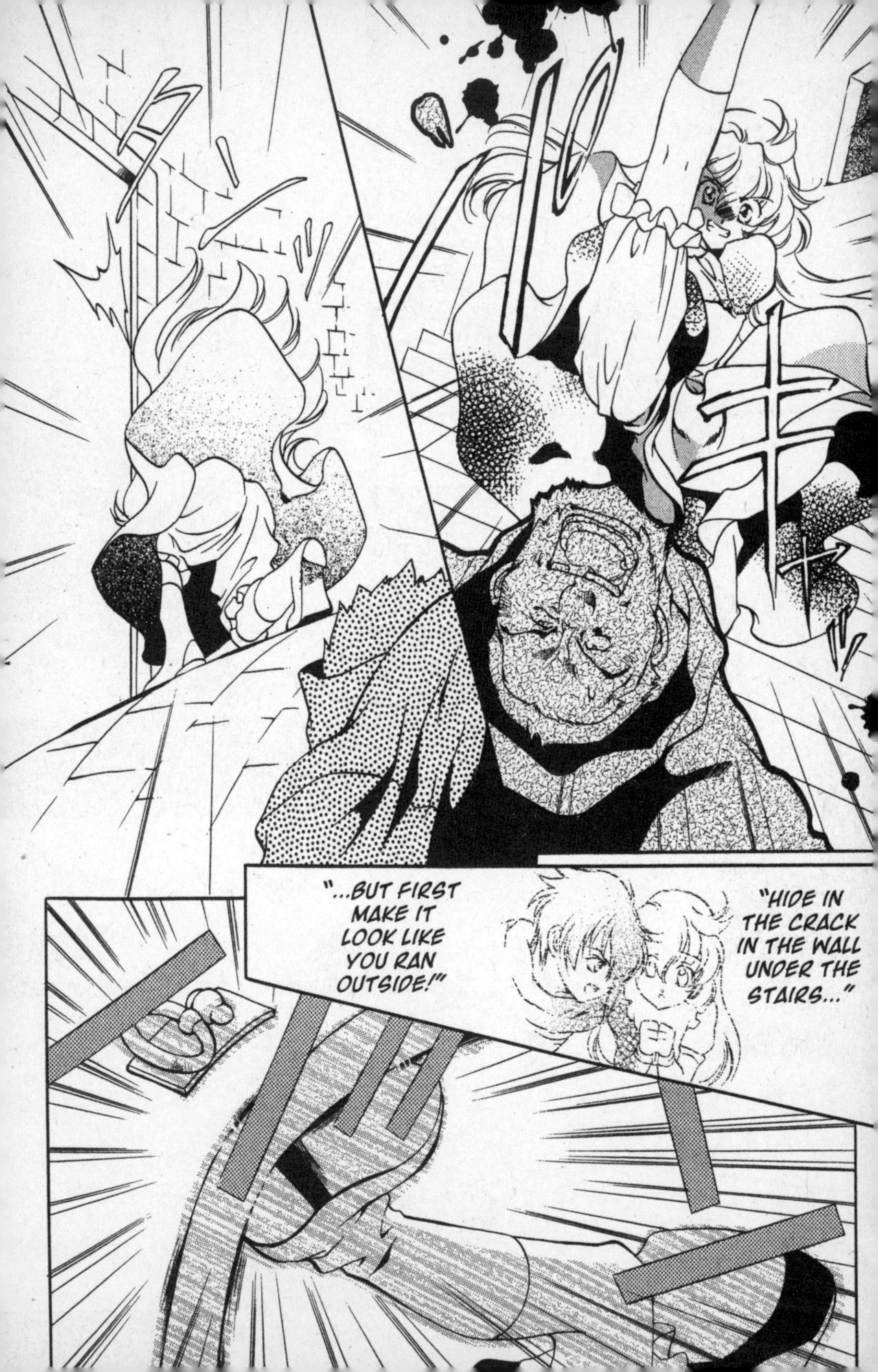
"HIDE IN THE CRACK IN THE WALL UNDER THE STAIRS..."
"...BUT FIRST MAKE IT LOOK LIKE YOU RAN OUTSIDE!"

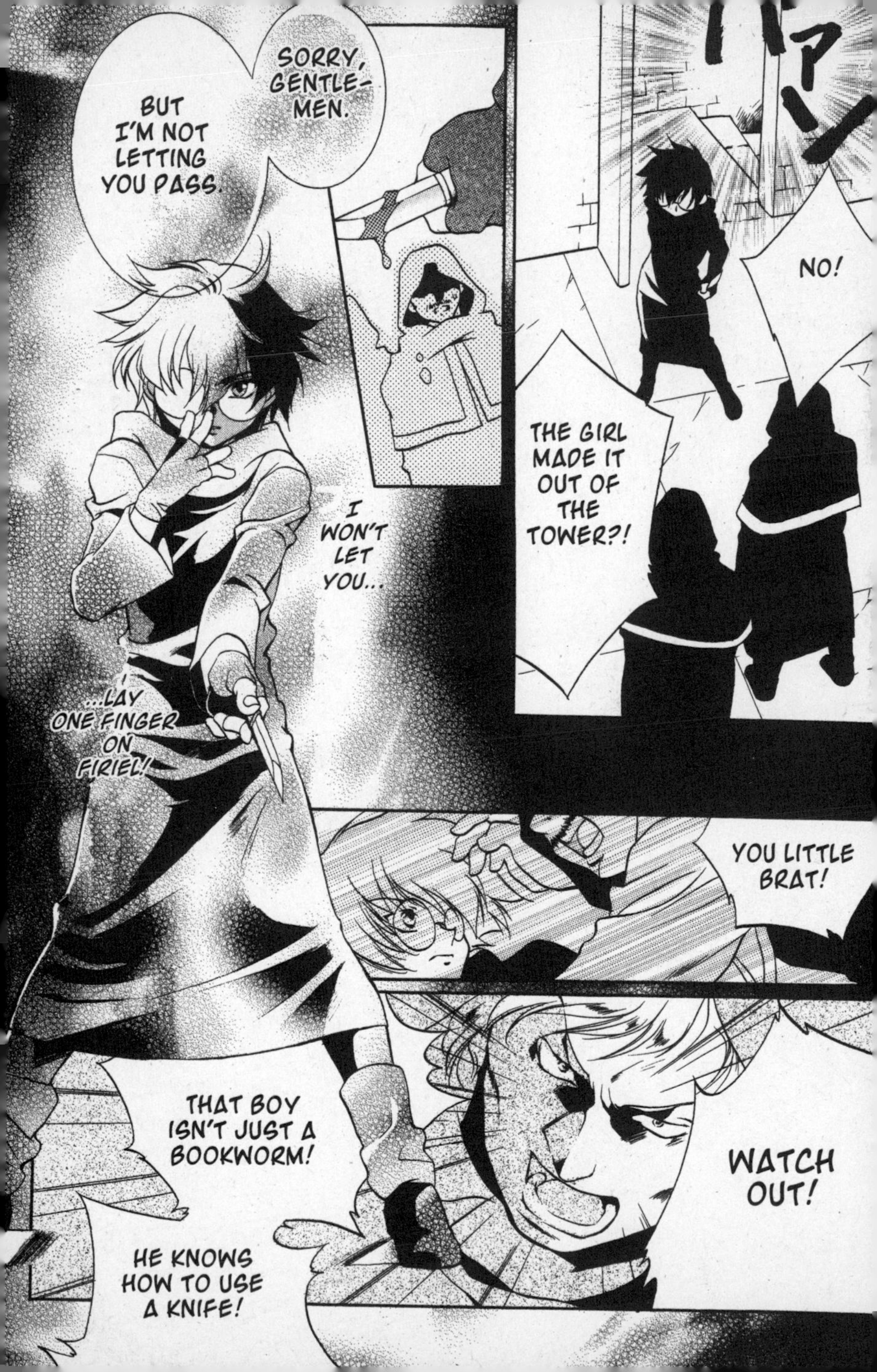
NO!
THE GIRL MADE IT OUT OF THE TOWER?!
YOU LITTLE BRAT!
WATCH OUT!
THAT BOY ISN'T JUST A BOOKWORM!
HE KNOWS HOW TO USE A KNIFE!
SORRY, GENTLE-MEN.
BUT I'M NOT LETTING YOU PASS.
I WON'T LET YOU...
...LAY ONE FINGER ON FIRIEL!

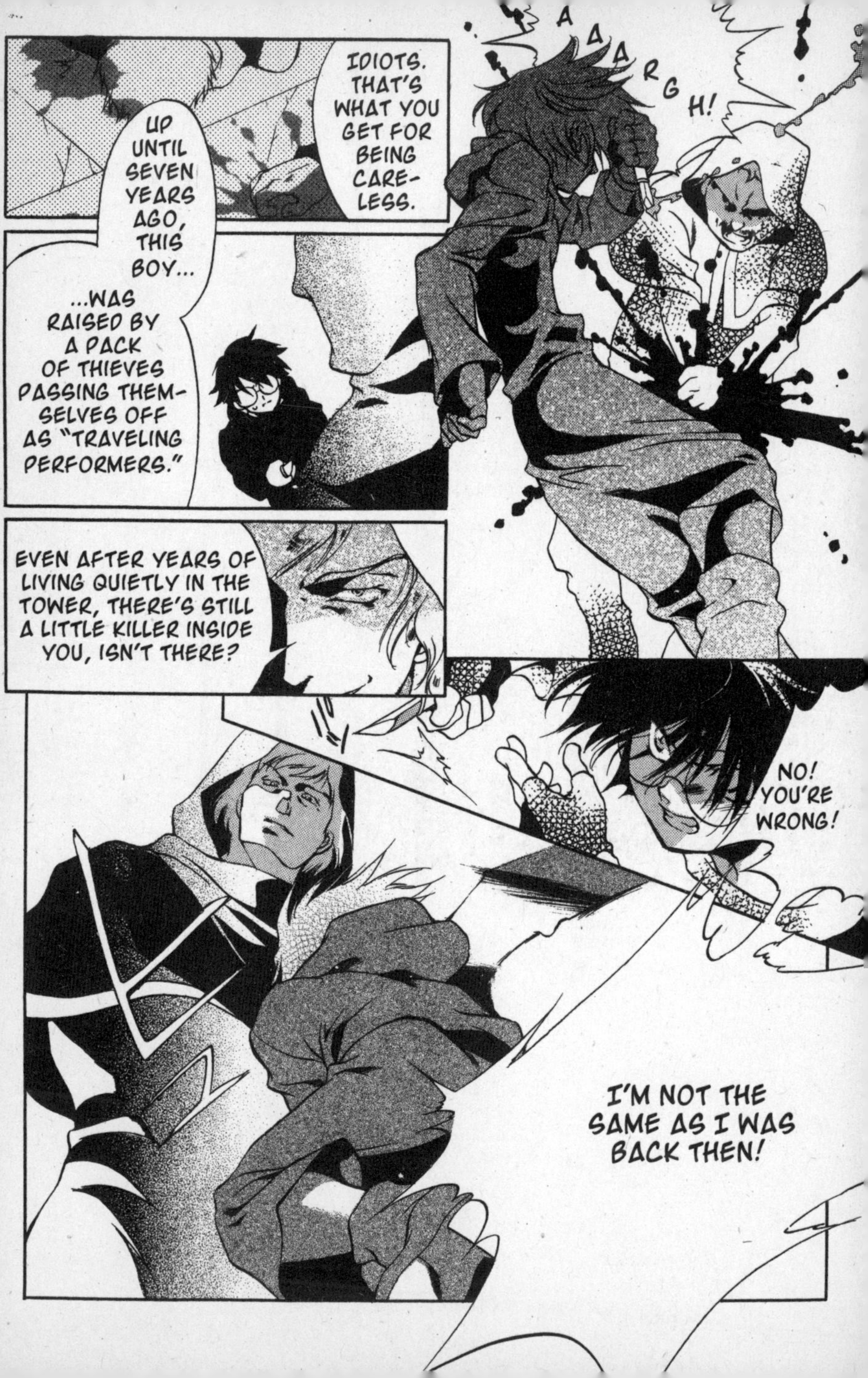
AAAARGH!
IDIOTS. THAT'S WHAT YOU GET FOR BEING CARE-LESS.
UP UNTIL SEVEN YEARS AGO, THIS BOY...
...WAS RAISED BY A PACK OF THIEVES PASSING THEM-SELVES OFF AS "TRAVELING PERFORMERS."
EVEN AFTER YEARS OF LIVING QUIETLY IN THE TOWER, THERE'S STILL A LITTLE KILLER INSIDE YOU, ISN'T THERE?
NO! YOU'RE WRONG!
I'M NOT THE SAME AS I WAS BACK THEN!

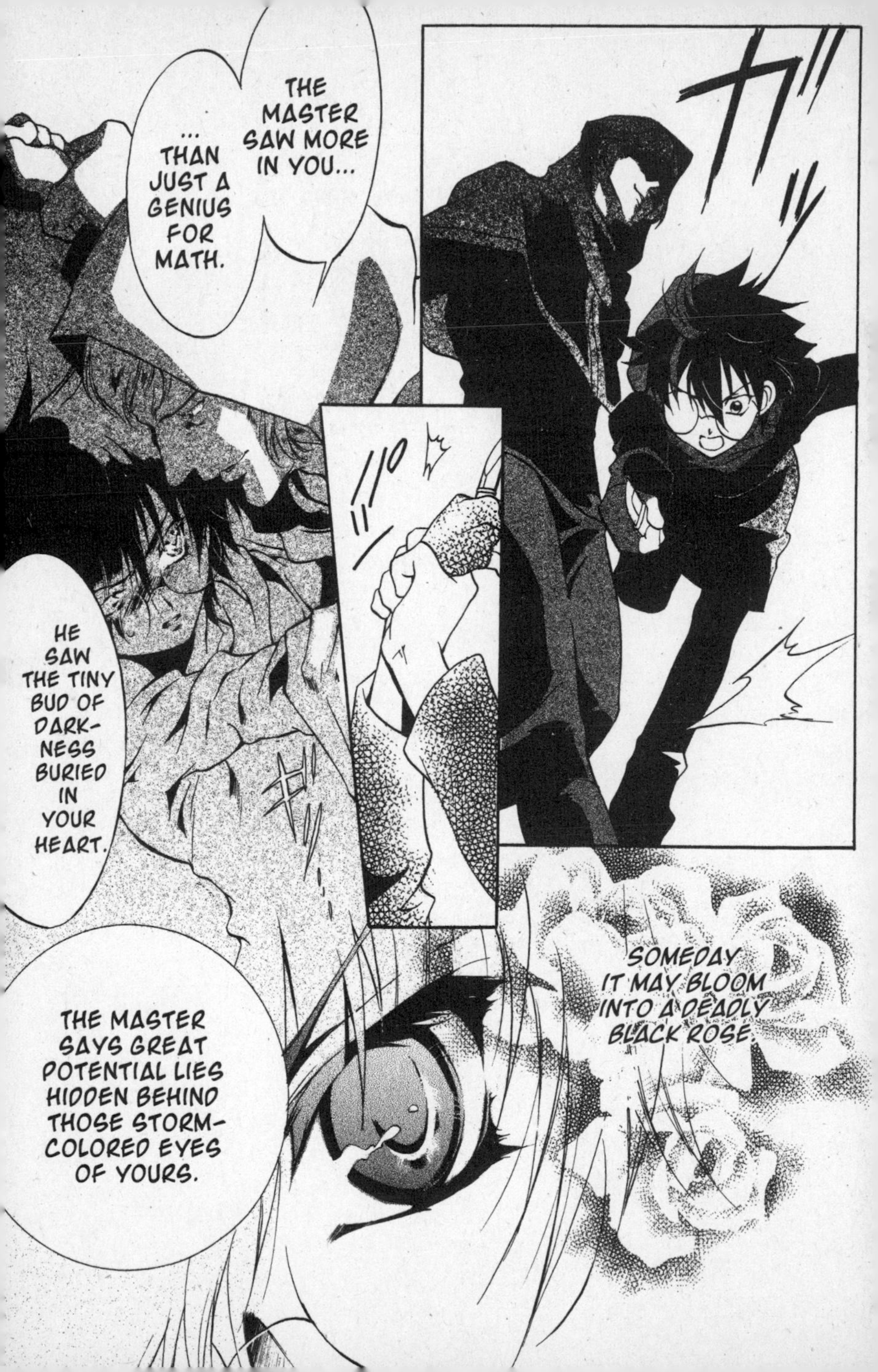
THE MASTER SAW MORE IN YOU...
... THAN JUST A GENIUS FOR MATH.
HE SAW THE TINY BUD OF DARK-NESS BURIED IN YOUR HEART.
SOMEDAY IT MAY BLOOM INTO A DEADLY BLACK ROSE.
THE MASTER SAYS GREAT POTENTIAL LIES HIDDEN BEHIND THOSE STORM-COLORED EYES OF YOURS.

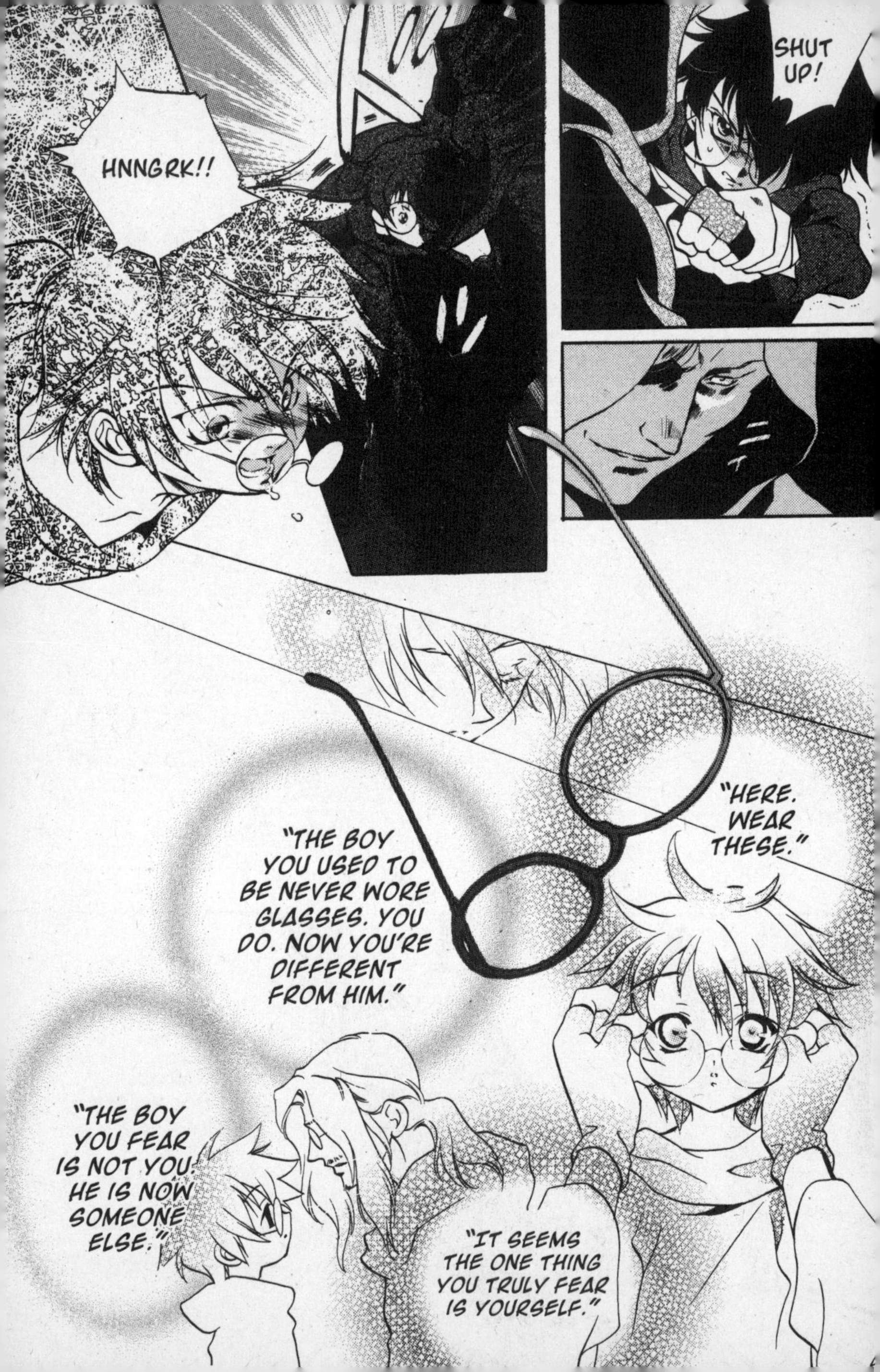
SHUT UP!
HNNGRK!!
"HERE. WEAR THESE."
"THE BOY YOU USED TO BE NEVER WORE GLASSES. YOU DO. NOW YOU'RE DIFFERENT FROM HIM."
"IT SEEMS THE ONE THING YOU TRULY FEAR IS YOURSELF."
"THE BOY YOU FEAR IS NOT YOU. HE IS NOW SOMEONE ELSE."

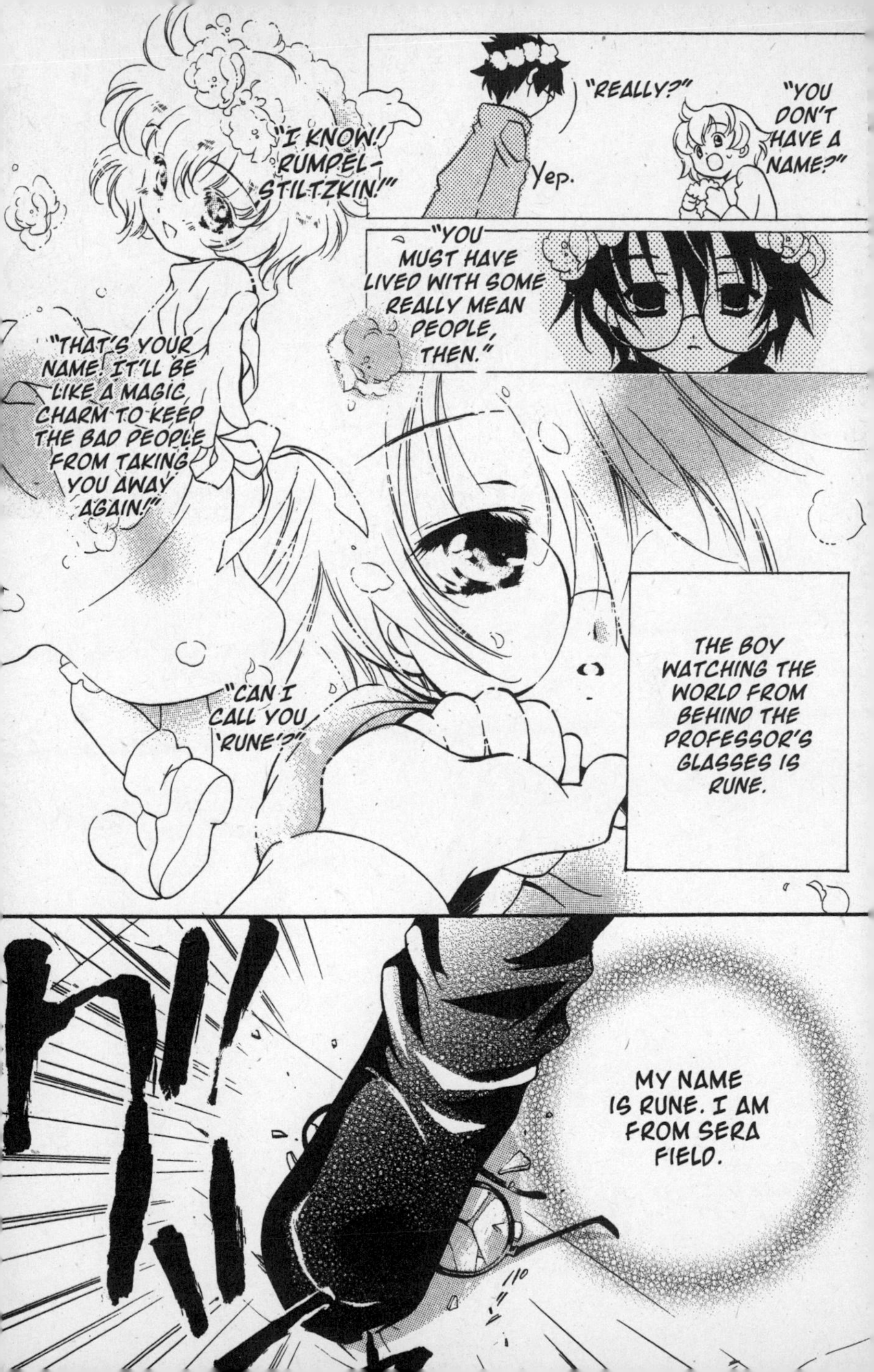
"YOU DON'T HAVE A NAME?"
"REALLY?"
Yep.
"YOU MUST HAVE LIVED WITH SOME REALLY MEAN PEOPLE, THEN."
"I KNOW! RUMPEL-STILTZKIN!"
"THAT'S YOUR NAME! IT'LL BE LIKE A MAGIC CHARM TO KEEP THE BAD PEOPLE FROM TAKING YOU AWAY AGAIN!"
"CAN I CALL YOU 'RUNE'?"
THE BOY WATCHING THE WORLD FROM BEHIND THE PROFESSOR'S GLASSES IS RUNE.
MY NAME IS RUNE. I AM FROM SERA FIELD.

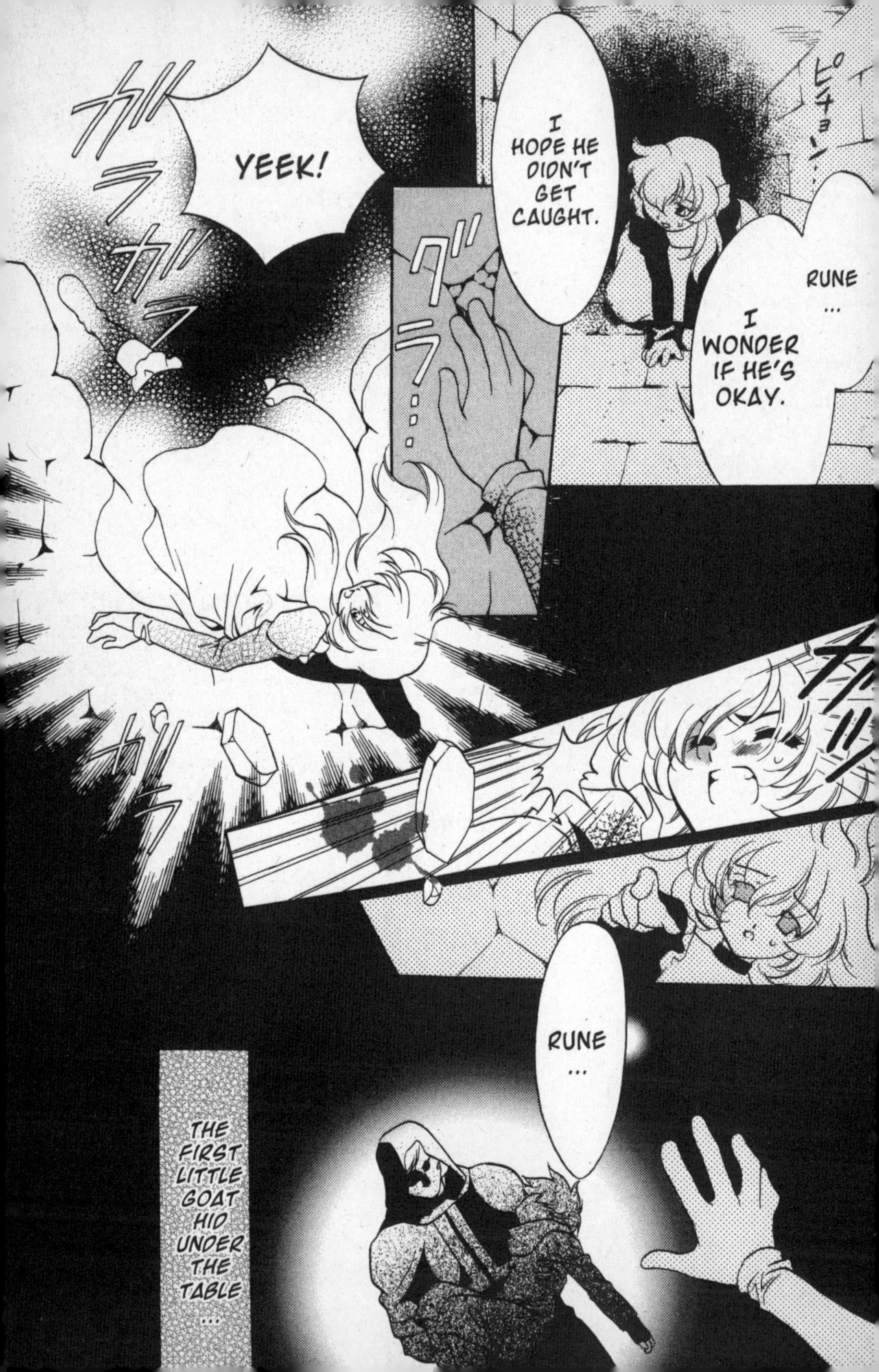
ピチョン…
RUNE ...
I WONDER IF HE'S OKAY.
I HOPE HE DIDN'T GET CAUGHT.
YEEK!
RUNE ...
THE FIRST LITTLE GOAT HID UNDER THE TABLE ...

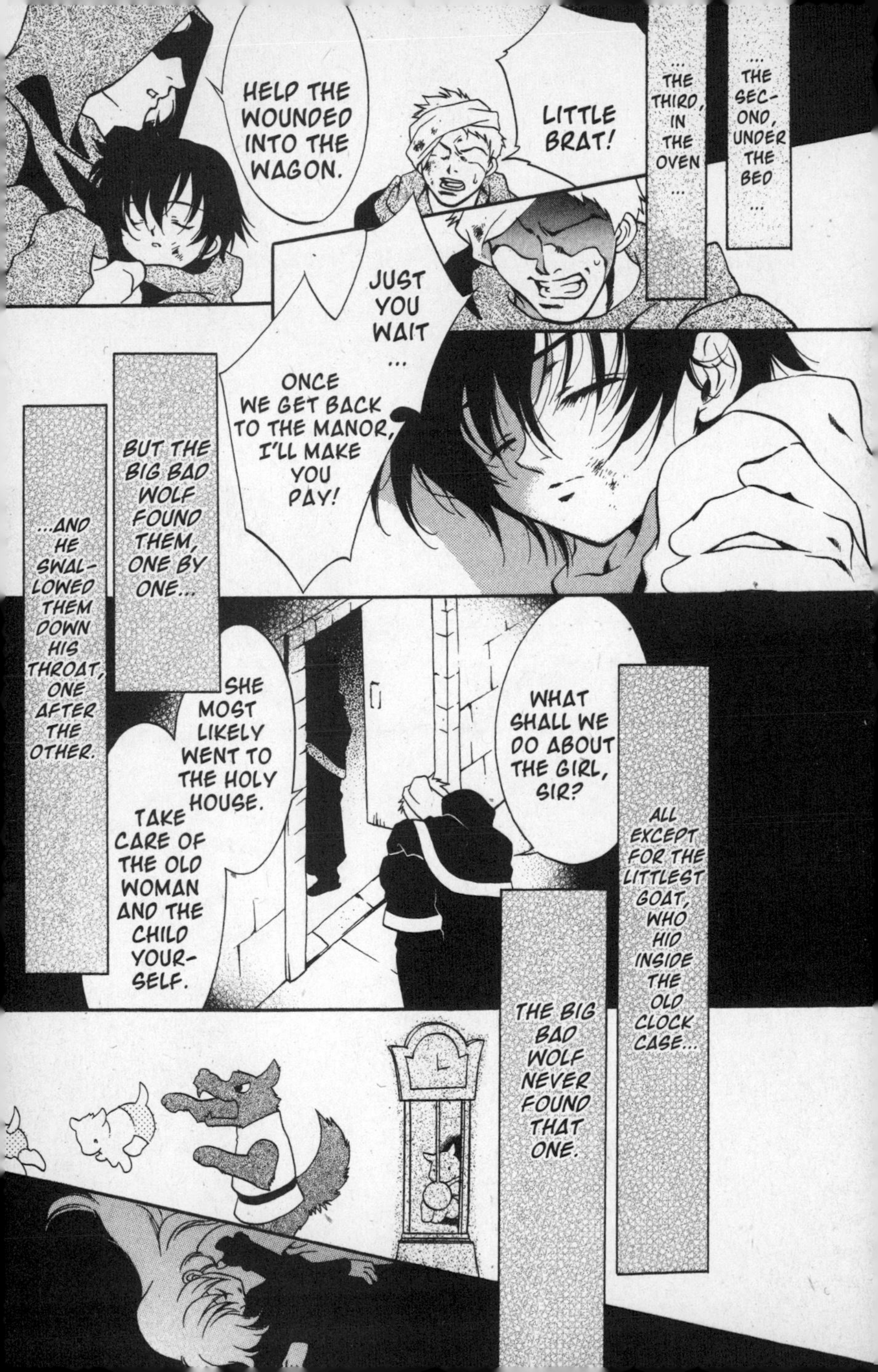
...THE SEC-OND, UNDER THE BED...
...THE THIRD, IN THE OVEN...
LITTLE BRAT!
HELP THE WOUNDED INTO THE WAGON.
JUST YOU WAIT... ONCE WE GET BACK TO THE MANOR, I'LL MAKE YOU PAY!
BUT THE BIG BAD WOLF FOUND THEM, ONE BY ONE...
...AND HE SWAL-LOWED THEM DOWN HIS THROAT, ONE AFTER THE OTHER.
WHAT SHALL WE DO ABOUT THE GIRL, SIR?
SHE MOST LIKELY WENT TO THE HOLY HOUSE.
TAKE CARE OF THE OLD WOMAN AND THE CHILD YOUR-SELF.
ALL EXCEPT FOR THE LITTLEST GOAT, WHO HID INSIDE THE OLD CLOCK CASE...
THE BIG BAD WOLF NEVER FOUND THAT ONE.

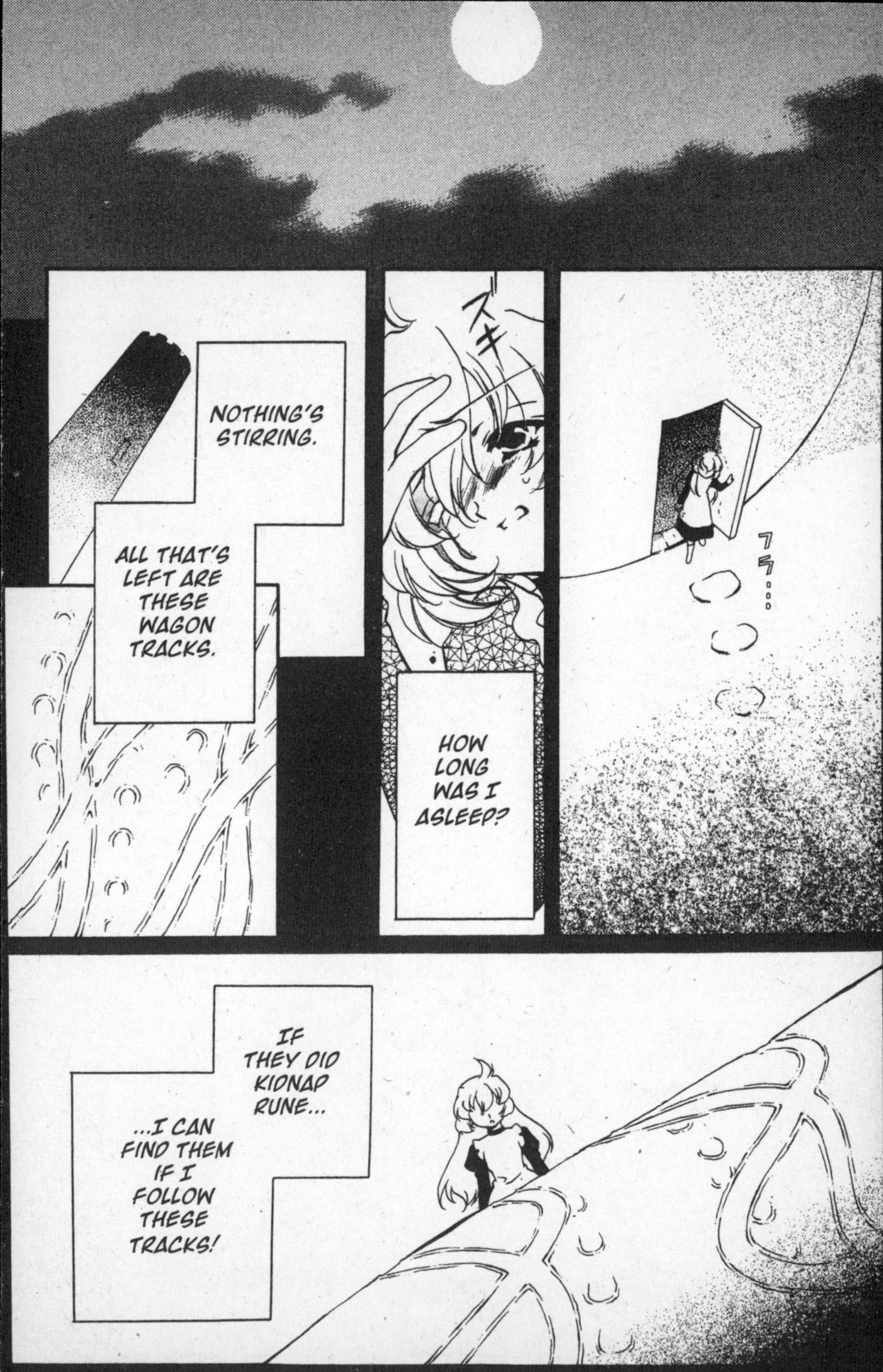
フラ...
ズキ
HOW LONG WAS I ASLEEP?
NOTHING'S STIRRING.
ALL THAT'S LEFT ARE THESE WAGON TRACKS.
IF THEY DID KIDNAP RUNE...
...I CAN FIND THEM IF I FOLLOW THESE TRACKS!

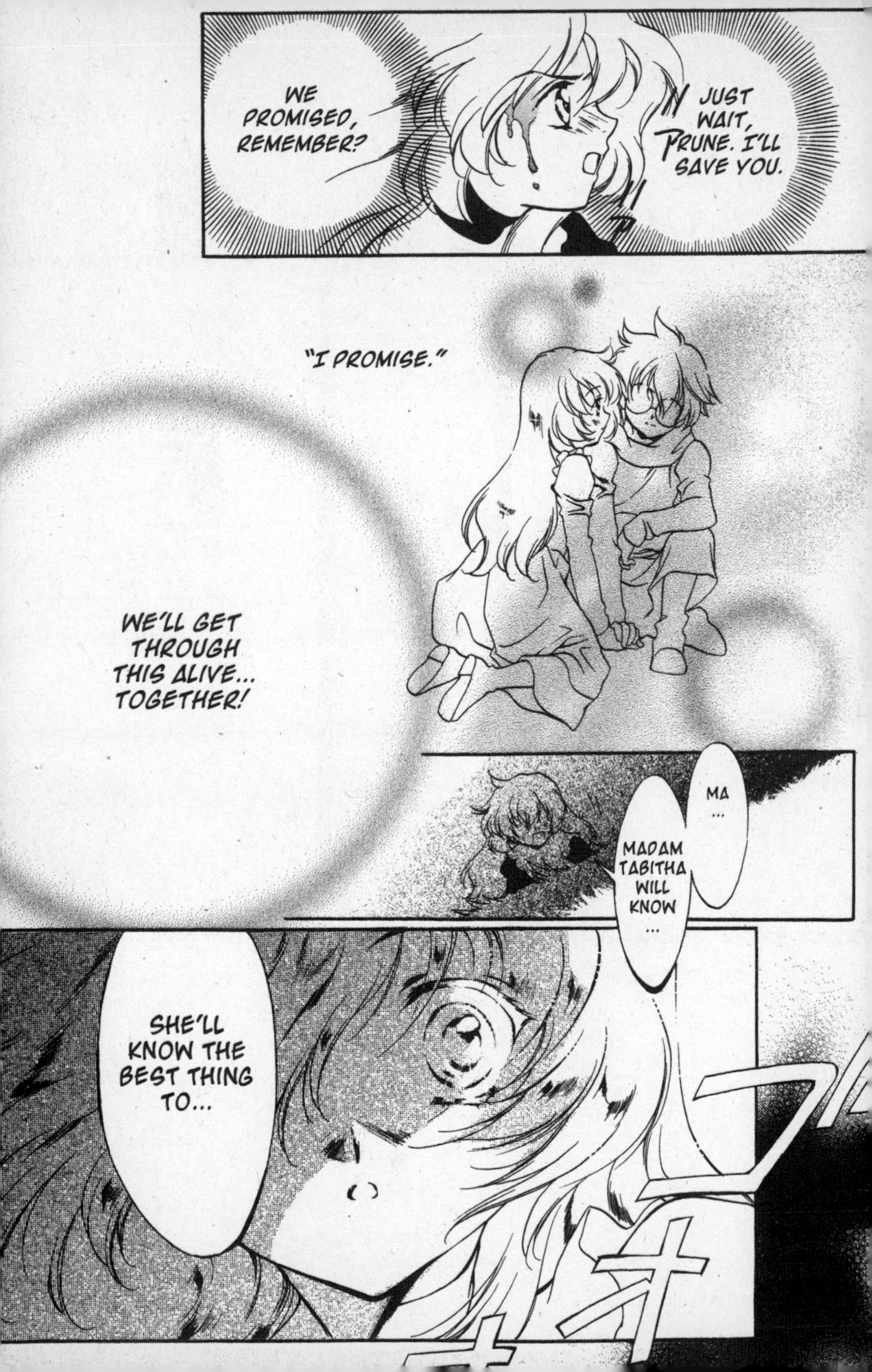
JUST WAIT, PRUNE. I'LL SAVE YOU.
WE PROMISED, REMEMBER?
"I PROMISE."
WE'LL GET THROUGH THIS ALIVE... TOGETHER!
MA ...
MADAM TABITHA WILL KNOW ...
SHE'LL KNOW THE BEST THING TO...

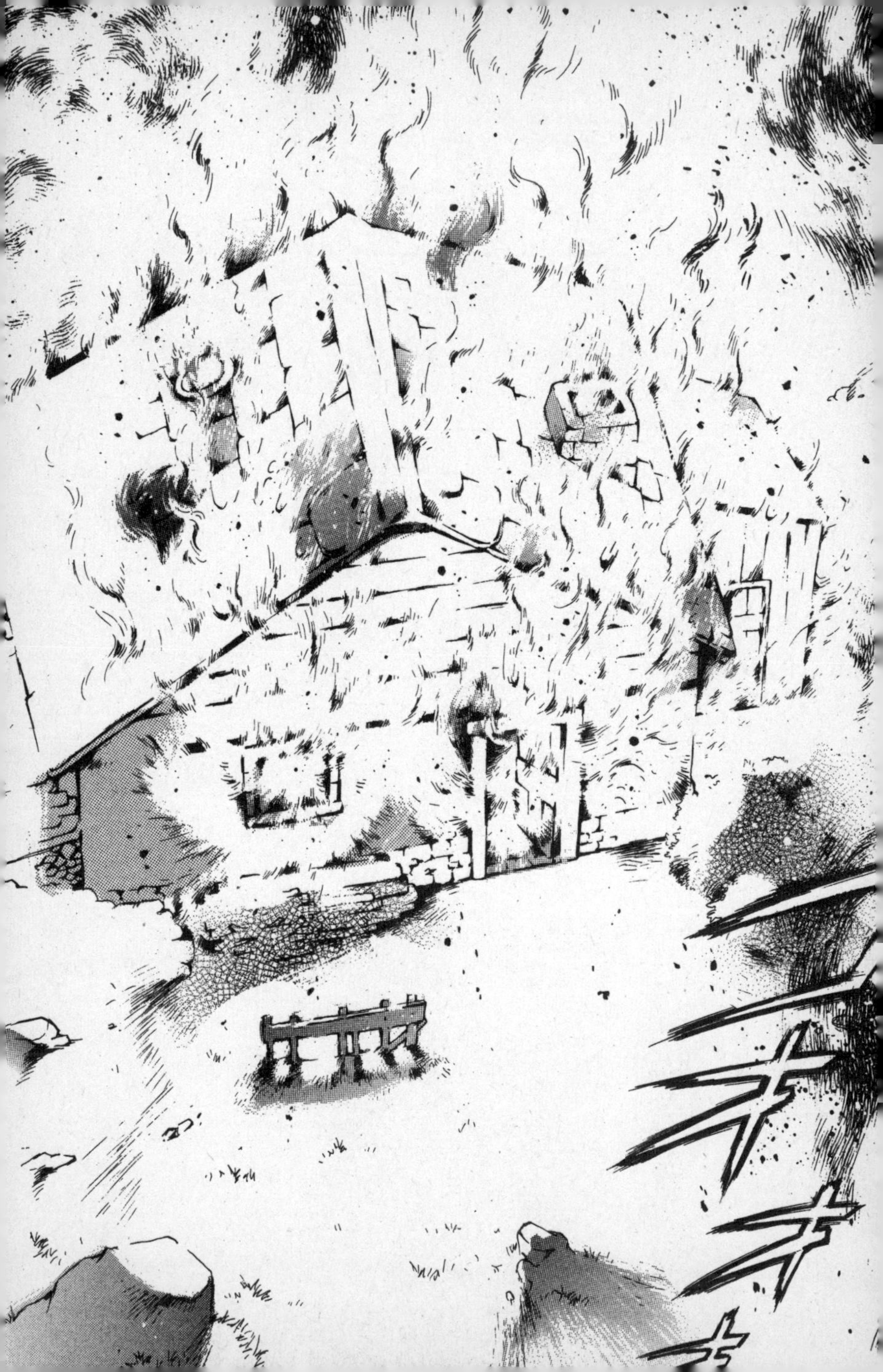

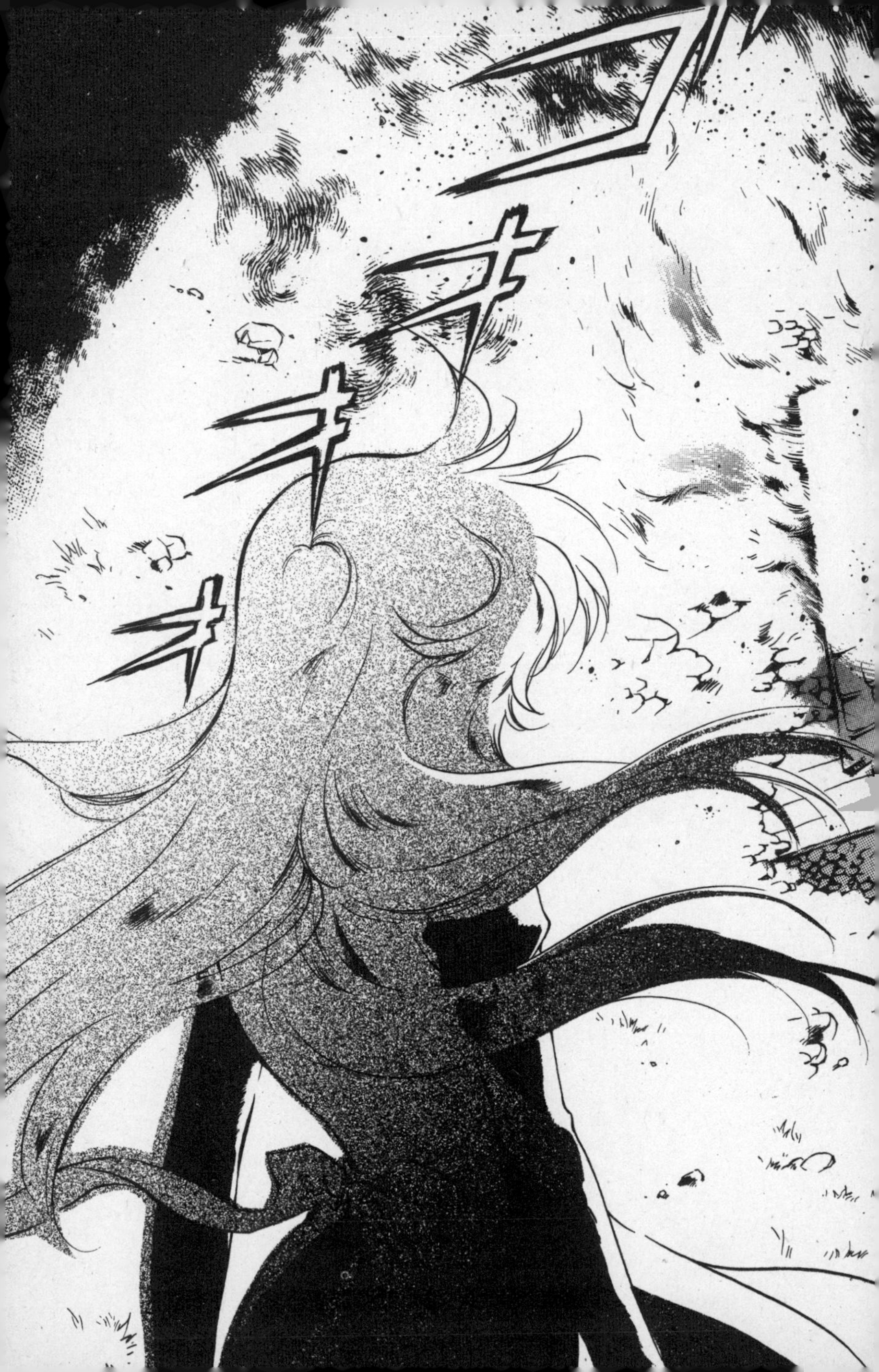

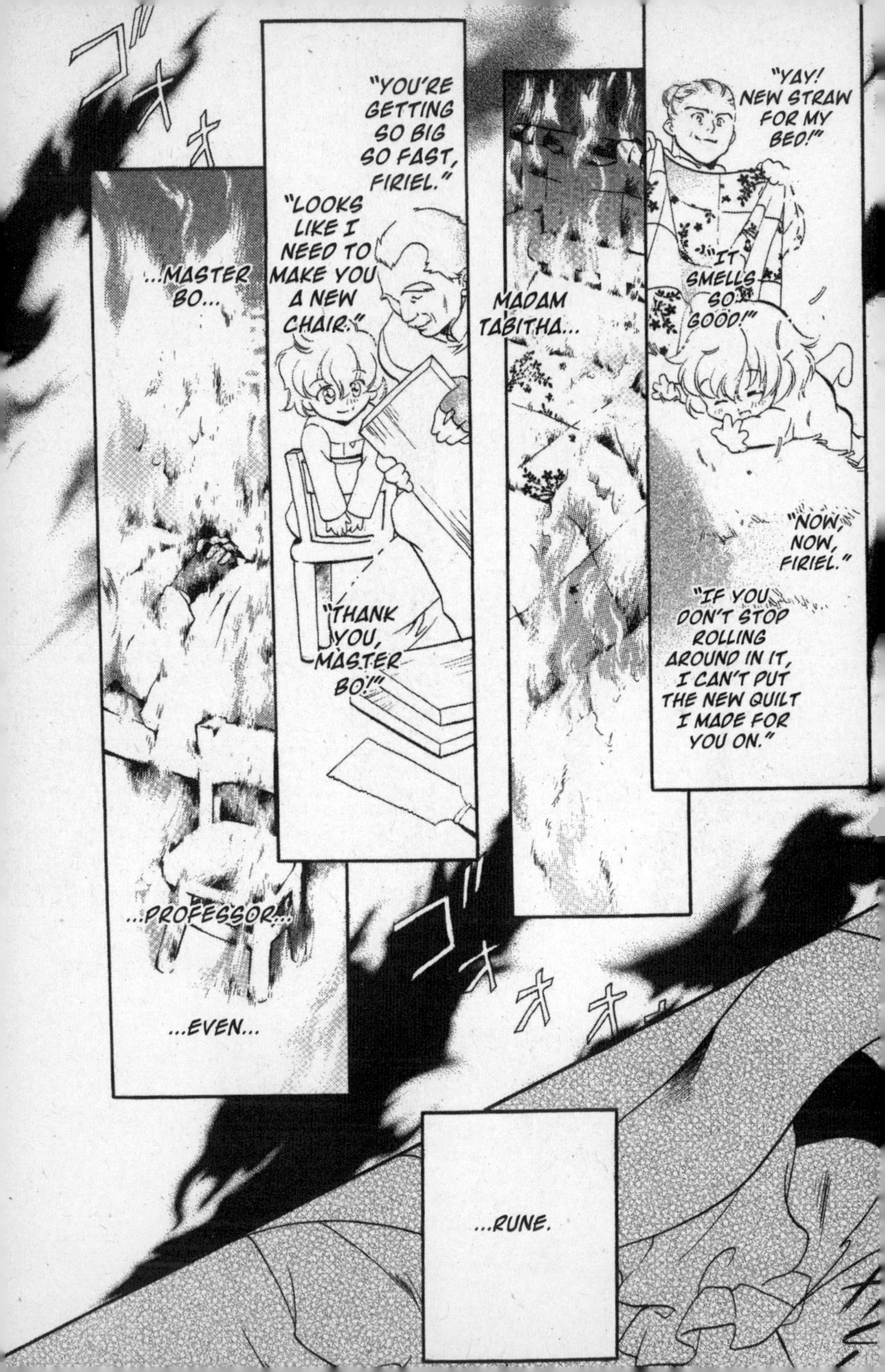
ゴォォ
"YAY! NEW STRAW FOR MY BED!"
"IT SMELLS SO GOOD!"
"NOW, NOW, FIRIEL."
"IF YOU DON'T STOP ROLLING AROUND IN IT, I CAN'T PUT THE NEW QUILT I MADE FOR YOU ON."
MADAM TABITHA...
"YOU'RE GETTING SO BIG SO FAST, FIRIEL."
"LOOKS LIKE I NEED TO MAKE YOU A NEW CHAIR."
"THANK YOU, MASTER BO!"
...MASTER BO...
...PROFESSOR...
...EVEN...
ゴォォォ
...RUNE.

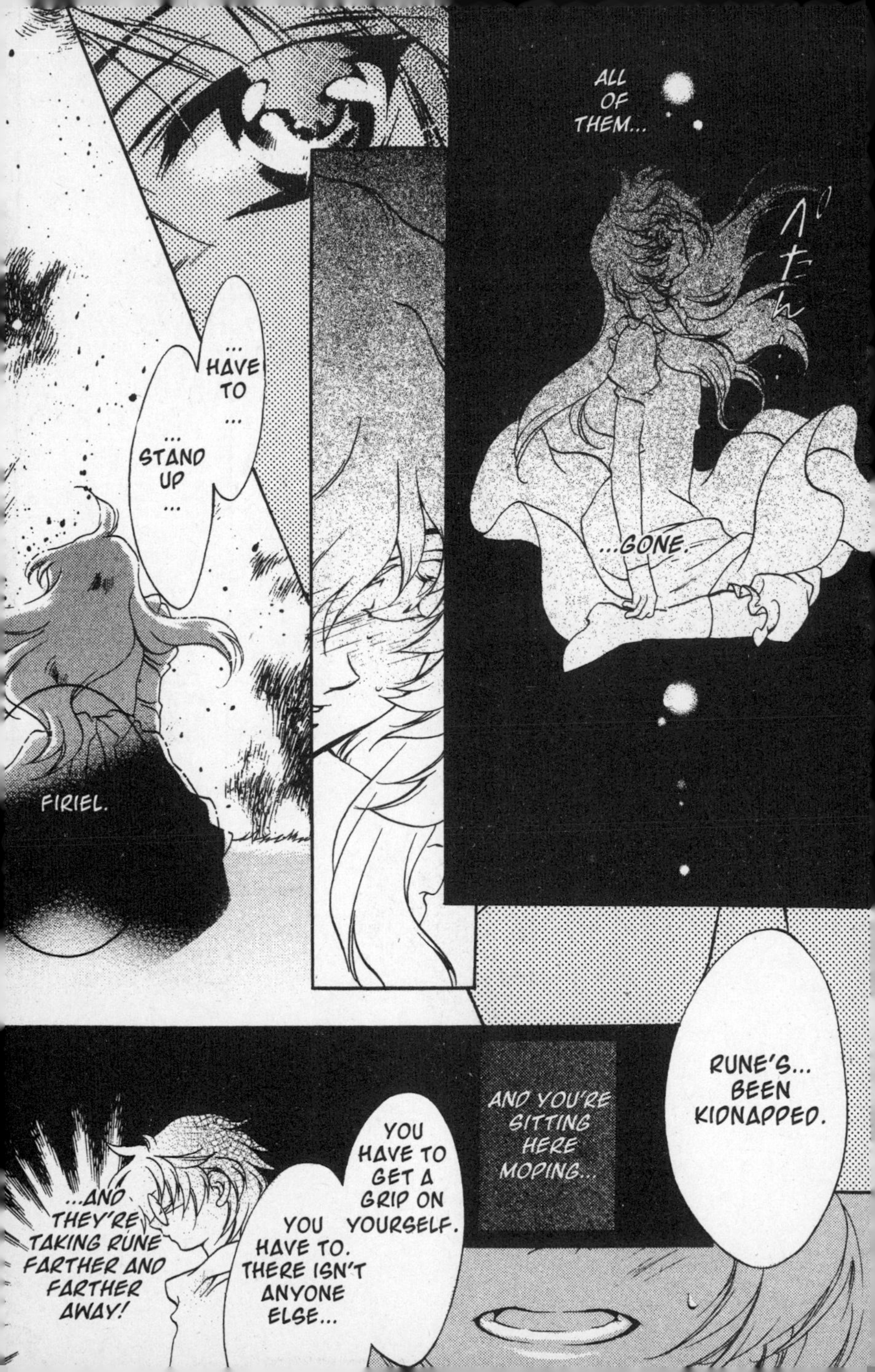
ALL OF THEM...
ぺたん
...GONE.
...HAVE TO ...
...STAND UP ...
FIRIEL.
RUNE'S... BEEN KIDNAPPED.
AND YOU'RE SITTING HERE MOPING...
YOU HAVE TO GET A GRIP ON YOURSELF.
YOU HAVE TO. THERE ISN'T ANYONE ELSE...
...AND THEY'RE TAKING RUNE FARTHER AND FARTHER AWAY!

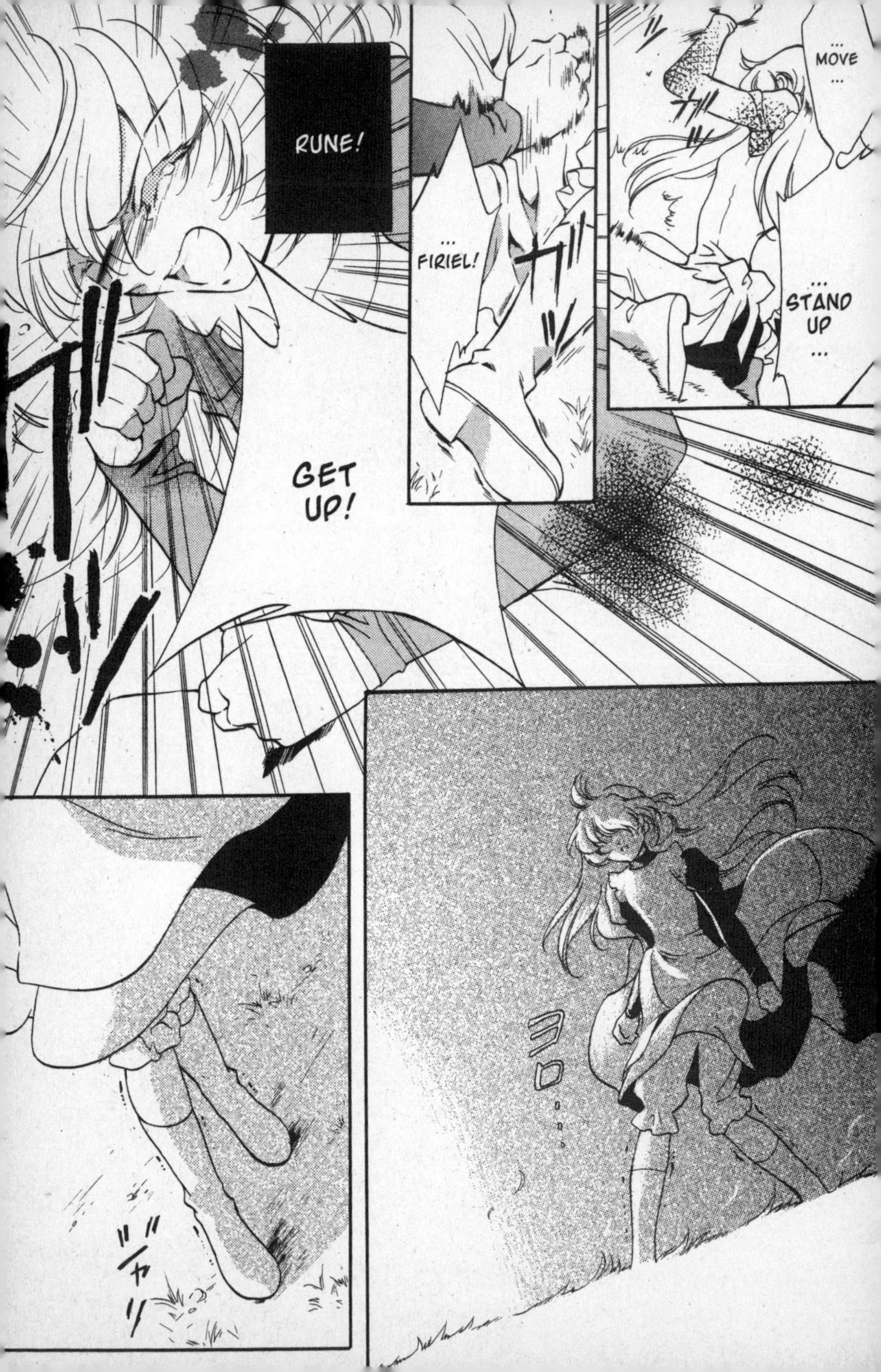
... MOVE ...
... STAND UP ...
... FIRIEL!
RUNE!
GET UP!

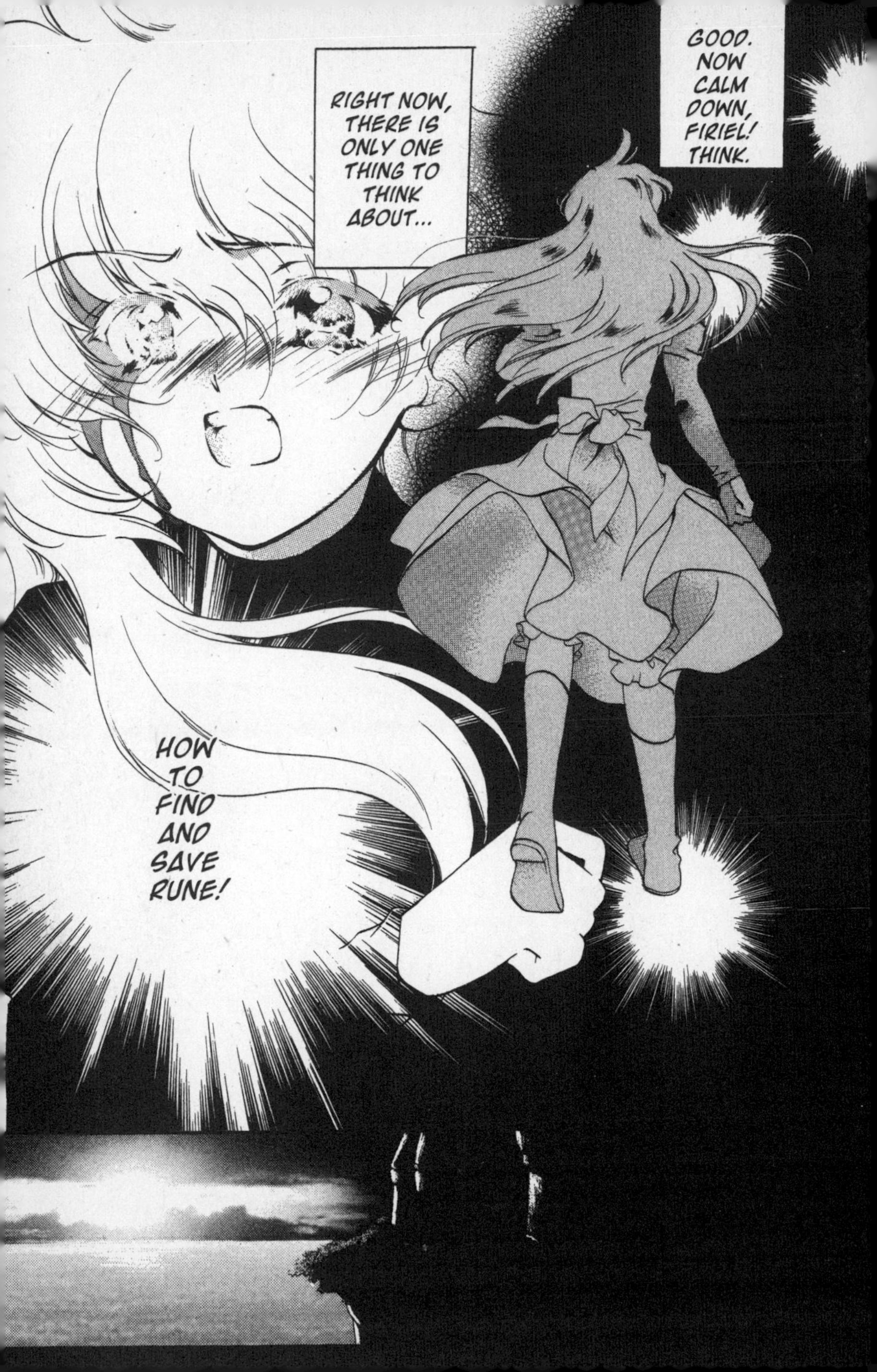
GOOD. NOW CALM DOWN, FIRIEL! THINK.
RIGHT NOW, THERE IS ONLY ONE THING TO THINK ABOUT...
HOW TO FIND AND SAVE RUNE!

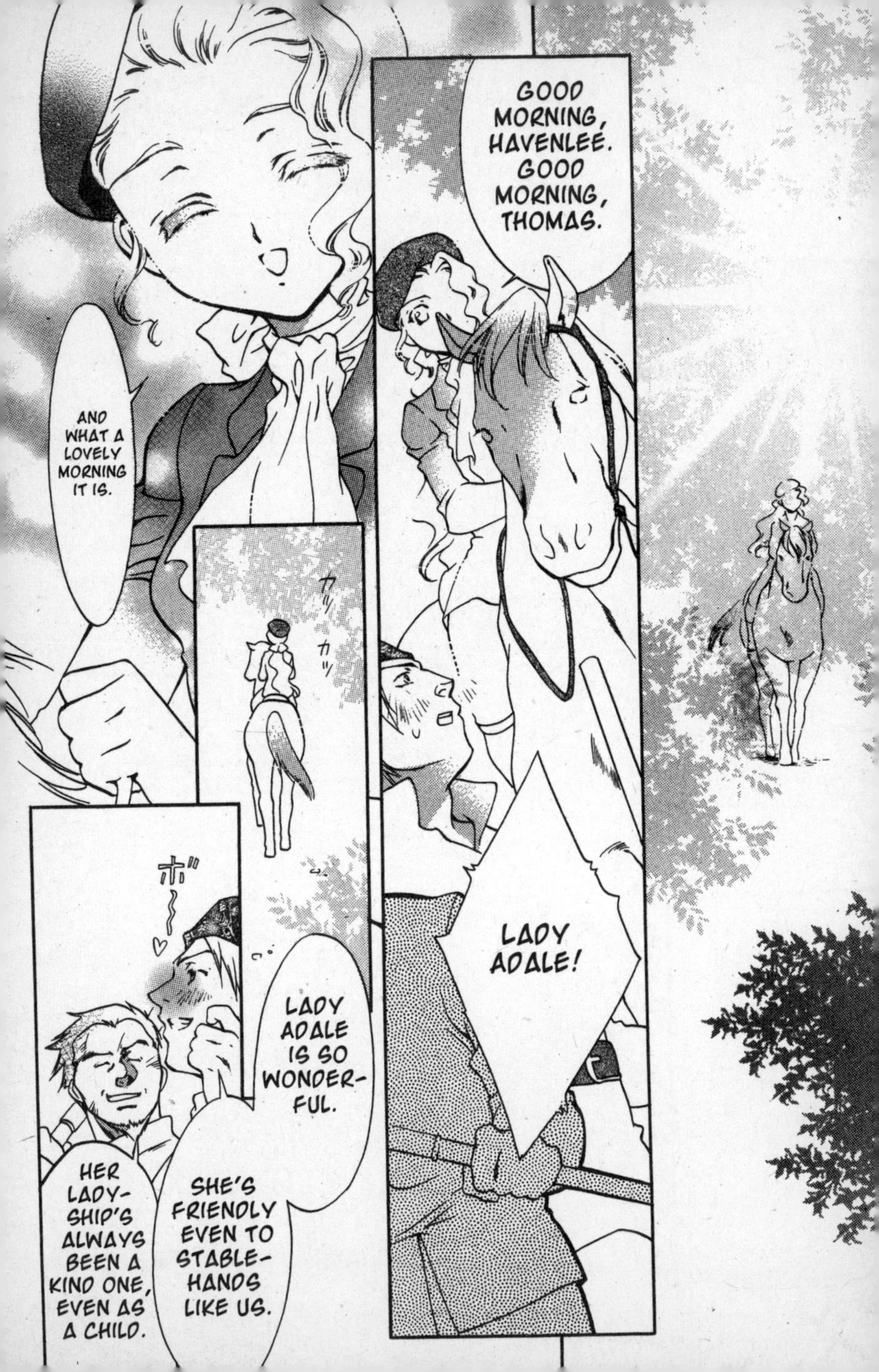
GOOD MORNING, HAVENLEE. GOOD MORNING, THOMAS.
AND WHAT A LOVELY MORNING IT IS.
カッ カッ
LADY ADALE!
ボ~
LADY ADALE IS SO WONDER-FUL.
SHE'S FRIENDLY EVEN TO STABLE-HANDS LIKE US.
HER LADY-SHIP'S ALWAYS BEEN A KIND ONE, EVEN AS A CHILD.

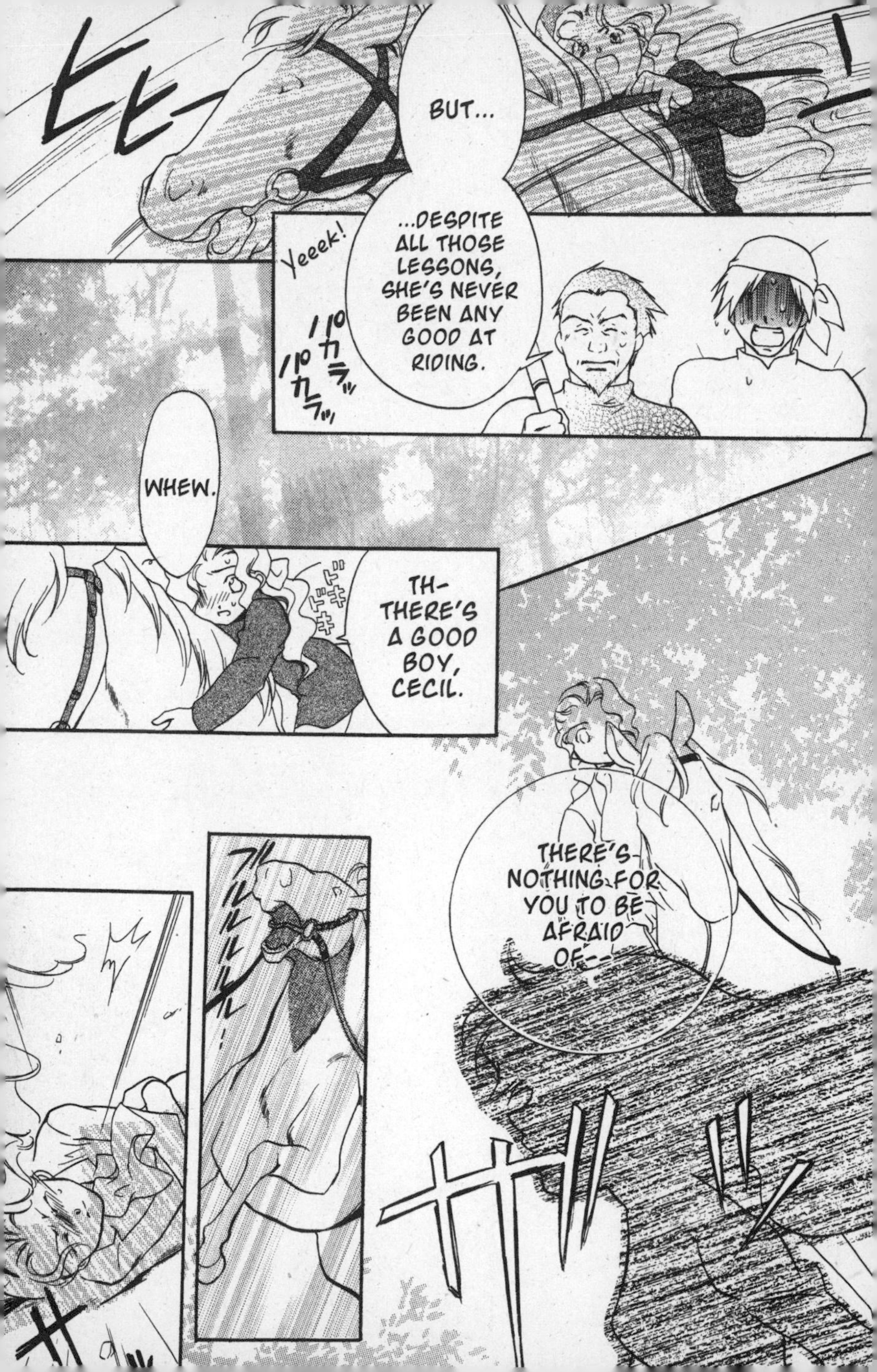
ヒヒー
BUT...
...DESPITE ALL THOSE LESSONS, SHE'S NEVER BEEN ANY GOOD AT RIDING.
Yeeek!
パカラッ パカラッ
WHEW.
ドキドキ
TH-THERE'S A GOOD BOY, CECIL.
THERE'S NOTHING FOR YOU TO BE AFRAID OF--
ザザッ
ブルルルル

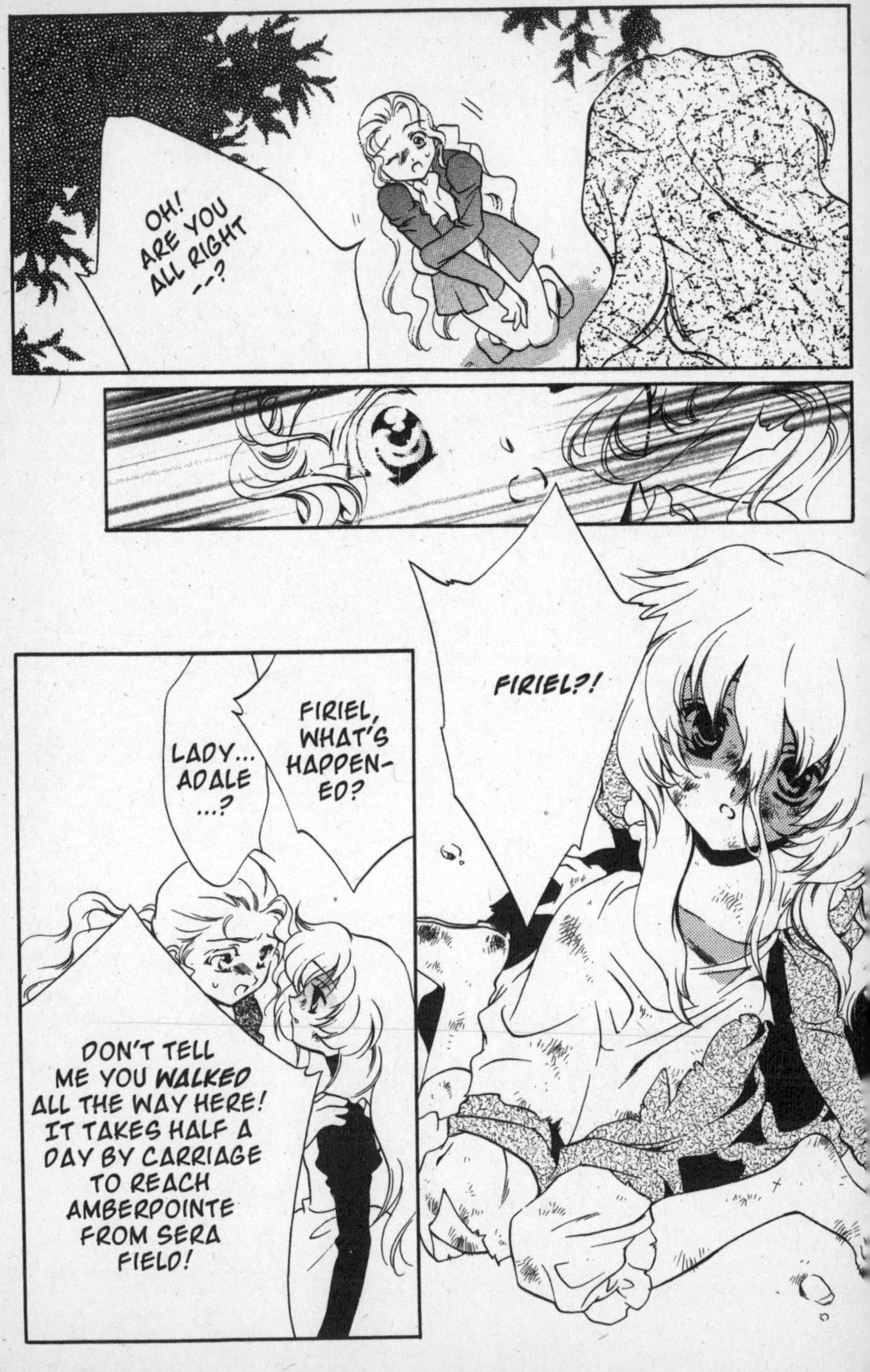
OH! ARE YOU ALL RIGHT --?
FIRIEL?!
FIRIEL, WHAT'S HAPPEN-ED?
LADY... ADALE ...?
DON'T TELL ME YOU WALKED ALL THE WAY HERE! IT TAKES HALF A DAY BY CARRIAGE TO REACH AMBERPOINTE FROM SERA FIELD!

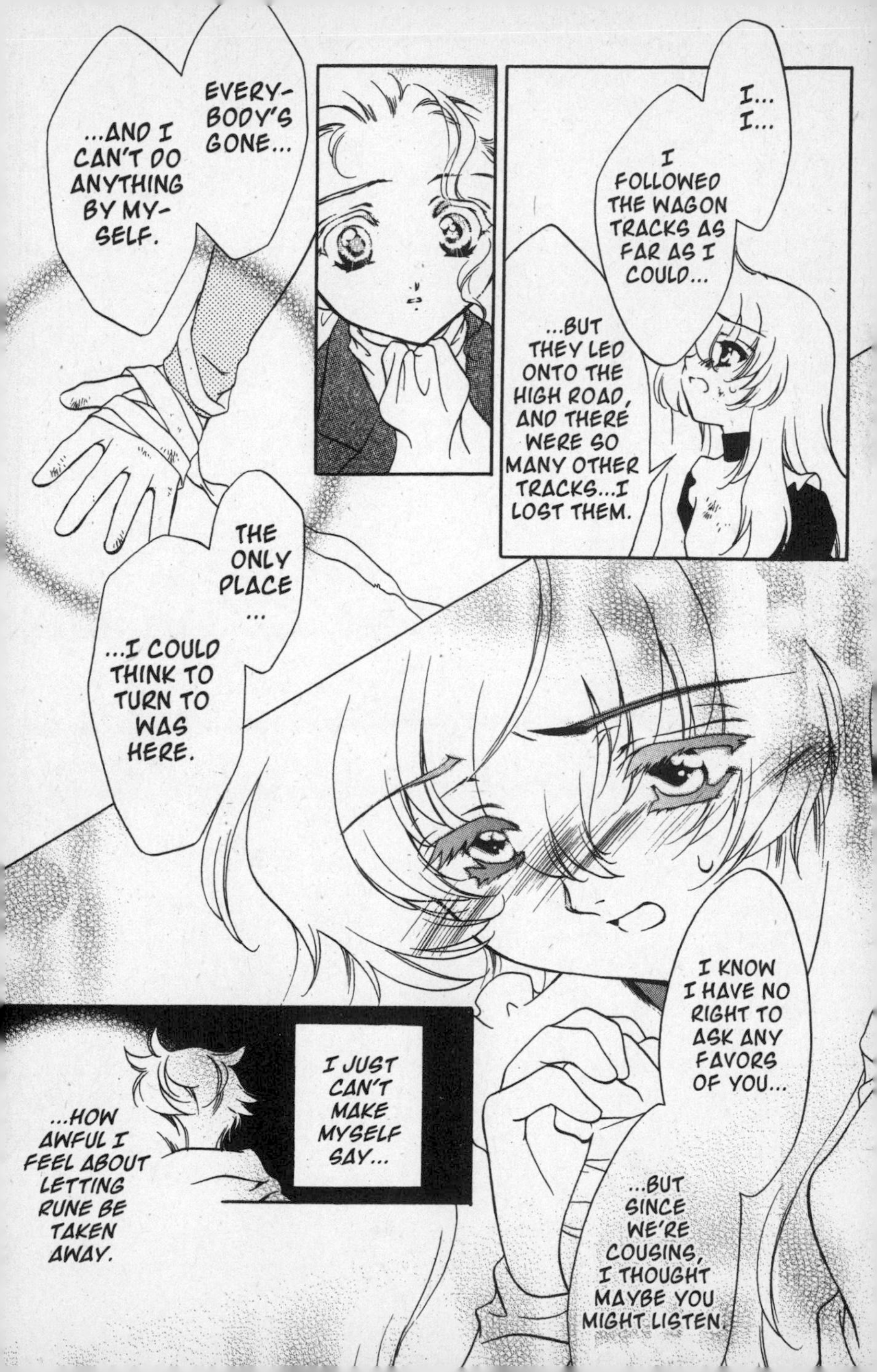
I... I...
I FOLLOWED THE WAGON TRACKS AS FAR AS I COULD...
...BUT THEY LED ONTO THE HIGH ROAD, AND THERE WERE SO MANY OTHER TRACKS...I LOST THEM.
EVERY-BODY'S GONE...
...AND I CAN'T DO ANYTHING BY MY-SELF.
THE ONLY PLACE...
...I COULD THINK TO TURN TO WAS HERE.
I KNOW I HAVE NO RIGHT TO ASK ANY FAVORS OF YOU...
...BUT SINCE WE'RE COUSINS, I THOUGHT MAYBE YOU MIGHT LISTEN.
I JUST CAN'T MAKE MYSELF SAY...
...HOW AWFUL I FEEL ABOUT LETTING RUNE BE TAKEN AWAY.

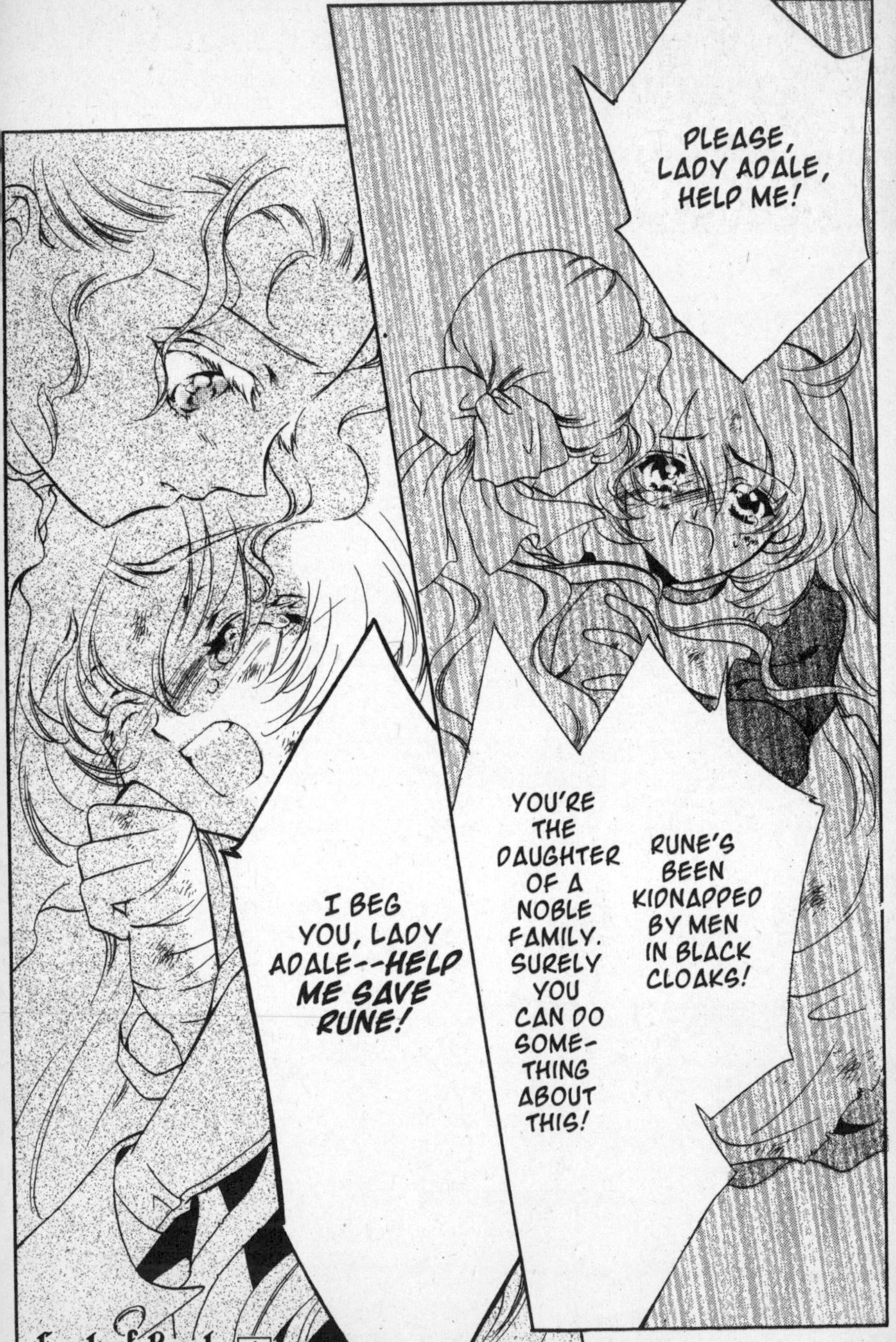
PLEASE, LADY ADALE, HELP ME!
RUNE'S BEEN KIDNAPPED BY MEN IN BLACK CLOAKS!
YOU'RE THE DAUGHTER OF A NOBLE FAMILY. SURELY YOU CAN DO SOMETHING ABOUT THIS!
I BEG YOU, LADY ADALE--**HELP ME SAVE RUNE!**

End of Book 1

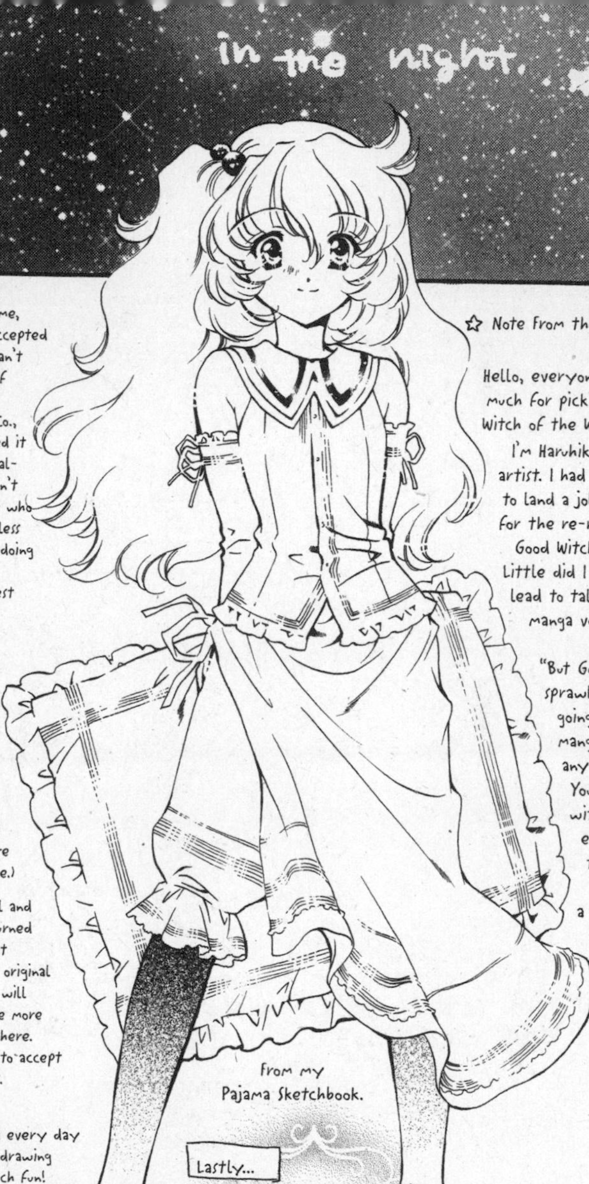
in the night.

☆ Note from the Author ☆

Hello, everyone! Thank you so much for picking up The Good Witch of the West volume one!

I'm Haruhiko Momokawa, a manga artist. I had the extreme good lu to land a job doing the illustratio for the re-release of Ms. Ogiwara Good Witch of the West novels. Little did I know that that woul lead to talk of doing a full-blo manga version of the books!

"But Good Witch is a huge, sprawling series! If you're going to make it into a manga, you can't let just any old artist work on it. You have to get someone with loads of talent and experience to do some-thing like that!"

I thought. I mean, I'm a major fan of the nove and I know I wouldn't want to read the manga unless it wa done by someone who loved the original stories.

I waffled back and forth for a long time, but I (obviously) accepted the offer. (I still can't help but wonder if that was the best thing for Firiel & Co., but...) What decided it for me was the real-ization that I couldn't stand it if someone who loved the stories less than me ended up doing the manga.

"I'm not the greatest manga artist out there, but I love Firiel & Co. more than anyone! I promise I'll put my heart and soul into it! Please, let me do the manga!" ...is how things ended up. (Basically, I begged for a job they were already offering me.)

After a lot of trial and error, the manga turned out to be quite a bit different from the original novels. I know this will irritate some of the more hardcore fans out there. I'm fully prepared to accept your angry letters.

Being able to spend every day thinking about and drawing Good Witch is so much fun! I can't wait to get started every morning. Ms. Ogiwara is a great help. She's so kind and understanding. My editor, Ms. Yagi, is another big fan of the books (we have the best phone conversations--all fun, nothing about work.) Thank you both so much!!

From my Pajama Sketchbook.

Lastly...

The original Good Witch novels are awesome! Go read them! Go become a fan like me and my editor and spend all night talking on the phone about them! They're the best!

Another big thank you goes to all my friends for all their support. I love you all!

Haruhiko Momokawa 2004 5.13 桃川春日子.拝.

☆ Bonus Under Cover Corner ☆

Of course I adore all the major characters, but there are some that I love more than others. I thought I might as well sneak a little corner about them here under the cover. (That's the original Japanese cover!) Plus, I want to get "I love that character too!!" fan letters...

- Captain Garland (love the austere type!)
- Kain Abel
- Lucel

They're all deep characters with ulterior motives (good ones) who have one particular person they're dedicated to following.

Oh, and my No. 1 favorite female character has to be Leandra. (Now that I think about it, the ones I like are all schemers...)

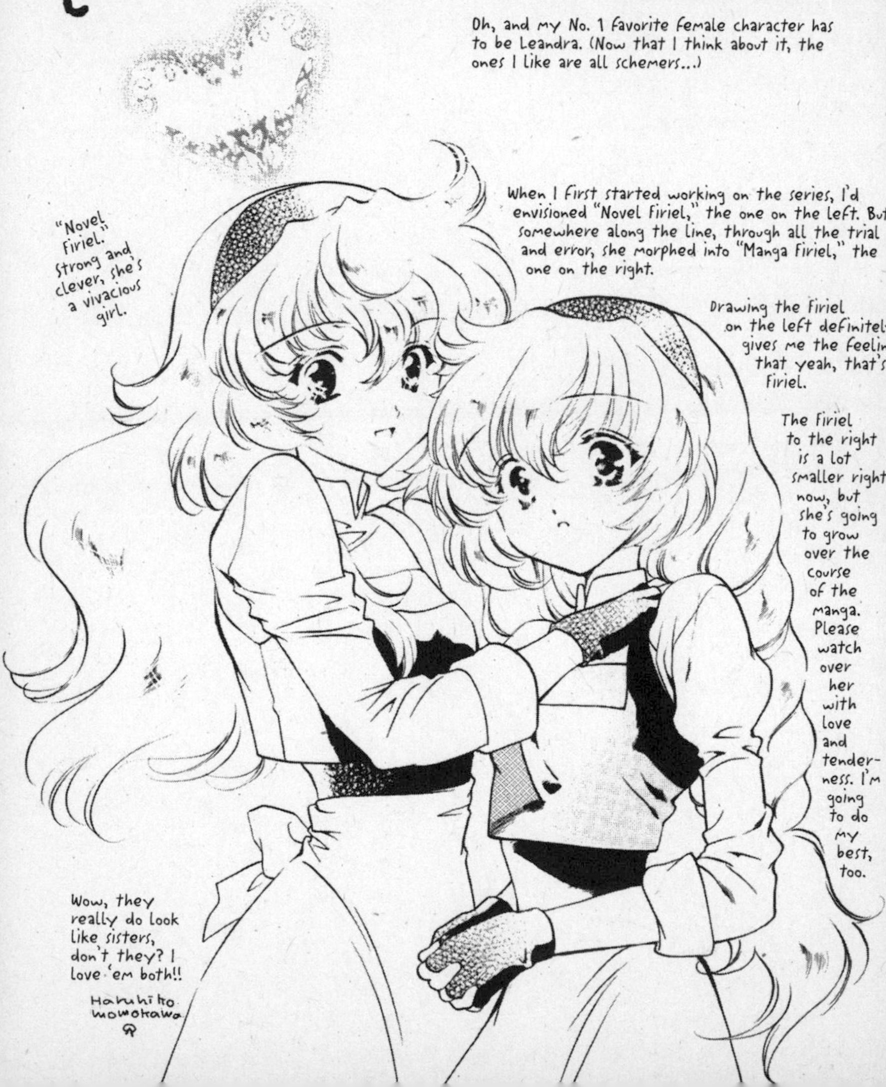

When I first started working on the series, I'd envisioned "Novel Firiel," the one on the left. But somewhere along the line, through all the trial and error, she morphed into "Manga Firiel," the one on the right.

"Novel Firiel." Strong and clever, she's a vivacious girl.

Drawing the Firiel on the left definitely gives me the feeling that yeah, that's Firiel.

The Firiel to the right is a lot smaller right now, but she's going to grow over the course of the manga. Please watch over her with love and tenderness. I'm going to do my best, too.

Wow, they really do look like sisters, don't they? I love 'em both!!

Haruhiko Momokawa

Dear Mother,

Where is Rune?
I've reached Adel's castle,
but no one will help me.
Rune's probability calculation couldn't
be wrong, so I must hope my rank
as Princess will convince Eusis to
stop being so snobbish and cruel
and help! If it were not for Adale's
bright smile, I would surely feel like
crying all the time. I miss Madam Tabitha,
Master Bo and the Professor so much!
If I must, I will become stronger,
if only for Rune's sake...

Firiel Dee

In the Next

THE GOOD WITCH OF THE WEST™

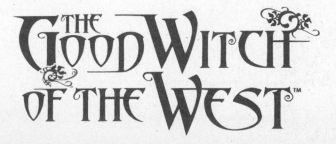

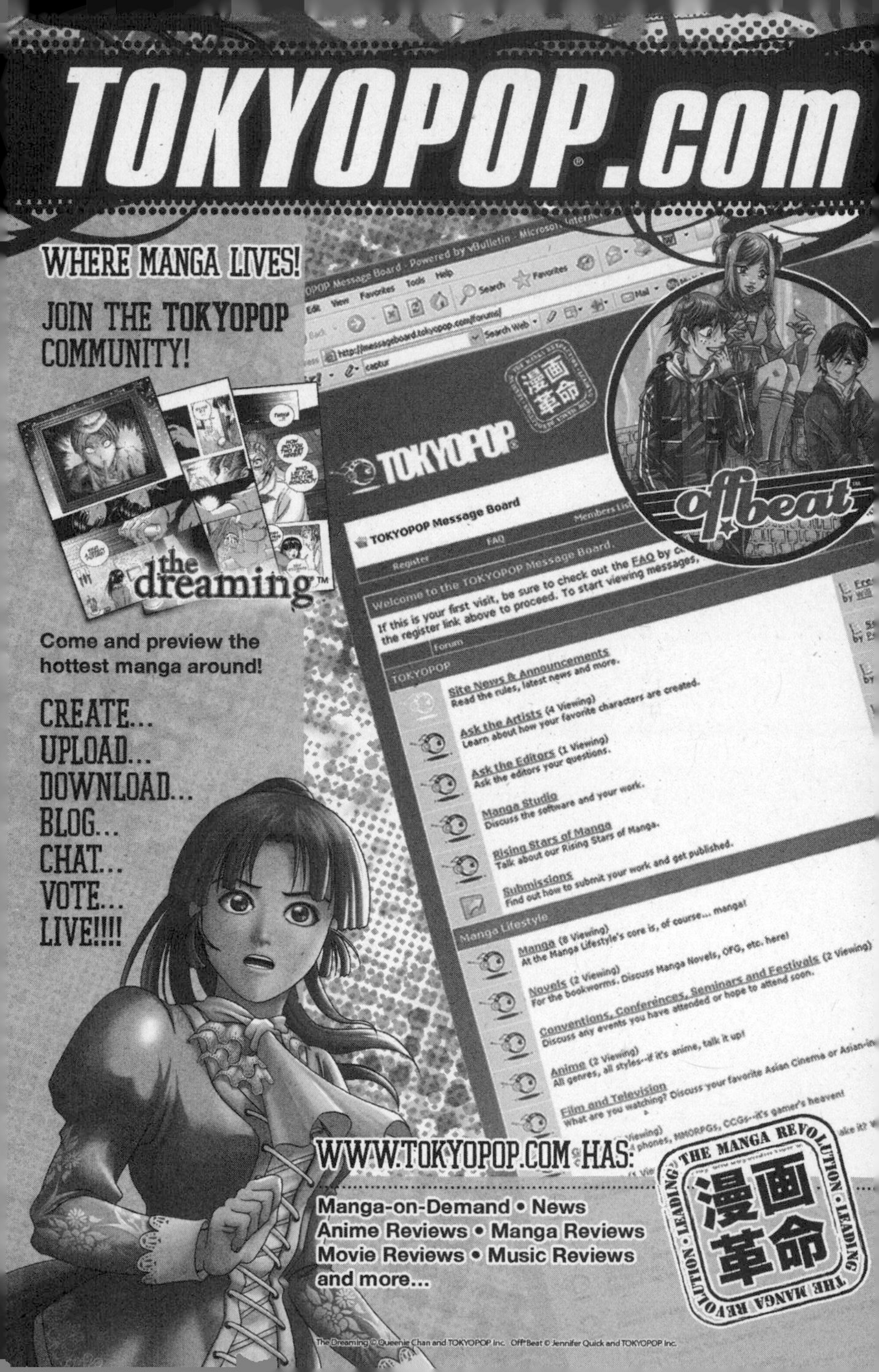
TOKYOPOP.com
WHERE MANGA LIVES!
JOIN THE TOKYOPOP COMMUNITY!
the dreaming™
Come and preview the hottest manga around!
CREATE...
UPLOAD...
DOWNLOAD...
BLOG...
CHAT...
VOTE...
LIVE!!!!
TOKYOPOP
TOKYOPOP Message Board
offbeat™
Site News & Announcements
Read the rules, latest news and more.
Ask the Artists
Learn about how your favorite characters are created.
Ask the Editors
Ask the editors your questions.
Manga Studio
Discuss the software and your work.
Rising Stars of Manga
Talk about our Rising Stars of Manga.
Submissions
Find out how to submit your work and get published.
Manga Lifestyle
Manga
At the Manga Lifestyle's core is, of course... manga!
Novels
For the bookworms. Discuss Manga Novels, OFG, etc. here!
Conventions, Conferences, Seminars and Festivals
Discuss any events you have attended or hope to attend soon.
Anime
All genres, all styles--if it's anime, talk it up!
Film and Television
What are you watching? Discuss your favorite Asian Cinema or Asian-in
WWW.TOKYOPOP.COM HAS:
Manga-on-Demand • News
Anime Reviews • Manga Reviews
Movie Reviews • Music Reviews
and more...
LEADING • THE MANGA REVOLUTION •
漫画革命
The Dreaming © Queenie Chan and TOKYOPOP Inc. Off*Beat © Jennifer Quick and TOKYOPOP Inc.

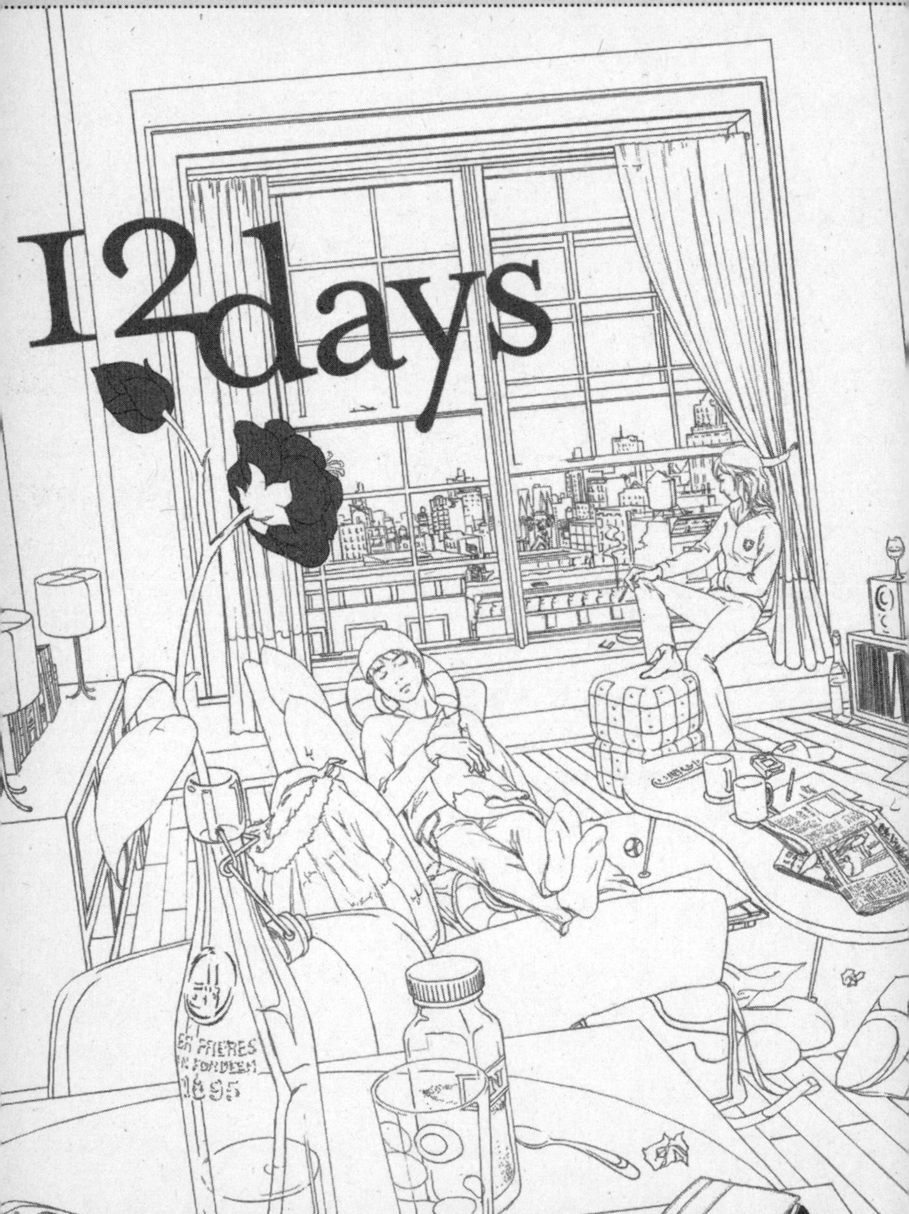
12days

How long would it take to get over...

losing the love of your life?

When Jackie's ex-lover Noah dies, she decides the quickest way to get over her is to hold a personal ritual with Noah's ashes. Jackie consumes the ashes in the form of smoothies for 12 days, hoping the pain will subside. But will that be enough?

From the internationally published illustrator June Kim.

ELEMENTAL GELADE VOL. 2
BY MAYUMI AZUMA

ELEMENTAL GELADE

A SKY PIRATE MANGA BOUND TO HOOK YOU!

Rookie sky pirate Coud Van Giruet discovers a most unusual bounty: a young girl named Ren who is an "Edel Raid"—a living weapon that lends extraordinary powers to humans. But just as he realizes Ren is a very valuable treasure, she is captured! Can Coud and Arc Aile join forces and rescue her without killing themselves…or each other?

THE MANGA THAT SPARKED THE HIT ANIME!!

ACTION

T
TEEN
AGE 13+

© MAYUMI AZUMA

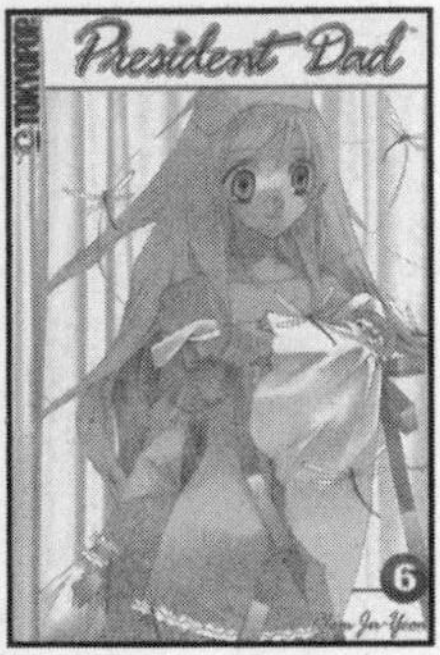
President Dad
TOKYOPOP
6

COMEDY
TEEN AGE 13+

PRESIDENT DAD

BY JU-YEON RHIM

In spite of the kind of dorky title, this book is tremendously fun and stylish. The mix of romance and truly bizarre comedy won me over in a heartbeat. When young Ami's father becomes the new president of South Korea, suddenly she is forced into a limelight that she never looked for and isn't particularly excited about. She's got your typical teenage crushes on pop idols (and a mysterious boy from her past who may be a North Korean spy! Who'd have thought there'd be global politics thrown into a shojo series?!), and more than her fair share of crazy relatives, but now she's also got a super-tough bodyguard who can disguise himself as anyone you can possibly imagine, and the eyes of the nation are upon her! This underrated manhwa totally deserves a second look!

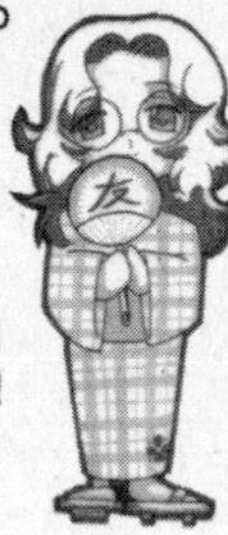

~Lillian Diaz-Pryzbyl, Editor

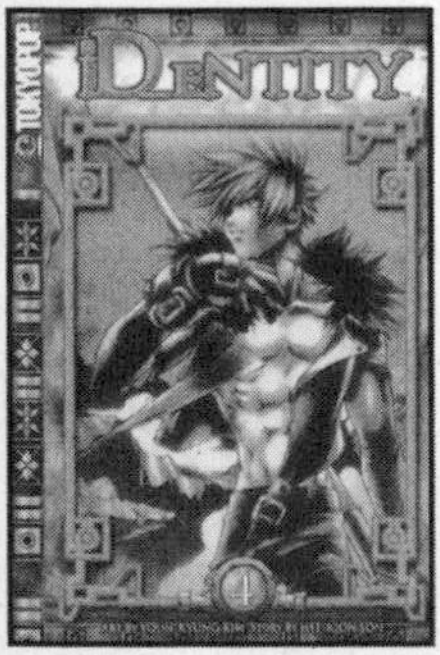
iDENTITY
TOKYOPOP
4

ACTION
TEEN AGE 13+

ID_ENTITY

BY HEE-JOON SON AND YOUN-KYUNG KIM

As a fan of online gaming, I've really been enjoying *iD_eNTITY.* Packed with action, intrigue and loads of laughs, *iD_eNTITY* is a raucous romp through a virtual world that's obviously written and illustrated by fellow gamers. Hee-Joon Son and Youn-Kyung Kim utilize gaming's terms and conventions while keeping the story simple and entertaining enough for noobs (a glossary of gaming terms is included in the back). Anyone else out there who has already absorbed *.hack* and is looking for a new gaming adventure to go on would do well to start here.

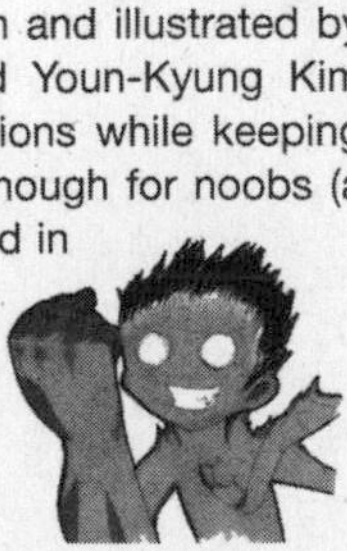

~Tim Beedle, Editor

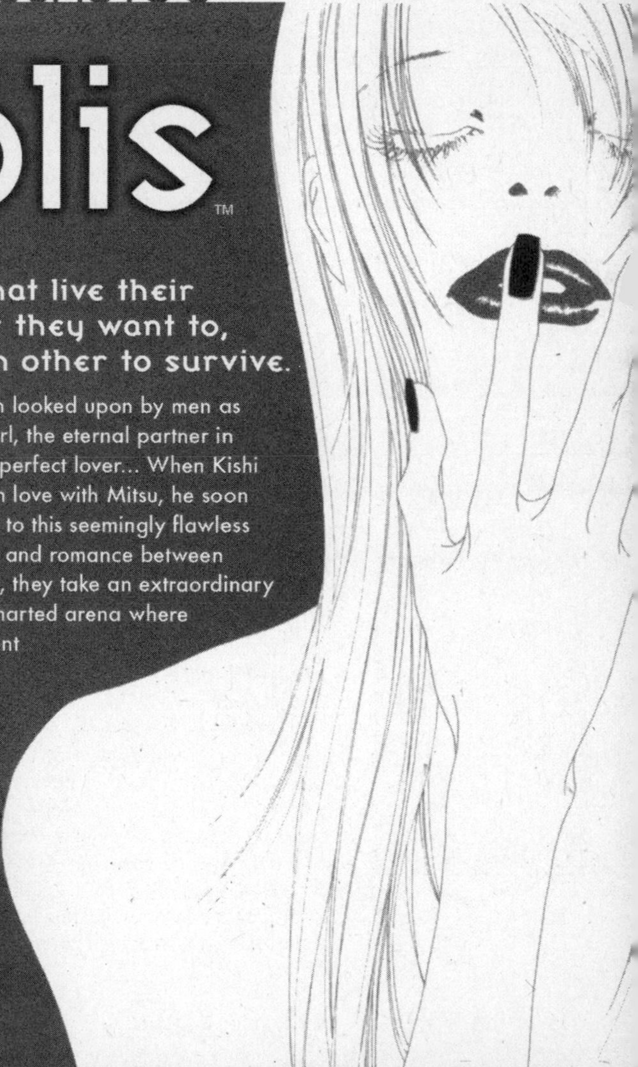

STOP!

This is the back of the book.
You wouldn't want to spoil a great ending!

This book is printed "manga-style," in the authentic Japanese right-to-left format. Since none of the artwork has been flipped or altered, readers get to experience the story just as the creator intended. You've been asking for it, so TOKYOPOP® delivered: authentic, hot-off-the-press, and far more fun!

DIRECTIONS

If this is your first time reading manga-style, here's a quick guide to help you understand how it works.

It's easy... just start in the top right panel and follow the numbers. Have fun, and look for more 100% authentic manga from TOKYOPOP®!

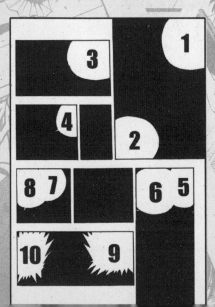